AGE OF HOPE

AGE OF HOPE

Labour, 1945, and the Birth of Modern Britain

RICHARD TOYE

BLOOMSBURY CONTINUUM
LONDON · OXFORD · NEW YORK · NEW DELHI · SYDNEY

BLOOMSBURY CONTINUUM
Bloomsbury Publishing Plc
50 Bedford Square, London, WC1B 3DP, UK
29 Earlsfort Terrace, Dublin 2, Ireland

BLOOMSBURY, BLOOMSBURY CONTINUUM and the Diana logo are trademarks
of Bloomsbury Publishing Plc

First published in Great Britain 2023

A catalogue record for this book is available from the British Library

Library of Congress Cataloging-in-Publication data has been applied for

ISBN: HB: 978-1-4729-9230-7; eBook: 978-1-4729-9229-1; ePDF: 978-1-4729-9228-4

2 4 6 8 10 9 7 5 3 1

Typeset by Deanta Global Publishing Services, Chennai, India
Printed and bound in Great Britain by CPI Group (UK) Ltd, Croydon CR0 4YY

MIX
Paper from
responsible sources
FSC® C020471

To find out more about our authors and books visit www.bloomsbury.com
and sign up for our newsletters

Contents

Acknowledgements

Robin Baird-Smith at Bloomsbury approached me with the idea for this book in September 2020. He noted that it was getting on for forty years since the publication of Kenneth O. Morgan's seminal study of the Attlee government, *Labour in Power, 1945–1951* (1984). Robin wanted to commission me to write a new history of that administration, which, as he noted, 'contributed so much to modern society in Britain as we know it'. Although there could be no question of replacing or supplanting Morgan's ground-breaking work, I felt that there would be value in creating a portrait of the era on a broader canvas, by tracking the origins and consequences of the 1945 election from the late nineteenth century through to the present day. Robin has been encouraging and supportive throughout and his comments on my drafts have always been thought-provoking and constructive.

I am grateful, too, for the invaluable help and guidance I have received from Natasha Fairweather of RCW Literary Agency. Innumerable archivists and librarians have assisted me. I would like to thank, in particular, Allen Packwood at the Churchill Archives Centre, Jeremy McIlwaine at the Bodleian Library, and Darren Treadwell at the People's History Museum. Among academic friends, Richard Jobson and Gary Love both took time out from their own research to consult some archival material on my behalf. Ben Jackson provided me with useful information. Julie Gottlieb kindly hosted me when I was researching in Manchester. She also kindly shared her unpublished research with me, as did Kit Kowol. There are now no survivors of the Attlee government or the 1945 generation of MPs, but Mary Jay kindly shared memories of her late husband Douglas Jay. Rosemary Addison generously put me up in Edinburgh and allowed me to consult the papers of her late husband, the historian Paul Addison, prior to their deposit at the Churchill Archives Centre.

Nick Fawcett carried out the copyediting with great efficiency. I am grateful to Fahmida Ahmed and others at Bloomsbury Continuum for their help in bringing the book into the world.

My father, John Toye, regularly discussed this project with me from its beginning, but did not live to see it completed. One of the last conversations I had with him, prior to his death in 2021, concerned the books that his own father used to borrow from his local London County Council library in the 1950s. These included Arthur Bryant's volumes based on the diaries of Lord Alanbrooke, which took some of the shine off the Churchill myth, and the memoirs of Hugh Dalton. This suggests some continuity of interests between the generations, and I owe my preoccupation with history and politics in part to John's encouragement. It is to his memory that I dedicate this book.

Witikon, Zürich, March 2023

Introduction

December 6th 1923. That was the date of the general election that brought Labour to power for the first time – though its leader Ramsay MacDonald did not take office as Prime Minister until the new year. Just shy of a century later, the party appears to stand on the verge of another historic victory. But whereas MacDonald could not command a majority in the House of Commons, and though his first tenure of No. 10 lasted only a matter of months, Keir Starmer may today be heading for a landslide to rival those of 1945, 1966 and 1997. Of course, nothing should be taken for granted – Rishi Sunak's Tories, though deeply divided, cannot be written off. At the same time, it would be a tragedy if Labour were to so underrate itself that it failed to properly prepare for the challenge it likely faces – winning big and then working to deliver on the hopes that its victory has raised.

An essential part of that preparation is considering Labour's past in an informed and realistic way, rather than a sentimental one. The record of the Attlee government will loom large in any such discussion, because of the scale of victory that brought it to office at the end of the Second World War, because of its achievements, but also because of its sad and anticlimactic end after six difficult years. That government, however, needs to be understood not only in its immediate context but in the long sweep of Labour's history. That is the aim of this book: to show how, in the face of adversity, the party succeeded in building both a credible policy programme and an atmosphere of popular optimism, yet also to show how that mood of hope dissipated, with consequences through to the present day.

In September 1945 *The Middletown Press*, a small-town Connecticut newspaper, published an article it had received from a locally born woman who had lived in Britain for some years. This lady, who was in her early thirties, was moved to write because she had heard 'that the news of Mr. Churchill's defeat in the recent general election aroused bewilderment and dismay among Americans'. Writing from her in-laws' home in Barry, South Wales, she did her best to set the record straight. She noted that, though the Conservatives had not expected to be defeated, they had worried that the Labour Party would win enough seats that, in combination with Liberals and Independents, it would be able to force a parliamentary stalemate. The Tories had therefore put Churchill himself at the front and centre of their campaign, hoping that his huge personal popularity would lead the voters to back his party even if they didn't like his policies. 'Yet, with all this support of Churchill's immense prestige, the Conservatives were beaten in one constituency after another, in their most resounding defeat for almost 40 years. Why?'

The article addressed this question by noting that, whereas Republicans and Democrats held similar economic outlooks, the two main British parties embodied antagonistic points of view. The Conservatives thought that industry should be in private ownership and run for profit, Labour that basic industries and public services should be owned and administered by the state. This had been the fundamental issue before the voters. 'It was quite impossible for them, no matter how much they were urged to do so by the Conservatives, to consider this election as merely an opportunity to say "Well done!" to their war leader.' Notwithstanding his recent descent into 'the recriminations and accusations of party politics', the wise and courageous Churchill deserved the British people's gratitude. But the election was about the future not the past: 'The people had to choose which policy would be their guide in the coming five years, and they have answered in no uncertain voice that they do not wish to go back to the "good old days" of private enterprise and devil take the hindmost.'[1]

The article's author was my paternal grandmother, Adele Toye (née Francis), known to family and friends as 'Dibby'. As a student at Connecticut College for Women, Dibby came to Britain in the early 1930s on a Junior Year Abroad. She studied at the University College of the Southwest, now the University of Exeter – where I work today – and it was there that she met her future husband Jack. Later in the decade, they honeymooned in Germany, even bringing back a Nazi banner as a souvenir. That was quickly removed from the couple's London house at the time of the 1938 Munich Crisis – an event that Dibby described in the first of her occasional articles for *The Middletown Press*. She vividly described the tension and then the joy when it was revealed that Neville Chamberlain was to make a final dramatic flight to meet Hitler. 'What a relief! Good old Nevvy! [...] We congratulated each other in extravagant phrases on having such a wonderful prime minister.'²

Yet the experiences of the next months and years changed Dibby's political perspective. She was moved when she met a group of Czech refugees from Nazism, became convinced that German aggression had to be resisted, and was unnerved by government missteps. Once war started, she and Jack were evacuated to Wisbech, a sleepy town in East Anglia, where they started a family. Dibby worked as a billeting officer, helping find lodgings for more than three thousand women and children made homeless by the Blitz. What effect this close-up view of social conditions had on her political opinions is unclear, but by 1945 she was a firm if moderate Labour supporter. She wanted to avoid a repeat of 'the deplorable state of affairs' that had occurred when the men came home in 1919. 'The Conservatives were in power then, and if they were not actually responsible for unemployment, doles, and all the dismal economic confusion, at least they were unable to prevent it or put it right.'³

To my regret, I never met Dibby, but the yellowing cuttings of her vivid writings have long intrigued me. We should not assume that her judgements on the reasons for Churchill's famous defeat were reliable or representative. Nevertheless, they shine a glimmer of light on the themes of this book, which offers a re-evaluation of the causes and consequences of Labour's 1945 victory. Three things stand out from the assessment that she offered. The first is the fact that, though people were dumbfounded by the *scale* of Labour's win, a good electoral performance by the party had been expected by many. Second is her failure to mention Labour's plans for a National Health Service, for housing, and for other social services. Given her own strong interest in social issues it cannot be that she thought these things were unimportant. But there was an overarching issue that she considered more significant. This is the third point – her presentation of the real issue of the election. 'A fundamental decision had to be taken', she wrote: 'shall the reconstruction of the country's economic life be made according to the principles of private enterprise or of public ownership and control?'[4] She had no doubt that, in plumping for the latter, the British people had taken the right decision.

Debates about why Labour won power at the war's end, and then lost it again, have mainly been conducted among those who are sympathetic to socialist or progressive ideas. Among those leftists who have been critical of the government's record, there are two broad schools.[5] The first asserts that the party underestimated the radical fervour of the people. In government it delivered a few sticking-plaster reforms, but no fundamental challenge to capitalism. Influenced by the conservatism of the trade union movement, and their own bourgeois assumptions, ministers gave in to a tepid managerialism and the logic of the Cold War.[6] And when, at the outset, they accepted commitments to international economic liberalization as the price of American economic aid, in an effort to prop up waning Britain's Great Power status, they sacrificed the opportunity to pursue an autonomous economic strategy.[7] The second school has it the other way round. In 1945, it is argued, the voters were not looking for a new form of society. They wanted simple things – above all else, the jobs and decent housing that made private family life worthwhile. They chose Labour because they thought the party could deliver this modest agenda, but its leaders misread the support they received as an endorsement of their own socialist beliefs.[8] Labour, ploughing on in sublime ignorance, in due course alienated the voters. When it was rejected at the polls, the party even came to feel that the People, lacking in high idealism, had somehow failed to live up to their destiny.[9]

My contention is different. It is quite true that ordinary people were often more interested in concrete, everyday improvements than in abstractions such as socialism. (And it must be borne in mind that less than half of voters actually opted for Labour.) At the same time, Labour needed a framing device to help them persuade the masses that it was the party best placed to deliver – especially given that its rivals were promising social reform as well. The frame it chose was – as my grandmother's article reflects – that of public versus private control. The 1945 party manifesto cast Labour's differences with the Tories as follows:

They say, 'Full employment. Yes! If we can get it without interfering too much with private industry.' We say, 'Full employment in any case, and if we need to keep a firm public hand on industry in order to get jobs for all, very well. No more dole queues, in order to let the

Czars of Big Business remain kings in their own castles. The price of so-called "economic freedom" for the few is too high if it is bought at the cost of idleness and misery for millions.'[10]

This was not just good rhetoric – it was sound economics. By emphasizing the monopolistic and anti-competitive behaviour of many influential firms, Labour did not turn itself into an opponent of free enterprise. Rather, it suggested that the very existence of free enterprise was a myth. As the party's speaker's handbook noted, opponents of state control condemned all public regulation as 'government interference' while simultaneously demanding subsidies, protective duties, and other measures that would benefit their private interests.[11] And they very often got them.

To say that Labour's diagnosis was broadly right is not, of course, to say that its policy solutions were perfectly thought out and ideally implemented. Its ideas about economic planning were vague and ill-thought-through. It was also assumed too readily that large-scale nationalization would in itself give the government the tools it needed to make a reality of public control. If there is one thing on which the party's right and left wings have generally been able to agree in recent decades, it is that the Attlee government's extension of public ownership is not something to be emulated. This is because right-wingers now prefer free market solutions, whereas left-wingers feel that the wrong model of nationalization was adopted – top-down and bureaucratic rather than participatory and liberating.

In fact, some rehabilitation of the record is required. There were significant failures, such as the takeover of the railways. Yet even in that case, the accompanying nationalization of some passenger shipping was a distinct success, as was, for example, public ownership of the gas industry.[12] It is a commonplace that the government ran out of steam in the late 1940s partly because there was little agreement on what, if anything, to nationalize next, once the items on the initial 'shopping list' had been crossed off. That is true enough, but it was an aspect of a wider problem: that Labour had not found a way to renew and refresh its formerly effective theme of public versus private control. It was not helped by the fact that rationing and other restrictions on personal freedom, though still necessary in the aftermath of the war, were naturally unpopular with many.[13]

Yet arguably, the harsh material conditions of the time were propitious for the launch of Labour's egalitarian project. As the historical economist Thomas Piketty has shown, the enormous destruction of capital in the First and Second World Wars laid the foundations for a fairer distribution of income: 'the reduction of inequality that took place in most developed countries between 1910 and 1950 was above all a consequence of war and of policies adopted to cope with the shocks of war'.[14] This is not to negate the importance of ideology or political will, but the tough times were in some ways congenial to the pursuit of economic justice.

This helps explain why the six years Attlee was in Downing Street were a foundational moment in the formation of modern Britain. His government still has a living legacy in spite of the frequently successful efforts by later administrations, notably that of Margaret Thatcher, to undo or undermine its achievements. Cultural factors also have to be taken into account. The Second World War still has a 'special grip' on British national memory and its meaning is still contested.[15] The fact that it has often been remembered as a 'people's war', the sacrifices of which could only be vindicated if a better world was rebuilt in its aftermath, helps explain the longevity of the welfare state.[16] Although the Labour Party has been relatively electorally unsuccessful in the post-war period, even in Opposition it has maintained pressure sufficient to ensure that the National Health Service, regarded as the 1945 government's crowning achievement, has remained in existence (albeit in now severely weakened form). The Attlee government has long departed this world, but it has passed on some of its DNA.

It is important not to surrender to nostalgia or mythmaking. As early as 1958, the cartoonist Michael Cummings predicted that one day socialists would speak of the 1945 government with the same longing that wistful Liberals then recalled the Asquith administration of 1908.[17] He had a point – Labour has sometimes seemed imprisoned by its history.[18] And it must be remembered that post-war problems, which were real enough, were sometimes made worse by genuine ministerial incompetence. Nevertheless, Labour would not have been able to achieve what it did – delivering economic reform, improved living standards and a decent measure of social security – had it not mobilized the language of optimism and inspired hope for the future. Shirley Williams – a Labour minister in the 1960s – recalled her youthful desire to make the world a better place: 'The deep satisfaction of growing up in the cold, austere, wonderful world of the Attlee government, the first-ever Labour majority government, was to watch that happening, to be part of that revolution by consent.'[19]

Of course, not everyone experienced the period that way. The novelist Evelyn Waugh remembered it as a time 'when the kingdom seemed to be under enemy occupation'.[20] He, who did not even admit the validity of democratic elections, was an extreme example – but many others also found the Attlee period profoundly uncongenial. It was not, then, that Labour magically united the nation in the pursuit of equality and justice, but simply that, for a time, it defanged the Opposition and bought itself some sympathy from waverers. Its honeymoon could not last. But in explaining why the optimism faded, we should probably place less emphasis than is usual on Labour's internal contradictions and weaknesses, and more on the new 'war of nerves' that broke out as relations with the Soviet Union plunged into crisis.[21] The speed with which the world moved from the conclusion of one global conflict to the threat of another remains shocking. The outbreak of the Cold War looks like an obvious policy failure, even if the blame was not to be shared equally. But, in the light of today's events in Ukraine, we should consider giving more credit to the players on *both* sides of the iron curtain for the fact that things did not turn out even worse than they did.

Clement Attlee, the man at the apex, has always been something of an enigma. The gibes are well known – 'a sheep in sheep's clothing', 'an empty taxi drew up in Downing Street and Mr. Attlee got out'. They have long been debunked, though aspects of the myth persist. The first man to lead a majority Labour government would not trouble someone else to fetch him a cup of tea if he could do it himself – but he had a very good opinion of his own judgement. Turning a standard joke on its head, his one-time assistant Douglas Jay quipped that he was 'an immodest man and had a lot to be immodest about'.[22]

Strikingly, there was no life of Attlee published between the appearance of Roy Jenkins' 'interim biography' in 1948 and Kenneth Harris's official Life in 1982.[23] A series of able biographies have followed, as well as a substantial study of Attlee's relationship with Churchill.[24] There have also been admirable works on many of Attlee's colleagues – Ernest Bevin, Aneurin Bevan, Stafford Cripps, Hugh Dalton, Hugh Gaitskell, Herbert Morrison, Harold Wilson and Ellen Wilkinson, to name only the most high profile. However, other key figures have eluded biographical attention until recently.[25] What is more, most Labour MPs of the 1945 generation did not leave diaries, memoirs or papers, let alone have their life stories written.[26] It has long been a cliché (of diminishing accuracy) that Attlee has been underrated; yet it must be remembered that the vast majority of the activists and politicians who made his victory possible have been swallowed up by a much deeper obscurity.

Three accounts of the Attlee government stand out: Kenneth O. Morgan's *Labour in Power* (1984) for its authority and clarity, Peter Hennessy's *Never Again* (1992) for its verve and humour, and David Kynaston's *Austerity Britain* (2007) for its interweaving of high politics with the lives of ordinary Britons.[27] In addition, there have been many themed monographs as well as a mass of academic literature on specific issues or episodes. Over the last several decades much of the sheen has come off some of the government's achievements. In particular, scholars are now rightly sceptical of the self-congratulatory approach towards Indian independence that ministers were retrospectively prone to take. A forced retreat was dressed up as an act of generosity; colonial exploitation continued elsewhere, while careful attention was paid to revising imperial terminology to make the system sound progressive and benign.[28] Some Labour politicians held appalling racial attitudes. In 1950, when offered the Colonial Office, Hugh Dalton turned it down, afflicted by 'a horrid vision of pullulating, poverty stricken, diseased n----- communities, for whom one can do nothing in the short run, and who, the more one tries to help them, are querulous and ungrateful'.[29]

To point this out is not to say that there was no difference between the Labour Party and its opponents. It is only to observe that, whereas it was formally committed to battling racial prejudice and imperialism, it failed, by quite some distance, to transcend the white supremacist assumptions and structures of the time. The development of the welfare state was wrapped up with these phenomena too. But rather than reduce the story to one of condemnation or exculpation, we should recognize these facts as part of its complexity. We need to understand the contradictions, rather than pretending that they did not exist. Labour was both visionary and pedantically pragmatic, genuinely internationalist and subject to Cold War paranoia, socially radical in some respects, petit bourgeois and conventional in others. Attlee himself encapsulated many of the tensions. When asked why he sent his children to private schools rather than state ones, he replied that 'the man who lives in the world as if it were already the world he hopes to achieve – is a crank'.[30]

We need to rethink our assumptions about what constituted mainstream politics in this period. For example, plenty of Labour MPs, including many of the government's leading lights, were secularists. But recent research has revealed that a good number of this generation of socialists were influenced, not merely by Christianity, but by esoteric belief systems such as Theosophy and Spiritualism.[31] To take but one instance, George Rogers liked to consult dead politicians via his wife's mediumship, and claimed they always told him accurately what his majority at each election would be. 'When I first entered Parliament in 1945 I was told I would be MP for North Kensington for 25 years and then the seat would be abolished.' He did serve until 1970 and the constituency ceased to exist four years later. The serious point is that he believed that Spiritualism could unite mankind and spoke up on its behalf in the Commons. He was probably right to suggest that many who shared his views would not say so in public for fear of alienating religiously orthodox voters.[32]

I have written this book, then, not to overthrow existing interpretations but to explore and enrich them, and to show how they emerged over time. I do this by casting the government in long-term perspective, starting in the 1880s, in order to explain how the personal paths of Labour's leading figures intersected with the movement's development and with broader social and political change. I describe the politics of the Second World War and the 1945 campaign in detail, and then, in the central chapters, relate the history of the government from bright dawn to eventual defeat. Finally, I explain how the nexus between history, politics, archives, publishing and the media has shaped understandings of Attlee's legacy until the present day. In the conclusion I offer some suggestions about what today's Labour Party can learn from its past as it fights to return to power in the 2020s.

I first started investigating the Attlee government when studying for my PhD, over twenty-five years ago. Writing this book required me to re-examine familiar sources, as well as to make use of new archival releases. The latter include a substantial new deposit of Attlee's personal papers at the Bodleian Library in Oxford. Although this material, or parts of it, has been available to some previous biographers, there is still new information to be extracted from it. Of particular value is a chronology of Attlee's premiership, compiled by civil servants, which gives a granular, day-by-day insight into his activities and routine. There is also a memoir (albeit only a few pages long) by Attlee's wife Violet of her time in Downing Street, as well as a transcript of the couple's memories as contributed to a 1963 radio programme. Official secrecy – especially concerning decolonization, the security services and the royal family – still places some limits on what we can know of the period.[33] This is frustrating, but one may at least be grateful for the wealth of information that is available for the study of most areas of policy.

As for my grandmother, after the war she built a career as a social worker. She and her colleagues strove valiantly to implement the provisions of the 1948 Children Act, which gave local authorities substantial new responsibilities for the care of underprivileged children. She served as the first president of the Association of Child Care Officers (ACCO). Writing of that body's launch, she recalled 'hope and confidence about the future, and a sense of elation, of satisfaction, that we were going forward in our profession'.[34] In 1972, the year before I was born, she died of a stroke at the age of 58. What would she have thought had she been told that, more than fifty years after her death, her analysis of the 1945 election would form a starting point for a serious work of history? I am not sure, but my guess is that, to use a favourite phrase of hers, she would have been 'tickled pink'.

Hymns of Hope

August 1st 1945. The first meeting of the fresh Parliament, not a week after the stunning news of Labour's election victory. 'The House was a strange sight', wrote the Tory MP and diarist Cuthbert Headlam, 'full to the brim with the new boys – the flight lieutenants and other callow youths who are to rule us all for the next five years at least.'[1] Many members were in uniform because, on account of being elected, they had not passed through demobilization centres and lacked the ration coupons needed to buy civilian clothes.[2] The Commons met, not in its regular chamber, which had been destroyed by a Luftwaffe bomb four years earlier, but in the red-benched House of Lords. The atmosphere was one of excitement and uncertainty – for the assembled MPs included a sea of new boys, and a sprinkling of new girls too.

These 345 neophytes didn't know their way around and showed their ignorance of the convention that members cheer rather than clap. They applauded Herbert Morrison, who was the senior government figure present; Prime Minister Attlee and Foreign Secretary Bevin were in conclave with Truman and Stalin at the Potsdam conference. Suddenly 'a wild commotion' spread like a wave along the Opposition benches. The Conservative MPs came to their feet, unleashing a violent cheer at the entrance of their leader. As Churchill took his seat, the cries mutated into a chorus of 'For He's a Jolly Good Fellow', as the Tories showed that they too were willing to breach Commons decorum. Then, led by the Yorkshire MP and former miner George Griffiths, the Labour side rose – literally – to the challenge, and broke out in a noisy rendition of

'The Red Flag'. Not all of those singing knew the words or, apparently, the tune. According to the *Manchester Guardian*, 'All the serried ranks were standing – all save one, the Ministers on the Treasury bench.'[3] As the *Aberdeen Journal* put it, 'The Labour Front Bench seemed to take a poor view of the "Red Flag" demonstration. They did not join it with any marked enthusiasm. In fact, there were prominent Labour front benchers who afterwards deplored the scene.'[4] Morrison later confessed that he had been 'mildly disturbed' by the outbreak of exuberance but he put it down to 'first-day high spirits'.[5]

For sure, the episode was fundamentally good humoured. The Tory Speaker, Douglas Clifton Brown, was quickly confirmed in his position with Labour's backing, and addressed the assembled MPs. 'I wondered whether I was going to be elected Speaker of the House or director of a musical show,' he quipped.[6] The conservative *Spectator* saw no reason for anxiety: the start of Parliament's proceedings, 'once a little superfluous exhilaration had boiled itself away, was quite as auspicious as could be hoped'.[7]

Still, the choral skirmish was a revealing moment. The chilly reaction of the front bench suggested a frisson of tension between the leaders and the led. This was not a simple split between backbench socialist enthusiasm and the moderation of ministers uncomfortable with singing about 'our martyred dead'. For example, the right-wing Bevin (though absent) was an enthusiast for what he called 'our labour song'.[8] Rather, it was partly a question of experienced MPs' disdain for the indecorous comportment of the newcomers. What was appropriate for a party conference or a public meeting was, to them, jarring within the hallowed precincts of the Commons. Thus, Jennie Lee, a left-wing MP who already knew the ropes, having served in Parliament from 1929 to 1931, correctly predicted that the incident would not be repeated. Soon the new members 'would know that this was not "done"', she wrote, just as they would know to mutter 'a parliamentary "hear, hear"' rather than to applaud.[9]

Yet there was an ideological aspect too. Far from being unprecedented, the 'Red Flag' affair represented a working out of stresses that had been present since the Labour movement's birth. The results of these tensions – between radicalism and caution, and between emotion and restraint – were by no means all negative. The 1945 victory can be seen as a consequence of the productive interplay of opposing forces. In that year – not quite uniquely in its history – Labour made successful appeals both to a 'social patriotism' that transcended class *and* to stirringly emotive ideals of worker solidarity.[10] Although the party's enemies liked to present socialism as an alien import, the antithesis of patriotism, by the end of the Second World War Labour had done much to negate the charge. Keeping the party's firebrand activists on board at the same time required a balancing act. 'The Red Flag' was not to be denied pride of place in the party's official songbook – but Attlee's preference was for William Blake's 'Jerusalem', which was included when the collection was updated in 1950.[11]

To understand the origins of the Attlee government we must begin in the 1880s, when 'The Red Flag' and 'England Arise!' (another key socialist hymn) were both written. This was the decade when Attlee and the other members of Labour's Big Five – Ernest Bevin, Herbert Morrison, Hugh Dalton and Stafford Cripps – were all born. It was, furthermore, a time when Britain's trade union movement made dramatic new strides and when socialist ideas were starting to gain a real foothold, as the working-class franchise expanded dramatically. Gross deprivation in the face of Victorian prosperity led social reformers to complain of 'poverty in the midst of plenty' – a slogan that retained its power through the 1930s and beyond.

The Social Democratic Federation (SDF) was started by businessman Henry Hyndman, who published a book ripping off the ideas of Karl Marx without giving him credit. SDF members who resented Hyndman's autocratic style split to form the Socialist League, with financial support from William Morris, the designer, writer and visionary. In 1884, the Fabian Society was founded, initially with the aim of 'permeating' the major political parties with its gradualist, evolutionary socialist ideas. This strategy failed, but the Fabians in due course became an intellectual powerhouse for the British Labour movement. Sidney and Beatrice Webb were crucial here. This ascetic, mind-melding power-couple pumped out books and reports while deploying spartan hospitality to win over Britain's shakers and movers to their brand of socialist bureaucratic efficiency. The food was plain, the conversation high-flown and intense. The Webbs remained formidable – intellectually and personally – down to the 1930s. Visiting them for lunch, Prime Minister Ramsay MacDonald could not summon the courage to ask where the toilet was and was obliged to relieve himself in a timber yard as he returned home.[12]

Some of the currents of the 1880s were thoroughly avant-garde. Edward Carpenter, the actively gay author of 'England Arise!' and an early Fabian, was a former clergyman whose sexual and spiritual awakening was influenced partly by the *Bhagavad Gita*. His ideas blended utopian socialism with an erotic romanticization of the working class. Carpenter became a public campaigner for homosexual equality, at a time when sex between men was subject to harsh punishment. Carpenter was a friend of Hugh Dalton's father, Canon John Dalton, who served as a tutor to the future George V. Carpenter's writings were also an influence on Hugh and the young men with whom he developed intense friendships when an undergraduate at Cambridge University. There is no evidence that Hugh ever had a sexual relationship with another man (though later in life he developed crushes on younger male comrades). Dalton's biographer has noted that it is hard to determine the exact influence of Carpenter on his beliefs about socialist fellowship and his feelings – if he had any – of sexual guilt. But if Dalton was more interested in Webbian practicality than in Arcadian schemes, the impact of utopian thought on his generation of leaders should not be dismissed.[13]

This is true even in the case of Clement Attlee, whose image was that of a functionary rather than a dreamer. Born in 1883 in Putney, the son of a solicitor, his first memory was of Queen Victoria's Jubilee, which he celebrated by putting a flag – not a red one – on his family's porch.[14] He attended Haileybury College, a public (that is to say, elite private) school. Its mission was to train imperial administrators – who were increasingly in demand as Britain grabbed vast new territories in Africa. So far, so conventional. Asked in old age to name the best prime minister of his lifetime, Attlee named Lord Salisbury, the Conservative who served for most of the period between 1885 and 1902.[15] 'Mother always tried to stop political discussion,' he recalled, 'father being a home ruler and all the rest of us Tories.'[16]

Yet, as his most recent biographer has emphasized, Attlee read not only mainstream authors Rudyard Kipling and Anthony Trollope but also the contrasting utopias of Edward Bellamy and William Morris. Bellamy's bestselling novel *Looking Backward* imagined a future society in which private property and capitalism had been done away with; Morris's *News From Nowhere* was a riposte that rejected Bellamy's vision of an industrialized modernity. Victorian utopianism helped form Attlee's sense that long years of struggle really could help create a better society; the more conventional writers helped place limits on the degree of change that he actually sought.[17]

The literature of the age, both factual and fictional, had a big impact on Herbert Morrison too. A native of Brixton, he faced harder struggles than either Attlee or Dalton, not least because he wrestled with a disability: an infection in infancy made him blind in his right eye. Though his background was modest he did not suffer the extremes of poverty. His Tory-supporting father was a policeman, a respectable calling that brought a reliable wage. Morrison also benefited from the new era of compulsory education, which helped make him more questioning of the established order than were his fatalistic parents. After leaving school he took a job as a shop assistant:

> Cheap books, pamphlets and essays written by authors whose object was to open the eyes of youngsters such as myself, were pouring from the presses. By day I watched the ordinary people as they came to the shop. By night I read voraciously the ideas of those who wanted to create a new society. This literature was without doubt the basic reason why my thoughts began to turn towards socialism.[18]

Ernest Bevin, by contrast, picked up his education piecemeal, and gathered his knowledge of public affairs, as he put it, 'from the hedgerows of experience'.[19] The oldest of the Big Five, he also had the hardest upbringing. He was born in Somerset; it is not known who his father was. His mother raised him as a single parent, but she died when he was a child. Thereafter he lived with his sister and her husband, left school at the age of 11, and eventually landed in Bristol, where he undertook a variety of unskilled work. He was highly intelligent but preferred to pick up information through conversation rather than by reading.[20] He was a regular attender at Chapel, and for a short period served as a Sunday School teacher and Baptist preacher. He furthered his education through Sunday and evening classes, including some run by the YMCA. This spirit of mutual aid and collective self-improvement was typical of both the nascent labour movement and of pre-1914 society as a whole. It was no great step for Bevin to move from adult education to the socialist meetings he started attending after the conclusion of the Boer War.

Yet if Bevin's nonconformist background was crucial to his development, it was Stafford Cripps, the youngest of the Five, who had the most powerful, long-lasting and publicly visible religious commitment. His mother died when he was four, having expressed the wish that her children be 'trained to be undogmatic and unsectarian Christians [...] taking their religious inspiration directly from the spirit of the New Testament'.[21] He was raised in this temper by his father, Alfred, a successful barrister who was to become a Conservative MP. Stafford, too, achieved renown at the Bar, but although he was a nephew of Beatrice Webb, and sympathized with the plight of the poor, he hesitated to become a member of the Labour Party as he was not a manual worker.[22] He eventually joined in 1929. Ultimately his Christian and his socialist beliefs merged, and he took the view that the Church should be 'the active protagonist of the Kingdom of Heaven, or the rule of God, here on earth, as the pioneer of social salvation, more concerned with creating the greatest sum of human good and happiness here and now, than with encouraging individual merit as a means to personal salvation hereafter'.[23]

One didn't have to be a religious enthusiast to be attracted to the labour movement, of course. Neither Attlee nor Dalton showed much interest in theological matters, despite their Anglican backgrounds. Morrison, a sometime atheist who settled into agnosticism, despised organized religion and perhaps even viewed socialism as a substitute.[24] To some, Christianity and socialism seemed antithetical. Among Welsh miners, for example, the growth of class struggle and socialism went together with the growth of secularism. Young radicals became alienated both from the nonconformist churches and from the Liberal Party with which they were strongly associated.[25] Yet for many people socialism and religious fellowship went hand in hand. The 'Labour Church' movement of the 1890s rejected the existing churches but it did not reject religion. Rather, it took the view that the emancipation of Labour could only be achieved through the embrace of the moral and economic laws laid down by God. The rise of the labour movement, then, was no simple story of class politics sweeping away primitive beliefs as society progressed inevitably towards modernity.[26]

The broader point is that adherence to the emergent labour movement – which did not necessarily involve socialism – was compatible with a wide range of belief systems, including mysticism and the occult.[27] Its members were united above all by a belief in justice and progress and by the idea that social problems, having human origins, could be remedied through purposive human action. Though many trade unionists were motivated by self-interest as much as by ideas or social conscience, the developing movement had a crusading essence. This spirit was familiar in British politics from, for example, the anti-slavery movement, the Anti-Corn Law League, and Chartism, as well as from Gladstone's multifarious campaigns. Labour, then, should be seen as a *spiritually inflected* movement, irrespective of the actual theological beliefs of all of its individual members.

A religious-type sensibility was crucial to Labour's *ethos* (or culture) though not to its *doctrine* (its formal set of stated beliefs and policies).[28] Thus, Beatrice Webb described the undergraduate Dalton as 'by nature an ecclesiastic – a sort of lay Jesuit – preparing for political life'.[29] Similarly, Cripps and Morrison, near opposites in spiritual matters, found common ground with Attlee in their admiration for Blake's 'Jerusalem', and the 'intense and courageous spirit of happy determination' that it represented.[30] Attlee may never have had a religious experience, and did not discuss religion in public: 'it is a matter on which I always prefer to be reticent'.[31] But he did not discard the Christian message entirely. 'Believe in the ethics of Christianity,' he told his biographer in retirement. 'Can't believe the mumbo-jumbo.'[32]

The last two decades of the nineteenth century saw both the union movement and the socialist movement make dramatic new strides, but it was not a foregone conclusion that this would lead to the creation of a new workers' party with potential mass appeal. Whereas older-style craft unions had been the preserve of the labour aristocracy, the so-called New Unionism was open to the unskilled. There was an outbreak of 'strike fever'.[33] The match-girls' strike of 1888 and the London dock strike of 1889 were key successes. The latter involved a new dockers' union that, considerably later, merged into the powerful Transport and General Workers' Union (TGWU) – which would be led brilliantly by Bevin.

The dock strike was one of the events that inspired Jim Connell, an Irish-born activist based in London, to write 'The Red Flag' that same year. Connell was a 'burly figure, with red tie, large moustache, and wide-brimmed hat', who claimed to have been educated 'under a hedge for a few weeks'.[34] Connell's preferred tune for the song was the lively Jacobite one 'The White Cockade' – but to his frustration it was 'O Tannenbaum' (also known as 'Maryland') that caught on.[35] Socialist critics of 'The Red Flag' saw this music as dreary and uninspiring. George Bernard Shaw once suggested it be republished as 'The Funeral March of a Fried Eel'.[36]

The leadership of the Trades Union Congress, founded in 1868, showed little inclination to live, let alone die, below the scarlet standard. It was dominated by 'Lib–Lab' MPs – a small group of working men who held Liberal Party seats and who resisted the growing pressure to establish a new party. Still, there were signs of progress. At the general election of 1892 Keir Hardie and John Burns were returned as independent Labour candidates. In 1893, the Independent Labour Party (ILP) was founded at a conference in Bradford; 5,000 people attended an accompanying Labour Church service.[37] But there was not much chance of parliamentary success on a large scale unless such a party was backed by union money. MPs were still unpaid, so if any working-class candidates were successful they would need their salaries to be met, in addition to the costs of campaigning.

The creation of the Labour Representation Committee (LRC) in London in February 1900 marked the foundation of the Labour Party, but it could have failed, as had a similar initiative of 1887, the Labour Electoral Association. The LRC's simple purpose was to create a Labour group in Parliament that would promote workers' interests. The committee included seven trade unionists, together with one representative from the Fabian Society, two from the SDF, and two from the ILP. It was not possible to join the new organization as an individual, though one could join the affiliated organizations.

Two factors were crucial to the LRC's success. First, the Taff Vale case of 1901, a legal ruling that made unions liable for the financial losses to employers caused by strikes. The unions now had a very powerful motive to help elect Labour MPs in order to get the judgement overturned by legislation. Second, the 1903 pact between Ramsay MacDonald, Secretary of the LRC, and Herbert Gladstone, the Liberal Chief Whip. This allowed Labour candidates a free run in a range of constituencies to ensure that the anti-Tory vote was not split. A broad Liberal–Labour consensus in favour of Free Trade, one of the defining issues of the day, meant that there was a genuine commonality of interest.[38]

At the general election of 1906, 29 Labour MPs were elected, and there was further progress four years later. For the time being, though, the party was stalled as the junior partner in the Liberal–Labour 'progressive alliance'. During an era of growing industrial militancy, and a time of heightened xenophobia, Labour was portrayed by its enemies as 'an anti-patriotic party, disowning the symbol of national unity, the Union Jack, and ostentatiously marching under a flag of its own, the blood-red banner of cosmopolitan socialism'.[39] In fact, the party's constitution did not commit it to achieving socialism. Labour was divided between those who wanted to abolish capitalism and those who saw the pursuit of common ownership as a dangerous distraction from the party's real mission of achieving gradual progressive reform within Parliament. This was a tension that has never been fully resolved throughout the party's history, but arguably it was the Attlee government that papered most effectively over the cracks.

The outbreak of the First World War saw the party split between those who supported the conflict and the minority – not all of them pacifists – who opposed it. MacDonald resigned as Chair of the Parliamentary Labour Party (PLP) and campaigned for peace, helping establish the Union of Democratic Control (UDC), which demanded transparency in foreign policy. The future Big Five took a range of paths. Attlee, by this stage, had abandoned Law for East End social work. Seeing the effects of poverty made him question the economic system: 'After trying to get hold of various ways by which one might do something without causing any particular trouble to one's own self, I became a socialist.' Now he joined up: 'I wasn't conscientious enough to be a pacifist.'[40] He served with distinction and was wounded twice. 'When we entered the war we were too credulous,' he later admitted – in his view the UDC was proved right.[41]

Dalton, having studied for his doctorate at the London School of Economics, ended up on the Italian front, and later published a book about his experiences.[42] Cripps, at the start of the conflict, took the view that, as he was married, he fell into a class of men who were not yet needed. But he acted as a recruiter and then performed ambulance service in France. Later, he ran a munitions factory; the strain caused his health to collapse. Morrison opposed the war, but though his disability would have excused him from conscription, he agreed to carry out non-military service as a gardener. This left him time for his work as Secretary of the London Labour Party, to which position he had been elected in 1918. Bevin supported the war but continued his work as one of the national organizers of the Dockers' Union. He was the only one of the five to contest a seat at the election at the war's end – but he was defeated. In the aftermath of the Russian revolution he was forced to contend with the allegation that a vote for Labour was a vote for Bolshevism. He also declared his hand on the 'alien question', i.e. the issue of immigration: 'he would make it illegal for any employer to employ a non-British subject at less than trade union wages and conditions, and no alien should be allowed in a British ship if there was a Britisher available to go to sea'.[43]

In spite of its divisions, Labour emerged from the war strengthened. It had gained governing experience as part of the Asquith and Lloyd George coalitions. It also adopted a new constitution, which facilitated individual membership. The constitution's famous Clause 4 expressed the party's belief in 'the common ownership of the means of production'. (The words 'distribution and exchange' were added later.) There was a substantial new policy statement, called *Labour and the New Social Order*. Labour stood to gain from the wartime extension of the franchise to all adult men and some women – but there was no guarantee that this would lead to the party overtaking the Liberals, and in fact the Conservatives proved adept at appealing to the new voters too.[44] The split between Lloyd George (coalition) Liberals and Asquithian (independent) ones was a crucial factor in Labour's success.

The 1918 election saw Labour make relatively modest progress, gaining over 20 per cent of the vote but only 57 seats. The PLP remained weak. The uninspired chairmanship of William Adamson (1917–21) and the rather stronger leadership of J. R. Clynes (1921–2) made little impression in the face of the enormous majority wielded by the Lloyd George coalition. According to its critics, Labour ran its parliamentary work merely 'as a side show to its trade union organization'.[45] There was increasing discussion of non-parliamentary methods and of radical alterations to Parliament.[46] Guild Socialism, based on the idea of 'functional representation', enjoyed a brief vogue.[47] The political theorist G. D. H. Cole was its chief advocate, as well as being 'a key figure in the socialist project of reviving an English radical past'.[48] Attlee recalled being 'a good deal influenced' by his writings.[49]

More important, however, was the concept of 'direct action' – the use of industrial power outside Parliament for political ends. This idea was not merely the preserve of extremists. In 1919, Morrison argued that British intervention in the Russian civil war 'should be resisted with the full political and industrial power of the whole Trade Union movement', a view endorsed by the Labour Party conference.[50] In 1920, Bevin backed the dockers of the *Jolly George*, who refused to load weapons onto a ship destined for anti-Soviet Poland.[51] Many advocates of direct action saw it as a complement to parliamentary methods, not as an alternative.[52] But Labour's opponents exploited every opportunity to present the party as a dangerous and potentially revolutionary force.

In 1922, Lloyd George's coalition broke apart, and the new Conservative Prime Minister, Andrew Bonar Law, called an election. Earlier in the year, Dalton had stood for Parliament, fighting and losing a by-election in Cambridge. Now – grieving the death of his four-year-old daughter earlier in the year – he contested Maidstone. He was making a name for himself as an advocate of a capital levy (a tax on fortunes) and he came within a thousand votes of the Tory victor, though he landed third. Major Attlee (as he was usually referred to at this time) had better luck. One of a number of former servicemen standing, he triumphed at Limehouse, having previously served as Mayor of Stepney, during which time his first book, *The Social Worker*, was published. Also among Labour's candidates were the intellectuals Bertrand Russell and Sidney Webb, trade unionists such as Margaret Bondfield (though not Bevin), the medical doctor Leslie Haden-Guest, and former MPs including MacDonald, Philip Snowden and George Lansbury. The *Daily Mail* labelled these various groups 'queer bedfellows', but the diversity was a sign of the way that the party was broadening its appeal.[53]

The Conservatives won a large majority, but Labour made a dramatic breakthrough too. Attlee took his place as one of 142 MPs, who between them now constituted the official Opposition. However, Labour still had to share the front bench with the Asquithian Liberals, and their respective party leaders literally jostled each other for space.[54] For Labour, that leader was now MacDonald. When the new session began, there was an election for the post, in which MacDonald beat the previous chairman, J. R. Clynes, by a margin of five votes. One of those who supported MacDonald was Attlee, who 'lived to regret that vote'.[55]

Attlee did, however, gain valuable new experience, as MacDonald appointed him as one of his parliamentary private secretaries. Now in his late thirties, Attlee had recently married Violet Millar. Vi, as she was known, found him 'an easy husband', though he was frequently absent and never willing to speak for more than two minutes on the phone.[56] In his maiden Commons speech, Attlee emphasized that unemployment, which had shot up after the collapse of a brief post-war boom, represented 'waste'. In the London area alone, 600,000 people were living in one-room tenements. Using the language of national efficiency, tinged with anxieties about the impact of poverty upon the characters of the poor, Attlee argued: 'You are not going to get an A1 nation under those conditions: you are not going to get a moral nation under those conditions; you are not going to get a sober nation under those conditions.' He pointed out that many of those on the dole were 'the same men who stood side by side in the trenches. They are the heroes of 1914 and 1918, though they may be pointed out as the Bolshevists of to-day.' Furthermore, 'As the nation was organised for war and death, so it can be organised for peace and life if we have the will for it.'[57] Attlee could later legitimately claim that this sentiment foreshadowed the approach and concerns of his 1945 administration.[58]

Attlee conceded that Conservatives were concerned about the problem of the dole queues, even if their policies were wrong. Not everyone agreed – a belief given credence by Bonar Law's refusal to meet the leaders of a group of unemployed Hunger Marchers. In the face of the social devastation wreaked in some parts of the country, many of the new Labour MPs – especially those from 'Red Clydeside' – were determined to present themselves in Parliament as the champions of the poor. There were quite a lot of middle-class recruits to the ILP at this time and the Clydesiders looked on them with suspicion. Attlee, however, was seen differently. His war service as an officer was held against him but the fact that he had combined his lot with that of the Stepney working class was in his favour. If they had their doubts about the Major they approved of the Mayor.[59] He, for his part, regarded his radical Scottish colleagues as 'great fun'.[60]

The Clydesiders were determined to denounce the government as heartless and uncaring. Controversy centred partly on the passion and stridency of their rhetorical technique. To their sympathizers, their eager contributions were 'a great demonstration of the workers' claim for a human life' and 'a measure of the difference between the old Ruling Class type of MP and the representatives of Labour'.[61] To their detractors, their street-corner style, in combination with class-conscious language, resulted in speeches of 'Bolshevist frightfulness' designed to bring Parliament into contempt.[62] Left-wingers depicted this as a morally forceful type of speech that was intended to awaken the Commons (and the nation) to its responsibilities. But it was privately deplored by moderates such as MacDonald and portrayed by Conservatives as a 'hymn of hate' chanted by sour and fanatical class warriors.[63]

What is more, some Labour members were keen to use parliamentary disruption tactics. They saw this as a proper use of the Commons to challenge capitalism and to 'put a fighting spirit into the working-class outside'.[64] 'By all night sittings, by organised guerrilla opposition, which anyone is free to call "obstruction," for all we care, Labour is making it impossible to forget the unemployed', declared the ILP weekly *The New Leader*.[65] The year 1923 saw some spectacular parliamentary 'scenes'. One of the most notorious of these involved 'actual scrimmages, and many threats of violence', and the singing of 'The Red Flag' within the Chamber. Eventually the Speaker suspended the sitting.[66] Some within the Labour Party, notably MacDonald, disapproved of such episodes (which may have been painted by the copy-hungry press as more exciting than they really were).[67]

Conservatives and Liberals presented all this as proof of Labour's innate extremism and unfitness to govern. The disrupters, they claimed, offended against the dignity and traditions of the Commons, and showed themselves devoid of the 'reverence for the ancient institutions of state'.[68] As one writer in the *Lloyd George Liberal Magazine* put it, 'To cause the recesses of the Chamber to re-echo the strains of the "Red Flag" is not the step that politicians would naturally take if they wished to convince the electorate that their party ought to be entrusted with the reins of government.'[69] Unwise or not, the MPs were giving voice to genuine anger among the workless. A few months earlier, for example, the Wesleyan evangelist Gipsy Smith had invited the unemployed to attend one of his services at Victoria Hall, Sheffield. One of them asked that 'England Arise!' be sung, and when this was ruled out of order, chaos ensued. When a hymn was announced, the unemployed responded with 'The Red Flag'. This happened repeatedly, and when one unemployed man appealed for Smith to be given a hearing, a hymn book was thrown at his head.[70]

Bonar Law, who was mortally ill, retired after a few months in office. Later in 1923, his successor, Stanley Baldwin, caused a political upset by calling a general election. He wanted to get a mandate from the voters to introduce protectionism to cure unemployment. It was a huge miscalculation, and he lost his majority (though the Conservatives remained the largest party). Morrison was elected for Hackney South, but Dalton was again narrowly defeated, this time at Cardiff East. The crowd sang 'The Red Flag' as he left for London. 'Ah! That is the funeral dirge of our Movement,' said MacDonald, who was travelling on the same train, and who prided himself on 'bringing the wild socialist Labour members to heel'.[71]

In January, Parliament met. In the gloom and drizzle a crowd of onlookers was 'edified by a series of char-a-bancs conveying East End Socialists using rattles and singing the "Red Flag" and "The Internationale" as they conveyed their elect to the august precincts'.[72] Baldwin's government brought forward a King's Speech but was defeated, clearing the way for Labour to take office. This had a calming effect on the PLP.[73] The Liberal MP William Wedgwood Benn, who himself joined Labour later in the decade, recorded in his diary: 'Notable restraint on the part of the Labour people, and a buoyant aggressiveness about the Tories.'[74] George V grumbled to MacDonald that 'The Red Flag' and the 'Marseillaise' had been sung at Labour's victory celebration at the Royal Albert Hall. MacDonald explained that he could not have prevented it without provoking a riot, and that it had taken all his efforts to stop his MPs singing 'The Red Flag' in the Commons on the night the Tory government fell. His followers had 'got into the way of singing this song,' he said; he hoped, 'by degrees [...] to break down this habit'.[75] Jim Connell, author of 'The Red Flag', was still alive, and told a journalist that although he had written better songs since, he was happy with the effectiveness of his most famous composition. 'It appeals, he says, to the emotions, and there are many people who cannot be appealed to through reason. A Scottish member of parliament has assured him that the song has done more for Socialism on Clydeside than anything else.'[76]

Jack Lawson was a former miner who, like Attlee, was to serve as a junior minister at the War Office. He recalled: 'The coming of that first Labour government was a terrific shock to the divinely ordained to rule element in the country.'[77] Yet there were clear limits to the challenge that the new administration presented to the established order. First, MacDonald faced difficulties finding enough ministers, especially from the Tory-dominated House of Lords. Therefore he recruited the Liberal Lord Haldane as Lord Chancellor and the Conservative Lord Chelmsford as First Lord of the Admiralty. He also turned to Cripps's father Alfred, who had been ennobled as Lord Parmoor, who became Lord President of the Council with responsibility for League of Nations matters. Second, there was MacDonald's lack of a majority. He tried to make the best of this, but soon became irritated with what he saw as excessive parliamentary discussion.[78] Third, there was the Prime Minister's own natural caution. Would it have been better to plunge ahead with bold schemes, in the interests of proving the party's radicalism, even though these would have inevitably been blocked by the Opposition? Not necessarily. MacDonald's plan, which was to demonstrate Labour's capacity for steady, competent government, can be seen as a strategic success.

There is a strong case that the experience of 1924 'legitimised Labour as the new representative of progressive forces in British politics, helped to dispatch the Liberal Party to political oblivion and shaped Labour [...] as the leading British political party of the Left'.[79] This conforms with the judgement of Attlee, who rejected, in his memoirs, the suggestion that Labour should have refused to take office as it lacked a majority. 'The electors at that time needed to see a Labour Government in being, if they were to appreciate that Labour was now the alternative to a Conservative administration,' he argued. 'Refusal on our part to accept responsibility might have given a new lease of life to the Liberal Party.'[80]

The government's domestic policy successes were, admittedly, limited. Although there was some extension of unemployment benefits, the problem of the dole queues was not tackled. There were some temporary public works schemes, but there was no fundamental break with economic orthodoxy, which the Chancellor, Philip Snowden, seemed to embody. The government's flagship success was its Housing Act, steered through by the radical socialist minister John Wheatley, which led to a dramatic expansion in building, peaking in 1927, when a record 273,000 houses were completed.[81]

Yet although the 1924 government deserves its due, its short life saw an increase in the tensions between the industrial and political wings of the labour movement. The Tory press labelled Bevin 'the strike dictator', and revelled in describing his stout physique, broad shoulders and long arms. 'His eyes are dark and his complexion sallow. When roused he roars at his opponents, and he has almost as many critics inside the trade union movement as outside.'[82] Bevin's existing scepticism about the leadership of the party now hardened. During the nine months of the government, his union participated in three strikes – one by busmen and tramwaymen, the others at the docks. He strongly resented the government's use of the Emergency Powers Act to force the dockers back to work. As far as he was concerned, it was the behaviour of the various employers that had obliged the union to act. But he had to contend with appeals not to embarrass the Labour government as well as the potential resentment of his members if he backed down. 'I only wish it had been a Tory Government in office,' said Bevin when the transport men went back. 'We would not have been frightened by their threats. But we were put in the position of having to listen to the appeal of our own people.'[83]

Away from home, the picture was somewhat happier. MacDonald served as his own Foreign Secretary and cut a figure on the international stage. MacDonald's technique for smoothing over differences was to speak eloquently but nebulously.[84] Nevertheless, he worked tirelessly to reconcile Germany's desire for rehabilitation with France's desire for security. This helped secure both French withdrawal from the Ruhr (which they had occupied the previous year) and a revision of German reparations payments. Labour's boast, by the end of its time in power, was to have improved the 'embittered relations between France and Germany left by the disastrous tangles of preceding Governments'.[85]

At this time, it still seemed possible to think that European peace and disarmament could be achieved via the League of Nations. MacDonald, and his French opposite number Édouard Herriot, could claim credit for gaining member states' preliminary approval for the Geneva Protocol for the Pacific Settlement of International Disputes. This would have established compulsory arbitration and strengthened the role of the World Court. However, the Conservative government that followed MacDonald's administration refused to ratify it. Although it is unclear if the Protocol would actually have worked, this failure enabled Labour to add another item to the anti-Tory charge-sheet. Attlee was one who judged MacDonald's actions at Geneva as a 'considerable success'.[86]

Though his own tasks as a junior minister were inevitably prosaic – he had particular responsibility for the Territorial Army – Attlee's experiences in 1924 cast light both on his own political development and on the tensions within Labour. Early in the government's life, Bristol MP Walter Ayles moved a Commons amendment to reduce the army to a token size, reducing it by 150,000. He argued that 'the time has come when we should dethrone Mars and exalt Christianity'.[87] Just a few months previously, Attlee himself had spoken in favour of the abolition of all armies.[88] Now he backed the government's line, which was to maintain the efficiency of the armed forces while pursuing a policy of peace. The amendment was defeated by 347 votes to 13, showing that there was only limited support for unconditional pacifism within the Labour Party. At the same time, there was broad support throughout the movement for disarmament as an ultimate goal. There was, though, a continuing debate on how to achieve it. This debate mapped roughly on to the divide between 'idealists' and 'realists' in the field of international relations theory.[89] The future Big Five were ultimately all foreign policy realists, though it took Cripps longer than the others to reach that position.

These foreign policy issues were wrapped up with Labour's evolving attitudes to communism, domestically and internationally. In order to pursue its revolutionary strategy, the Communist Party of Great Britain (CPGB) maintained a doomed campaign to affiliate to the Labour Party, but at the same time regarded 'MacDonaldism' and the Labour government as a bourgeois sham.[90] Meanwhile, Labour was keen to normalize British relations with the USSR – formal diplomatic ties were quickly established – but was increasingly hostile to the CPGB. The Soviets wanted to strengthen economic links with Britain but were prepared to lash out rhetorically when it suited them. Thus, in answer to a parliamentary question (and without any agenda of his own), Attlee estimated the strength of the Red Army at 1,300,000. Trotsky responded in a statement that in fact it had fewer than 600,000 men: 'Major Attlee is misleading British public opinion and that of the whole world. [...] If the head of our intelligence service provided such fantastic information he would be immediately cashiered and prosecuted.'[91]

Attlee had been something of a sceptic about the Bolsheviks in 1917. But in his public comments he remained positive about the Soviet regime for a remarkably long time.[92] Communism at home was different, in part because there was less need for diplomatic tact. In October 1924, Attlee opposed left-wing efforts to strengthen the control of Labour's annual conference and its National Executive Committee (NEC) over the PLP and the government. Writing in the *New Leader*, he lambasted the advocates of this idea, suggesting communist influence: 'they believe in the dictatorship of the proletariat, but in their own opinion they are the only proletarians'.[93]

In the face of bitter hostility from the Liberals and the Tories, the government succeeded in negotiating two treaties with the Soviets, which were intended to settle past disputes and create new trade relations. The Opposition could, at any opportune moment, decide to turn Labour out. Eventually they did so, defeating the government in the Commons over its decision to withdraw the prosecution for sedition of J. R. Campbell, editor of a communist newspaper. A general election followed. On 25 October, four days before polling, the *Daily Mail* published 'A "very secret" letter of instruction from Moscow, which [...] discloses a great Bolshevik plot to paralyse the British Army and navy and to plunge the country into civil war.'[94] Supposedly, this was a set of instructions to British communists from Grigory Zinoviev of the Communist International (or Comintern). It was almost certainly a forgery, but there were plenty of people within Britain's secret state who, whether they knew this or not, were prepared to use the letter to damage Labour.[95] Baldwin returned to Downing Street with a huge majority. Morrison was among the Labour casualties. Attlee held on in Limehouse. Dalton bucked the trend and, at the age of 37, entered the Commons for the first time with a victory in Peckham. He wrote in his diary: 'A strange sensation, this victory at last, while others are falling at the touch of the Zinoviev letter! The beginning of a new chapter in my life.'[96]

In fact, Labour's election defeat was not quite the disaster that it seemed. Though the party had lost 40 seats, it had slightly increased its share of the national vote. Ellen Wilkinson, a future Cabinet minister and a darling of the press, won Middlesborough East.[97] The real losers were the Liberals, who saw their vote collapse further and lost nearly a hundred and twenty seats. MacDonald withstood the efforts of Bevin and others to drive him out of the leadership. As the party turned left, the now ex-prime minister went to lengths to emphasize his own moderation. In 1925, he launched an attack on 'The Red Flag', declaring his certainty that Labour would never triumph so long as it marched to that type of music. 'We still [are in] want [of] our great Labour song – a Labour song that is not a ditty.'[98] The *Daily Herald* responded by launching a competition to find a replacement, but not one of the three hundred entries was judged good enough.[99] This was a relief to Jim Connell who had resented the attack on his composition by a man who, in his view, was devoid of literary and musical discernment. 'I have known him for 30 years,' Connell said, 'and yet have never had any proof that he had the slightest appreciation of Robert Burns.'[100]

The General Strike of 1926 posed a more serious threat to MacDonald's authority than did Connell's attack on his powers of appreciation. But this return to direct action quickly failed. The strike's rapid defeat suggested a clear lesson: that the unions needed to work hard for the return of a Labour government, not least to secure the repeal of the restrictive Trade Disputes Act that passed in 1927. *Labour and the Nation*, the party's substantial new policy programme, pledged to do away with this hated law. The title reflected Labour's efforts to build an image as a national party, which meant reduced autonomy for local parties in candidate choice and campaigning.[101] The document also tried to blunt the charge that Labour was revolutionary, while still appearing radical, by promising that the party would establish a *peaceful* revolution:

> It will carry its programme into completion by peaceful means, without disorder or confusion, with the consent of the majority of the electors and by the use of the ordinary machinery of democratic government. [...] The dangerous revolutionaries are not those who seek power to initiate reforms which are long overdue, but the reactionaries who dam the stream till it bursts its banks in a raging torrent.[102]

In February 1929, *Red Flag* author Jim Connell died at the age of 76. The song itself was sung twice at his funeral, once to the 'White Cockade' and once to 'O Tannenbaum'.[103] That year's general election saw competition for the young women's 'flapper vote', following equalization of the franchise the previous year.[104] The Conservatives, fighting on the slogan 'Safety First', liked to present the choice between their party and Labour as the choice between 'a Constitutional Government under the Union Jack, or a Socialist Revolution under the Red Flag'.[105] The Labour candidate for Dover tried to claim that the song in fact referred to the Red Ensign, the flag of British civilian shipping. 'When they said "The Red Flag" they meant the flag of their country,' he told his final rally. 'They of the Labour Party were the only patriotic party there was.'[106] If his argument did not carry conviction, it at least showed awareness of the need to neutralize the nationalistic weapons used by the Tories.

Indeed, on this occasion, Labour was reasonably successful in doing so. The Conservatives got slightly more votes than Labour but lost over 150 seats. Lloyd George's Liberals fought a bold campaign on the pledge to conquer unemployment but they were still divided and their partial recovery fell well short of their hopes.[107] Labour was now the largest party, but again lacked an overall majority. Attlee did not immediately obtain ministerial office. Dalton became Under-Secretary of State for Foreign Affairs, the deputy of Foreign Secretary 'Uncle' Arthur Henderson. Morrison, who had returned to the Commons, was appointed Minister of Transport. He performed well and was appointed to the Cabinet towards the end of the government's life. However, his proposals for a new London Passenger Transport Board earned him the enmity of Bevin, who was still leading the TGWU and whose importance as a powerbroker would continue to grow. Morrison wanted the Board to be appointed by the minister, purely on grounds of ability, though likely including trades unionists. Bevin wanted union representation as of right and was not satisfied with an attempted compromise.[108] The bitterness between these two moderate figures would have poisonous consequences over the next two decades, showing that Labour movement rivalries did not also fall along neat ideological lines.

One Commons newcomer was noteworthy as a passionate orator who was not afraid to take on Parliament's big beasts. This was Aneurin Bevan, a former miner, who used his maiden speech to attack both Lloyd George and Churchill, who had criticized the government's unemployment plans from different angles. 'Whereas we are accused from the Conservative Benches of not having sufficient ambition,' noted Bevan, 'indeed of being comparatively pedestrian, on the other benches we are accused of being enormously adventurous.'[109] But his smart debating points could not disguise the truth that the government lacked a credible strategy for dealing with Britain's economic problems. This was hardly Bevan's fault. MacDonald's open contempt for the union movement and the parliamentary party made a bad situation worse, but perhaps no government could have withstood the impact of the Wall Street Crash of October 1929, which sent unemployment skyrocketing.[110] There is still scope for debate about whether proto-Keynesian reflationary policies would have helped. If ministers were in general too constrained by economic orthodoxy, there was no off-the-peg alternative available that came with a guarantee of success.[111]

The post-1931 Labour Party consciously defined itself in opposition to the painful experience of these years. Yet, even if they were concerned about the government's drift, Attlee and his future ministers offered little open opposition to MacDonald at the time. Bevan and his friend John Strachey (MP for Birmingham Aston) were exceptions. Strachey was Parliamentary Private Secretary to the maverick former Tory Oswald Mosley, who had been appointed Chancellor of the Duchy of Lancaster with special responsibility for unemployment. When Mosley resigned in frustration, Strachey resigned with him. (Attlee was given Mosley's job and later served for a few months as Postmaster-General.) In September 1930, Strachey and Bevan travelled to the Soviet Union and were attracted by the apparent successes of the Five Year Plan.[112] In December that year they were among the 17 signatories to the 'Mosley Manifesto', which called for an emergency Cabinet of five, loan-financed public works, and a 'national economic planning organisation'.[113] They also co-authored a pamphlet in support of its ideas.[114] But when Mosley left Labour early in 1931 to found the ill-fated New Party, Bevan, like most of the other manifesto signatories, refused to abandon ship.[115] Strachey made the leap, but then broke with Mosley when he turned towards Fascism. Strachey then became a renowned popularizer of communist ideas, but re-joined Labour during the Second World War.

Strachey's political journey was unique, but the pressures of the times also drove many other socialists to question their former assumptions. The events that tore Labour apart in the late summer of 1931 had powerful emotional and ideological consequences. The immediate cause was a financial crisis. Although the Cabinet agreed on the need for spending cuts to restore market confidence, a minority of ministers objected to the proposal for a 10 per cent reduction in the rate of unemployment benefit. In the face of deadlock, the government fell at the end of August. However, MacDonald immediately formed a so-called National Government, remaining Prime Minister at the head of a coalition dominated by Conservatives. 'The spiritual and psychological effects upon the Labour movement of what became known as "the Great Betrayal" were, I am inclined to think, as serious as the thing in itself and its immediate electoral consequences,' recalled Morrison, who was himself suspected of having wanted to join MacDonald. 'It left in the Party a spirit of distrust of the idea of leadership, a determination that for the time being there should be no more great men, and seeking to tie up the leadership with conditions and checks of one sort and another.'[116] Crucially – and to the chagrin of Morrison, who may have fancied himself a Great Man – it also helped pave the way for the low-key leadership of Attlee.

In 1931, though Attlee was moving closer towards greater influence, he was still an obscure figure. MacDonald, who was expelled from the party, quickly called an election, and together with the Liberal and Conservative leaders called for a 'doctor's mandate' (or free hand) to cure Britain's economic ills. Labour's representation in the Commons was slashed to 52, including 6 unendorsed Labour and ILP candidates. (The ILP disaffiliated from the Labour Party the following year.) Labour parliamentary ranks now included only one former Cabinet minister, the veteran George Lansbury. And only two former junior ministers had held their seats. One was Attlee, with a majority of 551. The other was Cripps. In 1930 Cripps had been appointed by MacDonald as Solicitor-General, had taken the customary knighthood, and had won a by-election at Bristol East. He survived the general election with a majority of 429. These facts determined the composition of the party's leadership for the next few years.[117] Attlee became Lansbury's deputy. When Attlee felt that, for financial reasons, he could no longer keep up this unpaid position, he offered to stand down in favour of Cripps, whom he regarded as Lansbury's natural successor. Instead, the wealthy Cripps provided Attlee with a subvention so that he could continue in the role.[118] Had he chosen otherwise, Labour's subsequent history could have been very different.

Faced with the overwhelming numbers of the National Government side, Lansbury kept up his MPs' spirits by leading them into the voting lobby singing 'The Red Flag'.[119] The Deputy Leadership was a proving ground for Attlee, who rarely got home before midnight, and who had to master unfamiliar topics such as foreign affairs and finance. He recalled: 'In 1932 I filled more columns of Hansard than any other Member and, as I am generally considered to be rather a laconic speaker, it can be judged that my interventions in Debate were numerous.' When Lansbury was hospitalized, Attlee led the party for several months. Compared with his previous period in the House, Attlee judged, these years 'were like the Western Front in World War I contrasted with the South African War'.[120] There were some grounds for optimism – if only in the very long run. As John Maynard Keynes pointed out, Labour represented 'the only organised body of opinion outside the National Government' and would therefore 'be called on some day, presumably, to form an alternative government'.[121]

These were years of renewal, as well as ones of anxiety and division. On the one hand, the party embarked on a process of policy development that helped it move away from the 'radiant ambiguity' of the MacDonald era.[122] Think-tanks and outside experts, including academic economists and City figures, played a key role.[123] Though he was out of Parliament, Dalton made an important contribution, via his position on the NEC. His book *Practical Socialism for Britain* was significant as an example of a new wave of progressive literature. As Labour established itself further as the thinking party, the Conservatives, though electorally dominant, found themselves increasingly on the defensive in the war of ideas.[124] Labour also continued its efforts to establish itself in the countryside, and in the south-east, albeit with limited success.[125] A concrete sign of hope came in 1934, when Morrison led Labour to victory in the London County Council (LCC) elections.

On the other hand, in spite of the efforts of some leading figures to present a moderate face to the electorate, in important respects the party had in fact turned to the left. The lesson widely drawn from 1931 was that Labour needed to renew its socialist commitment and spell out in detail how it was to be achieved. Although some of the party's intellectuals showed interest in the reformist economic ideas of Keynes, there was also a fair degree of scepticism. The Soviet example impressed many, including Dalton, who visited and concluded: 'The thing is working, it is not a fantasy, nor a propagandist tale.'[126] Though the belief in centralized economic planning was now a commonplace, the economic aspects of Stalinism acted as an inspiration, not a blueprint. There was, however, a sincere and widespread belief within the party that capitalism could be replaced, and not merely modified.

Writing in 1937, Attlee acknowledged that 'revulsion from MacDonaldism caused the Party to lean rather too far towards a catastrophic view of progress and to emphasise unduly the conditions of crisis which were being experienced, and to underestimate the recuperative powers of the Capitalist system'.[127] A few years earlier, Attlee and Cripps had co-authored a memorandum in favour of nationalizing the banks – a key left-wing demand that had been backed by the party conference – which emphasized the futility of trying 'to persuade capital to hand over control to socialism by gradual and restrained measures'.[128] Though in retrospect some of Attlee's statements appear quite extreme, it was Cripps, the darling of the party activists, who hogged the headlines with wild statements that had to be repudiated by the party machine.[129] He suggested, for example, that a socialist government might need to prolong 'the life of Parliament for a further term without an election'.[130] 'Cripps seems quite unable to see that he is damaging the party electorally', complained Dalton to his diary. 'He has become very vain and seems to think that he and his cronies know what Socialism is, or how it should be preached.'[131] Eventually, persistent advocacy of working with the Communists led to Cripps's expulsion from Labour, shortly before the outbreak of war. Bevan was expelled at the same time but was quickly readmitted in exchange for promises of good behaviour.

The question of capitalism versus socialism was intimately connected to the foreign policy issues that dominated the decade. Labour was broadly united in opposition to the appeasement of Europe's Fascist regimes, but it was harder to agree on what should actually be done to stop them. The National Government favoured rearmament, but many socialists believed that it could not be trusted with the weapons as it was dominated by Capital. Labour's official position was not against force under all circumstances, but rather favoured 'collective security' under the League of Nations, which was said to render 'national armaments' unnecessary. To complicate the picture, Lansbury was an unconditional pacifist, and some left-wingers, like Cripps, criticized the League on the non-pacifist ground that it was 'nothing but the tool of the satiated imperialist powers'.[132]

The party therefore faced a serious dilemma following Mussolini's invasion of Abyssinia in 1935. Following MacDonald's retirement, the National Government was now headed by Baldwin. Faced with government declarations of support for strong action against Italy via the League of Nations, Labour had to decide whether or not it would countenance a 'League war'. At that autumn's conference, Bevin launched a stinging attack upon Lansbury, accusing him of dragging his conscience around asking to be told what to do with it. With the union block vote playing a critical role, the party overwhelmingly rejected the pacifist and extreme socialist positions by 2,168,000 votes to 102,000. Lansbury resigned, and was replaced pro tem by Attlee, who led the party into the general election that followed. Labour found it hard to establish the distinctiveness of its position during the campaign; the government stole the party's political clothes and then abandoned Abyssinia once it was safely back in power. But Attlee demonstrated some of the qualities that would make him a successful leader. In a cinema newsreel speech – a precursor of TV election broadcasts – he offered cutting comments on the government's performance. 'The government's election programme, apart from increased armaments, consists of promises to undo some of the evil things they have done, and to do some of the many things they have neglected.'[133]

Labour gained 38 per cent of the vote and won 154 seats. Thus its recovery was strictly limited, in spite of ongoing social distress from which the party might have been expected to benefit. The journalist Ivor Brown commented: 'In many cases Poverty Corner has not only refused the Red Flag, it has even fought shy of the pink ribbon which was Major Attlee's not very fiery standard.'[134] However, Attlee had secured the confidence of his parliamentary colleagues. When the House reconvened there was a ballot to determine who would serve as leader on a continuing basis. Attlee beat two rivals who had returned to the House: Morrison and Arthur Greenwood, the former Minister of Health, who became Deputy Leader. Attlee may have owed his victory in part to the assumption that, in comparison to the others, he would be easier to displace. Dalton, who had campaigned for Morrison, told his diary: 'A wretched disheartening result! "And a little mouse shall lead them"!'[135] However, the *Manchester Guardian*'s political correspondent wisely noted: 'Mr. Attlee is no showman, but he has much patient merit, and in the opinion of many may be found capable of rising surprisingly in stature under the calls of leadership.'[136]

Attlee's victory completed a generational shift. The future Big Five were by this time in their forties and fifties – though the eldest, Bevin, was not yet in the Commons. Labour now had an increasingly sophisticated media operation and a more credible set of policies.[137]

The slim pamphlet *Labour's Immediate Programme* (1937), which laid much of the groundwork for the 1945 manifesto, stressed public control of finance, land, transport, coal and power.[138] But the party still had a mountain to climb. In the context of historic struggles such as the Spanish Civil War, the singing of 'The Red Flag' made powerful emotional sense, but its symbolism helped Labour's opponents in their mission to portray the party as unpatriotic.[139] At the start of 1939, Neville Chamberlain, who had replaced Baldwin in Downing Street, seemed electorally impregnable in the wake of his seeming triumph at the time of the Munich Crisis. That May, Dalton told an eve-of-conference rally:

> You have in office a Government which has imperilled your lives as well as your livelihood and dragged the name of Britain through the mud, and no supporter of it should ever again without shame lift up the Union Jack at a public meeting or on an election platform. We, the Labour Party, are alone entitled to lift not only the Union Jack which stands for Britain but the red flag, which stands for socialism and democracy.[140]

This echoed Bevan's earlier claim that 'the conjunction of the Red Flag and the Union Jack in the hands of the Labour Party is reaching consummation'.[141] We may doubt that such a consummation was ever truly reached – but the Second World War offered new opportunities for Labour to present itself convincingly as the real national party.

2

'And – Yes, There Was Hope'

March 1st 1940. Canterbury Hall, Cartwright Gardens – home of the London School of Economics. A lecture by Attlee on War Aims.[1] Beatrice Webb, the Grand Old Woman of Fabian Socialism, now in her eighties, was present and unimpressed. The Labour leader's talk, she told her diary, was 'pitiable. He looked and spoke like an insignificant elderly clerk, without distinction in the voice, manner, or substance of his discourse.' She had little time for the 'reactionary' Morrison or the 'untrustworthy' Dalton either, but upon Attlee she poured out particular contempt. 'To realize that this little nonentity is the Parliamentary Leader of The Labour Party, the representative of His Majesty's Opposition at £2,000 a year, and presumably the future P.M., is humiliating.' It is not surprising that Webb, who had developed a powerful enthusiasm for Stalin's Russia, had little enthusiasm for Attlee's 'string of vague assertions'.[2] Nor was her dismissal of Attlee's personality remarkable – hers was a commonly shared view, though his 'patent sincerity' was recognized.[3] What *was* striking was her prediction, however reluctant, that one day he would enter Downing Street. The possibility, although obvious given that he was Leader of the Opposition, seems to have occurred to very few other people. One can hardly say that Attlee's triumph was inevitable. But it was considerably more probable than most well-informed observers seemed to think.

It is something of a cliché that Attlee's secret weapon was his 'deceptive capacity for not being noticed'.[4] Plenty of his colleagues *did* notice his leadership style and, like Webb, found it totally underwhelming. But those who tried, at various times during the war, to get rid of him were too obviously self-interested and divided among themselves to succeed. Attlee was no Machiavellian genius, but he was strategically and tactically astute, flicking away challenges to his authority with curt, dismissive confidence. He made it to No. 10 not simply because of his political survival skills but because he headed a party well placed to benefit from the social upheavals wrought by the war. He could shape and channel these to some extent, but they were forces beyond anyone's individual control. They worked out, in the end, to the advantage of Labour. But there was another surprise outcome in 1945 – the fashioning and entrenchment of a new form of two-party system. Everyone was so shocked at the short-term triumph of one particular party that they failed to notice this equally fundamental set of changes.

To put it another way, Labour's victory served as the death-knell of an older style of politics. During the nineteenth century parties had formed, and broken apart, as the result of manoeuvres within Parliament. This is not to say that social and ideological forces were uninvolved, but MPs were far less beholden to party managers than they are today. They were more inclined to exercise independent judgement, with the result that splits emerged and new alliances were forged in response to the major issues of the day. Thus, in 1886, Joseph Chamberlain and his 'Liberal Unionists' sheered off from Gladstone's Liberal Party in opposition to Irish Home Rule. In time, the Liberal Unionists allied themselves with the Tories, with whom they subsequently merged. Party labels were flexible, adapted according to the candidate's preference and local circumstance. In the first part of the twentieth century, single-party, majority government was by no means the obligatory rule.[5] At key moments, the Conservatives chose to govern in coalition, even when they had the Commons numbers to rule in their own right. They could present this cross-party veneer as evidence of their ideological latitude and patriotic credentials, the latter explicitly emphasized in the term 'National Government' after 1931. This model seemed to work well up until 1939 – had the election due in 1940 not been cancelled due to the hostilities it seems probable that Labour, once again, would have been beaten handily.

This should not disguise what Labour, building on the achievements of its founding generation, had already achieved. The party's generally underwhelming record when it comes to winning elections, plain throughout its history, often distracts us from an obvious point. Against the odds it successfully established itself as the second party in the state and defended that position against serious threats. The fact that, during the 1930s, it saw off its 'National Labour' rival, and also prevented any kind of Liberal renaissance, should not simply be taken for granted. Though Labour was surely not on the edge of power when war broke out, it was gradually regaining favour through social reform at the municipal level, growing local presence, and its highlighting of the problems caused by mass unemployment.[6]

Some of this can be explained by Labour's own internal strength. Lacking its rivals' roots in aristocratic politics, it operated differently to the other parties. The Conservatives and Labour were both mass-membership organizations, but Labour had a more centralized structure.[7] Ruled (in theory) by its annual conference, it was on the face of things more democratic than the Tories and the Liberals, although the role of the union block vote called this theory into question. Labour's leaders did not merely 'emerge', but were elected, albeit by MPs rather than by the wider membership. The party sought ideological discipline, trying to unify around agreed policy programmes, though this aspiration often went unmet. ('It is indeed a necessary feature of democracy that the minority should acquiesce in the decisions of the majority', wrote Attlee.[8]) Parliament, thought to be too much of a 'talking shop', was to be turned into a machine for processing legislation that had already been outlined in the governing party's election manifesto.[9] The Tories had often run on the basis of their record in government and the character of their leaders; Labour became increasingly adept at using policy pledges to create a 'sense of promise'. Whereas its trade union basis meant that it could be labelled as a sectional, class party, Labour stood to benefit from the upsurge in union membership triggered by wartime full employment.[10] The party, in 1939, retained many weaknesses and contradictions; the well-funded Conservatives were still formidable opponents. But Labour had key strengths on which it could capitalize in wartime conditions, helping it develop a modern, forward-looking and patriotic image.

When war broke out, Labour had two important advantages. First, the party was fundamentally united in support of the war. Unlike in 1914, there was no split. Second, the party was equally united in opposition to Neville Chamberlain. He made no secret of the fact that he despised the

Labour Party; its leaders returned the feeling wholesale. It was easy, then, to resist his offer to join the government. Dalton noted:

> if, for instance, members of the Labour Party were given, say, one seat in the Inner Cabinet, plus the Postmaster-General and the Secretaryship of State for Latrines, we should not only be un-influential within, but we should lose most of our power to exercise influence from without [...] Further, we should lose much of our own credit amongst our own people, who would be filled with suspicions at our official participation.[11]

Labour did agree to an electoral truce, whereby the main parties would not put up candidates against each other at by-elections. But this was not a *political* truce: the party retained the liberty to criticize the government. And despite the inevitable disruption caused by conflict conditions, it gained at least a slight organizational edge over the Tories at the constituency level over the course of the war.[12]

The decision to hold aloof from the government was crucial to Labour's ultimate success. Throughout the 1930s, Labour had made efforts to burnish its patriotic credentials.[13] The party's own foreign policy record had not been perfect, but there was no doubt about its vociferous opposition to Chamberlain, on whom the blame for the failure of Appeasement inevitably fell. On 2 September 1939, it seemed to some that the government was hesitating to declare war. In the Commons the mood turned ugly. Frustrated at Chamberlain's apparent dithering, the Conservative Leo Amery urged Arthur Greenwood (who was deputizing for Attlee) to 'Speak for England'.[14] Over time, Labour and the Left succeeded in labelling the Conservatives as the party of Munich (and of mass unemployment), a label the Tories failed to shake off even when under new management.[15]

During the Phoney War, Labour still had plenty of problems. Attlee, returning after a long illness, fended off an incompetent coup attempt in which Dalton and Morrison were prime movers. Yet despite their rivalries, Labour's leaders, far from sitting on their hands, were actively working to gain office as part of a post-Chamberlain coalition.[16] This should not be confused with a mere quest to obtain government jobs for themselves. They could have had those earlier if they had been prepared to accept them from their old enemy. Rather, they offered a broad critique, in which a successful war effort *required* social and economic transformation of the kind that Labour had always demanded. Attlee suggested that the creation of a stable future peace required 'nothing less than the establishment of a New World Order'.[17] Labour and the TUC stepped up their attacks on the government.[18] Labour demanded rationing of all essential foodstuffs, and not merely of butter and bacon, as the government proposed.[19] At the same time, Attlee was forced to address grass-roots concerns that the party was supporting the National Government: 'We are supporting this country against aggression, but I must remind you that we are still deeply critical of this Government's past, critical of their present, and distrustful of their future.'[20]

Perhaps most worrying for the government – tone-deaf to the impact of its own rhetoric – was the spectre of industrial unrest. Addressing TGWU members in Bristol in February 1940, Bevin slammed appeals for working-class sacrifice 'after the bankers had scoped £13,000,000 extra profits out of the country in the first days of the war'. He went on:

I should be extremely sorry in a war of this character to find myself in a first-class political conflict with the Government, but if the Government is going to take this occasion of this war to invade the liberties of the people I will lead this movement to resist them or any other Government. This is not the only Government that can win the war.[21]

In April, Hitler launched a lightning strike against Norway. The British counter-invasion was a fiasco. During the Commons debate on the matter on 7–8 May, Chamberlain and the government suffered slashing criticisms, including from its own side. Labour forced a division and the government majority fell to 81 – enough to show that a reconstruction of the administration was necessary. Behind-the-scenes negotiations followed, in which the Labour leaders made clear that they would serve in a coalition – provided it wasn't led by Chamberlain. By coincidence, the Labour Party conference was meeting. Attlee travelled to Bournemouth, where the NEC backed his line. Attlee confirmed the decision to No. 10 by phone. This was the death-knell, and Chamberlain finally determined to resign.[22] In his diary for 10 May, Dalton noted with satisfaction: 'the last blow which dislodged the old limpet was struck by us at Bournemouth this afternoon'.[23]

Churchill became Prime Minister that same evening. Attlee and Greenwood then had a long discussion with him. 'I was an old Gallipoli man and I had a strong impression that one of the reasons for the failure of Gallipoli was that at a crucial moment the Liberals and Conservatives were squabbling over the allocation of seats in the Coalition Government,' remembered Attlee. 'And I said, "I will not haggle about seats."'[24] Nevertheless, the two Labour leaders 'made it clear that in a War Cabinet of six or seven they would both expect places'. Churchill indicated that he also wanted to give jobs to Bevin, Morrison and A. V. Alexander (who had served as First Lord of the Admiralty in 1929–31 and now took the role again). Attlee and Greenwood suggested repeal of the despised Trades Disputes Act but chose not to push their luck.[25]

There were also a generous number of junior appointments. Churchill bragged that his government stretched 'from Lord Lloyd of Dolobran on the Right to Miss [Ellen] Wilkinson on the Left'.[26] Wilkinson was one of the few real Labour enthusiasts for Churchill, and later admitted to being 'prejudiced in his favour'.[27] She was initially given a role at the Ministry of Pensions and later at the Ministry of Home Security. Cripps, still outside the Labour Party, was made ambassador to the USSR. There were some notable absentees from the government's ranks. Emanuel Shinwell, a future Attlee Cabinet minister, turned down a job and focused on criticizing the government from the backbenches.[28] Bevan was not offered a position. Throughout the war he boosted his profile with attacks on Churchill, who branded him 'a squalid nuisance'.[29]

The War Cabinet, as finally settled, had five members: Churchill, Attlee, Greenwood, Lord Halifax and Chamberlain (who remained in the government until the autumn as Lord President of the Council). Attlee and Greenwood gave Churchill vital support in the secret late May debates about whether to explore peace terms with Germany, but Greenwood wrestled with a drink problem. Generally ineffectual in his role as Minister Without Portfolio, he left the government early in 1942. Attlee held the post of Lord Privy Seal until 1942, when he became Secretary of State for the Dominions and Deputy Prime Minister (a role he kept for rest of the war). From September 1943 he was Lord President of the Council. Wilkinson was once asked how things were different when Attlee was standing in for Churchill when the latter was abroad. 'When Mr. Attlee is presiding in the absence of the Prime

Minister the Cabinet meets on time, works systematically through the agenda, makes the necessary decisions and goes home after three or four hours' work,' she explained. 'When Mr. Churchill presides we never reach the agenda and we decide nothing. But we go home to bed at midnight, conscious of having been present at an historic occasion.'[30]

Attlee didn't make a great impact on the public and was rarely name-checked in the Ministry of Information's assessments on domestic morale. One of the few reports that did mention him noted: 'as soon as Mr. Attlee has to "make an important speech in the House, the country knows that Mr. Churchill is abroad"'.[31] Outside the War Cabinet, Morrison was initially given the Ministry of Supply; within a few months he was made Home Secretary. Dalton was given the Ministry of Economic Warfare, and then, in 1942, the Presidency of the Board of Trade. Arguably, the most significant appointment was Bevin's. 'When I was asked if I would go into the government', he recalled, 'I asked what office they wanted me to undertake and they told me that of Minister of Labour and National Service. I said, "I do not think I shall have any competitors for that job or cause any jealousy or heart-burnings."'[32] This was because the management of wartime labour supply threatened to be an extremely vexed task. Attlee recalled of Bevin: 'After 1931 he had a great suspicion of politicians and, indeed, failed to understand the conditions in which they worked [...] But when we became fellow members of the War-time administration we soon became friends and during the War we worked together in great harmony.'[33] Bevin, a large man, was assigned a Morris 10, a relatively small vehicle, as a ministerial car. He recalled: 'I said to the then Chancellor that if I could not get a bigger car, I would ask him to purchase a shoe-horn to enable me to get into it.'[34]

We now take the significance of Labour's membership of the Churchill government for granted. In the 1960s and 70s, historians of very different complexions put forward arguments that helped establish its importance.[35] As a result of this work, it became clear that Labour's victory had been the product of profound changes dating back to the early years of the war, and was not merely the product of Tory slip-ups in the run-up to polling day in 1945. Scholars now understood the birth of the coalition as 'the medium through which the Labour Party became the dominant intellectual and political force' in the post-war years.[36] Today it seems remarkable that anyone might ever have thought differently, but of course, at the time, it was impossible for contemporaries to grasp the full significance of the events that they themselves were experiencing. Labour's leaders did understand, though, that the war offered the chance to secure objectives that would otherwise have been out of reach – as long, of course, as Britain could survive.

After the British evacuation from Dunkirk, and the subsequent fall of France, Labour benefited from the backlash of opinion against former Appeasers, notably Chamberlain and Halifax, who remained in the government. The bestselling pamphlet *Guilty Men* epitomized this popular anger, which was also reflected in the press. Not wanting his government destabilized, Churchill used his influence with the press to get the campaign halted.[37] But the damage to Chamberlain was already done. In the Commons, Labour MPs cheered Churchill, whose personal popularity was stratospheric, louder than the Tories did, perhaps to try and show where the loyalties of the 'serried ranks of Mr. Chamberlain's friends' really lay.[38]

Chamberlain, who was mortally ill, retired in the autumn, and died quickly afterwards. Halifax was removed from the scene at the end of the year, despatched as ambassador to the USA. But the MPs who had backed the government during the Norway Debate were still in place, and the Conservative Party would not be allowed to forget it. Come 1945, the Tories would still be haunted by the ghosts of their past.[39] 'They were badly frightened in 1940 when it looked as if the Nazis whom they had befriended and appeased were going to beat us', wrote one successful Labour candidate. 'But gradually as, with the advent of Labour into government the situation was saved, they recovered their self-assurance and began once more to obstruct and oppose every measure for the advancement of the people's welfare.'[40]

During the Phoney War, Labour figures had already been thinking about the shape of the post-war world. Now as ministers they were involved in running the war economy – and the decisions made would have implications for whichever government was in power when peace finally came. It fell to Attlee to introduce the Emergency Powers (Defence) (No. 2) Bill (1940), which gave ministers the power to 'make such Defence Regulations making provision for requiring persons to place themselves, their services' at the government's disposal.[41] There was, perhaps, an element of gesture politics in this broad-brush, sweeping 'enabling' Act; some of the key powers that it granted actually existed already.[42] Nevertheless, it was a significant rupture with Whitehall's interwar assumptions.[43] What was more, the creation of wartime emergency powers in general created a set of economic tools that the Attlee government extended and continued to use in peacetime. This wasn't mere happenstance. Labour had a broad and genuine ideological preference for 'physical' controls — that is to say, detailed regulations governing prices, labour, use of raw materials, imports and exports, and so forth. Socialists liked these better than attempts to regulate the economy via budgetary or financial macroeconomic management, of the kind that we might loosely call 'Keynesian'.[44] Keynes's ideas, expressed most famously in his *General Theory* of 1936, had had a mixed reception in Labour circles. But even the most enthusiastic (who included a number of the party's young economists) saw macroeconomic methods as a complement to physical controls, not as a substitute for them.

Even during wartime, ministers could not achieve their objectives simply by issuing decrees. On his appointment, Bevin had driven a hard bargain with Churchill, insisting that the Ministry of Labour must 'be in a position to make its contribution to the actual organization of production so as to ensure the right utilization of labour, and not merely be regarded as an institution to supply the personnel'.[45] But it was hard going. Elected for Wandsworth Central at a by-election — the last of the Big Five to become an MP — Bevin soon found that his inexperience of Parliament put him at a disadvantage. Although open criticism was limited in time of coalition, there were still some vociferous attacks. Conservatives felt that Bevin's 'voluntaryist' tactics were being abused by the unions; Labour dissenters placed the blame for production failings on management. Eventually, in January 1941, Bevin toughened up his approach with the introduction of the Essential Work Order (EWO). On the one hand, this gave the minister power to prevent any individual leaving a job that was designated 'national work'.[46] On the other, a business or factory could only be registered under the EWO if the minister was convinced that the conditions of work and welfare were satisfactory. Despite this effort at even-handedness, tensions between employers and workers continued to mount.[47]

The PLP started flexing its muscles as well.[48] In December 1941, following a renewed crisis over labour shortages, there were 'secret excursions and alarums within the Labour Party' leading to a major backbench revolt. Bevin was proposing an extension of National Service;

a substantial crew of rebels backed an amendment that would have matched this with 'public ownership and control of all industries vital to our war effort'.[49] Bevan, no friend of his near-namesake, justified the revolt with the argument that the forces of property had not yet been forced to make any concessions in the interests of winning the war. 'The time has come for Labour to insist on the adoption of its own policies or to regain its independence', he wrote.[50] Ministers insisted that no necessary measure had been ducked, but Attlee's efforts to bring his MPs into line exposed the limits of his authority. There were rumours that he might resign, 'since he told his Party meeting that if a substantial number voted against the Government, he would find his own position impossible'.[51]

Attlee held on, but the imbroglio was an indication of the strains within the Labour movement, which prefigured later splits between 'fundamentalism' and 'revisionism'.[52] These in turn cast light on the wider questions that have preoccupied the historians of these years. Three key issues stand out. First, what was the extent and meaning of the wartime 'swing to the left' in public opinion? Second, what was the significance of the wartime 'movement away from party', as manifested at multiple by-elections? Third, was there a 'wartime consensus', representing ideological convergence between parties, and laying the groundwork for the Attlee government's reforms?

Over the last several decades, scholars have proved quite effective at demolishing the myth of a 'People's War', in which the experience of the Blitz stimulated an orgy of radicalism and participatory democracy. The relationship between national identity and political change was complex and contested.[53] Pointing this out is not quite enough. It is surely true that the mass of the British people were never explicitly converted to the Labour Party's vision of socialism, that their views were inchoate, and that apathy and resentment at politicians were rife.[54] But as one Liberal analyst admitted at the time:

This Socialist programme must have been present to the minds of voters, however little its implications and possible consequences may have been understood by some of them. It follows, therefore, that however numerous were the Labour supporters who gave their votes for reasons other than a positive desire for Socialization, all were nevertheless aware that they were helping to install a Socialist government and were not unwilling to do so.[55]

So, if even most Labour voters did not move beyond a vague form of progressivism, the party's leaders did succeed, by a combination of luck and judgement, in exploiting this feeling to their own advantage. They did this in spite of their own divisions. Perhaps in the end they misread the meaning of their own victory. They may not have fully understood the public mood – perhaps no party ever truly does. But they put themselves, far more effectively than the Liberals or Conservatives, in a position to benefit from it.

It seems obvious, in retrospect, that the war saw 'a steady strengthening of left-wing feeling'.[56] At the time, Attlee claimed that the party's own actions had created this trend. Forced to defend Labour's continuing participation in the coalition, he argued that the 'great swing to the Left' was 'due very largely to the fact that Labour men like Morrison, Bevin, [Tom] Johnston, Alexander, and Dalton, have taken on difficult jobs, have carried them through, have not been afraid to brave criticism by doing unpopular things'.[57] The party, he claimed, was acting responsibly, but there was a risk that in so doing it would be associated with the status quo. In 1942, the Ministry of Information received a report from the Midlands on the growth of 'a kind of home-made Socialism, which does not owe allegiance to any particular political party, but which expresses a resentment of the system which has given so much power to so few people'.[58] Officials were sufficiently concerned to ask Regional Information Officers to ask if the same was true elsewhere. The replies confirmed that 'this amorphous doctrine' was widespread. It was said to have a 'non-political character' (i.e. it wasn't in support of a particular party). It had been boosted by the growing prestige of the Soviet Union, which had entered the war the previous year. It was the enemy of 'vested interests', 'privilege', and the remnants of the pre-war Establishment known as 'the old gang'.[59]

This 'movement away from party' was particularly pronounced during 1942.[60] Although the US entry into the war after Pearl Harbor seemed to signal the inevitability of victory, the fall of Singapore in February came as a profound shock. In the quest for new or better leadership, the people for a brief while put their faith in Cripps, who had just returned from his spell as Ambassador to Moscow.[61] As Tom Harrisson, founder of Mass Observation (MO), noted: 'He brought back with him an aura of success from the most successful country in fighting Germany so far, and he came back as the one British politician who has kept right outside the controversies and difficulties of the past two years of war.'[62] A rough-and-ready MO survey in the spring found that Cripps had the unreserved approval of 79 per cent of those asked. The figure for Churchill was 32 per cent, for Bevin 27 per cent, and for Morrison 18 per cent.[63] As for Attlee, it seems nobody thought to ask the question. Cripps was appointed to the War Cabinet. This was seen in some quarters as selling his principles for office, and, perhaps inevitably, his star soon waned.[64] After he fell out with Churchill over war strategy, he was demoted to the Ministry of Aircraft Production. But his brief period in the spotlight reflected the public's dissatisfaction with the status quo.

This manifested itself in a string of by-election victories for independent candidates. Then, in July, Sir Richard Acland MP, a former Liberal, launched a new party called Common Wealth. With grandiose aspirations for a new social order in which 'Fellowship' would 'replace competition as the driving force in our community', it threatened to outflank Labour from the Left.[65] It too secured a series of by-election wins. However, the organizations of the two main parties proved robust in the face of these challenges.[66] Labour also resisted the renewed attempts of the CPGB, which had gained a flood of new members, to affiliate to the party.[67] Still, Labour's leaders might well feel anxious. The 'anti-party' feelings of the public demanded a reaction, and there was no guarantee that Labour would benefit from this inchoate mood of discontent unless it found a way to channel them to its own advantage. The problem was that, to many, the party's own leaders appeared to be part of the Establishment. What appeared to Attlee and his colleagues as pragmatic compromise looked to others like a stitch-up.

This brings us to the vexed question of 'consensus'. Those who challenge the notion can easily point to the bitterness of wartime politics and to the profoundly held differences of view both within and between parties. On the other hand, Labour and the Conservatives did share some key assumptions about the conduct of politics and both were fundamentally pragmatic in their approach to societal change.[68] But although it is tempting to compare speeches and policy statements in an effort to determine whether or not politicians fundamentally agreed with each other, it is perhaps more useful to examine how the term was actually used at the time. The first uses of the term 'consensus', in the sense that we are discussing, can be found in 1942. In May of that year *The Times* commented on the Labour Party report *The Old World and the New Society* in approving terms: 'the leading features of the report reflect a broad consensus of opinion on vital issues transcending party divisions and party programmes'.[69] A few days later, the former Archbishop of Canterbury, Cosmo Lang, spoke in the Lords. He commented on Labour's report and on others by the Federation of British Industries and the London Chamber of Commerce: 'it is really remarkable what a consensus there is among all these different bodies as to the main outlines of any economic settlement after the war'.[70]

The idea of consensus, then, was not a retrospective nostalgic invention – but it would be naïve to take these statements as proof that consensus existed. They were not merely descriptions of a state of affairs; they were interventions in ideological debate. The *Times*'s comments were made in an editorial that urged Labour to stick to a moderate path and to avoid disrupting the coalition government by pursuing partisan proposals. Lang, for his part, made clear his own preference for state economic control, but also deprecated vested interests and the pursuit of party advantage. This denigration of partisanship was a well-worn theme in British politics. What is interesting is the way in which Labour managed to rework it to its own benefit, given that it had traditionally suffered from its image as a 'sectional', class-based party.

A sense of how the party did this can be gained from a letter sent by Attlee to Churchill, in the aftermath of the publication of William Beveridge's bestselling report in November 1942. Beveridge's proposals for a major expansion of social services 'sent a thrill through the Labour movement'.[71] Churchill took the view that it would be wrong for the coalition government, which lacked a fresh electoral mandate, to implement decisions on post-war policy. Attlee wrote to him that this had not been his understanding when he joined the government and argued that the government had already legislated on areas over which agreement could be reached. The people of Britain, moreover, were prepared for radical change, a point borne out, he suggested, by a recent review of public opinion circulated by the Minister of Information. 'In particular it showed a remarkable consensus of opinion on many points between people of different political parties and different economic and social backgrounds', Attlee wrote. 'I have myself been in contact with a number of prominent business men and with many people not of my own political views and have found it possible to arrive at a very large measure of agreement.'[72]

Attlee's technique, then, was to use the 'consensus' idea to paint the Prime Minister as someone who was isolated from the main currents of national opinion and who formed an obstacle to measures that were needed if disaster were to be avoided at the end of the war. His audience in this case was only the unreceptive Churchill (and perhaps his political advisers) but the letter illustrates what was at stake between the two men and their respective parties. They were involved in a battle over 'national' values, both attempting to portray themselves as representative of mainstream opinion. Churchill hoped to draw Liberal and other moderate voters to his side by casting the fight as '"socialists v. the rest" rather than "Tories v. the rest"'.[73] Attlee wanted to paint the Tories as the party of property and privilege and Labour as the modern, classless embodiment of the entire nation.

Attlee faced his own problems over Beveridge. In February 1943, despite a 'superb' speech by Morrison, there was a major revolt by Labour backbenchers who demanded that the government commit itself definitely to the principles of the report.[74] But in the end it was Churchill who was pushed onto the back foot. Grudgingly, and to counter the perception that he was an obstacle to reform, he made a broadcast in which he talked in broad terms about post-war planning. Morrison managed to push him into stating that legislative preparation should start before the war was over.[75] The first Gallup poll on voting intentions was carried out in June. Labour was 18 points ahead and stayed in the lead until the general election.[76]

Further landmarks of cross-party cooperation followed. One of these was the Education Act of 1944, pioneered by the Conservative R. A. Butler and his Labour junior minister James Chuter Ede. Aiming to improve equality of opportunity, they had to navigate a range of religious sensibilities, and certainly succeeded in improving upon the previous system. The introduction of the Eleven Plus exam, which allocated children to different types of school according to their ability, now looks retrograde. Yet this was not a major point of concern at the time for Labour MPs; the movement in favour of 'multilateral' (or comprehensive) schools had yet to gather pace.[77] More controversial was the Employment White Paper of 1944, which included the (somewhat ambiguous) commitment to maintain a high and stable level of employment after the war. This could be seen, loosely, as a commitment to Keynesian policies – which involved management of overall demand rather than detailed regulation of the economy – although there were limits to how far Labour had moved.[78] Dalton and Morrison, who would be the chief economic ministers after the war were in agreement 'that we should very much keep in mind the technique of unbalanced budgets'.[79] This position, which was in marked contrast to Labour attitudes in the 1930s, was reflected in an official party policy statement, but the new belief in contra-cyclical budgetary policy was matched by a continuing faith in physical planning and controls.[80]

One can debate whether the coalition's blueprints represented humane and enlightened social reform, or were simply a means by which the authorities neutered a more genuine form of grass-roots radicalism.[81] To some extent, this argument reflects the contemporary Labour divisions between those who saw the coalition as marking a great social advance and those who saw it as selling out socialism. Bevan parodied the Employment White Paper as 'Jobs For Some' and described it as 'a piece of elaborate and cynical deception' designed to overcome the scepticism of the fighting forces. Bevin revealed in the Commons that he had pledged to men embarking for D-Day that they would not return to the dole queues after the war. 'I hope those words will never haunt Ernest Bevin in the years to come', Bevan wrote. 'It is an audacious, or an irresponsible, man who would use such language to soldiers going into battle, about a proposal to deal with unemployment to which the Tories had given their approval.'[82]

After the success of the Normandy landings, and with the end of the war clearly in sight, the tensions within the coalition and within the Labour Party increased. In October 1944, the Liberals and Labour both announced that they would fight the next election as independent parties. This confirmed that there would be no 1918-style 'coupon election' and had 'soothing effects' on Labour critics of the coalition.[83] Exactly when the party would leave the coalition – at the end of the German or the Japanese war – was left unclear. The assumption, at this point, seems to have been that Churchill would win the election, but that Labour would benefit from a period of Opposition while the government would face post-war economic problems. The calculation of left-wingers, according to the *Observer*'s political correspondent, was that 'Another election will then become necessary and that will be Labour's chance to come back with a sweeping majority for a long stay.'[84] Yet Churchill's victory was not taken absolutely for granted. One possibility canvassed was 'A coalition of Labour and other Left-wing elements', the assumption here being that the Liberals would do reasonably well.[85]

By this stage, the NEC's Policy Committee was at work on 'Points for inclusion in a Short Programme', which would become the 1945 manifesto.[86] *Labour's Immediate Programme*, published seven years before, appears to have been the prototype, and there was considerable overlap in the policy content.[87] Although a general election was not yet at hand, such a document could be used as a manifesto if necessary. The Short Programme was not ready when the party conference took place in December. Delegates debated another NEC document, *Full Employment and Financial Policy*, instead. Many found it insipid and not explicit enough in its commitment to nationalization. Future MP Ian Mikardo moved a resolution in favour of 'the transfer to public ownership of the land, large-scale building, heavy industry, and all forms of banking, transport and fuel and power'.[88] The motion was carried over the NEC's opposition. Afterwards, Morrison had a word with Mikardo. 'Young man,' he said, 'you did very well this morning. That was a good speech you made – but you realise, don't you, that you've just lost us the general election.'[89]

According to Labour myth, this was a story of the party's grassroots using its power to prevent the leadership from betraying socialism. In fact, the detail of Mikardo's motion did not make it into the policy programme that it now fell to Morrison to draw up. All the same, the conference revolt made it easier for Dalton to press a sceptical Morrison to include a commitment to the nationalization of the iron and steel industry.[90] The resulting document was called *Let Us Face the Future*. It has been described as 'perhaps the most effective election manifesto in Labour's history'.[91] Michael Young, the Director of the Labour Party Research Department, was charged with putting the final draft together. He later claimed that if the Labour Party had had a decent organization he would not have been landed with the job and recalled that the document 'sort of wrote itself'.[92] 'I didn't think it was particularly good,' he said. 'It wasn't well written, but nor did it need to be. Almost anything the Labour Party said then was going to carry them.'[93]

The manifesto steered around the consensus issue by arguing that, although all parties paid lip service to full employment, only Labour would be ready to interfere with private industry to the degree necessary to make it happen. In terms of detailed policies, there was a strong commitment to economic planning and to nationalization. The fuel and power industries came first in the list of those to be brought into public ownership. Given that the NHS is generally seen as the Attlee government's crowning achievement, the topic received surprisingly short shrift. The best healthcare should be available free to everyone, voters were told. 'In the new National Health Service there should be health centres where the people may get the best that modern science can offer, more and better hospitals, and proper conditions for our doctors and nurses.' Foreign policy was discussed in broad internationalist terms; there was rather too much optimism about the prospect of future cooperation with the USSR. The prospect of decolonization was foreseen and welcomed, though the actual pace of change probably was not, and the topic received few words: 'the Labour Party will seek to promote mutual understanding and cordial co-operation between the Dominions of the British Commonwealth, the advancement of India to responsible self-government, and the planned progress of our Colonial Dependencies'.[94]

That such important topics received so little space should not startle us too much. Labour was, in fact, quite advanced in terms of the level of detail it provided (and there was more information given in separate documents).[95] Whereas the other main parties had often been happy to campaign on the basis of broad principles and the records and characters of their leaders, Labour's manifestos had always been fairly policy-heavy. Although *Let Us Face the Future* did not come with the 'costings' and other niceties that parties are expected to provide today, it marked a step-change in British electioneering.[96] It was intended not only as a way of winning votes but as a tool to be used once the party was in power. If the party obtained a mandate from the people for a specified set of policies, that would make it easier to overcome the resistance that it expected to encounter. To this end the document stated, 'we give clear notice that we will not tolerate obstruction of the people's will by the House of Lords'.[97]

Somewhat improbably, *Let Us Face the Future* succeeded in (more or less) satisfying Labour's Left without turning into a weapon to be used by the party's enemies. The weekly *Tribune*, founded by Cripps in 1937, generally took an uncompromising line, but was now gratified that Labour was starting to disentangle itself from the coalition. The statement about the Lords gave the policy declaration 'a steel edge'. 'At last we are moving in the right direction,' the paper argued, 'even if the pace of advance is not so quick as some of us would like.'[98] At Labour's next conference, in May 1945, Mikardo commended the NEC for its 'good and workmanlike job'.[99]

Let Us Face the Future slipped under the radar of the mainstream press, because it was not perceived to be very new or radical. The *Economist* suggested that it simply restated 'in rather cautious terms, well-established Labour principles and policies, which might have been taken from any Labour manifesto during the past twenty years'.[100] The headline in the *Daily Mail* was 'LABOUR LIMITS PLEDGES'.[101] The Tory Party's *Notes for Speakers and Workers* criticized the 'boastful rhetoric and misleading innuendo' of the manifesto and attempted to debunk its claims.[102] But the Conservatives focused their main attacks elsewhere, and meanwhile nearly 1.3 million copies of the pamphlet were distributed.[103] How many voters actually read it is unknown, but it served a propaganda function simply as a physical object. Its striking cover, featuring the 'V for Victory' symbol, was designed by John Armstrong. He was also responsible for the iconic election poster based on the same theme.[104]

In May 1945, shortly after VE Day, Labour and the Liberals left the coalition. This was not the time of Attlee's own choosing, and the Labour leaders were divided among themselves. Churchill offered two options: an election at once or the continuation of the coalition until the end of the war with Japan. Attlee, Bevin and Dalton favoured staying in; Morrison favoured withdrawal and won the day in the NEC. Churchill resigned as Prime Minister and formed a new caretaker government that would last until the election in July. Wilkinson approached Dalton and suggested Attlee step aside in favour of Morrison, but Dalton did not encourage her. Harold Laski, Professor of Political Science at the LSE, and current Chairman of the NEC, wrote to Attlee directly to tell him he should resign in the interests of the party. Attlee's reply has become legendary:

Dear Laski
Thank you for your letter, contents of which have been noted.
C.R. Attlee[105]

Attlee's restrained and low-key personality was in tune with the mood, conventions and emotional codes of the day.[106] In spite of the bitterness of much of the politicians' rhetoric, the election campaign was diminuendo. Mass meetings and personal contact with the public remained important, but voter participation and rowdiness were lower than in previous elections.[107] In comparison to today, there was relatively little interference from party HQ in individual constituency battles. Future Prime Minister Jim Callaghan, who fought Cardiff South, remembered: 'We fought our own election. We were isolated. There weren't all these quantities of leaflets or instructions or things you ought to concentrate on.'[108] However, Labour's finances had improved radically during the war, allowing it to develop a newly sophisticated publicity, propaganda and media effort.[109] Newsreels were important – cinema attendance grew during wartime and peaked in 1946.[110] Churchill's filmed election speech may have been seen by 20 million cinemagoers, and it is likely that Attlee got a similar audience.[111] Cinema, though, was considered second in importance to radio. The various parties' election broadcasts received an average of 45 per cent of the domestic audience and were widely reprinted in the press.[112] In addition, they were recorded and rebroadcast on shortwave so that the men overseas would have the same chance to listen as those at home.[113]

Hence the impact of Churchill's first radio speech, which has come to rank with the most notorious of his utterances. He said that a Labour government 'would have to fall back on some form of Gestapo, no doubt very humanely directed in the first instance'.[114] Churchill had given his government a 'National' veneer by recruiting a number of non-Tories, and the speech was partly an attempt to appeal to Liberal opinion. But, even if carefully calculated, it was clearly misjudged. Churchill had just spent five years working closely with Labour colleagues, but now he seemed to suggest that electing them would unleash Nazi-style horrors. The liberation of the concentration camps had made a huge impression on the British public, but was not understood at the time in the context of the 'Final Solution'. (In fact, Belsen, which made perhaps the greatest impact, was not an extermination camp.) Left-wingers tended to view the camps in light of what had been known about them in the 1930s – that is, that they had been used to repress Social Democrats and other political opponents of the Nazis, even as the Conservatives had continued to pursue their policy of Appeasement. In this context, socialists could be far more persuasively portrayed as the likely victims of Nazi-style political terror than as its likely perpetrators, so Churchill's Gestapo comment was particularly inopportune. As the historian of Belsen's liberation has suggested, the news from the camps played into Labour's hands.[115]

Yet, in their rebuttals, Labour's leaders did not criticize the Prime Minister on grounds of poor taste. Morrison, instead, suggested it was the product of a mental lapse. He labelled it 'Churchill's crazy broadcast', which became the following day's *Daily Herald* headline.[116] Attlee was due to broadcast the day after Churchill. 'The unexpectedly violent attack by the Prime Minister on his late colleagues and on all that they stood for raised the question as to what line I should follow,' he recalled. 'I decided not to alter my original script but only to add a few words of comment on the line taken by my opponent.'[117] Those 'few words' were devastating:

> When I listened to the Prime Minister's speech last night, in which he gave such a travesty of the policy of the Labour Party, I realized at once what was his object. He wanted the electors to understand how great was the difference between Winston Churchill, the great leader in war of a united nation, and Mr. Churchill, the party leader of the Conservatives. He feared lest those who had accepted his leadership in war might be tempted out of gratitude to follow him further. I thank him for having disillusioned them so thoroughly.

In the final section of his speech, Attlee contested Churchill's claim that his government was a 'National' one. Not only was the government a Conservative government, he argued, but the Conservative Party was 'a class Party' that had rarely drawn any MPs from 'the ranks of the wage-earners' and continued to represent 'property and privilege'. Moreover, 'The Labour Party is, in fact, the one party which most nearly reflects in its representation and composition all the main streams which flow into the great river of our national life.'[118]

It must not be assumed that all listeners were turned off by Churchill or persuaded by Attlee. Nor is it necessarily true that the Conservatives fought dirtier than Labour. A range of socialist figures themselves compared the Tories to Nazis or Fascists. For example, Cripps, who had re-joined Labour earlier in the year, now declared it sinister that there was no mention of the word 'Conservative' in the manifesto of Churchill, who was running a highly personalized campaign. 'In Cumberland I saw someone was running as a "Churchill candidate",' he said. 'We seem to be getting nearer and nearer the Fuhrer idea.'[119] It's worth noting, too, that the Nazi comparisons had been kicked off not by Churchill, but by Attlee. During the debates over whether or not the coalition should be continued, Churchill had proposed a referendum on whether the life of the current Parliament should be prolonged. Attlee had publicly rejected the suggestion. 'I could not consent to the introduction into our national life of a device so alien to all our traditions as the referendum, which has only too often been the instrument of Nazism and Fascism', he wrote, adding: 'Hitler's practices in the field of referenda and plebiscites can hardly have endeared these expedients to the British heart.'[120]

Labour's sometimes brutal rhetoric could, of course, be seen as a necessary response to long-standing Tory tactics. The Labour Party *Speaker's Handbook 1945* summoned up memories of the Zinoviev letter and other such stunts, warning that the Conservatives might 'spring scares as they have so unscrupulously done so often before'.[121] It was a good prediction. There were suggestions that Labour would confiscate individual savings held with the Post Office. And with the so-called 'Laski scare' the Tories seem to have thought they were on to a winning ticket. Churchill was due to meet with Stalin and Truman for a conference at Potsdam, near Berlin. The conference was to start after polling day but before the results were known (there was a three-week delay in order to allow the votes of servicemen abroad to be counted). As a courtesy, Churchill invited Attlee to come too. Then Laski stuck his oar in. He announced that, as the conference would be debating issues that the NEC and the PLP had not yet discussed, the Labour Party could not be committed to any decisions made at Potsdam.[122] The Tory papers painted the socialist professor as a revolutionary extremist who would be the power behind the Labour leader's throne.[123]

This was a (doubtless intentional) misreading of Laski's powers. As Chairman of the NEC, serving for a single year on the basis of Buggins' turn, he was a functionary with ideas above his station. Though Laski may be given some credit for helping ensure that the Left remained loyal to Labour, Attlee regarded him as a self-important nuisance.[124]

In a lengthy public correspondence with Churchill, Attlee schooled the Prime Minister on the niceties of the Labour Party constitution. Churchill liked to release his missives late at night, to try to prevent the replies appearing alongside them in the press the next day, but Attlee always managed to respond in time anyway.[125]

The fact that the Laski scare was silly was not, in itself, any guarantee that it wouldn't work. For fear tactics to function, though, they normally need to be coupled with a more positive approach. In 1945, the Conservatives struggled with this. 'I am worried about this damned election,' Churchill admitted to his doctor. 'I have no message for them now.'[126] It has been said that Churchill 'was useless as a social reformer'.[127] Actually, though he failed to prioritize such issues during the war, he had a considerable interest in them and a track record dating back to Edwardian times.[128] Indeed, the Conservatives had plenty of policies. The party's manifesto devoted more space to health than the Labour one did. It pledged: 'no one will be denied the attention, the treatment or the appliances he requires because he cannot afford them. We propose to create a comprehensive health service covering the whole range of medical treatment.'[129] Such a health service, if put into practice had the Tories won, would probably have been much more limited in scope than the one that came into being.[130] Still, there was enough overlap between the parties to make it necessary for Labour to stress the differences. As A. V. Alexander warned, 'Programmes may appear to be similar, but it is the *principles* upon which decisions have to be made at this time.'[131] The Tories suffered not only because they failed to package their policies in an attractive and dynamic fashion, but also because Labour successfully cast doubt on their sincerity and highlighted the limitations of their ideas.

Churchill was met by huge crowds – and a certain amount of heckling – on his national election travels. Attlee made a tour of his own, chauffeured in an Austin 7 by his wife, a notoriously poor driver. Bevin was probably the most prominent of the Labour leaders. The Labour Party issued a pamphlet praising his record as Minister of Labour; there was no equivalent for Attlee.[132] The authors of the academic study of the general election – the first attempt at such an analysis – wrote that 'the hero' of the Opposition press 'was undoubtedly Mr. Bevin'.[133] Housing, in the wake of the Blitz, was an urgent issue for many voters. Bevin declared that 'if returned to power I would tackle housing just as I tackled aeroplanes and shells for the war'.[134] When he slammed the steel industry's price-fixing cartel it was the main headline in the *Daily Mirror* – attacks on Big Business were a significant election theme.[135] Bevin was now taking a growing interest in foreign policy too.[136] 'In the realm of foreign affairs you have been told that only certain men can handle these problems,' he told radio listeners. 'Was ever such nonsense uttered?'[137] According to the diary of *Daily Express* journalist Albert Hird:

> It is of course a commonplace that Attlee only holds his position as leader of the Labour Party in the House of Commons because the party cannot make up their minds on Bevin or Herbert Morrison as leader. Many of them mistrust Bevin and do not like either the man or his methods, while still more distrust Morrison, whom they feel will 'rat' upon them whenever the prospects seems good enough.[138]

The election results were declared on 26 July. Chuter Ede recorded: 'at 12 noon came the staggering announcement: "The government holds 24 seats, the Opposition 100 ..."' He wondered if he would wake up and discover he had been dreaming.[139] Labour had won 393 seats, the Conservatives and their allies 213, and the Liberals a mere 12. For the winners it was a moment of elation, for the losers a time of shock and grief.[140] Barbara Castle (elected for Blackburn) claimed in her memoirs that 'no one in the Labour Party, except Aneurin Bevan, believed that the party could snatch victory from the wartime Prime Minister'.[141] It is quite true that the *scale* of Labour's triumph was an incredible surprise. It is also true that the Gallup polls, which had consistently predicted such a result, were not taken seriously.[142] But it has been forgotten that in fact there were a range of optimistic predictions from the Labour side, and above all a good deal of uncertainty.[143] As one Conservative MP wrote: 'My reason tells me that there will be a Tory debacle; my instinct urges me to remember that the Socialists are hopeless tacticians and may blunder at the eleventh hour.'[144]

Shortly before polling day, Morrison claimed that victory was within grasp.[145] This may have been mere bravado, but Labour agents throughout the country were predicting a marked swing to the Left.[146] The *Manchester Guardian* judged that although the chances of Labour getting a majority were remote, the party might be able to form a government together with the Liberals.[147] (The poor Liberal performance came as much as a surprise to many as the poor Tory one.) Some journalists speculated privately that the enthusiasm shown towards Churchill on his tour might not translate into votes, 'and that when it came to marking the ballot paper the hold of the Trade Unions in the North would tell'.[148] After polling day, Labour was reported as claiming it had achieved a balance in the new Parliament; one unnamed party figure predicted a 1929-style result.[149] At the end of the campaign, Ede had noted: 'I have alternating waves of pessimism & optimism, but cannot accept the apparent view of neutral opinion that we are winning.'[150] The existence of this 'neutral opinion' suggests that although surprise at the size of the majority was real, Labour's win did not come out of a clear blue sky. Attlee recalled returning from his election tour 'confident that we should do well, but with no great conviction that we were going to sweep the country'.[151]

This is important because it helps explain why, during the campaign, Labour mostly avoided the internal recriminations typical of a party that thinks it is going down to defeat. If Churchill had achieved his upper prediction of an 80-seat majority, this would still have meant substantial Tory losses.[152] Even Dalton's pessimistic prediction of a Conservative majority of one hundred involved Labour picking up 80 constituencies.[153] Labour therefore behaved, not as a party confident of winning, but as one that believed it was on a significant upward curve. It made sense to imagine that a post-war Churchill government would prove as disappointing as Lloyd George's had after 1918 and that Labour could then step into the breach. Labour, then, was positioning itself for power, even in the belief that one more heave would likely still be needed.

Multiple, interlocking factors explained Labour's win. The Conservatives, of course, tried to explain it away. They argued that the Army Bureau of Current Affairs (ABCA) had, through its efforts at citizenship education, radicalized servicemen and paved the way for Labour's landslide. But the numbers of servicemen who voted could not have accounted for Labour's majority, even if 100 per cent of them had plumped for Labour.[154] The party certainly benefited from the public's war-weariness. Churchill's pitch was that he was the man best placed to fight the war with Japan to the finish. 'We've beaten the Hun,' said one Tory leaflet, 'but there's more to be done.'[155] But the voters lacked interest in the Japanese conflict, perhaps felt that the war was effectively over, and preferred to focus on domestic horizons. 'We beat Hitler', wrote Labour's candidate in Blackpool South. 'Let Us Beat Poverty!'[156] That slogan didn't gain Labour this safe Tory seat. But it reflected the party's winning national message that the 'great people' that had saved itself 'in the face of mortal danger' should now 'give Labour power to lead the way to a peaceful world and a just social order'.[157]

Not everything can be pinned on Tory misjudgements, given that, if the Gallup polls are to be believed, the Conservatives actually recovered ground during the campaign. The incumbents were naturally vulnerable to the 'swing of the pendulum' and the emergence of a new generation of voters, as there had not been a general election for ten years. Labour's campaigning and organizational advantages were matched by improved press coverage, though the media playing field was still not level. The London papers that backed Labour had six million readers between them, and the Tory-supporting ones six million eight hundred thousand.[158] The anti-establishment line of the populist *Daily Mirror* was significant, although the paper did not declare its formal support for Labour until the campaign's final days.[159] The government probably suffered from 'the feeling of sheer blind weariness and fed-upness at continued shortages, discomforts, uncertainties'.[160] At the same time, many voters were probably persuaded by Labour's claims that the Conservatives would relax controls too soon, thus putting an end to 'fair shares'. Labour's successful national appeal – though dependent on a rather fragile party unity – was the key to attracting middle-class votes and extending its appeal in London and the south-east.

Above all, Labour had succeeded in shifting the narrative. Crucially, it turned the dominant image of the 1930s into one of dole queues, slums, foreign policy failures and broken promises.[161] Although this was to some extent a caricature, it was based on genuine memories of suffering, injustice and government indifference. The further distress caused by war and bombing accentuated the thirst for positive visions of what was to come. As Mass Observation reported, once the first shock of the outcome had waned, there was a widespread feeling of optimism for the future, 'that here was something new, that was to be seriously and earnestly tried out'.[162] One Labour-supporting soldier recalled hearing the results on All India Radio in a tented camp on the Indian–Burmese border: 'I sat in our mess drinking warm gin and watching the senior officers sinking deeper and deeper into gloom. Every Labour win brought on an enormous cheer from the troops. They knew Britain was going to be different and better.'[163] Another remembered 'coming back from Jerusalem across the Sinai Desert and reading in the *Palestine Post* that Tom Reed had been elected [in Swindon] with an 11,000 majority. And – yes, there was hope. Hope.'[164]

3

New Masters

April 2nd 1946. Sir Hartley Shawcross, several months into his role as Attorney-General, was speaking on the Third Reading of the new government's Trades Disputes and Trade Unions Bill. The Bill's purpose was simple – to repeal the Act of 1927, passed in the wake of the General Strike, and seen by many as a purely vindictive piece of legislation. It had hurt the Labour Party's income, as union members now had to 'contract in' to the payment of the political levy that funded it, rather than passively paying it unless they 'contracted out'. During the war, the unions had repeatedly pressed the government to do away with the hated law. Churchill had responded by challenging Labour to submit the issue to the verdict of the people – clearly believing that, if his opponents made it an election issue, they would never win. Now they had done so. Shawcross accused Churchill of trying to wriggle out of it. He told MPs that the former Prime Minister was acting like Humpty-Dumpty, who claimed that the meaning of words was determined by who was master. Then Shawcross rubbed it in: 'We are the masters at the moment, and not only at the moment, but for a very long time to come, and as hon. Members opposite are not prepared to implement the pledge which was given by their leader in regard to this matter at the General Election, we are going to implement it for them.'[1]

In spite of his later, probably ironic, recollection, Shawcross was never 'a red hot socialist'.[2] Dalton, who thought him arrogant and vain, called him 'Sir Peacock'.[3] (They had something in common though: Shawcross put his feet up in the chamber 'with something like the abandon of that champion sprawler Mr. Hugh Dalton'.[4]) Because of his right-wing tendencies, he later attracted the nickname 'Sir Shortly Floorcross', quit Labour, and sat as a cross-bench peer. Strikingly handsome, and with 'expressive hands', he had made his name as a star barrister.[5] In his forties at the war's end, he was mildly disappointed to be given the Attorney-Generalship rather than a more political role, but legal expertise in the government ranks was in short supply. This job involved him personally leading the prosecutions of high-profile traitors and of the 'acid-bath murderer' John Haigh. He also led the British prosecution team at the Nuremberg trials. But these responsibilities did not preclude him from involvement in partisan politics, as long as he didn't politicize the legal aspects of his job. Hence his willingness to put the boot into the Tories, which, together with his haughty disposition, got him into trouble.

After Shawcross's speech, the independent MP W. J. Brown alleged in the *Evening Standard* that Shawcross 'in an exultant voice, told the House that "We are the masters now"'.[6] This was a slightly inaccurate rendition of the words but rather a catchy one. Though Shawcross's gaffe did not gain notoriety immediately, within a year or so the improved version was being flung back at Labour as evidence of its high-handedness and 'shockingly class-conscious' attitude.[7] It gave the title of a polemical book, *Our New Masters*, by the journalist Colm Brogan, which was admired by the young Margaret Thatcher.[8] 'At all events the misquotation stuck and has followed me around all my life,' Shawcross recalled ruefully in his nineties. 'If I had not been so politically naïve and unsophisticated in the art of public relations I should have realized that the phrase could be used against me.' At the time 'it all seemed good fun' and the backbenches lapped it up.[9]

This apparently trivial wave of spin and counter-spin symbolized much about the Labour government's first year. Despite the threat of national bankruptcy, Attlee and his ministers seemed to carry all before them. Wielding their huge mandate from the electorate, they set about fulfilling their pledges with abandon, pausing here and there to grind their opponents' noses into the dirt. After a few months in office, the new Prime Minister's own stock stood higher than ever, while Churchill and his Conservative colleagues failed to find their feet in Opposition. At the same time, during the honeymoon period – which Attlee knew from the start would be a short one – trouble was building for the future.[10] On the one hand, the government, under pressure, took economic decisions that would return to bite it. On the other, the hubristic language of ministers like Shawcross gave Labour's enemies a stick with which to beat it. Meanwhile, ministers' optimistic and occasionally brash demeanour disguised internal tensions that Attlee, nonetheless, largely kept under control.

Attlee can have been under no illusions as to the rivalries within his new Cabinet. Two days before the election results were declared, Morrison had sent him a letter. 'A number of our colleagues have approached me, provisionally,' he wrote, 'asking that I should accept nomination for the leadership of the Parliamentary Party.' Posing as the defender of the interests of Labour MPs, and claiming to have given the matter deep thought, Morrison stated that he had decided to agree to be nominated. 'That I am animated solely by considerations of the interest of the party, and regard for their democratic rights, and not by any personal unfriendliness towards yourself, I need hardly assure you.'[11] If Labour had gone down to defeat, a leadership contest would have made perfect sense. But even after the victory was known, Morrison's vanity drove him to press on.

In the afternoon of 26 July Churchill conceded he had lost the election. When the news reached Transport House (Labour's HQ) Morrison argued that, according to party rules, Attlee should not accept a commission from the King to form a government until the PLP had met and elected its leader. 'We cannot have that man as Prime Minister,' he insisted.[12] Morrison then spoke to Cripps on the phone and reported to Attlee and Bevin that he had his backing. When Morrison left the room, Bevin asked Morgan Phillips, the party Secretary, if he, Bevin, would win if he stood against Attlee. It was quite possible, judged Phillips. Bevin 'went blue in the face' and said to Attlee: 'Clem, you go to the Palace straight away.'[13]

Attlee saw the King at Buckingham Palace at 7.30. 'I've won the election,' he told him. 'I know,' the King replied. 'I heard it on the six o'clock news.'[14] When Attlee spoke at Labour's Central Hall victory rally later that evening he announced: 'I have this evening accepted His Majesty's commission to form a government.'[15] The acclamation he received put paid to Morrison's hopes. Backbencher Ian Mikardo judged that had Morrison been nominated, 'Attlee would have defeated him by an overwhelming majority.'[16] The setback did not stop Morrison from making a final, vain effort during a party committee meeting the next day.[17] Had he succeeded, even if only to the extent of delaying Attlee's triumph, it might have confirmed the suspicions raised by the 'Laski scare' – that the Labour leader's strings were controlled by a cabal who put the party's constitution above that of the country. As Attlee put it in retirement: 'If you're invited by the King to form a Government you don't say you can't reply for forty-eight hours. You accept the commission and you either bring it off successfully or you don't, and if you don't you go back and say you can't and advise the King to send for someone else.'[18]

Attlee gave instructions that No. 10 was to be left at Churchill's disposal until he was ready to move out. In the meantime, he decided to occupy offices at the Treasury and lived in a flat in Storey's Gate.[19] For Vi, who had never discussed with her husband what would happen if he became Prime Minister, the next two months were 'a nightmare'. The amount of post was 'colossal' and she had no secretary to help her. 'I also had no peace from the Press – and photographers.' It was only in mid-October that the couple moved into Downing Street. 'It was such a relief to be there and to be with my husband again.'[20]

Labour's victory caused shock not only around the world, but also at home in Northern Ireland. There, the protestant Unionist regime had just won a substantial victory in elections for the Stormont parliament, on a strong anti-socialist ticket – though the Northern Ireland Labour Party had put in a good performance too. The Unionists maintained their dominance at the Westminster election but were apprehensive of a London government with an uncongenial agenda.[21] The result caused bafflement in the USA. However, as the British embassy reported, even right-leaning American papers 'concluded in not unfriendly tones that no radical break with the past is involved in this "middle-class revolution" and that the British tradition of orderly progress and moderation will prevail'. Attlee's personality, said to be 'as British as Oxford, warm beer or cold toast', was often cited as evidence for this view. He was now spoken of as 'the British Truman', another understated character who had risen from obscurity, and whom Attlee himself liked and admired.[22]

But those on the free enterprise wing of Truman's government – labelled 'conservatives' by the New Deal radicals – were wary. As Arthur Krock of the *New York Times* summarized, they believed that the United States should stand by Britain. 'But it must safeguard all its commitments against a demoralized British economy that might result from the attempt to carry out the promised Labor party program. It should not "underwrite State Socialism."'[23] To Canadian Prime Minister W. L. Mackenzie King, though, Churchill's defeat came as a relief: 'at Imperial Conferences and peace conferences I know I will not have to be bucking centralized Imperialism again'.[24]

As part of its election pitch, Labour had claimed that it could handle relations with the Soviets better than Churchill and his reactionary colleagues: 'Let it not be forgotten that in the years leading up to the war the Tories were so scared of Russia that they missed the chance to establish a partnership which might well have prevented the war.'[25] Moscow radio welcomed the result of the election as a new chapter in the life of Britain, noting: 'The Labour Party leaders are at great pains to refute statements abroad suggesting that Britain might be willing to resume the leadership in an anti-Russian coalition.'[26] But when, just a couple of days after taking office, Attlee returned to Germany for the conclusion of the Potsdam conference, it was clear that there would be no new dawn. On the British side there was continuity not only in personnel – the same civil servants were present as before – but in policy. The UK and the USA worked hand in glove, doing their best to counter harsh Soviet demands over Italy, Poland and Germany. Attlee thought Stalin regretted the result of the election. 'But despite that we did try very hard to get alongside him. It proved perfectly impossible.'[27] At the close of proceedings there came the question of which country would sign the communiqué first. 'I favor alphabetical order,' quipped Attlee; 'that is where I would score over Marshal Zhukov.'[28]

Potsdam was sandwiched between two rounds of Cabinet-making. Attlee made his most high-profile appointments before leaving London. Dalton had expected to go to the Foreign Office, but instead picked up the keys to No. 11, though Bevin had wanted the Treasury. On 28 July, the Czech Foreign Minister told an American journalist that 'he had spent a long time last night with Bevin and Bevin had assured him he would not accept the post of foreign minister because it would divorce him too completely from Labor Party activities and the trade union movement. [...] Before midnight Attlee announced that Bevin was his foreign minister.'[29] There is an apocryphal story that another US reporter burst into Bevin's Commons room an hour after his appointment and asked him his views about communists. 'I hate the buggers,' he supposedly replied. 'Now you bugger off.'[30]

Bevin's legendary toughness was seen by many as a vital qualification for what was clearly going to be a Herculean job. Edward Hulton, proprietor of *Picture Post*, wrote of his joy that 'Labour has not thought fit to appoint some goody-goody Left-Wing intellectual, rather too full of "uplift," to this post; but Ernest Bevin, whose massive limbs are like those of the Englishmen who fought at Agincourt.'[31] The Northern Irish Unionists were reassured because Bevin, one of their most consistent critics, would be occupied elsewhere.[32] But why the Bevin–Dalton switch? The King recorded in his diary that at the meeting at which he asked Attlee to form a government, 'I asked him whom he would make Foreign Secy. & he suggested Dr. Hugh Dalton. I disagreed with him & said that Foreign Affairs was the most important subject at the moment & I hoped he would make Mr. Bevin take it.' Supposedly, Attlee said he would.[33] Alan Lascelles, a key courtier, was convinced that 'the King persuaded Attlee to put Bevin, and not Greasy Dalton, into the Foreign Office'.[34]

Attlee later claimed not to have been influenced by the King's suggestion, nor even, in his distracted state, to have remembered it.[35] Perhaps this was disingenuous, but he did have sound reasons for his decision, irrespective of any royal influence. In autobiographical notes written towards the end of his time as Prime Minister, Attlee explained that Bevin's enmity with Morrison was a crucial factor. The latter 'had some hankering after a departmental job, but I convinced him that his proper position was that of Lord President [of the Council], leader of the House and Deputy Prime Minister with general supervision over Home Affairs'. In that case, though, he had to be kept from clashing with the man who so thoroughly loathed him. 'I was not convinced that Dalton's temperament really fitted him for the Foreign Office, but as Chancellor of the Exchequer Bevin would certainly have got into controversy with Morrison.'[36]

Chuter Ede, to his 'great surprise', was given the Home Office, rather than Education, as he would have wished: that job was given to Ellen Wilkinson.[37] (Attlee believed that 'you should have some women in and there are certain jobs like Education or National Insurance where a woman will fit better than others'.[38]) Cripps, having only recently re-joined Labour, had to be content with the Presidency of the Board of Trade. With his icy competence and poorly disguised contempt for the Opposition, W. J. Brown compared him to 'a disembodied Brain, which functions with enormous efficiency, but no warmth whatever'.[39]

The most surprising – and inspired – appointment was that of Nye Bevan as Minister of Health and Housing. It was remarkable because Bevan's track record was not that of an administrator, but of a brilliant yet destructive critic. Nor had he shown a strong interest in medical issues. In October 1940, the pioneering Black dentist Edward Tull-Warnock responded to one of Bevan's articles in *Tribune*, saying he was 'astonished to find that in demanding State service for banking, railways, mining, etc., he made no mention of "Health"'.[40] Bevan took the point, but as one biographer has argued, healthcare was always secondary to his broader goal of creating a socialist society.[41]

Emanuel Shinwell, who became Minister of Fuel and Power, had, like Bevan, been a critic of the wartime coalition, and indeed had refused to join it. Not known for his generosity of spirit, he nonetheless acknowledged that the new Prime Minister had wholly suppressed his personal feelings when making his Cabinet: 'In the event Attlee appointed each man to the post most suitable, and contrary to their own ambitions.'[42] That said, Shinwell failed spectacularly in his new role, and of course Attlee did not neglect factors such as the relative popularity of his appointees within the Labour Party. In fact, with some later promotions, Attlee received press criticism, as a Haileyburian, for being too influenced by the Old School Tie.[43] He was not shy about this in his memoirs, in which he explained his choice of Geoffrey de Freitas as his PPS: 'There was a wide choice, but, other things being equal, I saw no reason why I should not select someone from my old school.'[44]

Most of the new ministers were in their sixties, and between them had much government experience. Bevan, at 47, was the youngest. The oldest, at 76, was Lord Addison. (As a Liberal he had served under Asquith and Lloyd George; he was now to be a more-than-usually significant Leader of the House of Lords.) Seven were ex-miners. It was the first Cabinet to have a nonconformist majority.[45] In the Cabinet there was a Minister of Defence, but the ministers for the three armed services were left outside.[46] There was no drastic overhaul of the machinery of government. The wartime system of Cabinet committees was maintained, but there was no immediate move towards major constitutional change.[47] There was, of course, civil service continuity. The new government inherited an arrangement whereby Cabinet Secretary Edward Bridges also served as Permanent Secretary to the Treasury and head of the civil service. Norman Brook served as an additional secretary to the Cabinet and in practice took on the work of recording its decisions. In 1947 Brook took over as full Cabinet Secretary and served for 15 years, becoming known as the 'man of a million secrets'.[48]

Labour's opponents would not have agreed that the party was constitutionally conservative. Rather they saw the government's determination to drive through its plans by seizing control of the parliamentary timetable as a sign of its imperious, arbitrary and authoritarian character. From the point of view of a new backbencher, the new regime had its discouraging aspects. As Jean Mann, MP for Coatbridge, recalled:

> On our arrival we were taken around by some of the old hands and were told what was expected of us – exactly nothing! 'Keep mum and let the Bills get through.' With a bunch of women which included Jennie Lee, Barbara Castle, Bessie Braddock, Leah Manning, and Jean Mann, that was going to be difficult. Hence the warning – there wouldn't even be the tiniest Private Member's Bill allowed![49]

In a 1930s memorandum, Attlee had written that 'The essential quality in a PM is that he should be a good Chairman able to get others to work.' He judged that 'The vice of the modern cabinet is allowing things to drift because of differences of opinion.'[50] As Prime Minister, he stuck closely to his preferred model, placing the importance of reaching a decision above that of arriving at any given policy outcome. His technique was not perfect, as it led him to be reactive, rather than giving the strong positive lead that was sometimes needed. All the same, it was the method that helped Labour achieve all its manifesto pledges in a remarkably short space of time, aided by the abilities and outsize personalities of Attlee's top team.

Attlee conducted himself in an extremely self-effacing way but, argued George Strauss, this was not the same thing as modesty, 'of which he had little'. Strauss had been appointed to the Ministry of Transport and recalled in his memoirs the pep-talk that he and other junior ministers received from the Prime Minister. Attlee's opening words were 'warm and wise' but then, almost as an afterthought, he added a personal request. 'If I walk past you in the corridors of the House without greeting you, please don't take offence. Remember I'm shy.'[51] Woodrow Wyatt, a new MP fresh out of the army, made the mistake of addressing him as he would a superior officer. 'Don't call me "Sir", call me "Clem", snapped Attlee, presumably trying to put me at my ease.'[52] *New Statesman* editor Kingsley Martin recalled Attlee as 'very cold and icy with a tough tongue which upset people'.[53] Yet as Evan Durbin, Dalton's PPS, noted, Attlee's aloofness was 'one of manner, not of spirit, for he knows an immense amount about all his colleagues in the House of Commons as *individuals* – their gifts, their weaknesses, their family circumstances'.[54]

Two months after taking power, although 'allergic to the press', Attlee appointed Francis Williams, former editor of the *Daily Herald*, as his Public Relations adviser. Like Strauss, Williams judged that Attlee's lack of vanity and disregard for the trappings of office was not a product of self-doubt: 'He had in fact great self-confidence and a strong streak of ruthlessness, and although he was an administrator of ideas rather than a creative political thinker he knew exactly what he wanted to do.'[55] Williams persuaded Attlee to have a news agency ticker-tape service installed in No. 10, offering the incentive that it would help the Prime Minister keep up with the cricket. The next week Attlee dashed into Williams's office in a state of anxiety: 'You know my cricket machine at the Cabinet door? When I checked it just now for the lunch-time score at Lord's it was ticking out the decisions and subjects discussed at the Cabinet meeting this morning. How can it do that?'[56]

In the room next to Williams's was another former journalist, Douglas Jay. For the government's first few months Jay served as Attlee's economic adviser, before becoming an MP and later a minister. In his memoirs, Jay remembered the strains of this initial period, dominated by financial crisis and global shortages. 'So far from pulling great levers, the PM at this time found himself hemmed in by relentless economic or physical forces, and faced with problems which had to be solved, but could not be solved.' Attlee's position was 'more that of a cornered animal. Or a climber on a rock face unable to go up or down, than that of a general ordering his troops wherever he wished around the landscape.'[57] In the face of huge challenges, it was remarkable how much assurance and aplomb the government seemed to possess at this stage.

So long as the war with Japan continued, Britain continued to be kept afloat by American Lend-Lease aid. Days after Labour took power, Assistant Secretary of State for Economic Affairs Will Clayton arrived in

London for financial conversations with the new government, Clayton – 'tall, strikingly handsome, beautifully attired, articulate, affable, assured' – was an enthusiastic advocate of an open global economy.[58] Too much so for the British – Dalton dubbed him 'Doctrinaire Willie'.[59] Cripps chaired a meeting at which Clayton and John Maynard Keynes – the distinguished economist and Treasury adviser – began to thrash out the main lines of policy regarding post-war US assistance to Britain.[60]

Cripps, with his pinched features, rimless spectacles and clear, but rather academic manner of talking, presented, at first glance, a striking contrast with Clayton, the tall, well-built Southerner, with grey hair, and handsome, rugged features. Cripps had a 'somewhat wintry humour and cordiality, a slight attitude of superiority and contempt', whereas the suave, earnest Clayton was 'patient, reasonable, smooth as butter' in the face of criticism.[61] Yet they also had a certain amount in common. They were both rich men, of self-denying habits and fierce intelligence, and both worked harder than could possibly have been good for them. Both, from strikingly different perspectives, had a political zeal that verged on the fanatical. And although the solutions they advocated – freer trade versus planned trade – were radically different, there were similarities in the ways they viewed the world's problems. Economic rivalries caused war; international cooperation to eliminate them would help guarantee peace. And both men appreciated that compromises would be needed in order to achieve this. After the shock of Labour's landslide Cripps made a reassuring broadcast to the USA that was 'quoted as evidence of the firm democratic foundations of the British way of life'.[62]

Still, the Truman administration would face trouble at home if it was seen to be 'subsidising socialism'. The US government was determined to extract, as the price of any aid, British commitments towards multilateral and non-discriminatory trade and payments regimes. In simple terms, the Americans wanted to reduce the barriers to the free flow of goods and money that they believed had helped cause the war, which itself had only made the problems worse. Post-war help from them to the UK was bound to be conditional on progress towards these ideals. Britain would have to join the new financial institutions negotiated at the 1944 Bretton Woods conference. It would also have to work with the USA to establish an International Trade Organization (ITO).

There was one big sticking point: Britain's imperial preference system. Though of limited economic significance, this was an arrangement that offended the core principle of non-discrimination, because Empire countries favoured each other's trade at the expense of the non-British world. And it was a bugbear for those hostile to British imperialism. Attlee and his colleagues had no special attachment to it but would not do away with it unless they could get a big cut in US trade barriers in exchange. To them, the United States looked like a high-tariff nation preaching a low-tariff gospel. 'The Americans had a great idea,' Attlee quipped to an interviewer in retirement. 'They believed in free trade for the rest of the world but not for themselves.'[63]

Despite these tensions, the prospects for Anglo-American partnership on international economic questions seemed fair. Then came the twist. On 6 August the US Air Force dropped an atomic bomb on Hiroshima and three days later another on Nagasaki. Attlee had had only limited knowledge of the 'Tube Alloys' project before, at Potsdam, Truman told him of the successful test that had taken place in New Mexico. Attlee had no role in the decision to drop the bombs, but said later that he would have agreed if called upon to do so, not knowing of the effects of radiation, and believing that the continuation of the war would cost many more lives.[64] Emperor Hirohito announced Japan's surrender on the 15th. On the 22nd, the *New York Times* reported a statement by Truman's press secretary: 'The President has directed the Foreign Economic Administration [FEA] to take steps immediately to discontinue all lend-lease operations and to notify foreign Governments receiving lend-lease of its actions.'[65] To the British, this seemed to threaten 'stark ruin' or – as Keynes had already vividly foreseen – 'a financial Dunkirk'.[66]

The decision has been blamed on Leo Crowley, Anglophobic head of the FEA, who took advantage of the absence of rival officials such as Clayton to influence an inexperienced President.[67] Truman admitted in his memoirs that he had been bounced.[68] But although a less dramatic cut-off might have been possible in theory, it would have been a challenging sell politically, given the comparative fragility of the Anglo-American relationship, and the administration's repeated pledges to Congress that Lend-Lease would be used for war purposes only.[69] Each country had its own interpretation of the late war. As far as the British were concerned, they had held the fort in 1940–1 while the Americans watched the world burn, and now their US cousins didn't 'like being reminded that they didn't win the war unaided'.[70] Stateside, there was not much love lost for those who begged for handouts, showing little gratitude for America's past generosity. 'Mr. Attlee and Mr. Churchill in parliament greeted the news that lend-lease is ended with mingled apprehension and moral indignation', observed the *Chicago Tribune*, a paper permanently sceptical of foreign entanglements. 'Their feelings seem to be akin to those of a pair of impecunious nephews on learning that a rich and elderly bachelor uncle had just taken a bride.'[71]

In fact, ministers and officials were divided and ambivalent. They pondered making 'clear to the people of this country the shabby fashion in which we were being treated by the Americans'. But some of them, at least, understood that 'the attitude of Congress made it inevitable that lend-lease should be terminated as early as possible after the Japanese war'. Thus, 'the present action of the United States Government merely amounted to clearing the decks for new arrangements'.[72] There was some recognition that it would be good tactics to argue for aid to Britain on the grounds that it would benefit the whole world – by creating the conditions for a stable global economy – and not just the United Kingdom.[73] At the same time, the British wanted, as far as possible, to concentrate on immediate financial questions and to decouple them from discussion of future international monetary and trade planning.

For the Americans, these things were all wrapped up together. Indeed, they believed that Britain, under Article VII of the original Lend-Lease agreement, had committed itself to cooperate in the building of a new international economic order in which goods and payments could move freely.[74] Efforts to trade on US goodwill were not likely to get very far, especially if the UK appeared to be reneging on its earlier pledges. Clayton told Bevin and Dalton frankly that 'he did not believe that public opinion in the States would support retroactive measures to compensate the United Kingdom for expenditure in 1940. He thought that the most that could be got would be credit on very liberal terms.'[75]

But how much and on what conditions? Keynes, in a memorandum submitted to the Cabinet just before VJ Day, advised 'that those members of the American Administration who are in touch with our financial position are already aware that we shall be in Queer Street without aid of somewhere between $3 and $5 billion and contemplate aid on this scale as not outside practical politics'. He objected to the idea of the US providing this as a credit. If it involved interest payments and 'stipulated terms of repayment' there was a danger that Britain would not be able to live up to its obligations. 'If, however, the term credit is no more than a camouflage for what would be in effect a grant-in-aid, that is another matter.'[76]

Keynes was a genius and had the flaws of genius. Difficult and mercurial, suffering from a heart condition, and more than a little contemptuous of the Labour leaders for whom he was working, he was enamoured of his own persuasive powers. If the well-meaning but obtuse Americans were to grant Britain the justice she so richly deserved, who better than the smooth-tongued polymath himself to win them over to the light? As it was easy for the Cabinet to believe that Britain should be treated generously – which would, after all, save the country from being plunged into harshest austerity – it was easy also to believe Keynes's apparent promise that despatching him to Washington would lead to the UK getting an enormous free gift or, at minimum, an interest-free loan. Bevin, though, is said to have remarked: 'When I listen to Lord Keynes talking, I seem to hear those coins jingling in my pocket; but I am not so sure that they are really there.'[77]

When the British delegation arrived in North America for talks, negotiations with Canada (a source of generous economic assistance) were dealt with quite straightforwardly. But things were not easy in DC, and the British attitude to the Americans was *de haut en bas*. (When Lord Halifax, the ambassador to Washington, learned that a friend's hairdresser found it hard to believe that goods were still rationed in the UK, he told his diary: 'It is a pretty heart-breaking business trying to educate and inform 130,000,000 people of whom the vast proportion make no attempt to educate themselves.'[78]) A back-up team, sent out to deal with trade policy, arrived at the end of September. One of its members, the economist Lionel Robbins, immediately realized that a simple grant-in-aid would not be forthcoming. It was clear, too, that Keynes himself now accepted this. 'I had no difficulty in refraining from saying I told you so,' noted Robbins. 'But I perceive that we shall have great difficulty in dehypnotising London.'[79]

In his memoirs, Dalton recalled:

we retreated, slowly and with a bad grace and with increasing irritation, from a free gift to an interest-free loan, and from this again to a loan bearing interest; from a larger to a smaller total of aid; and from the prospect of loose strings, some of which would be only general declarations of intention, to the most unwilling acceptance of strings so tight that they might strangle our trade and indeed, our whole economic life.[80]

The British embassy provided some wise advice, and technology kept Keynes and his colleagues in rapid touch with London, but quick communication could not prevent a descent into 'mutual incomprehension'.[81] 'Foreign Secretary, have you got the telegram?' demanded Dalton during one of the late-evening sessions dedicated to the negotiations. 'I've got 'undreds,' replied Bevin.[82]

While the talks were bogged down in misunderstandings and recriminations, domestic politics seemed to exist in a parallel universe. Dalton was loathed by his civil servants for his 'bloody-mindedness & insults' – 'he shits for England in the Olympic Games', ran the Treasury joke.[83] But to many Labour backbenchers he was a hero. His policy of 'cheap money' – holding down interest rates to boost business activity and keep down the cost of servicing the national debt – was not yet controversial (though he later alienated the City by pushing it to extremes).[84] His interim Budget in October was, he said, a staging post on the way to 'a fuller national life'.[85] It may seem surprising that a radical Labour Chancellor should have tried to achieve this by reducing taxes. Yet these had reached remarkable heights in wartime, and Dalton accepted the standard logic that tax cuts would boost morale and create incentives to effort.[86] He relieved over two million people from income tax altogether and at the same time made the system more progressive. He maintained subsidies and raised surtax (which applied to higher earners). 'This last got the loudest cheer of all', he wrote in his diary. 'How right I was to go against the advice of all these foolish unpolitical officials!'[87] 'LABOUR BRINGS IN PEOPLE'S BUDGET TO SPUR PRODUCTION' was the *Daily Mirror* headline, and even the *Mail* hailed Dalton's actions as a 'tonic to trade'.[88]

Within a week, Dalton was once more at the despatch box, this time to introduce a Bill nationalizing the Bank of England. The fact that Britain's central bank, though acting in effect as a public institution, was owned by private shareholders was an incongruity, though not a unique one. (The Bank of France was nationalized by Charles de Gaulle's government almost simultaneously.[89]) But for Labour, the new legislation went beyond the mere rectification of an anomaly. The Bank – and its notorious Governor Montagu Norman, who served from 1920 to 1944 – was blamed both for the deflation of the interwar years and for the collapse of MacDonald's government in 1931.[90] Nationalization, supposedly, was the mechanism by which finance could be made the servant rather than the master of the economy. It had, of course, been pledged in *Let Us Face the Future*, which Dalton now brandished, 'with the scarlet V slashed across it', at the Conservative MPs ranged sullenly opposite.[91] 'Tories despised Hugh's gesture as a piece of theatre, especially as it came from an old Etonian who, they sneered, had deserted his class,' recalled Jim Callaghan, who had recently been elected for Cardiff. 'But they could neither deny our manifesto nor our majority and whatever they thought we newcomers loved it.'[92] Another neophyte, Barbara Castle, remembered that as the voting progressed 'the strains of the Red Flag floated into the chamber from the government lobby. We were jubilant.'[93]

Yet the victory was rather hollow. Nationalization was a symbolic act rather than one that had practical meaning, and the ambiguities of the Bank–Treasury relationship were not resolved.[94] At the same time, the promised National Investment Board (NIB), which was supposed to 'determine social priorities and promote better timing in private investment', never came into being.[95] Instead, Dalton founded a toothless National Investment Council, with a purely advisory role. This was partly because he wanted to ensure that physical and financial resources continued to be controlled separately, but also because of the weight of conventional Treasury wisdom.[96]

This is not to say that the decision was wrong, but the fact that the NIB was so quickly abandoned exposes the fact that Labour's post-1931 vision of a socialist planned economy had always been rather vague. Many of the policies that it had led to – such as nationalization – were indeed implemented but did not bring about the economic and societal step-change that had been hoped for. The Attlee government's economic strategy never amounted to more than the sum of its parts; it would be better remembered for its welfare reforms. These, however necessary, had never been intended as the centrepiece of Labour's revolution. A social security scheme, as Morrison had said during wartime, was at best 'nothing more than ambulance and salvage work, rescuing and patching up our social casualties [...] In our true policy for the future, social security can play but a part, and, if we succeed, it will and should be an ever lessening part.'[97]

Post-conflict dislocation vastly complicated the government's tasks. The war and the Holocaust had forced millions of civilians across national frontiers. Afterwards, multitudes of ethnic Germans were expelled from Eastern Europe and many of the Jews in Poland fled from a new wave of persecution. Those lucky enough to survive these migrations faced months and years in limbo as the authorities wrestled with the logistical, political and moral difficulties involved in returning them home – or in finding them a new one. All these people had to be fed – and shipping was a problem in addition to that of locating and paying for supplies. With mass starvation looming in Germany, a humanitarian campaign led by publisher Victor Gollancz gained traction. But ministers were slow to react. With the occupation of the British Zone already set to cost £80 million a year, and with the American financial talks incomplete, they expressed sympathy but had little inclination to act in the face of their own feelings and those of much of the British public.[98] ('Some people were so anti-German that they talked of killing dachshunds in the street.'[99]) It would be many months before the true severity of the situation finally dawned.

Britain was faced with multiple challenges simultaneously. There were refugee and supply issues not just in Europe but in Asia and the Middle East. At the same time, nationalist/anti-colonial pressures intensified in many parts of the Empire, setting the scene for a sequence of unfolding crises. Not all ministers were prepared for the reality of imperial decline. Asked by a journalist if the Labour government was going to preside (in Churchill's phrase) over the liquidation of the British Empire, Morrison replied: 'No fear. We are great friends of the jolly old Empire and we are going to stick to it.'[100] More pressing, in the autumn of 1945, was the issue of demobilization. Millions of armed forces personnel were distributed across the globe, many of them carrying out essential tasks, but their labour was also needed to assist with reconstruction at home. The resulting tensions – combined with the need to manage press and public pressure to get the men home quickly – led to some of the first serious arguments within the Cabinet.

The Minister of Labour, the trades unionist George Isaacs, faced a dilemma. He was under pressure on the one hand to release manpower to help boost exports and rebuild the country, and on the other to put the brakes on demobilization so that Britain could meet her defence obligations around the world. Bevin favoured the latter. As Bevin had successfully run Isaacs' ministry during wartime, and as Isaacs was in his first ministerial post, it was Bevin who (as chair of the Cabinet's Manpower Committee) ended up calling the shots.[101] He was determined to maintain his original demob scheme, whereby priority for release (for a man in Class A) was based on a combination of his age and how long he had served. Men in Class B (who had special skills or qualifications) would be released only in limited numbers. New, younger men would continue to be conscripted.[102] The government determined to stick to these principles, but to accelerate the overall rate of demobilization. Meanwhile, the government came under friendly fire, when the Labour MP and journalist Garry Allighan published an article in the *Daily Mail* alleging muddle. One of his major complaints was that servicemen had been bewildered and disappointed by confusing official announcements.[103]

In Cabinet, Isaacs said he was disturbed by the wider press campaign. Bevin suggested sending for the editor of the *Mail*. Bevan, though, was worried about the housing programme, which depended greatly on Class B releases. Unless the scheme was modified, building workers might soon be unemployed because of a lack of technical and supervisory workers. 'Trouble not caused by the article but by facts,' Bevan said, and warned about the dangers of interfering with the press. Thousands of men were bored with the delays, he pointed out. 'This scheme *has* broken.'[104] A broadcast by Attlee – who sounded 'like a tired man with a headache' – failed to give enough clarity about who would be coming home when.[105] The Opposition upped the pressure by asking for a Commons debate, in which Churchill urged: 'we must bring the men home, and set the men free'.[106]

Bevin believed that until the international situation became easier, Britain would inevitably be short of men at home: industry would simply have to improvise and adjust. He was also desperate to avoid the problems that had afflicted the demob process after the First World War. In November, and with the loan negotiations still unresolved, he put his foot down. He sent a long personal minute to Attlee complaining that some ministers on the Manpower Committee were 'seeking to force us to break our undertaking to the troops that we would call up men between the ages of 18 and 30 in order to allow the other men who have been in the war so long to be demobilised'. He was being pressured to send the unconscripted into agriculture, housing, and other fields. This, he argued, would violate Labour's election pledges and Bevin's own solemn wartime promises to the servicemen. What is more, 'I should have great difficulty in being associated with an administration that would go back on its word to these men who have done so much for us.' In short, stick by my plan or I resign.[107]

This was a threat that Attlee could not ignore, and the original principles remained in place, though the rate of release was again speeded up and more Class B men were allowed back in civvies.[108] The crisis had been managed, though the basic problem – that there were not enough workers in the right industries to generate dollar-earning imports – was unresolved. There is a critique of the Attlee government that suggests it squandered Britain's post-war opportunities by frittering away cash on expensive 'New Jerusalem'-type schemes and on its continued pretensions as a world power.[109] The latter criticism is the more plausible, given that Britain's post-war welfare state was not especially generous in international perspective, nor did its institutions suck up excessive real resources such as steel.[110] According to one influential analysis, 'the "welfareness" of British state spending did not return to early 1930s levels until 1970', welfareness being defined as the ratio of welfare to defence expenditure.[111] In his memoirs, Jay dismissed the idea that the government had splashed cash on the old and the poor and neglected industry. From the beginning, Downing Street's effort was fixed on preaching the word that the only way to recover from war damage and pay Britain's debts 'was by the steady, unromantic slog of production and exports'.[112]

Propaganda and entreaty were the tools ministers used to square the gap between their belief in central planning and their belief in individual freedom. The government's PR efforts were often clumsy, and attempts to woo workers into unpopular industries, such as coal, textiles and agriculture, ran into inevitable resistance.[113] As one historian of Scottish nationalism has noted, 'The Attlee government's focus on production for exports was consistently singled out by the SNP as demonstrating the misplaced priorities of a British state that was not economically self-sufficient in the way that Scotland – with its lower population – could be.'[114]

Exhortation and appeals to public spirit were not wholly fruitless, though. After the cut-off of Lend-Lease, the TUC General Council was persuaded to accept the continuation of wartime Order 1305, which remained in place until 1951. This enforced binding arbitration when negotiations between employers and unions failed. The TUC's decision was not entirely selfless, as arbitration normally led to at least a small pay increase.[115] Still, it showed that moral suasion could have an effect, albeit rather more on high-level union leaders than on ordinary workers. Ultimately, the technique would show diminishing returns. Industrial unrest had not vanished. For example, the government used troops to unload cargoes during a dock strike in the autumn of 1945. The dispute ended with the daily minimum wage in the industry being increased from 16 to 19 shillings, though falling short of the 25 shillings that had been demanded.[116]

While the economy struggled to return to normal, the autumn was marked by a combination of optimism and fear. The first of a series of meetings of Foreign Ministers (of the UK, USA, USSR, France and China) brought little result. At an embassy reception, a drunken Molotov appeared to let slip that the Soviets already had the secret of the A-bomb.[117] In an essay published in *Tribune*, George Orwell coined the term 'cold war'.[118] While recognizing the terrible threat posed by the Bomb, ministers were at first hopeful that its horrendous destructive power could be subjected to control by the United Nations. Over this, though, they would prioritize maintaining what they saw as Britain's unique relationship with the United States, which, of course, was already strained by the ending of Lend-Lease. The British had provided vital knowledge and expertise that had kickstarted the wartime Manhattan Project but had received little in return save for ambiguous promises of future cooperation. As a report from the Washington Embassy noted, even sympathetic internationalists in the Truman administration saw Britain merely 'as a valuable junior partner', though she received more solicitude than did the Soviets or the Chinese.[119]

When Attlee, who still favoured joint control by the UK, USA and the USSR, wrote to Truman asking to confer on the 'momentous' nuclear question, he got nowhere.[120] But when he wrote again, asking for a summit without Soviet participation, he was rewarded with a joint British–US–Canadian meeting in DC.[121] Truman worried about how to entertain the Prime Minister at the White House for an entire weekend and decided on a trip down the Potomac in the presidential yacht. One of his assistants quipped that 'he might run aground and that would take up the evening'.[122] On the face of it, the visit was a success, notwithstanding the *Chicago Tribune*'s accusation that the British were questing for 'Uncle Sam's atomic bomb and Uncle Sam's dollars'.[123] Attlee was granted the honour of addressing a joint session of Congress and, more importantly, appeared to get what he wanted in the form of a joint declaration promising 'full and effective cooperation in the field of atomic energy'. He came away believing that the UK and Canada, unlike other countries, would be allowed to share US know-how.[124] This proved illusory. Though deeply disappointing to the British, the McMahon Act of 1946, which banned the sharing of nuclear technology, was really a confirmation of existing American practice rather than a radical new departure.[125]

Back at home, Labour's ascendancy was confirmed when the Conservatives put down an ill-advised motion of censure in the Commons. After Churchill had spoken, Attlee mocked his 'quiet note of injured innocence'. He went on:

> The burden of the right hon. Gentleman's speech is this: He said: Why, when you were elected to carry out a Socialist programme, did you not carry out a Conservative programme? To the right hon. Gentleman everything that is Conservative is normal, anything that sees a changing world and wishes to change it must be wrong. We are always asked to rally round, to be patriotic and keep things as they are. We were not returned for that purpose.[126]

When the motion was heavily and inevitably defeated, the *Daily Herald* revelled in the Tory flop. The cheers that greeted Attlee when he sat down were a 'demonstration of affection, admiration and support such as few men have been given in recent years'.[127]

And now finally – after considerable last-minute drama – agreement was reached on the terms of the American loan. The UK was to receive a line of credit of $3.75 billion at 2 per cent interest, repayable in 50 annual instalments from 1951. In return, Britain was to ensure by 31 December 1946 that her use of quantitative trade controls did not discriminate against the United States; make sterling generally convertible for current transactions within one year after the effective date of the agreement (i.e., by 15 July 1947, as it turned out); and commit herself to joint Anglo-American proposals on progress towards multilateral trade. It was further understood that she would ratify the Bretton Woods agreement, thus allowing the International Monetary Fund and the International Bank for Reconstruction and Development to come into being.[128]

Although the results of the financial talks are often presented as a setback for the British – they fell far short of what Keynes had suggested might be possible – the proposals on trade that emerged from the negotiations were more ambiguous. The UK team had successfully insisted that, given her economic weakness and the state of her domestic opinion, Britain could neither afford to eliminate imperial preference outright, nor be seen to do so in exchange for American financial aid. She could only consider the reduction or elimination of the system in exchange for major reductions in US tariffs. And they argued that, due the contractual nature of the 1932 Ottawa agreements, which undergirded the preference system, the UK could not pledge unilaterally to abolish preferences, but could only promise to negotiate in good faith for their abolition.[129] Secretary of State James Byrnes seemed to accept this interpretation of the position, and Attlee spoke to this effect in the Commons.[130] The waters were muddied, though, as the US negotiators had drawn up a statement that the British agreed could be used if the necessity arose. This 'provided that if the Dominions were to adopt an unreasonable position regarding the elimination of preferences, the United Kingdom would denounce their agreements with the Dominions'.[131] In fact, the Americans never did come to see Dominion behaviour as sufficiently unreasonable to justify this. But, partly on account of the mixed messaging, there remained a large gap between the two sides' views on how far the UK was obliged to go.

The loan terms as a whole were seen by many at the time as harsh, as a sign of American ingratitude, even as 'our economic Munich' (as the Tory MP Bob Boothby put it).[132] Retrospectively, some have viewed this as the moment when Labour dispensed with any effort 'to find an autonomous economic strategy in association with a defence policy concerned mainly with national survival rather than with the defence of the international capitalist system as the chief lieutenant of the US'.[133] True, the convertibility requirement was a major error that would come back to bite. But the Truman administration had strained at the limits of the politically possible, given the need to get the loan through

Congress, and the strong strain of popular opinion that baulked at bailing out a dying empire with socialists at the helm. And although it is fair to say that a more autarkic alternative based on bilateral pacts with third countries was now ruled out, it is by no means clear that in that direction lay the route to the socialist millennium. As Dalton told Labour MPs, the alternative to the loan was 'too grim'.[134] He wrote in his autobiography that he was under no doubt about the consequences had the talks failed:

> We would go deeper into the dark valley of austerity than at any time during the war. Less food, except for bread and potatoes [...] Heavy and growing unemployment in many industries. Worst of all, from the point of view of public morale, practically no smokes, since eighty per cent of our tobacco cost dollars. [...] Soon, I knew, the tide of public feeling would turn. The Tories would exploit all the inevitable privations. Every shortage would be attributed to the Government's incompetence. Our feet would soon be on the downward slope, leading towards sure defeat at the next election.[135]

Sheer political realism aside, it was not the case that the government had been forced, as if at gunpoint, to accept a capitalist international order. The fact was that – though Bevin was a notable sceptic – most Labour ministers in the wartime coalition had supported efforts to establish new international economic organizations out of ideological conviction. For them, the Bretton Woods institutions, and the proposed ITO, represented a form of 'international planning' that could complement a planned economy at home. To be sure, trying to reconcile socialist objectives with the necessity for cooperation with capitalist countries was no easy proposition, but some form of compromise was inevitable. The post-war international economic regime headed by the United States was, in fact, no *laissez-faire* anarchy, but rather a form of 'embedded liberalism'. This sought a middle way between state control and the unhindered free market. Its proponents sought a framework that would safeguard domestic stability and employment while avoiding the beggar-my-neighbour external policies that had bedevilled the years between the wars.[136] Though the result was imperfect, the aspiration was consistent with Labour's ambition to reform the global economy in the interests of preventing future wars.

Not everyone within the Labour Party agreed. There was a certain ideological overlap, or unholy alliance, between socialist advocates of bilateralism and Tory advocates of imperial protection.[137] Shinwell told the Cabinet that the loan conditions would be fatal to the construction of a planned economy at home. Britain would be 'in pawn' to the US for years, he said. (To that extent he was right: the loan was finally paid off in 2006.) Bevan backed Shinwell up.[138] But neither man felt compelled to resign. Some of the new Labour MPs refused to be won over, though. Barbara Castle believed that 'we were faced with yet another attempt to cripple economic recovery by forcing us into a financial straitjacket in obedience to an orthodox doctrine which I knew had destroyed the 1929 Labour government'.[139] Remarkably, Morrison informed the PLP that 'should any Member who held strong views on this matter find it necessary to vote against the Government's proposals [...] disciplinary action would be inapplicable on this occasion'.[140] The reason for this became clear to Jim Callaghan when he tackled the Chancellor about his doubts: 'In reply, Hugh Dalton gave one of his portentous winks. He did not mind, he said, if some of us voted against the loan and the Agreement. It would show the Americans that the Labour Government was not a pushover, and had its own domestic problems.'[141]

The government gained from the fact that the Conservatives were divided too. Their leaders supported the loan, but told Tory MPs to abstain, in the hope of preventing them from voting against it.[142] Winding up the Commons debate, Bevin – who had by now dropped his own hostility to Bretton Woods – raised a laugh by saying that he had never expected to meet Churchill 'in the capacity of an abstainer'. He also challenged him to say whether he thought a Conservative government would have got better terms from the USA than the Labour government had. Churchill fell into the trap and said yes. 'Then that is a libel on the Administration of the United States,' Bevin shouted back, banging on the despatch box. 'I will not believe, nor will I have it said about them without challenge, that the American Government conduct their foreign policy in the light of a change of Government brought about by the free vote of the people of Great Britain.'[143] The government's motion passed by 345 votes to 98, with 71 Tories voting against the loan and 8 in favour.

The government had secured a breathing space. The wranglings over demobilization faded away. After the government had been seven months in office, the Treasury civil servant R. W. B. ('Otto') Clarke judged: 'By and large [...] the government isn't doing too badly – it is trying in a sort of haphazard way to get the big things right.'[144] It was getting its programme on to the statute book. The Bank of England Act received Royal Assent on 14 February 1946 – a socialist Valentine. The Trades Disputes Act – the piece of legislation that had prompted Shawcross's 'masters' remark – passed the same hurdle in May, though the Stormont government refused to follow suit in Northern Ireland.[145] The Coal Industry Nationalisation Act followed in July, and the National Insurance Act (which offered a broad extension of social security) in August. Introducing his second Budget, Dalton told MPs of his determination to help revive areas that had suffered high unemployment between the wars: 'I will find, and find with a song in my heart, whatever money is necessary.'[146] This happy phase would not last. As Jean Mann recalled: 'The great majority given to Labour in 1945 engendered in all of us a false sense of security.' She and her colleagues believed in the maxim of the pioneering figure of Robert Blatchford, who said, 'The British people will take a long time to become Socialist but when they do they will stay that way.'[147] They believed they were swimming with the tides of history – but were soon to be battered by the surf.

4

Cards on the Table

May 29th 1947. The Labour Party conference in the seaside resort of Margate, Kent. For a few days, the rank-and-file delegates had been rubbing shoulders with Cabinet ministers at dances and receptions and addressing them by their first names. In the warmest weather for years – a blessed relief after the freezing winter – Attlee, accompanied by his wife and detective, indulged in a round of mini-golf.[1] Bevin was a latecomer, arriving bronzed from a holiday in nearby Folkestone, in time for the foreign affairs debate.[2] Though the Foreign Secretary's health was by now a matter of public comment – he suffered from angina and a host of other problems – he was in good form. On the conference agenda were a slew of resolutions critical of his foreign policy, and he was ready to tackle his opponents head on.

Two rival pamphlets were in circulation. One, *Keep Left*, was published by a group of MPs headed by Richard Crossman, Michael Foot and Ian Mikardo. It complained that the government's stance abroad had 'only been half-heartedly socialist'.[3] It reflected a common belief at this time that Europe as a whole was moving Left. If cooperation with the Soviets in fact proved impossible, then a democratic socialist Europe, headed by Britain and France, could emerge as a Third Force, as a counterweight to the new superpowers.[4] The other tract, *Cards on the Table*, was by Denis Healey, the young Secretary of the party's International Department, firmly anti-communist and not noted for his shyness in debate. Distributed to every delegate, Healey's punchy defence of Bevin's stewardship took its title from his professed willingness to avoid secret diplomacy and to put Britain's 'cards on the table face upwards'.[5]

As he clambered to his feet to confront his critics, Bevin had two key advantages. On the one hand, the Keep Left group and its allies – lacking powerful alternatives to his policies – seemed to have an appetite for no more than a half-hearted revolt. On the other, the Soviets had played into Bevin's hands. For some time, they had been clumsily encouraging the Labour Left 'to force Bevin out and demand that he be replaced by someone who would "get along with the USSR"'.[6] Now, a long article in *Izvestia* made a ferocious attack on him. If it was intended to ginger up the critics, it achieved the opposite of its purpose.[7]

A Labour Party or trades union conference was Bevin's natural habitat. Healey recalled: 'Though short in stature, he was built like a battle tank, with the rolling gait and thick stumpy fingers typical of a stevedore. Slow and soft of speech in private, he could roar like any sucking-dove at a public meeting.' Though his stream-of-consciousness approach to public speaking was a torment to his officials, he was much more effective in front of a Labour movement audience than in the Commons, where his efforts could be dull and obscure. 'Rambling and ill-constructed though they were, such conference speeches invariably won overwhelming support from his audience, whatever the price paid by his diplomatic advisers in nervous breakdowns.'[8]

There was, perhaps, more art in Bevin's speeches than appeared on the surface. *The Economist* noted how, on this occasion, he did not launch straight into denouncing those who had crossed him. Instead, he treated his audience to an impressive if baffling *tour d'horizon*. 'Mr. Bevin took his listeners all round the world, touching in brief detail on a vast variety of topics and if the delegates were not confused at the beginning of his survey, they certainly were at the end, and probably went away glad that Ernie and not they had to deal with the problems.'[9]

Only towards the end of his disquisition did Bevin's anger break on his opponents like a storm of hailstones out of a clear blue sky. He referred to a rebellion by MPs the previous autumn, in which the brilliant but mercurial Crossman had been a prime mover. That challenge had occurred when Bevin had been in Washington, negotiating over the urgent issue of Britain's wheat requirements

– bread rationing, which had not been necessary even during the war, had been introduced earlier in the year. As his West Country burr rose to an indignant shout, Bevin declared: 'The very day I was trying to get the agreement with the Americans to prevent the bread rationing going down was the day I was stabbed in the back in the House of Commons!' (This was a favourite trope: if Bevin had been stabbed in the back as often as he claimed he'd have had more holes than a colander.) To thunderous applause, he punched his outstretched palm and continued: 'I do say that if you expect loyalty from ministers, however much ministers may make mistakes, ministers 'as the right to expect loyalty back, and fair treatment.'[10] An exultant Dalton told his diary that a kerfuffle about whether *Cards on the Table* had been approved by the National Executive was 'submerged in the tidal wave of the Bevin speech on Thursday. He scored a very great personal success and swept away all opposition. He has a most astonishing – and unique – conference personality. There was no come-back.'[11]

Years later, Crossman told an interviewer:

Well, I've never felt a Conference as hostile. I was sitting behind the T & G delegation. You could feel their knives going into my front. And you knew it was tough – it *is* tough when you are at conference and you're wiped out. But I remember that evening I was – the dance was on – the Mayor's Reception – and when one's licked one feels a bit gloomy, and I was standing alone by one of the pillars and in comes Ernie [from] the other side of the hall, and he spotted me and he waddled right across the hall and he says to me: 'No ill feelings.' And you know I was furious at the time, but now I think it was rather nice of him.[12]

As Michael Foot, one of the victims, was quick to point out at the time, Bevin's triumph involved some sleight of hand. Foot, ironically, had recently been attacked himself by Left colleagues for being excessively anti-Soviet. Like Bevin, he had a nice line in vitriol.[13] The Foreign Secretary, he wrote, lacked a beautiful voice, gracious gestures and logical arguments. But these were nothing to the weapons he did wield:

The massive marshalling of indisputable and irrelevant facts, the calculated lapses into downright good humour, the brazen denial of allegations which have never been made, the mobilisation of all the most reputable emotions in support of the most dubious causes, the sweeping assertion of platitudes as if they were maxims for a new revolution and, finally, an injured ego parading all its bleeding wounds and courageously refusing to succumb to them.

Bevin had got his American agreement, Foot pointed out, 'stab or no stab'. What, then, was he complaining about? Furthermore, Bevin had failed to mention that, also at the vital moment, the TUC Congress had 'recorded a vote against his foreign policy larger proportionately than that achieved by the rebellion in the House of Commons'. Thus, Bevin's attempt to 'divide the Labour Movement between the loyal trade unionists and the rebellious intellectuals has no basis whatsoever in fact'.[14]

These were good debating points, but they could not alter the reality: after two rocky years at the helm of the Foreign Office, Bevin had finally established his ascendancy, even as he reached the point where it seemed, due to a heart condition, he could not continue long in office. And this was not just the result of his remarkable persona or his well-honed ability to browbeat anyone who got in his way. The fact was that most of the opposition was not based on any great gulf of principle. True, the ranks of Labour did include a few genuine fellow-travellers with Soviet communism. These included the multilingual MP Konni Zilliacus (born in Japan to Finnish parents), who quipped that the government's true policy was 'Cards *Under* the Table'.[15] But the authors and signatories of Keep Left, who deprecated British subservience to America and the division of Europe while deploring the actions of the Stalinist police state, shared many of the government's fundamental objectives, even while they criticized its way of trying to obtain them. A key difference was that the Keep Left group thought that Britain could influence the world by moral example, such as by a rapid withdrawal of troops from the Middle East, rather than by *realpolitik*. 'Having proved the sincerity of our Socialist intentions, we should try to negotiate a settlement of the great Power Conflicts', they wrote.[16]

This made things sound rather easy. But though the pamphlet was confused and naïve in some ways, those who wrote it should not be judged too harshly. One senior figure at the FO wrote an assessment of its foreign policy arguments. Much of it, he said, would have seemed sensible eighteen months or two years previously.

> Indeed, all our own papers were then based on the assumption that there should in no circumstances be any Anglo-American 'line-up' against the Soviet Union, or indeed against 'Communism', until such time at any rate as the Soviets should have made it absolutely clear that they did not intend to co-operate with the West. It will be recalled with what passionate conviction the Foreign Office represented this thesis to the Chiefs of Staff, and what care was taken to prevent even the smallest whisper getting around that we favoured the Americans rather than the Russians.[17]

Yet it would be wrong to think that Bevin had come into office in a state of innocence only to be roughly disillusioned. Nor, despite his established reputation as a foreign policy realist, should we see him as a straightforward exponent of brutal power-politics and expediency. Neither position fully captures the complexity of his views, which combined the canniness of the union negotiator with more than a dash of socialist idealism. He saw the necessity of making pragmatic compromises and was optimistic that other countries could be persuaded to do likewise in the interests of human progress. In this sense he stood as part of a long-standing Labour patriotic-cum-internationalist tradition that has encompassed almost all of the party's leaders and Foreign Secretaries. He became frustrated with the Left in part because of his personal prejudices and resentments but also because he felt his critics failed to recognize the hard-nosed methods needed to accomplish the objectives that he and they genuinely had in common. In the conditions of the early Cold War, this meant being constantly torn between high hopes, bitter realities, and the imperatives of national survival as British power ebbed.

Bevin did not underestimate the scale of his task: 'it was not only a question of the state of our foreign relations but almost the reconstruction of the world', he noted.[18] Certainly, he and other Labour leaders had given significant hostages to fortune during the election. 'The whole world is moving Left,' he told a meeting in Yorkshire. 'France is voting Left and Russia would have greater confidence in us if we had a Labour Government than a Government comprised of the historical men of Munich.'[19] This needs to be read, at least in part, as calculated electioneering. The Tories, at the same moment, were claiming that the route to peace was 'to send our Churchill to meet his buddy Stalin'.[20] This is evidence of the widespread realization that relations with the USSR would require very careful management.

Bevin made clear, in the first survey that he offered the Commons, that his keynote would be continuity with the policy of the coalition.[21] One Labour MP quipped, 'How fat Anthony has grown' – referring to the similarities with Eden, the previous Foreign Secretary.[22] 'When Conservatives murmur "Hear hear" Bevin is pleased', wrote Crossman. 'When, very rarely, we do he is almost embarrassed.'[23] Bevin's approach caused dismay among some European socialists and American liberals.[24] According to *Pravda*, his speech was a blow to 'any illusions created during the British election campaign about change in British foreign policy'.[25] (On the other hand, Moscow radio pointed out that jubilation in Spain over Bevin's 'extreme circumspection' towards the Franco regime ignored the fact that the British government would prefer the return of democracy there. 'The Spanish puppets of Mussolini and Hitler evidently overdid it.'[26]) According to the Soviet paper *Red Star*, the speech satisfied the Conservatives 'but not all the Labour members, who clearly expected from Bevin more definite statements about co-operation with the USSR'.[27] But although some Far Left Labour MPs vented their criticism within the PLP, the majority seemed contented at this point.[28]

Over time, it was increasingly suggested that the new Foreign Secretary had failed to make the required clear-out of the diplomatic Establishment, the members of which held 'the most fantastic feudal prejudices and an aristocratic contempt for their temporary masters'.[29] Bevin, it was alleged, was ill-equipped to counter the wiles of the mandarins, and had succumbed to the Foreign Office embrace. But we might speak less of beguilement and more of a *rapprochement*. It was initially a wary one, as can be seen from the memoirs of Gladwyn Jebb, the same man who provided the shrewd FO analysis of *Keep Left*. Jebb was 'good-looking, quick-witted, articulate and sardonic', though sometimes arrogant and tactless, and was known for relentless 'brains-trusting' (the throwing out and exploration of ideas).[30] Educated at Eton and Oxford, he entered the diplomatic service in the 1920s. During the second Labour government, he was the 'perfect Private Secretary' to

Dalton, who, during the Second World War, appointed him as head of the Special Operations Executive (SOE), tasked with stirring up resistance in occupied Europe.[31]

But Dalton was another Etonian; the hedgerow-schooled Bevin, 'all shrewdness, experience and personality', was a different kettle of fish.[32] Though Jebb had seen Bevin at Potsdam, he did not have the opportunity to speak to him until, back in London, he was summoned to brief him on UN affairs. (Jebb had been seconded to serve as the new body's Acting-Secretary General in preparation for the first General Assembly in London.) The two men's encounter was, to begin with, a little frosty. When Jebb sat down, Bevin silently cast his eyes over him, before at last remarking: 'Must be kinda queer for a chap like you to see a chap like me sitting in a chair like this?' Jebb gave a mere shrug and smile, but Bevin wouldn't let it drop. 'Ain't never 'appened before in 'istory,' he scowled. Jebb decided he couldn't let it pass.

'Secretary of State,' I said on the spur of the moment, 'I am sorry that the first time I open my mouth in your presence is to contradict you. But you're wrong. It has.' 'What do you mean, young man?' 'Well,' I said, 'it was a long time ago – rather over four hundred years I think. But there was then a butcher's boy in Ipswich whose origins, I suspect, were just as humble as your own, and he became the Foreign Secretary of one of our greatest kings. And for that matter, a Cardinal too. His name was Tom Wolsey. And incidentally, now I come to think of it, he was not unlike you physically.' 'Well,' said the Secretary of State, visibly impressed, 'I must say, I never thought of that.'

From this point onwards, Jebb could scarcely do wrong in Bevin's eyes. 'Whatever you may say about Gladwyn,' he once said, 'he ain't never dull!' Many of his officials, including Jebb, came to love 'Uncle Ernie', who was always quick to grasp a point, never objected to a challenge by a subordinate, but was brutal to his enemies. They were not blind to his faults, which included, according to Jebb, vindictiveness, vanity, and prejudice against Jews and Catholics. (To these could be added his repetitious, rambling habits of speech.) Bevin claimed to quite like the upper class, to love (of course) the working class, but to loathe the 'self-righteous and narrow-minded' middle class.[33]

'Above all, he stood up fearlessly for his staff,' noted the writer and former diplomat Robert Bruce Lockhart, after chatting with officials early on in Bevin's tenure. 'His view of the Foreign Office clerks was that there were too few of them – and that they were too badly paid.'[34] According to one account, when a friend said that Dalton as Chancellor might object to an all-round pay rise, 'Bargainer Bevin roared: "I'll take the worthy doctor by his pants and swing him around my head till I get it!"'[35]

Bevin, then, was a breath of fresh air, not a hurricane. Lord Halifax and Duff Cooper, both Conservative political appointees, were kept on as ambassadors to Washington and Paris until 1946 and 1948 respectively. But though there was no dramatic clear-out, Bevin noted the criticisms and made tactful changes when opportunities arose.[36] Lord Killearn, the long-serving and high-handed High Commissioner for Egypt and the Sudan, was bewildered to be 'yanked out' of Cairo and 'dumped' in a 'rather nebulous capacity' in the Far East.[37] Sir Rex Leeper, a strong supporter of the Greek monarchy and a particular bugbear of the Labour Left, was quietly moved from the Athens embassy to Buenos Aires. At the Margate conference, Bevin was careful to boast about the people selected for diplomatic posts since he had taken office: 'Mr. Churchill will be upset when I say that there is not one entry from Harrow and only one from Eton.'[38] By the end of 1947, Bevin had forced 17 senior retirements.[39] Women were allowed to enter the Foreign Service for the first time, though they were normally expected to resign upon marriage, and their numbers were temporarily restricted to 10 per cent of the intake as a safeguard against 'a sudden disproportionate inflow' of female recruits.[40]

The fact that Bevin backed his officials boldly in public, and that he shared many of their precepts about Britain's place in the world, should not distract us from the fact that he and the Labour critics had certain assumptions in common.[41] These tended to be concealed by the minister's duty (as he conceived it) to guard the honour of his department to the utmost. Valentine Lawford served as his Private Secretary at the start of his term in office. As Lawford had also served Bevin's two immediate predecessors, Lord Halifax and Anthony Eden, he was well placed to make comparisons. In an article about the three published in the 1950s, he noted the warmer intimacy that Bevin established with his civil servants, and delighted in describing his 'weathered, or molten, nose', and the 'equally unpremeditated, geological, quality about the mouth below'. Lawford also observed that, behind closed doors, Bevin liked to play the role of the sceptical layman fallen among slippery experts.

> It might happen that the very day after he had stoutly defended the honesty and intelligence of his Department before an incredulous, almost outraged, audience at a Labour Party Conference, he could himself have been found listening with a look of the direst suspicion (like a tribesman at a parley in the tents of another tribe) while some senior member of the Foreign Office hierarchy uncomfortably drew his attention to the many previous occasions when a course of action now proposed by his Secretary of State had proved to be impracticable; or irritatingly warned him of the awkward precedents that would be created by some genuinely original plan which he had recently conceived, in his bed or his bath or on a train.[42]

Bevin's way of working with his staff was affected by his comparatively low level of literacy. Witness accounts conflict. 'He had a fluent tongue but not a facile pen,' recalled Duff Cooper. 'He also read slowly. These disadvantages increased enormously the burden of his work.'[43] Sir David Scott, Deputy Under-Secretary of State, judged differently: 'He reads with amazing rapidity, remembers what he reads, cross-examines the experts, and having once mastered his brief, acts with vigour.'[44] Permanent Secretary Alexander Cadogan wrote that Bevin was 'prepared to read any amount, seems to take in what he does read, and is capable of making up his own mind and sticking up for his (or our) point of view against anyone'.[45] Bevin did struggle with writing, though. He held the pen clumsily between his first and second fingers and the results, painstakingly obtained, could be virtually illegible.[46] 'Not for him the long and carefully drafted minutes by which a Curzon or an Austen Chamberlain would convey their instructions to their subordinates.'[47]

Dictation was the obvious, though not straightforward, solution. Lawford recalled being summoned to his room in advance of Bevin's Commons debut as Foreign Secretary, where 'one of the Private Secretarial ladies', Miss Eames, was in attendance. At Bevin's invitation she sat down next to him and positioned her pencil in readiness. But her natural nervousness turned into a look of outright anguish as Bevin, smoking a cigar and gazing at the ceiling, launched into a barely coherent monologue, 'uninhibited by considerations of grammar or syntax, and punctuated less by any recognisable vocal equivalent of commas or semi-colons or full stops than by the occasional pauses required for blowing smoke, coughing, removing tobacco-leaf from his tongue or dusting ash from the lapels of his coat'. At last, with a wink, and a manner 'like a kindly chiropodist', Bevin indicated to Eames that her ordeal was over. 'And Lawford here,' he remarked finally, 'will just turn that into English if he can.'[48]

On another occasion, a civil servant who had just received instructions came back straight away seeking more guidance. 'Ha,' Bevin replied, 'the ink is hardly dry on the words out of my mouth, and here you are again!'[49] Sometimes, in conversation, Bevin's meaning could be obscure, but Attlee later claimed that there had only ever been one occasion on which he had failed to understand him. This was in a meeting with Dalton and another Labour MP, Dai Grenfell, which ended with Bevin announcing, 'We'll leave it all to YEWANDEYE.' Attlee didn't know if this meant 'you and I', 'You and Dai', 'Hugh and I', or 'Hugh and Dai'.[50]

If the FO under Bevin's captaincy was a happy ship, he sometimes complained of his ministerial colleagues that 'None of them seemed interested.'[51] His relationships with his ministerial colleagues ranged from the friendly to the dysfunctional. Famously, when someone remarked that Nye Bevan was 'his own worst enemy', he replied: 'Not while I'm alive, he ain't.' Bevan repeated a saying about Bevin: 'He's a big bumble bee caught in a web and he thinks he's the spider.' But in spite of occasional Cabinet rows, their mutual dealings never reached the point of breakdown.[52] By contrast, Bevin continued to regard Morrison as 'a scheming little bastard'.[53] He appears to have got on alright with Cripps, surprisingly in view of their past history on opposite sides of Labour's Left–Right battles of the 1930s. But Cripps, whose monkish exterior disguised his warmer side, had moderated his opinions since then. Attlee recalled that 'he and Stafford hit it off very well. [...] Both, of course, were tremendous egotists – Ernest having the egoism of the artist, Stafford the egoism of the altruist.'[54]

Dalton, on the other hand, had been one of Bevin's foreign policy allies before the war. But the two men's personal relations had always been ambivalent, and now the Chancellor (with some sympathy for the incipient Keep Left group) wanted military spending cuts that the Foreign Secretary was determined to resist.[55] Dalton was delighted when Bevin complained to him about Morrison and Cripps, and told him that 'Attlee is very weak'.[56] But according to George Brown, Dalton's PPS, his boss became frustrated because he couldn't get Cabinet support for his preferred expansionary economic stance. 'Bevin, who detested him, was his particular bugbear,' he recalled. 'Dalton used to come back from No. 10 seething with rage about what he called "the incompetent little Prime Minister" who just sat there doing nothing to influence a decision "while I had to sit listening to rambling monologues from your friend Ernie Bevin".'[57]

Bevin's comment about the 'very weak' Attlee – if reported correctly – takes some of the shine off the legend of his loyalty. It is undeniable, though, that he never attempted to seize No. 10 for himself, even if there were moments when he would likely have succeeded had he tried. The fundamental strength of the Attlee–Bevin relationship is evidenced by the fact that when Attlee wrote about it, when reviewing the first volume of Alan Bullock's biography, his prose for once took to life. 'Ernest Bevin's great contribution to the Labour Movement was to emphasise the importance of power and, having emphasised it, set about obtaining it', he argued. This was the power 'of voice, fists and feet', Attlee explained, in what was, for him, unusually visceral language. 'Ernest certainly knew that I would give up being leader at any time this seemed in the interest of the party, and I think this appealed to him. I also think he liked the fact that I didn't talk much.'[58] Not that the two were peas in a pod. One evening, at a dinner with the eminent socialist politician Léon Blum, whom the Nazis had imprisoned during the Occupation, 'Bevin told a great many stories, all more or less obscene, which made Attlee rather nervous and which were difficult to translate into French.'[59]

Despite what some people thought at the time, Attlee had not handed Bevin 'sole control' of British foreign policy.[60] When his queries to the Foreign Office failed to get quick responses he made his views known.[61] When Bevin complained about something Francis Williams had told Lobby correspondents, Attlee fired off a curt memo: 'If your office was doing its job properly Francis would not need to intervene.'[62] More substantively, Attlee and Bevin had serious differences of opinion over some important strategic issues. Within a year of taking office, the former came to favour the withdrawal of British troops from the Med and the Middle East. The plan was to avoid friction with Stalin's regime by putting (as Dalton approvingly noted) 'a wide glacis of desert and Arabs between ourselves and the Russians'.[63] This was in line with the sentiments of the party's Left, but there was an obvious risk that the Soviets would simply step into the vacuum. Bevin and the Chiefs of Staff, seeing a threat to the Empire's power, and mindful of the question of oil, were strongly opposed. This was not a simple 'Internationalist' versus 'Imperialist' debate, though: Attlee wanted to refocus the available forces in British Africa.[64]

On the above issue, Bevin eventually won out. But when, hating the notion of leaving India, and doubting the 'competence of Indians to govern that great Sub-Continent', he resisted setting a fixed date for independence, Attlee hit back.[65] 'I am not defeatist but realist', he wrote. 'If you disagree with what is proposed, you must offer a practical alternative. I fail to find one in your letter.'[66] Bevin seems to have recognized India as Attlee's sphere, in return for more freedom elsewhere, and the two men's occasional run-ins never led to bad blood.[67] They talked over problems in private, but Attlee would only intervene in exceptional cases or when Bevin wanted his help. 'There's a lot in the proverb: "If you've got a good dog you don't bark yourself."'[68]

And Attlee's astute management of the parliamentary party helped shield Bevin as discontent over foreign policy grew in the government's early years. His technique was ably described by Emrys Hughes, who won a by-election at South Ayrshire early in the government's life. For years, the witty and iconoclastic Hughes had edited the Scottish socialist weekly *Forward*, writing much of the paper himself. Before that he had been jailed as a conscientious objector during the First World War. Still an unconditional pacifist, as well as being an advocate of World Government and an opponent of 'the old game of power politics', Hughes was a colourful addition to the ranks of the foreign policy sceptics.[69] He had been little impressed by Attlee's leadership during the war and, not having seen him in person for over two decades, now found him aged and shrunken. But the Prime Minister's seeming indifference to what was going on around him was misleading. When the moment came in debate, Attlee would leap up as if he had been stung, 'snap out some sharp, curt effective reply' and then recline and start his habitual doodling again. Crucially, Attlee never lost touch with his own MPs. He unfailingly went to PLP meetings and 'addressed us as comrades and when in difficulties knew how to urge the party to work together as a team'. Speaking softly, he never appeared to lose his cool: 'it was very difficult for any critic to make a direct attack on him or the policy that he was advocating without losing the sympathy of the party. [...] He was very good at summing up a discussion with short concise little speeches that seemed to be just common sense.'[70]

This was a rare skill at a time when international developments were a source of confusion and alarm, as the incipient end of Empire intersected with the beginnings of the Cold War. Labour had devoted a part of one sentence in its manifesto to promising 'the advancement of India to responsible self-government'.[71] The word 'decolonization', not yet a standard political term, was only gradually entering use.[72] Whatever this process was going to be called, ministers' elusive goal was above all to control it, and to ensure that the Empire, even if reconfigured as 'partnership', should continue to operate in Britain's interests.[73] The Cabinet wanted to avoid appearing *forced* to act through weakness, lest this triggered a wider liquidation of the Empire. Freedom for India needed to be presented as 'the logical conclusion, which we welcomed, of a policy followed by successive Governments for many years'.[74]

It was impossible in practice to avoid the Tory charge of 'scuttle'. Yet rising tensions with the USSR had a side-benefit. The Americans tended to prioritize anti-communism over anti-imperialism; the British could play on the fear that too-rapid withdrawal from Empire would be exploited by the Soviets. But although we can now see that Labour's anti-colonialism was less radical and more contradictory than the party later liked to claim, it should not be portrayed as purely reactionary either.[75] In addition, Attlee, Bevin and their colleagues sincerely wanted to make the new United Nations Organization work.

To understand the government's external policy in its first two years requires an imaginative leap into the sheer uncertainty of the period. Scholars differ over when exactly the Cold War broke out. Part of its origins lay in the nineteenth-century Great Game between the Russian and British Empires, and growing Russian–American tensions pre-1914, which were overlain but by no means suppressed by the Bolshevik revolution. Some scholars, including Soviet/Russian ones, have dated the start of the Cold War to that very point, October 1917. But the fact of the Second-World-War Anglo–US–Soviet alliance, however instrumental and however difficult, cannot be ignored, even if many of the proximate causes of the later conflict emerged during the war itself. The most plausible conclusion is that the Cold War started at some point in the first two years after VJ Day.[76] Though total precision is impossible, there were a series of important markers. These included the February 1946 speech in which Stalin told the Soviet people to prepare for a new war brought about by the contradictions of capitalism; Churchill's 'iron curtain' speech the following month; and Truman's landmark speech to Congress of March 1947.[77]

At the moment that the Labour government took office there were major tensions with the USSR, but these were thought to be potentially manageable. For a long time, Bevin refused to green light an anti-Soviet propaganda onslaught as he wanted to avoid provocation.[78] At the same time, he shared the general Foreign Office conviction that, if the United Kingdom was temporarily weakened, there was a good hope of long-term recovery. Britain and its Empire, it was thought, deserved to be treated as the equal of the USA and the USSR, though achieving this would require enlisting the support of France and other 'lesser' European powers.[79] It was tempting, in retrospect, for left-wingers to claim that, from the start, they recognized Bevin as a 'cold warrior' with a 'pathological hatred of communism'.[80]

This misses the fine grain of the pattern. Bevin's loathing of communism was real, but it was aimed mainly at British communists, whom he saw as a threat to the strength and cohesion of the Labour movement.[81] (The Soviets, for their part, abhorred and despised social democrats.) He should be credited with both a sincere initial intention to get along with the Soviet leaders and with the somewhat arrogant belief that, with so many years of union negotiations behind him, he knew how to handle them. Even Healey, a strong admirer, acknowledged there was truth 'in the jibe that Bevin thought the Soviet Union was a breakaway from the Transport and General Workers' Union'.[82] And sometimes his technique seemed to work. On one occasion, when Bevin told Molotov that he 'didn't want the thing to go like it had with "'Itler"', he appeared to get a more-than-usually cooperative reaction.[83]

At an early stage, left-wingers began protesting Britain's subordination to the power of America. But the formation of an Anglo-US alliance was no foregone conclusion. Though Bevin experienced greater difficulties with the Soviets, he had real troubles with the Truman administration too.[84] He has often been accused of subservience to the Americans, but this is inaccurate.[85] According to one official's diary, at Potsdam Bevin showed 'a perhaps too pronounced slant towards Russia and against America, and a wholly delightful assumption that, of the 3, we were still the biggest'.[86] Truman for his part found Bevin 'crude and uncouth', whereas Stalin and Molotov, though 'rough men', at least 'knew the common courtesies'.[87] Secretary of State Byrnes was at first shocked by Bevin's bluntness and aggression, but soon came to admire him as someone who 'lived up completely and wholeheartedly to his agreements – he had debated vigorously and sometimes harshly before entering into them, but having once committed himself he would carry out his contracts to the full'.[88] Bevin did not fully reciprocate this respect.

American strategy towards the Soviets was still based on trying to avoid provocation, though the administration was divided and Truman himself ambivalent. Often, the US simply failed to consult the British, as when Byrnes asked the Soviets to host a meeting of foreign ministers in Moscow, without checking what Bevin thought or even if he would be able to come.[89] A particular point of conflict was the US demand that the British allow large-scale Jewish immigration into Palestine. Another, less high-profile issue was Byrnes's pressure on Britain to cede the Americans strategic bases around the world – including, embarrassingly, in India, where Britain was on the verge of surrendering its own imperial control.[90] Asked in retirement what had been Bevin's most important contribution as Foreign Secretary, Attlee unhesitatingly replied, 'standing up to the Americans'.[91]

The difficulties notwithstanding, it became easier over time to work with the US as the two countries' leaders developed a shared (if not uniform) Cold War mentality. Attlee, who was determined to exercise tighter prime ministerial control over MI5, was kept informed about the communist connections of MPs. Building on earlier precedent, trades unionists, members of the peace movement, and other radicals, were subjected to surveillance on an almost industrial scale. In 1948 there began a purge of communists in the civil service.[92] (This targeting of small fry appears almost as a displacement activity by the Security Services, which had themselves been penetrated at a high level by Soviet intelligence.) Labour's leaders, who had long viewed the CPGB and its acolytes as menacing and dishonest, found it easy to fit current developments in Eastern Europe into a narrative of communist chicanery that drew on their own previous experience and rhetoric.[93]

When Bevin suggested in the Commons that Soviet territorial demands posed a danger to 'the throat of the British Commonwealth', left-wingers suspected him of trying to out-Churchill Churchill.[94] One local Labour Party passed a resolution condemning his policies and, in an accompanying letter, told him that the workers would not stand by and watch the creation of an Anglo-American anti-Soviet bloc. 'Your talk about putting cards on the table is puerile, when you keep the trumps up your sleeve.' In his reply, Bevin made clear his belief that such statements were stirred up by the communists: 'I do know that when directions are given I get a whole host of resolutions, all couched in similar terms, which are obviously all inspired and not the real feeling of the people of this country.'[95]

Having been bounced into the Moscow conference, Bevin arrived in the city in mid-December 1945. As he walked painfully slowly across Red Square in the bitter winter cold, his comment on Saint Basil's Cathedral was: ''Orrible building.' Valentine Lawford, who accompanied him, noted that he had a reputation with the local people for anti-Soviet hostility. 'I noticed that almost everyone that we passed in the street, noticing our OGPU guard, muttered to their companions, "Bevin".'[96] In his diary account of the conference, the hawkish US diplomat George Kennan described how Bevin 'looked highly disgusted with the whole procedure, and it was easy to see by his face that he found himself in a position he did not like'. He said that Bevin looked on Byrnes as a 'cocky and unreliable Irishman', and when the Americans sent a document on atomic energy to the Soviets before it had been cleared with the British, 'Bevin could view this only as an instance of direct bad faith and was furious.' Molotov, meanwhile, leant across the table with the look of a poker player with a royal flush in his hand. A cigarette hanging from his lip, and with his eyes glinting with delighted self-assurance, 'he glanced from one to the other foreign minister, obviously keenly aware of their differences between each other and their common uncertainty in the face of the keen, ruthless, and incisive Russian diplomacy'.[97] Bevin felt able get on with Stalin but could not stand Molotov. 'There's nothing there to warm yourself with,' he remarked.[98]

At least negotiations were alive again, following the breakdown that had occurred in London in the autumn. Byrnes believed he had achieved a breakthrough, but the results were limited at best.[99] The Soviets agreed to US proposals for a UN Atomic Energy Commission. In a bid to secure Anglo-American recognition of the Romanian and Bulgarian governments that they sponsored, they agreed to the inclusion of some token figures from the opposition – but in practice conceded nothing that would weaken their own influence in those countries.[100] In a confidential briefing for British journalists, Bevin said that Russia was 'quite clearly as imperialistic as the greatest of the Czars'. US policy, on the other hand, combined an idealistic desire to work through the UN, 'at the same time making secure as many bases as she can in case the United Nations don't work'. So 'you have two great imperialisms without, I am afraid, quite all the experience that this stupid old country has got'. Asked if Britain was prepared to fight Russia, Bevin replied, 'Good God, no.'[101] Back in London, and addressing the UN's inaugural General Assembly, Bevin showed little concern for the diplomatic niceties. *Time* magazine compared him favourably with the 'habitual compromiser' Byrnes: 'He spoke up to the Russians as a great many plain people in pubs and corner drugstores had often wanted to speak. Gasped one European delegate: "My God! We are playing chess, and Bevin is playing darts!"'[102]

Playing tough with the Soviets did not mean that Bevin despaired of inducing them to mend their ways. The outcome of the developing Iran Crisis seemed to provide evidence this could work. The Red Army had failed to pull out from Northern Iran under the terms of a wartime deal, and instead the USSR tried to pressurize the Iranians to grant them a favourable oil concession. It appears that the Soviets decided to withdraw at the point that they thought – wrongly, as it turned out – they had secured the deal they wanted. More broadly, Stalin was probably motivated less by communist ideology than by balancing British influence in Iran on a spheres of interest model.[103]

It seemed on the surface as though the Americans had forced the Soviets to back down by standing up to them in the UN. Scholars now tend to attribute more agency to the Iranians themselves, of whom the British were contemptuous, but who were the ones who caused the Soviets to be hauled before the Security Council, 'rather as if a rabbit had bitten a stoat'.[104] Given the shortage of reliable intelligence about Soviet intentions, it was understandable that British and American thinkers and policymakers should conclude the worst. 'Like most Western observers at this time, I believed that Stalin's behaviour showed he was bent on the military conquest of Western Europe', wrote Healey in his memoirs. 'I now think we were all mistaken. We took too seriously some of the Leninist rhetoric pouring out from Moscow, as the Russians took too seriously some of the anti-Communist rhetoric favoured by American politicians.'[105]

In March 1946, as the Iran crisis came to a head, Churchill delivered his famous 'iron curtain' speech at Fulton, Missouri, in the presence of Truman. As yet, his warning about the USSR's 'expansive and proselytising tendencies' was not one that the British government, nor even Truman himself, could openly endorse.[106] Ministers were embarrassed because copies of the speech had been distributed through British official channels (though they themselves had not seen it in advance). Bevin seemed irritated that Churchill's comments, rather than his own most recent speech, might be taken as a statement of government policy.[107] In Cabinet, though, only Nye Bevan gave any hint that he disagreed with the actual sentiments. In the Commons, Attlee fell back on the claim that the government was 'not called upon to express any opinion of a speech delivered in another country by a private individual'.[108] However, to Mackenzie King of Canada he acknowledged: 'It will certainly have done good if it encourages the Americans to think and to recognise the need for the United States and the British Commonwealth to work together.'[109]

Indeed, the speech contributed indirectly to the passage of the US loan through Congress. It made both Democrats and Republicans more willing to assist Britain in the face of the growing Soviet threat and, in addition, Churchill privately lobbied Senators and Congressmen directly to support the deal.[110] Though he complained, quite unfairly, that he was not consulted enough, Churchill privately stated that he was 'completely in agreement with the Government's foreign policy'.[111] He even conceded that Bevin 'was able to talk more firmly and clearly to Russia than he [Churchill] could have, by virtue of being a Labour government'.[112] Such comments would have confirmed the worst fears of many left-wingers, had they known of them. Eden, to whom Churchill left many of his day-to-day Opposition duties, admired Bevin and his 'rough-hewn' opinions and was sensitive to his problems.[113] He recalled: 'In parliament I usually followed him in debate and I would publicly have agreed with him more, if I had not been anxious to embarrass him less.'[114]

Although the notion of the 'post-war consensus' has been much disputed, the concept seems quite valid for foreign (if not imperial) policy.[115] The dynamic was noted in Moscow at the time. When the Council of Foreign Ministers met in Paris in May 1946, the influential Republican Senator Arthur Vandenberg witnessed how 'Bevin suddenly put all his cards on the table', challenging Molotov on the future of various disputed territories.[116] Bevin said that 'Nineteenth Century imperialism was dead in England, which was no longer an expansionist country', but voiced his 'suspicion that their place was taken by others'. This was a clear dig at the Soviets. He added: 'As a Social Democrat, he was not envious.' Molotov hit back, saying Bevin had forgotten 'there were Twentieth Century imperialist tendencies in the world, including in Great Britain. When Churchill calls for a new war and makes militant speeches at home and abroad, he represents the worst imperialist tendencies of the Twentieth Century, and it is to be noted that Churchill approves M. Bevin's foreign policy.' He pointed out that the UK had troops and bases in Greece, Denmark, Egypt, Iraq, Indonesia and other places. Forgetting his own country's recent behaviour in Iran, he said that Soviet troops were stationed abroad only in line with treaty requirements. When the diatribe was over, Bevin said only that 'he hoped that now that Mr. Molotov had gotten that off his chest, he felt better'.[117]

Bevin's own chest was in a sorry state. In July 1946 he collapsed with a heart attack, just after leaving the Chamber of the House of Commons. Reported in the press as 'a slight indisposition', this came on top of a litany of other health issues, which were exacerbated by lack of exercise and heavy smoking and drinking. (One of his secretaries said Bevin used alcohol 'like a car uses petrol'.[118]) As a result, Attlee initially had to head the British delegation to the Paris Peace Conference, though Bevin soon recovered sufficiently to take over.

The debates with the Soviets were bitter, but the conference did result in treaties settling the borders of Romania, Hungary, Bulgaria, Finland and Italy, as well as the future of former Italian colonies. Bevin's dull and downbeat parliamentary survey of the outcome won a mixed reception (though a surprisingly restrained one in Moscow).[119]

The *Daily Mail* judged that Bevin's speech lacked a clear definition of policy, and that it 'bore the marks of the weariness he must be feeling after his tremendous efforts of the last year, and which will earn him the sympathy of his countrymen'.[120] The *New Statesman* complained that Bevin had too often 'aired impeccable general principles' only to ignore them in practice.[121] Though it seemed that Bevin still had the bulk of his party behind him, his words were 'received coldly by a considerable number of Labour MPs'.[122] The stage was being set for a showdown.

It is worth recalling the sheer range of issues with which Bevin had to deal, from the future of occupied Germany and Japan, to Anglo-Egyptian relations, to the matter of British troops in Indonesia (which were withdrawn when Dutch rule resumed). It was the question of Palestine that was a major sore point both with the Americans and with Richard Crossman as organizer of the incipient Labour rebellion. Britain had conquered Palestine from the Ottomans at the end of the First World War and subsequently ruled it as a League of Nations mandate. With the Balfour Declaration of 1917, the British committed themselves to supporting 'the establishment in Palestine of a national home for the Jewish people', though pledging also that the rights of existing non-Jewish communities would not be prejudiced. Arab–Jewish conflict intensified throughout the interwar years and a 1939 government White Paper only exacerbated the tensions. This document restated support for a 'national home' but, to the outrage of Zionists, limited Jewish immigration. During the war and in its aftermath, many Jews were driven to escape Europe. At this stage, Labour policy gave strong support for a national home and was insensitive to the interests of Palestinian Arabs.[123]

Bevin himself had no sympathy for Zionism. His views were likely reinforced by the Arabist tendencies of the Foreign Office and by acts of Zionist terrorism. He personally was to become a target of a letter-bomb campaign by the notorious Stern Gang.[124] He enraged Truman and many other Americans with a series of inflammatory public statements, including the suggestion that the US was only demanding that 100,000 Jews be allowed into Palestine because 'They did not want too many Jews in New York.'[125] There has been much debate over whether Bevin was personally anti-Semitic. The evidence is mixed, given that, among other things, he had deplored the Nazi persecution of the Jews in the

1930s.[126] Nevertheless, the evidence of Christopher Mayhew, an MP who became close to Bevin and generally admired him, seems decisive. According to Mayhew, Bevin 'tended to attribute the characteristics of his Zionist enemies to the Jewish people as a whole', detested Jews in general, and even claimed 'they taught Hitler the technique of terror'.[127] Yet it is doubtful whether his individual prejudice had a dramatic impact on the outcome of British policy in Palestine. The decision eventually taken – to remit the question to the UN – was ironically similar to that advocated in the *Keep Left* pamphlet.[128]

Bevin's views on Palestine contributed to his growing enmity with Crossman. The latter's career as an Oxford academic had ended after he divorced his first wife and married the former wife of a colleague. In 1940, he was recruited by Dalton to work on propaganda at the Ministry of Economic Warfare, and five years later he was elected for Coventry East. His friend Barbara Castle noted that his scholarly mind-set turned every political discussion into a tutorial, but she 'loved him for the way he would use his first-class brain and intellectual clarity to scythe through political evasions, muddle-headedness and hypocrisy'.[129] Fiercely intelligent but unpredictable and erratic, he was labelled by his enemies 'Double Crossman'. Bevin appointed him to an Anglo-American commission on Palestine's future, though he came to regret doing so, and rejected the committee's recommendation to admit 100,000 Jews. He concluded that Crossman's ideas were the product of arrogance and poor judgement.[130] Crossman's later verdict on Bevin was scathing: 'Driven by a frightening mixture of anger and violent self-pity, he became convinced that the Jews were organising a world conspiracy against poor old Britain and, in particular, against poor old Ernie.'[131]

Attlee was hardly more receptive to Crossman than Bevin was. Though he granted Crossman's (rather presumptuous) request for a 30-minute interview, the Prime Minister's only response to his lengthy description of his Palestinian experiences was: 'I saw your mother last week.'[132] This was not a purely random remark. The two families had long been friendly and had spent many Saturday afternoons on the Crossmans' tennis court at their house in Essex. Tam Dalyell, Crossman's friend and biographer, described Richard's difficult relationship with both mother and father. He wrote that 'The Attlees never forgave him for causing his parents so much pain' and noted that both Vi and Clem 'were shocked by what both of them always regarded as the irresponsibility of his public and, even worse, of his private life'. Asked his opinion of Crossman's tennis-playing, Attlee replied: 'Erratic – like his politics.'[133]

In October 1946, Crossman and 20 other MPs sent an open letter to Attlee. The signatories included left-wingers such as Foot, Castle and Jennie Lee (who was married to Bevan) and future right-wingers Callaghan and Wyatt. The letter should be read partly in the context of the recent forced resignation of Henry A. Wallace, US Commerce Secretary and former Vice-President, after a speech in which he rejected the 'Get tough with Russia' approach that Truman was now moving towards. The MPs expressed concern at the reactive nature of the government's foreign policy and stated: 'we believe that, by our example, we can bridge the antagonism between the United States and the Soviet Union by the vigorous pursuit of socialist policies at home and abroad and that we can live on terms of amity with both'.[134] The critics then put down an amendment in the debate on the King's Speech, which attracted 57 signatures.[135]

As an inexperienced MP, Crossman may not have realized the momentousness of this action, which amounted to proposing a vote of no-confidence in the government's foreign policy. Addressing the PLP, Attlee seems to have temporarily lost his touch – according to Mayhew he gave a 'Straight ticking off – not very well done and [a] rather plaintive, querulous style.'[136] He would have done better to make the argument that he had recently addressed to the readers of *Picture Post* – that the government was 'trying to bring a new socialist outlook into world affairs', but that the necessity of compromise with other countries led to solutions that socialists might not favour if they had a free hand.[137]

The rebels pressed ahead, and in the debate Crossman urged 'that a Socialist Britain which puts into effect an independent British policy and refuses to join any ideological bloc is the only power which can break the present deadlock and save this country and the world'.[138] He and his sympathizers did not actually vote against the government and instead merely abstained, but it was naïve to imagine that this would lower the political heat. The rebels totalled no more than 80. Their numbers were likely swelled by some MPs' concern over Palestine.[139] Though Bevin claimed to have been terribly undermined by the rebellion while he was absent in Washington, the reaction in the USA was muted. There was concern in official circles about the extent of the revolt, and some conservatives drew comparisons with the Wallace affair, but there was 'little disposition to assert that a reversal of Britain's foreign policy is impending'.[140]

According to Castle, the episode had two results at home. The first of these 'was that it drew an excited response from the rank and file in the party, many of whom wrote in supporting us'. The second was the strengthening of right-wing opposition to Attlee, especially from union leaders who thought he hadn't slapped down the rebels hard enough. Castle claimed that three key union bosses, including TGWU boss Arthur Deakin, decided the Prime Minister 'must be replaced by someone who would be tougher with the left, though they had to bide their time'.[141] Douglas Jay recalled: 'This was the beginning of the end of the enthusiastic harmony between Government and Party which had glowed so brightly after the 1945 election.'[142]

That harmony was also inevitably damaged by the domestic crisis that unfolded over the winter. In February 1947, the British informed the new American Secretary of State, George C. Marshall, that they could no longer afford to provide aid to Greece and Turkey and proposed that the Americans adopt the burden.[143] The Truman administration, fearing a communist takeover, determined on its own $400 million aid package. In front of Congress, the president articulated his new doctrine – 'that it must be the policy of the United States to support free peoples who are resisting attempted subjugation by armed minorities or by outside pressures'.[144] However, even as Britain went into retreat, Bevin successfully resisted Attlee's proposal for evacuation from the Middle East – indeed, the Chiefs of Staff threatened to resign if such a withdrawal took place.[145] Simultaneously, a small committee of ministers determined to proceed with the development of a British nuclear weapon.[146] Bevin took the view that an A-Bomb was needed, no matter what the cost, so that future Foreign Secretaries would not be humiliated *by the Americans*. Recalling his treatment at the hands of Byrnes, he said: 'We've got to have the bloody Union Jack flying on top of it.'[147]

Crossman later argued that the secretive and high-handed nature of the decision-making process showed that Attlee had been the first occupant of No. 10 to exercise 'prime ministerial government' (as opposed to

Cabinet government) in peacetime.[148] The counterargument, advanced by George Strauss, was that, far from being hidden, the decision was announced (in 1948) in response to a parliamentary question. In addition, a range of ministers were aware of the details.[149] Crossman was right, though, to draw attention to the absence of discussion and debate, which the government surely welcomed. Paradoxically, the bomb was Bevin and Attlee's way of pursuing the independent foreign policy that Crossman and Co. were urging upon them. This was true even if the method was one that the critics would have probably disapproved of had they truly been aware of it.

At this point, Attlee still had some hopes of reaching an accommodation with the Soviets, noting how Britain had been in conflict with France at the end of the nineteenth century, only to agree the *entente cordiale* in 1904.[150] Bevin seemed on the verge of giving up on achieving an understanding with Stalin ('a dreadful fellow') but was still willing to put in a few months' more effort to that end.[151] According to Dalton, Bevin was now 'physically unable to go on much longer' and became exhausted after walking up two flights of stairs.[152] But it was too soon to write him off. Late one night at the Paris Embassy, Lady Diana Cooper (wife of Duff) escorted Bevin to the lift. All of a sudden he 'clasped me into his arms with the strength and immobility of a bear and buried his podgy face in my neck'. Then, after an agonizing pause, 'with a very slow utterly relentless gesture he shifted his mouth to mine. No struggles could have affected the situation.' She was deeply embarrassed when he asked her to spend the night with him and couldn't believe he thought she might agree. She was, however, forgiving: 'there's life in the dear old dog and courage and character and humanity and a lot of other nice things, and if he likes to be foolish late at night, he should be indulged'.[153]

To some analysts today, Bevin's political attitudes appear as distasteful as his wandering hands. There is some truth in the charge that, throughout this period, Bevin remained a conventional imperialist.[154] But as time passed he was increasingly prepared to speak the language of colonial freedom, if only to ensure that Labour took the credit for developments that had largely been forced on it.[155] The legend still circulates that, under Bevin, the Labour government 'pursued an unquestioning pro-USA policy'.[156] The Anglo-American relationship was at this stage far less secure than the conventional wisdom would suggest, and far from being in thrall to US power, Bevin was determined that Britain maintain its world-power role and independence of Washington. At Margate he steamrollered his opponents less because he was offended by their views than because he regarded virtually any challenge as a form of treachery. Using force of personality, he manipulated Labour movement traditions to turn the accusation of disloyalty into a deadly weapon. And during the crisis year of 1947 the party needed every ounce of unity at its disposal.

5

Up the Garden Path

November 13th 1947. Hugh Gaitskell, 41 years old, had been an MP for a bit more than two years and Minister of Fuel and Power for just a few weeks. It was an important role, but Gaitskell did not have a seat in the Cabinet and attended only for items that concerned his department. On this day, he was there for a discussion on wages policy. The problem at stake was that of how to encourage workers to move into industries where they were most needed without provoking inflation via wage rises; that is, how to reconcile the government's policy of economic planning with the tradition of free collective bargaining that the unions and many ministers held dear. Cripps had tabled a paper arguing for the abandonment of 'the old traditional "hierarchy" of income levels in favour of a new relationship which is more consonant with the national interest'. To this end, he proposed the creation of a Central Appeal Tribunal, to which the decisions of other bodies such as wages councils could be referred.[1] In his diary, Gaitskell wrote that the discussion, which ended inconclusively, 'dragged on and on very heatedly. Cripps and Morrison being calm and sensible, Ernie [Bevin] flying into a furious rage and accusing Cripps of leading us down the road to fascism. (It was as though Cripps had touched a fuse off.)' Dalton, though present, did not take part. 'In the middle of all this I saw HD sitting rather silent and looking rather tired.' Gaitskell had worked for Dalton as a temporary civil servant during the war. 'I caught his eye and he smiled at me,' Gaitskell continued. 'I did not know then that he must have been in appalling mental agony.'[2]

Within hours, Dalton had quit his job. 'DALTON RESIGNS; CRIPPS IS CHANCELLOR', announced the next day's *Daily Mail*, with the explanation: 'Budget leak sensation starts political storm'.[3] It was all due to a few indiscreet words Dalton had uttered to a friendly journalist as he was about to enter the Commons chamber to deliver – as it turned out – his final Budget. The London correspondent of the *Belfast News-Letter* claimed that nothing that had happened since 1945 had hit Attlee and his ministers as hard as Dalton's 'completely unexpected and sensational departure'. The government had been dealt 'a deep and grave wound'.[4] This was an exaggeration. Certainly, the episode was a personal tragedy for Dalton, though he returned to the Cabinet in a lesser role within months. The loss of a single minister, as the product of a minor lapse rather than of a dispute over policy, could easily be withstood. It was, nevertheless, a watershed. The rise of Cripps not only strengthened the government's authority. It also cemented the association between the government and the policy for which the new Chancellor stood. That policy can be summarized in a single word: Austerity.

There were real contrasts of style between the exuberant Dalton ('a large stentorian-voiced Barnum-type showman') and the chilly, upright Cripps (who 'tended, after having formed his decision, to imply that it had been imparted to him by some higher wisdom').[5] But Cripps had a private warmth and sense of mischief that were at odds with his public persona. He once obliged his PPS, Barbara Castle, to eat a substantial bowl of raw carrot that hotel staff had thoughtfully provided for him, their famously vegetarian guest. "We mustn't hurt their feelings," he insisted impishly. "Eat it up." His redeemingly human side, together with his refusal to be 'panicked out of his principles', helped reconcile his colleagues to the messianic and moralistic aspects of his personality.[6]

Cripps secured bipartisan respect in a way that eluded Dalton – and he was a cannier politician than has sometimes been allowed. Somewhere in their joint history, the two men had switched tracks. Dalton, the 1930s moderate, came to be welcomed by Keep Left types as a counterweight to Bevin. 'His spirit of aggression against the Tories satisfied the most exacting standards', and he openly relished implementing policies unpopular with the City and the better-off.[7] Cripps, the former Socialist League firebrand, now modelled a stern statesmanship based on appeals to Christian faith and the British national character. Yet on economic policy, their differences were ones of tone, degree and emphasis; there was no deep ideological split. In fact, although his focus was mainly on cutting defence spending rather than reducing domestic consumption, Dalton had begun 1947 desperate to economize, and had complained about his colleagues' 'bad failure to face unpleasant facts'.[8]

Understanding the successive crises of that year, which wore Dalton out even though they were not the direct cause of his resignation, requires stepping back to consider the impact of the US loan. Part of the problem was that the sum lent, though big enough to buy Britain time, was insufficient to restore equilibrium to a war-damaged country with massive external obligations. At the same time, there were massive, uncontrolled capital outflows, in the form of foreign investment to the Sterling Area, which greatly exceeded receipts from the loan.[9] Dalton was at first guilty of over-optimism about how long the loan would last, about the risks of inflation, and about the dangers of convertibility (due to take effect in July 1947).[10] Yet soon he was relying on sleeping pills to stop him lying awake making calculations about how long the reserves would last.[11] He persistently tried to alert his colleagues to the looming storm clouds, though perhaps he didn't have the personality necessary to make his warnings effective.

Dalton was accused by Conservatives and the right-wing press of frittering the loan away on socialist experiments. In fact, the emergent welfare state was quite cheap. Yes, it took a rising share of public spending (which fell overall until 1950). But it involved a switch from private to public consumption, not a major increase in the use of real resources like steel.[12] The financial journalist Paul Einzig was one of those who attacked Dalton unjustly for his remark about sanctioning expenditure with 'a song in his heart'. Einzig later confessed that Dalton made this comment in respect of comparatively small sums devoted to the former depressed areas. However: 'This remark was quoted against him on innumerable occasions and was presented by his critics – including myself – as being characteristic of his general attitude towards public spending.'[13]

This is not to say that the government's economic management was perfect. Ministers were hazy about how to turn their long-held aspirations into practice. The commitment to implement a planned socialist economy, a reaction against the evolutionary gradualism of the MacDonald years, remained ill-defined. Attlee stated that 'In matters of economic planning we agree with Soviet Russia' – even though there was nothing in Labour's programme that resembled Stalin's crash programme of centrally directed industrialization, and even though officials had advised the Cabinet that the two countries' economies were so different that it was hard to draw lessons from the USSR's example.[14] Ministers did recognize the conflict between planning (which suggested direction of labour and resources) and union/labourist traditions of free collective bargaining and choice of employment. They tended to imply that some unique British compromise would solve the contradiction. Morrison spoke in riddles: 'We in Britain stand for free planning and for planning as a means to fuller freedom.'[15]

Cripps 'talked a lot about the need for an Economic Plan', seemed more interested than his colleagues in the quantitative planning of production, and worried that the government's existing actions did not amount to planning. But, from his base at the Board of Trade, he lacked the ability to do much about it in the face of the Treasury's power.[16] Dalton had a long-standing interest in planning and continued to insist that it was a practical proposition.[17] Yet, on the face of it perversely, he insisted that the new annual Economic Surveys – intended to compare available resources with the claims likely to be made on them – be prepared on a calendar-year basis rather than in line with the financial year. This separated budgetary policy and broader economic planning in what seemed like a rejection of joined-up thinking.[18]

Arguably, this was not a rejection of planning as such, but rather a genuine attempt to share authority with Morrison (who had responsibility for the Surveys). The results may have been incoherent, but, in line with Labour's ideology, Dalton wanted to subordinate finance to the needs of the real economy: 'we must know what the distribution of our physical resources is to be, before we can match our financial policy to it'.[19] Without a clear lead from the top, civil servants fought it out among themselves. At the Treasury, Assistant Secretary Otto Clarke noted a division within Whitehall. There were those he labelled 'Thermostatters', who saw planning in terms of aggregate demand management, and 'Gosplanners' such as himself, who favoured more direct physical planning. (Gosplan was the Soviet planning agency; the label was a little tongue-in-cheek.) Clarke wrote: 'Unfortunately, it seems unlikely that the conflict will go to Ministers. The danger is that Ministers will think we are planning when we are not.'[20]

This illusion was understandable given the progress that was being made on other fronts. It seemed obvious that the more industry passed into public ownership the greater the government's ability to control the economy. Yet Morrison's preferred arms-length model of nationalization meant that the relevant minister would set terms of reference but not give detailed direction. Run by appointed boards, the industries were expected to operate on commercial principles rather than as part of a coordinated national plan. Nationalization, which became an early target of Labour revisionists, may be the Attlee government policy that has had the worst press. (Yet the creation of the NHS involved taking hospitals into public ownership.) Disappointment set in early, the authors of the pamphlet *Keeping Left* (1950) acknowledging that 'the public corporations have not, so far, provided everything which socialists expected from nationalised industries'.[21]

At the time, however, nationalization seemed like good sense rather than dogma, designed as it was to improve the efficiency of the staple industries, which, during the interwar years, had looked to many as though they were obviously failing. Government schemes promoting amalgamations and rationalization did not have the hoped-for results and public ownership appeared a logical next step.[22] Whereas Conservatives liked to frame the choice as one between socialism and free enterprise, Labour pointed to anti-competitive behaviour such as cartels, price-rings and 'octopus-like monopolies'.[23] The question in socialist eyes was not one of nationalization versus *laissez-faire* but rather the substitution of public control for wasteful capitalist exploitation – and the elimination, not of competition, but of its unhealthy varieties.[24]

In the important case of coal, nationalization was a long-standing union demand, and it was widely assumed that it was needed to win the cooperation of the miners in the interests of improved production.[25] But although the issue had been debated for decades, Shinwell found, when he arrived at the Ministry of Fuel and Power, that aside from a few pamphlets and memoranda, Labour had no detailed plan to put the policy into effect. 'For the whole of my political life I had listened to the Party speakers advocating state ownership and control of the coal mines, and I had myself spoken of it as a primary task once the Labour Party was in power,' he recalled. 'I had believed, as other members had, that in the Party archives a blue-print was ready. Now, as Minister of Fuel and Power, I found that nothing practical and tangible existed.'[26] This was, in fact, no obstacle to rapid action. The Coal Industry Nationalisation Act received royal assent in July 1946, and 'vesting day' – the moment of formal acquisition by the state – occurred on 1 January the following year. The miners were rewarded with a reduction to a five-day working week. Attlee said that the new Coal Board was a fine team but admitted that it was 'going to bat on a distinctly sticky wicket'.[27]

The takeover of coal, which met only weak political opposition, had a particular importance because it could be seen as the 'great test case' of the nationalization principle.[28] Though it certainly did not live up to the highest hopes of its sponsors, scholars have shown that the policy was more successful than has been generally allowed. The picture of the typical miner as an irreconcilable militant, and the industry as peculiarly strike-prone, is misleading.[29] At the beginning, the leadership of the National Union of Mineworkers (NUM) felt an obligation to make the new order work. For the first 25 years after nationalization there was a notable harmony in worker–management relations.[30] There was even a shared understanding of how job losses should be handled in an industry that all knew to be in decline.[31] But nationalization occurred at a moment when events conspired immediately to discredit it. Coal entered public ownership and immediately crisis struck.

It was impossible, of course, for the change of ownership to wreak a revolution. The negative reputation of the industry under private ownership may have been overstated, but absenteeism was rife, not surprisingly given the appalling conditions that persisted. Some mines did not get pithead baths until the 1950s, at a time when many private houses still lacked bathrooms of their own; putting this right was one of the achievements of nationalization.[32] There was scope for bringing backward collieries up to the high technical standards of the best, but for the time being it was necessary to work with the existing stock of capital.[33] During the war, many men left the pits for the services, and the government tried to fill the gap by sending conscripts to replace them (the often reluctant victims being known as 'Bevin Boys'). As President of the Board of Trade, Dalton feared a coal shortage and tried to push through fuel rationing, but his scheme was frustrated by the opposition of the Coalition's Tory supporters.[34] The exceptionally harsh winter of 1946–7 was another factor putting pressure on coal stocks. In mid-January, the country was hit by severe snowfall; snow landed somewhere in the country every day for 55 days from 22 January. In

March, when temperatures rose, there was serious flooding across many areas in central and southern England.[35] Lost exports were estimated at £200 million.[36]

Yet when all is said and done, it is undeniable that government incompetence, in particular that of Shinwell, helped tip an ongoing chronic situation into near catastrophe. Shinwell, it should be said, had some impressive qualities. He was born in 1884 in London but his family soon moved to Glasgow. At age 11 he left school to work (unpaid) in his father's tailoring business. An autodidact, he grew interested in socialism in his late teens and became an effective union organizer. During the post-First-World-War anti-Bolshevik hysteria he was falsely convicted of incitement to riot and spent several months in prison. First elected to Parliament in 1922, he was an able parliamentarian, 'ready-witted, agile, versatile, disconcertingly alert'.[37]

Shinwell served as a minister in MacDonald's minority governments, including two spells as Mines Secretary (outside the Cabinet). During the war, from his place on the backbenches, he gained a reputation as a critic of the coalition and as the MP to write to if you had a grumble with officialdom. Once in the Cabinet, he alternated between riling up the Opposition with provocative comments about 'political sewage', and statesmanlike conciliation, as when he said that Conservative amendments had improved the Coal Bill.[38] From the Tory benches, Harold Macmillan quipped about being captivated by 'this pleasing inconstancy, this ravishing instability'.[39] Shinwell himself joked that his efforts to restrain himself in the Commons led to outbursts on the platform: 'many years ago I studied Freud, Hume and Adler and other psycho-analysts, and I know a good deal about the effects of repression'.[40]

A Freudian analysis of Shinwell's behaviour in the months before the fuel crisis might be more rewarding than simply blaming it on his 'disastrous, bone-headed perversity'.[41] In his memoirs, Shinwell listed a series of alarm-calls he had sounded to his colleagues about the state of production. He therefore claimed that 'whatever were the causes of the crisis [...] unawareness was not responsible'.[42] This was true enough. There was reliable information about all the variables. As early as Christmas 1945 it was clear that, barring radical action, a crisis was likely early in 1947. The problem was that others, notably Douglas Jay at No. 10, were simultaneously pointing out that Shinwell's warnings were not severe enough and that his proposed remedies were inadequate.

He blocked the employment of Polish miners ('over my dead body') and told Attlee, 'you should not let yourself be led up the garden path by the statistics'.[43] In the summer of 1946, he advised the Cabinet that 'conditions in the coalmining industry are over the worst', and told the Commons that 'we can get out of the wood'.[44] That autumn, he told a luncheon of the Coke Oven Managers' Association that 'everybody knew there was going to be a serious crisis in the coal industry – except the Minister of Fuel and Power'.[45]

Shinwell did not later deny making optimistic statements but justified himself on the basis of a remark by the King, who asked him about press stories of an expected coal famine: 'I told him the facts, of course, and he remarked: "It's sometimes difficult for a Minister to say in public what he knows and says in private."'[46] Yet he was unreliable in private too. Gaitskell was appointed as a junior minister in his department some months into the government's life. In his diary, he acknowledged Shinwell's sharp-wittedness and rhetorical skills, but deplored the suspiciousness and aggression he directed at his colleagues. He didn't just pass the buck: 'He picked it up and hurled it.' Furthermore:

> Because of his strong personality, free language and love of a fight, one expects first of all to find that he will be a 'strong' Minister. This is not so. He will always try and evade an unpopular decision, procrastinate, find a way round, etc. Of course there often is a case on political grounds for this. But S.'s hesitations go beyond natural prudence and amount to sheer weakness and moral cowardice.[47]

Coal was not the only issue that was a cause for alarm as 1947 dawned. There was a shortage of labour, and if the gap between requirements and available workers was not closed, some government programmes were bound to fail. The ministerial committee on economic planning (Dalton, Morrison, Cripps and Isaacs) was given a series of recommendations by officials. These focused on cuts in the housing programme and in the armed forces, a delay in the raising of the school leaving age, and conscription of women for industry.[48] The committee largely accepted the proposals, and the expectation was that they would be incorporated in a published White Paper: the *Economic Survey* for 1947.[49]

When the Cabinet considered the plans, Morrison and Bevin were away sick. Those two heavyweights could have helped force through the committee's ideas – but these were rejected, as was a compromise on the size of the armed forces.[50] Giving a clear hint that he might resign if his concerns were not met, Dalton protested to Attlee that 'Much of the report was brushed aside [...] in an atmosphere of emotional impatience and intellectual levity. No-one welcomed, even "in principle", this first attempt to make a detailed National Plan.' The government, though it had started 'wonderfully well', was drifting towards the rapids, he wrote. 'But we look like finishing wonderfully badly – worse, perhaps, than in 1931.'[51] Then, on 7 February, Shinwell dramatically asked the Cabinet's permission to tell Parliament that all electricity was to be cut off from large swathes of industry, and that domestic consumers would also be cut off for several hours a day. Dalton recorded: 'This is a complete thunderclap, following the usual rather hopeful tales we have had from him during the past week.'[52]

Though unemployment briefly spiked at two million, within a few weeks the government was saved by improved weather, though some restrictions on electricity use continued for months.[53] There had been severe consequences for sport and leisure, broadcasting, and the periodical press, and this removal of small pleasures further polarized politics.[54] The government's poll ratings remained surprisingly robust: Labour stayed neck and neck with the Tories until the summer.[55] Attlee did not sack Shinwell, apparently because he believed he had the confidence of the miners, but perhaps also because of political weakness.[56] (A few months later he moved Shinwell sideways to the War Office, hence Gaitskell's promotion.) When the *Economic Survey* was published in the midst of the chaos it was less a plan than an exhortation to the public to work harder.[57] Even though there was a 'popular' version with a coloured cover, it was unrealistic to expect members of the public to read it, grasp the government's objectives, and change their behaviour accordingly.[58] It was written in officialese; it is doubtful that the majority of the population could even understand what it meant.[59]

The day before Shinwell's bombshell announcement, a more personal tragedy struck, with the death of Ellen Wilkinson in St Mary's Hospital, Paddington. The daughter of a cotton worker, Wilkinson had overcome class and gender barriers to study History at Manchester University. As 'a sharp-tongued little fury just out of college' she was briefly a member of the Communist Party but soon switched to Labour.[60] She was the party's only female Labour MP when first elected in 1924. 'A tiny figure with flaming red hair and wearing a bright green dress which shocked the other members', she attracted the nicknames 'Red Ellen' and (less famously) 'Miss Perky'.[61] The press often seemed more interested in her fashion sense than in her political ideas, a fact she exploited for the publicity it might bring her radical causes.[62]

Among her many campaigns, Wilkinson was most renowned for the 1936 Jarrow Crusade, when she marched to London alongside unemployed constituents to draw attention to the economic devastation wreaked by the slump. Fiercely independent, and often short of money, she never married, but had a long-running affair with Herbert Morrison, under whom she served for three years as a junior minister during the war.[63] Was it this, or simply her admiration for Churchill, that led her to moderate her politics?[64] As Attlee's Education Secretary, and in poor health, she focused on putting the 1944 Act into effect rather than pushing forward dramatic new change.[65] But she should be credited with the raising of the school leaving age to 15 and for her conviction that education was about more than technical specialization; in her view its purpose was to cultivate common sense and sound judgement.[66] She once wrote of 'the surge of sheer hate' that welled up in her when she thought of her own schooldays, and of her resentment at having been treated like 'a little sausage in the vast educational sausage factory'.[67]

Wilkinson died from an overdose of sleeping pills, probably taken by mistake in an attempt to relieve the severe suffering caused by her asthma. The coroner's verdict was Accidental Death.[68] Rumours of suicide have continued to circulate but seem doubtful.[69] Told of the news, while in hospital himself, Morrison 'did not say anything, but he suddenly looked years older'. He sent no flowers.[70] Bevin, in his filmed newsreel tribute, was visibly moved: 'Farewell, Ellen, great little courageous soul. We will carry on your work.'[71] Attlee never appointed another woman to the Cabinet.[72] Wilkinson's successor, George Tomlinson, proved effective in expanding the number of school places, but with her death a brilliant flame had been put out.

It would be wrong, though, to turn her loss into a clumsy symbol for the decline of a government that, in fact, had key successes still ahead of it. Nor should we imagine that, as a minister, Wilkinson had always been treated kindly by her own side. 'I can recall that just after receiving a barrage from the Labour benches, Ellen came down to the Lady Members'

Room, shaking and upset,' Jean Mann wrote in her memoirs. 'In the ruthless attack on her there were no holds barred and no regard made for the fact that Ellen was suffering from extreme physical disability.'[73]

The stresses on the government at home intersected with the ongoing maelstrom abroad. The first cuts in British troops in Greece were announced a few days before the electricity went off. In March, Field-Marshal Montgomery and his fellow Chiefs of Staff put in a memorandum of protest to the Cabinet's Defence Committee. They were perhaps emboldened by the success of their previous threat to resign over the proposed withdrawal from the Middle East. They predicted that a series of commitments reached over the previous months would, collectively, have far-reaching and dangerous effects. These included the withdrawal of support to the Greeks, the referral of the Palestine question to the UN, and the decision to hand over power in India by June 1948. They warned that 'the security, not only of the Commonwealth but of the UK itself, are gravely threatened'.[74]

Ministers seem to have shrugged the memo off, and events moved even more quickly than the Chiefs feared. Things had already been unravelling for some time. In March 1946, a Cabinet Mission had arrived in India to negotiate. It was led by Cripps, who was very much in charge; A. V. Alexander and F. W. Pethick-Lawrence (the Secretary of State for India) played second fiddle. The British group attempted to find a solution for an independent India that would maintain the unity of the country and satisfy both the Hindu-dominated Congress party and the Muslim League (which favoured an independent Pakistan). The Viceroy, Viscount Wavell, found Cripps to be 'much the ablest of the party, with an extremely acute legal intellect, very quick to seize on a point, very persuasive, convinced of his ability to make both black and white appear a neutral and acceptable grey, a clever draftsman and very good at finding a compromise solution to any problem'. But he also thought him biased towards Congress, ambitious, and rather unscrupulous. The key politicians were Jawaharlal Nehru for Congress and Muhammad Ali Jinnah for the League. On the Congress side M. K. Gandhi's folk hero status gave him an effective right of veto, though he held no official position. When Gandhi torpedoed the talks and cast doubt on the British ministers' good faith, Cripps was 'shaken to the core'.[75] He was taken to hospital with a severe attack of colitis, the chronic bowel condition from which he had long suffered.[76]

Though the Cabinet mission failed to achieve accord on the future shape of a united India, an interim government led by Nehru was quickly created. The League joined soon after it was formed. But by the time this provisional administration came into being, the 'Great Calcutta Killing' had already triggered a wave of intercommunal violence and retaliation, especially in Bengal, Bihar and Punjab.[77] This helped persuade Congress that partition might be preferable to civil war and the British that the country was ungovernable.[78] Meanwhile Cripps and Attlee were losing faith in Wavell, and by the end of the year they were sounding out a replacement: the glamorous and pushy naval officer Lord Mountbatten. Born Prince Louis of Battenberg, Mountbatten was a descendant of Queen Victoria, and had headed South East Asia Command (SEAC) from 1943 to 1946. Progressive in imperial matters, he initially resisted the offer of the Viceroyalty. He later gave a dramatic account of how he was persuaded to accept. When he demanded a free hand to act as he wished, without reference to the India Office,

> Mr Attlee consulted Sir Stafford Cripps, and even after twenty-two years I can remember his next words: 'You are asking for plenipotentiary powers above His Majesty's Government. No one has been given such powers in this century.' There was silence for quite a while, then he went on: 'Surely you can't mean this?' 'Escape at last,' I thought as I firmly replied that I did indeed mean just that and would quite understand if as a result the appointment were withdrawn. But Cripps nodded his head and Attlee replied, 'All right, you've got the powers and the job.'[79]

This story has been called into question. The term 'plenipotentiary powers' had no real legal meaning and was not referred to in official documents. In practice, Mountbatten did consult London, even flying back for discussions with ministers. (The loquacious Pethick-Lawrence was replaced by Lord Listowel, who thus became the last Secretary of State for India.) But as Mountbatten's biographer points out, it is quite possible the crucial words were used informally, and the new Viceroy did enjoy unusually wide latitude in his decision-making. Furthermore, Mountbatten should be credited for insisting on June 1948 as the latest date for the handover, as opposed to the somewhat vaguer deadline the Prime Minister had previously favoured.[80]

On 20 February 1947, Attlee told the Commons of the new appointment and the timeframe for independence. He was heard almost in silence, but uproar followed when he declined to give the reasons for Wavell's abrupt sacking. 'Mr. Churchill loomed up again to press his point, with hearty vigour and thumps on the despatch box', and when he renewed his attack, 'the Prime Minister lay back on the Treasury Bench, tight-lipped, a flush on his cheeks'.[81] The setting of the date improved ministers' credibility in India. The *Hindustan Times* praised them for having 'at last seen the light' and for having 'put an end to all doubts about the bona fides of the present British Government or fear that it may yield to reactionary Counsels'. The Muslim League's official newspaper *Dawn* was more sceptical, suggesting that the statement was unclear about how partition would work. Yet it still conceded 'one cannot help feeling that it represents a new approach to the Indian problem'.[82] There was also a body of opinion that held that, by not doing enough to achieve agreement between Muslims and Hindus, the British had paved the way for civil war. One Hindu newspaper suggested, 'It looks as if the Britishers have determined to leave India in flames.'[83]

There were many more twists and turns before the assent of Indian politicians could be won. The Indian Independence Act was rushed through at breakneck speed. Despite Churchill's die-hard tendencies, he and his Shadow Cabinet decided not to oppose the Bill for reasons of tactical political advantage.[84] In June, believing that any delay risked the collapse of the fragile agreement between Congress and the League, Mountbatten announced a quicker timetable. On 14–15 August, India and Pakistan gained their independence, on the basis of a partition plan drawn up in rough-and-ready fashion. Both countries joined the newly emerging Commonwealth, thus allowing the British to preserve a degree of *amour propre*. Even the *Daily Mail* gave 'Great credit' to Attlee 'for the firmness of his Indian policy'.[85]

Partition had a brutal aftermath. Attlee had foreseen the possibility of bloodshed, but the scale of it was staggering.[86] In addition to massive population transfers across the new borders, there were large-scale killings of and by Hindus, Sikhs and Muslims, often accompanied by disfigurement, rape and the burning of villages. Up to one million people died.[87] Churchill put the blame on Attlee and his ministers for the 'series of hideous massacres, the like of which have never stained the British Empire in all its history'.[88] Given the rushed, flawed nature of the independence process it might be tempting to endorse such judgements. That viewpoint not only presupposes that Britain had a duty to keep order but that it had the ability to do so, when in fact it was the very erosion of that capacity that was the reason for the hurried exit. Throughout the life of the Raj, divide-and-rule tactics had stoked up religious and ethnic hatreds; only the promise to quit quickly could restore any measure of trust in the British.

Horrible as the consequences were, what Churchill called 'scuttle' may have been the only way to prevent India descending into the even more disastrous condition of disintegration and civil war. In 1948, both Ceylonese and Burmese independence were attended by much less upheaval. With little fuss, the Irish Free State left the Commonwealth and became a republic in 1949. That same year Newfoundland voted to join Canada, having been ruled directly by Britain after an economic collapse in the 1930s.

There was no generalized move towards decolonization, however. Though the Gold Coast and Nigeria were viewed as exceptions, elsewhere in Africa the combination of troublesome white settlers and supposedly unsophisticated African nationalists was thought to preclude swift moves towards independence. Attlee patronized members of the Northern Rhodesian African National Congress by telling them there was 'a long way to go' and that there were 'no short cuts to political maturity'.[89] Nor was violent coercion suddenly dropped as an instrument of policy. For example, the Malayan 'Emergency' (1948–60) saw British forces battle pro-independence communist rebels. This was long seen as a successful counterinsurgency operation which won over 'hearts and minds'. Scholars now tend to paint a very different picture. Members of the Chinese population were interned in large numbers, had their property destroyed, and were subject to lethal violence (as in the Batang Kali massacre, which has been the subject of historical amnesia in Britain). The authorities permitted civilian casualties to mount, in the belief that they were helping to achieve military goals.[90]

Malaya was important for its production of rubber, which could ease Britain's financial woes by earning precious dollars for the Sterling Area. Though ministers liked to cast things in terms of 'partnership' rather than exploitation, the residual Empire remained important to them for the economic benefits it could bring for the metropole. The

1945–51 period was a high point of Britain's economic exploitation of its imperium. Living standards in the colonies were squeezed in order to cut their dollar spending while boosting their earning capacity.[91] The notorious East African groundnuts scheme, which became a byword for state waste and failure, is instructive here. The aim was to save dollars by growing an oil-producing peanut crop, suitable for making margarine, over a vast area of Tanganyika (administered by the British as a UN Trusteeship). It was based on a technocratic enthusiasm for scientific development, which it was thought would help Africans and ease the world food shortage, though its sponsors in fact ignored expert advice. Yielding fewer peanuts than had been used as seed, this 'megaproject' wasted tens of millions of pounds before it was finally abandoned.[92]

There was undoubtedly a belief that the British had at least a medium-term future in Africa. But the groundnuts episode spoke above all to the desperation for anything that looked like a quick fix for the dollar problem. The actual solution – if only a partial one – came from the USA. On 5 June 1947, Secretary of State Marshall made an address at Harvard. Though given with little fanfare, it signalled a crucial change in the Truman administration's policy. The State Department had been warned, in a report by Will Clayton, that Europe's ongoing economic crisis threatened revolution. Such anxieties were accentuated by a communist coup in Hungary. Marshall's speech highlighted the continent's shortages of food and fuel and warned that obstacles to trade were threatening the breakdown of civilized life. He suggested that America could help draft an assistance plan but remained ambiguous about what this meant in practice. 'It would be neither fitting nor efficacious for this Government to undertake to draw up unilaterally a program designed to place Europe on its feet economically,' he said. 'This is the business of the Europeans. The initiative, I think, must come from Europe.'[93]

The speech was little reported in either the USA or Britain, and the British Embassy declined to pay the cost of cabling it to London.[94] This gave rise to a legend that its world-historical significance might not have been recognized had Bevin not spontaneously realized its possibilities, and that perhaps even Marshall himself had not fully known the implications of his own words.[95] In fact, the lack of advance publicity was due to the fact that Marshall feared the speech would be seen as 'a Santa Claus offer', which would provoke outrage in the Mid-West.[96]

The Reuters news agency described it as the most important US proclamation since the Truman doctrine, and as its logical extension.[97] Under-Secretary Dean Acheson had earlier briefed the Embassy's Head of Chancery, who sent a surface mail report that arrived at the Foreign Office on the day of the speech: so economizing on the telegram did no harm.[98] Acheson also spoke to friendly British journalists, and one of these, Leonard Miall, gave a BBC talk outlining the offer's significance.[99] Bevin recalled hearing this report 'on a little wireless set alongside the bed [...] it was like a lifeline to sinking men'.[100] He deserves credit, to be sure, for the nimbleness of his response, but he had more to rely on, when reacting boldly, than simply 'his own intuitive judgement'.[101]

Marshall recalled that the competition for leadership of the European response 'became more or less of a race' between Bevin and French foreign minister Georges Bidault.[102] The Soviets were offered the chance to participate in the recovery programme but turned it down. A new body, the Organization for European Economic Cooperation (OEEC), was soon founded to administer and distribute Marshall Aid. Between 1948 and 1951 the United States was to disperse $12.5 billion in grants and loans, each country receiving funds according to the size of its dollar deficit. Britain received 23 per cent of the overall sum (and France 20 per cent).[103] Around 40 per cent of Britain's share went on food and drink and tobacco. Raw materials accounted for a further 40 per cent, machinery for 7 per cent, and oil and related products for the majority of the rest.[104] But the money did not come on stream soon enough to avert the woes of summer 1947.

Sterling convertibility – one of the key conditions of the 1945 loan – came into effect on 15 July. Dalton and his advisers believed that this new situation was sustainable; they had a strong incentive to do so, as there was no mechanism for postponement. In fact, market actors started swopping pounds for dollars with ever increasing speed. Almost at once, the drain increased to over $100 million a week.[105] On 29 July, Dalton told the Cabinet that the loan might be exhausted by late September. Beyond that, Britain had only limited reserves, and it could not be guaranteed that Marshall Aid would be available to fill the gap. Efforts to boost production would not be enough. Cuts in the import of foreign films, and in currency allowances for overseas travel, might be necessary for symbolic reasons but would not lead to sufficient savings. It was necessary to take 'bold and unpleasant decisions' such as the halting for a period of a wide range of food imports.[106] Desperate to avoid a repeat of 1931 – at a time when rumours of coalition were flying – Dalton courted the Keep Left group and set up a clash with Bevin by urging cuts in overseas military spending and manpower. Bevin, by contrast, thought that maintenance of Britain's global presence was the necessary price of getting help under the Marshall Plan.[107]

The Prime Minister seemed to lack a grip on the situation. According to Edwin Plowden, an industrialist who had recently been appointed head of the government's new Central Economic Planning Staff (CEPS), 'During these weeks neither Attlee nor Morrison as "economic overlord" gave any lead to their colleagues and the Cabinet fell into disharmony and disarray, its confidence shattered.'[108] Dalton went to Attlee and told him that he would resign if he did not get his way, though 'with much heart-searching' he determined to continue. On the recommendation of his doctor, he also started taking Benzedrine – a brand name for a type of amphetamine. This restored his energy and spirit but made him insensitive to the opinions of others.[109] At a dinner on 12 August, Gaitskell found him 'superficially sunburnt and boisterously indiscreet – a contrast with the pale exhaustion of last week'.[110] On 20 August, with the reluctant consent of the Americans, convertibility was suspended. So too was Britain's ability to draw down the remaining $400 million of the loan (though this was later restored).[111] It was an inevitable but humiliating step. In 'pathetically depressed tones, almost in tears', Bevin said privately that 'It has knocked my whole policy, my whole work for two years sideways.'[112]

On the morning of the day convertibility ended, a front-page article by veteran journalist Wilson Broadbent appeared in the *Daily Mail*:

ATTLEE RESIGNING SOON
BEVIN TO BE PM

Broadbent stated that Attlee would be stepping aside due to ill-health, his decision reinforced by his inability to placate potentially rebellious MPs. Cripps was tipped as Chancellor, Dalton as Foreign Secretary, and Bevan as Minister of Supply. The change was supposedly going to take place the following month.[113] These predictions were quickly falsified. The paper's editor, Frank Owen, was later grilled about the story by the Royal Commission on the Press. He said that he published it only after

Broadbent assured him that it was based on conversations with some of the ministers concerned and their friends. 'It did not happen, and it did not happen because, when it was printed, the parties agreed not to carry out what they had intended,' Owen claimed.[114] One possible source was Cripps's wife Isobel, who was suspected of leaking to the *Mail*.[115] The details may have been badly wrong, but Cripps and Dalton were certainly ready to put Bevin in No. 10. Not long before, George Brown and Patrick Gordon Walker (Morrison's PPS) had already 'set out to organize a revolt by collecting signatures in the tea room to a resolution demanding the resignation of Mr Attlee and his replacement by Bevin'. When Bevin found out, he was enraged. He wrongly believed that 'that bastard Dalton' was behind the attempted putsch and Brown was unable to persuade him otherwise.[116]

Cripps had improved his national standing during the August crisis with a powerful Commons speech in which he urged: 'it is by our faith in the deep spiritual values that we acknowledge in our Christian faith, that we shall be enabled and inspired to move the present mountains of our difficulties'.[117] Douglas Jay wrote in his autobiography of the remarkable effect that this declaration of Cripps's personal convictions had on MPs of all parties: 'This speech [...] made the reputation which sustained Cripps's super-human efforts over the next three years.'[118] There was a stark contrast with Dalton, whose eyes, according to his enemies, blazed with insincerity.[119]

On 5 September, Cripps went to Dalton and insisted that, unless Attlee was replaced by Bevin, 'the Govt., the Party & the country are all sunk'. He proposed that he, Dalton and Morrison should make a joint deputation to Attlee and tell him to step aside. Cripps had thought out a series of ministerial changes: Attlee was to be made Chancellor, Dalton was to go to the FO. When Dalton saw Morrison the next day, the latter spoke 'very bitterly' against Attlee but thought that, he, Morrison, should be Prime Minister. He 'wanted to be PM, not out of any reason of vanity, but simply because he felt he could do the job better than anybody else could'. He also argued that the PLP should be allowed a vote and not simply presented with a *fait accompli*. Morrison and Cripps then tried to cast each other in a bad light in an exchange of letters, Morrison hinting that Cripps had been responsible for the story in the *Mail*, and Cripps recording that Morrison wanted Attlee to go but wanted to be Prime Minister himself. On 9 September,

Cripps confronted Attlee alone, and told him that Bevin should be PM and Minister of Production. Attlee coolly declined to move to the Treasury, saying that 'he had no head for these financial questions, EB didn't want to leave the FO, that the Party wouldn't have him [Bevin] as Leader, and that he and HM would never get on in close proximity in the same Cab[inet]'. After further discussion, Attlee suggested that Cripps should become Minister of Production himself. Cripps realized that if he took the job it might look as if he had plotted to steal many of Morrison's responsibilities. But, having reflected, he accepted anyway, albeit his new title was actually Minister of Economic Affairs.[120]

In the wake of the failed coup, Attlee made a few attempts to shore up his support among MPs by making visits to the Commons tea and smoking rooms. It didn't last: he was reduced to 'staccato monosyllables' unless someone brought up the subject of cricket.[121] Bevin had consistently refused to be involved in the plotting and, as we have seen, actively tried to shut it down. His standard line was that he did not want to do a man out of his job. Legend has it that Attlee, during the crucial meeting with Cripps, rang Bevin: 'Ernie, Stafford's here. He says you want my job.' In this version Bevin replied in the negative and then Attlee said 'Thought not' and hung up. Attlee clarified to his biographer that the call did take place, but he in fact said, 'Stafford's here: he says you want to *change* your job.' Bevin then answered that he wanted to stay at the Foreign Office.[122] According to one source, he told Cripps and Dalton, 'If the country is in a mess, it is you buggers who are responsible. Why don't you go away and clear it up?'[123]

But although Bevin never acted against Attlee, he twice sounded out Christopher Mayhew, now a junior minister. Mayhew told him that 'though he could no doubt make himself PM if he wished, my view was that he should let Clem stay, as the best means of keeping the party united'. Bevin agreed, with apparent sincerity, that the unspectacular but honest Attlee should remain. Given that he was now fed up not only with Morrison, but also with Cripps and Dalton (the last of whom opposed his foreign policy), it was a wise choice. 'Yes, I'd probably get a split party. It's all this intriguing I won't do.' Mayhew remarked that it was a big decision to make. 'Not for me it ain't,' answered Bevin, 'with a huge grin and a gleam in his eye.'[124]

Cripps's new role was announced at the end of September. In the meantime, he had to deal with a new threat. Since April, international talks had been taking place in Geneva with the aim of freeing up world trade. The aim was both to make progress on a charter for the planned International Trade Organization (ITO) and for countries to swap tariff and other concessions in a multilateral process. Initially the British had been quite enthusiastic, in the belief that 'our prosperity depends upon a world policy of trade expansion to be based upon an extensive international division of labour'.[125] But as the economic position worsened, ministers increasingly doubted if the country could cope with increased trade openness. In the aftermath of the convertibility crisis, junior trade minister Harold Wilson warned that the UK would have to fall back on methods, such as bilateral agreements, that 'may appear to be opposed to the principles and methods of the draft charter'.[126]

At the same time, the British were unwilling to negotiate away the imperial preference system except in exchange for substantial American tariff cuts, which US negotiators would not offer. The Americans thought that the British were merely paying lip service to the negotiations, while intending 'to get away with just as little performance as possible'.[127] This led to a showdown when US ambassador Lewis W. Douglas told Cripps and Bevin that, unless she changed her attitude, Great Britain might well get left out of any help given to Europe under the Marshall Plan.[128] They called his bluff, Bevin saying that 'The Marshall Plan was a US plan and if it now broke down they would suffer.'[129] As it turned out, the Americans didn't want to sacrifice the gains that had already been made in talks: 'This total accomplishment just had to be saved somehow.'[130]

Eventually, a compromise was thrashed out, in which imperial preference was reduced but not eliminated. With the trade bargain saved, Britain, the USA and 13 other countries signed the General Agreement on Tariffs and Trade (GATT). This was supposed to be an interim agreement, providing a framework for tariff reductions in advance of the creation of the ITO. But though an ITO Charter was agreed the following year, the US never ratified it, and it proved a dead letter. Thus, the GATT, an 'accidental organization', continued as the basis on which much world trade was regulated, until it was superseded by the World Trade Organization (WTO) in 1995.[131] The Attlee government's contribution to this outcome was one of its less heralded achievements.

Cripps's new appointment was heralded on the Left as a welcome sign that the government was finally committing itself to proper central planning.[132] Robert Hall, the recently appointed head of the Cabinet Office's Economic Section, thought 'The changes are very good in the sense that Cripps is a realist and able to understand a problem extremely quickly.'[133] Cripps and Dalton made the new arrangements work, though it is doubtful that they could have been sustained over time. Having two powerful ministers divide economic responsibilities between them was a recipe for conflict. But the situation would not last long. On 12 November came the chance occurrence that upended Dalton's career.

As the Chancellor was on his way to the Commons chamber to deliver his fourth Budget, he encountered John Carvel, the Lobby Correspondent of the *Star*. According to Carvel, he asked Dalton, 'Well, what is the worst you have for us to-day?' or words along those lines. Dalton's recollection was a little different:

He asked me: 'How about the Budget?' [...] He then began to ask me about particular taxes. I think he first asked about tobacco. But I cut these questions short, and told him, in a single sentence, what the principal points would be – no more on tobacco; a penny on beer; something on dogs and pools but not on horses; increase in Purchase Tax, but only on articles now taxable; Profits Tax doubled.

This was an unintentional breach of the code of Budget secrecy. What Dalton had not anticipated was that Carvel would succeed in ringing through the information and getting it printed in the Stop Press column in papers that hit the streets shortly before the Chancellor got to the relevant part of his speech. This was a matter of a few copies, and there was no evidence that stock market movements were affected.[134] Dalton forgot all about the episode until the next day, when he was passed a note in Cabinet, saying that a Budget leak had taken place and that a Conservative MP had put down a private notice question. This was when Gaitskell saw him sitting silent and looking tired. After the meeting, Dalton told his colleagues he must resign. That afternoon, he replied to the Commons question by making a full admission and apology. Afterwards, he pressed his resignation on Attlee, who said he felt he had to accept it. 'He said he hated – hated – he repeated this word several times – hated to lose me.'[135] By the end of the day, the shock announcement was made.

Dalton's biographer has argued that Attlee was not really obliged to accept the resignation. Even though the Tories decided to exploit the leak by demanding an enquiry, the embarrassment could have been surmounted. Though it may be a stretch to say that the Prime Minister agreed to the Chancellor going 'because he wanted to be rid of him', it's clear that Dalton was exhausted, had frayed relations with his colleagues, and was a declining asset to the government.[136] For Dalton, stepping down may have been a form of psychological escape.

Francis Williams made a note of ministers' reactions to the debacle as they gathered at the Prime Minister's room in the Commons. They were characteristic. 'Behaved like a fool,' commented Attlee. 'Can't see why anyone should want to talk to the press.' 'This is a bad business, Francis,' said Morrison. 'How do you think it'll affect the Gravesend [by-election] result?' Then Bevin came in. 'Poor old Hugh,' he said. 'It's easy done. Might just as well have been me. I'm always opening my bloody mouth too wide.' Finally, Cripps showed up. He beckoned to Williams and said, 'The P.M.'s asked me to take over the Treasury. I'd be glad if you could come over to see me in the morning. There are several things I'd like to discuss with you.' He did not refer to Dalton at all. A few days later, Williams saw Bevan and observed that it was strange that a politician with as much experience as Dalton should have made such a silly mistake. Bevan didn't agree. 'Something like that was bound to happen to him,' he said. 'There's no immaculate conception of disaster.'[137]

Some people have a phrase for everything.

6

Vermin

July 4th 1948. Belle Vue, Manchester. Nye Bevan was addressing a Labour Party rally called to celebrate the government's three years in power. The following day the new National Health Service would come into being. In confident mood – when was he not? – the Minister of Health pushed the socialist version of British national exceptionalism. 'We now have the moral leadership of the world, and before many years are over we shall have people coming here as to a modern Mecca, learning from us in the twentieth century as they learned from us in the seventeenth century.' He threw red meat to his audience by pledging that the government would carry out all its manifesto pledges, including the most controversial item, the nationalization of the steel industry. Then he got personal, recalling the bitter memories of his youth. He was the sixth of ten children, four of whom did not survive to adulthood. He recollected a period when he had had to survive on the earnings of an elder sister and was advised to emigrate. 'That is why no amount of cajolery and no attempts at ethical or social seduction can eradicate from my heart a deep burning hatred for the Tory Party that inflicted those bitter experiences on me,' he declared. 'So far as I am concerned they are lower than vermin.'[1]

The comment was incendiary. Enraged Tories seized the label as a badge of pride, setting up 'Rat Clubs' or 'Vermin Clubs'; over one hundred were said to have been formed within a few weeks. Vermin Club members wore badges in the shape of an insect with a top hat carrying a cane.[2] The words 'Vermin Villa, home of a loud-mouthed rat' were painted in black on the door of Bevan's house in Chelsea.[3] Bevan never disowned his remark but he did qualify it. Speaking at the Durham Miners' Gala, he explained: 'When I speak of Tories I mean the small body of people who, whenever they have the chance, have manipulated the political influence of the country for the benefit of the privileged few.' Bevan said he might be ready to be polite in 20 years, when he could look back on a long period of socialist government. 'Then maybe I won't have enough energy to be rude but while we have the energy to be rude, let us be rude to the right people.'[4] A few years, later, he made a further concession: it was a mistake to assume that Conservatives were wicked people. 'A Tory is often a good man doing bad things. To meet they are quite pleasant people – good husbands and fathers.'[5] He had often socialized with them, in fact, once leading Churchill's chum Brendan Bracken to flay him as a 'Bollinger Bolshevik' for guzzling Lord Beaverbrook's champagne while claiming to be a socialist.[6]

Bevan's indiscretion earned him a written rebuke from Attlee. 'It had been agreed that we wished to give the new Social Security Scheme [i.e. the NHS] as good a send-off as possible and to this end I made a non-polemical broadcast', the Prime Minister wrote. 'Your speech cut right across this.' Attlee agreed that the attacks Bevan had suffered for his handling of the British Medical Association (BMA) as he designed the system had been unfair. 'You had won a victory in obtaining their tardy co-operation, but these unfortunate remarks enable the doctors to stage a comeback and have given the general public the impression that there was more in their case than they had supposed.' This was a shame, Attlee said, because it had distracted from Bevan's legislative achievement without doing any positive good. He concluded with a sentence that was probably intended to be fatherly but that could be read as slightly menacing: 'Please, be a bit more careful in your own interest.'[7]

One biographer has speculated that it had been Bevan's deliberate intention to sabotage Attlee's effort to claim a bipartisan heritage for the NHS (which owed many of its origins to the coalition period). The Tories had voted against the National Health Service Act in the Commons and the 'vermin' phrase was a way of holding their feet to the flames.[8] We might note, though, that Bevan usually improvised his speeches, so the outburst may not have been pre-planned. Another theory, advanced by the *Manchester Guardian* at the time, was that whereas 'virulent political abuse was extremely common' before 1914, 'we have become milder in our verbal habits and more easily shocked'.[9] Arguably, then, Bevan found himself at odds with the dominant contemporary political culture, which now prized emotional sobriety and self-control.[10] But if so, he was not alone. Churchill took the chance to slap Bevan with the label 'Minister of Disease' and to say that he needed psychiatric help – the author of the Gestapo speech was himself a master of political venom.[11] Conservative MP Cyril Osborne deprecated Bevan's 'cheap gibes' while himself referring to 'this bloated Welsh Hitler'.[12] One Labour Party worker pointed out: 'Parasites, scum of the earth, and riff-raff are terms often applied to the workers by many of the Tory class, so one cannot be surprised when the compliment is returned.'[13]

Bevan was a magnificent platform orator who could 'make a revivalist meeting out of housing statistics'.[14] But he was vulnerable to the charge that comments unexceptional from a harassed speaker on a street-corner soapbox were inconsistent with the dignity of a Cabinet minister.[15] There were class-based and possibly anti-Welsh dimensions to such criticisms – though Bevan often adapted his accent in the direction of Received Pronunciation (RP) his unruly Celtic tongue was considered *indecorous*.[16] Even making due allowance for prejudice, the 'vermin' line undeniably put fire in the bellies of Labour's enemies and risked alienating a mass of voters.

What's more, Bevan needed the cooperation of many Conservatives at a local level to make the NHS function. (And he was determined to make appointments on the basis of expertise above all else.[17]) Ultimately, there was a simple explanation for Bevan's insult. 'More than any other part, the colliery towns and villages of South Wales were places of hopelessness and despair,' Beaverbrook journalist and Tory MP Beverley Baxter acknowledged sympathetically. 'There is no reason to doubt that Aneurin's heart was genuinely filled with hatred against a system of society which permitted men to live so wretchedly.'[18] At the same time, Bevan had 'a kind of natural arrogance' and suffered from 'wild impulses' that, by his own admission, he struggled to control.[19]

The 'vermin' furore occurred not quite halfway through the life of the Attlee government. It symbolized an important fault line within Labour, less over the radicalism of policy (which in the case of Health commanded wide agreement by this point) than over the aggression of political tactics. Yet its occasion, the launch of a health service now seen as the party's crowning achievement, also represented the government's renewed confidence, once the disasters of 1947 had been overcome. Cripps at the Treasury was the face of its deepening commitment to austerity and the rhetoric of national spiritual struggle and renewal.[20] Bevan at the Ministry of Health was the face of its willingness to court charges of class warfare when tackling vested interests in the service of reform.

It was housing rather than health that had been the bigger issue in 1945. This was natural, given the damage wrought by the Blitz, on top of the widespread persistence of slum conditions. The failure of the Lloyd George coalition to deliver 'Homes for Heroes' after 1918 was both a bitter memory and a powerful Labour talking point. In his 1944 pamphlet *Why Not Trust the Tories?* Bevan devoted a chapter to housing (but made only a few scattered references to health). He implied that a target of half a million houses per year would be fairly easy to achieve and poured scorn on what he saw as the coalition's lack of ambition for the post-war building programme.[21] In fact, there was plenty of planning taking place in Whitehall, and there would be considerable continuity of policy between war and post-war.[22] The influence of the building unions, whose ideas of guild socialism and industrial self-government had been significant in Labour circles during the first interwar years, was now minimized.[23]

The Ministry of Health was overburdened, but its housing responsibilities were not allocated to another ministry until early 1951. 'I never spent more than an hour a week on housing,' Bevan once claimed. 'Housing runs itself.'[24] This sounds like an exaggeration for effect. He spoke to civil servants in the Housing Division soon after the government took power. One of them, Enid Russell-Smith, noted that he made

> an excellent & very clever speech, saying that he knew what a bad time we had had during the war and that the last thing he had in mind was to give a pep talk, & then going on to give an excellent pep talk just the same. He certainly got it over that he was keen about housing & that he really cared about the way in which the people lived.[25]

The shortages of labour and materials made Bevan's task extremely taxing, and during the early part of his tenure he wisely declined to give hostages to fortune by publishing targets for completions. 'Nye said privately at the time that it would have been better to build no houses in the first year or two after the war,' recalled Bevan's wife Jennie Lee, who was also an MP. 'That would have given time for the orderly switch back from war to peace work in the factories, for the assembly of the hundreds of diverse parts that go to the making of a house, and quicker progress would in the end have been made than by the improvised methods he was forced to adopt.'[26] But such a delay would have been politically impossible.

Bevan was a student of power, from the day that, when he was a boy, his father pointed out a 'portly and complacent' gentleman and told young Nye that he was important because he was a councillor. Yet when Bevan made it to the council himself he found that the power had gone elsewhere, and it continued to prove elusive, well beyond the point that he entered the Commons. 'The ordinary man in Great Britain has been spending his life for the last couple of generations in this will-o'-the-wisp pursuit of power,' he observed, 'trying to get his hands on the levers of big policy and trying to find out where it is, and how it was that his life was shaped for him by somebody else.'[27] Now that his own hands were on those levers, he wanted to use the state to deliver the housing programme, minimizing the role of the private sector.

In an October 1945 Cabinet memo, Bevan set out his priorities. 'For our immediate programme we look mainly to the building of houses by Local Authorities for letting to the lower income groups', he wrote. In due course, though, councils would be encouraged to build for the better-off as well, in the interests of developing 'balanced communities'. Moreover: 'We must secure an improved standard over that provided before the war, both in equipment and in size. I shall lay down a standard of not less than 900 feet super for the ordinary three bedroomed houses. This represents an increase of 100 feet super over the pre-war standard.'[28]

This meant trading higher size and quality against the number of completions. Dalton branded Bevan 'a tremendous Tory' for insisting that each three-bedroom council house should have two WCs.[29] After 1951 the Conservatives achieved the spectacular headline figure of 300,000 houses a year at the price of smaller house sizes and lower-quality fittings.[30] 'If we reduce the size of the houses to rabbit hutches, of course we can build more,' Bevan pointed out, adding: 'The question always has been, how far should we sacrifice permanent values to short-term needs?'[31]

Early on, Bevan came under pressure not only from the Opposition but also from his own colleagues as progress seemed to stall. At No. 10, Douglas Jay provided Attlee with a series of warnings, suggesting that the Ministry of Health was disorganized and that the outlook was bleak. Bevan, though, was able see off the objections of other ministers and to prevent them having too much influence on his work. The delivery of the housing programme required the involvement of, and consultation with, a variety of other government departments, not least the Treasury. But an interdepartmental Housing Committee lasted only a few months before being disbanded and replaced with a new Prime Minister's Committee, which soon ceased to meet regularly. Serious problems developed, substantially the product of a failure to match the planned programme to the available labour and raw materials. It was too easy to start building houses without the certainty that the resources would be available to finish them. Yet Bevan successfully resisted pressure to establish a National Housing Corporation and continued to work via his chosen instrument, the local authorities.[32]

The extremity of the housing shortage was highlighted by an outbreak of squatting in 1946, in which returned veterans played a prominent role. Until September this took the form of homeless families – more than 45,000 people – occupying disused army camps on an impromptu basis. Then the movement spread, often with communist leadership and involvement. The government was less sympathetic to these organized efforts than to the spontaneous ones. The most spectacular case occurred when a thousand or more people occupied Duchess of Bedford House, a London block of luxury flats. It was under the control of the Ministry of Works but was due to be returned to the original owners. Allegedly, members of the police assisted the illegal entry.[33] While the crowd outside threw stones and flicked lighted matches at mounted policemen, squatters in Abbey Lodge, Regent's Park, shouted, 'We want Bevan. Give us blankets.'[34]

Picture Post contrasted the Mullins family, with three children, who joined in the Duchess of Bedford House takeover after a year waiting for accommodation, and the Underwood family, who did not become squatters, and who were stuck paying 25 shillings a week for two unfurnished rooms in a partially condemned building without sink, bathroom or sanitation. The article suggested that squatting was a direct threat to the government's authority that had to be stopped. But it admitted that 'going about London a week after the new campaign began, it was clear that councils had received a considerable impetus in the task of seeing what empty properties could, and should, be taken over for use in an orderly re-housing programme'.[35]

Some of the strongest ministerial condemnation came from Ellen Wilkinson, who said that the government couldn't 'countenance anarchy of this kind – the direct negation of everything the Labour Party stands for'.[36] Bevan expressed some sympathy for the squatters' situation, but argued that squatting 'brought disorder and confusion into a situation already sufficiently difficult'.[37] Special Branch recorded one CPGB speaker saying that Bevan had forgotten his working-class background: 'Mr. Bevan had remarked that he would require a whole army of policemen if he were to deal with black marketeering – yet he could find the policemen to deal with the squatters.'[38] In fact, the government took care not to be too heavy-handed. The movement was given a blow when five communists were charged with conspiring to incite and direct trespass. They were subsequently convicted but were merely bound over. By the time these token punishments were delivered the Duchess of Bedford House squatters had left and the trespass was finished. The Director of Public Prosecutions dropped a hint that harsh sentences were not required – there was no point in martyring the activists.[39]

By the time of the 'vermin' speech, Bevan could boast that the authorities were 'now building houses, permanent new houses, at the rate of over 20,000 a month – at the rate of 240,000 houses a year – and the vast majority of them to let'. Furthermore, 'We have carried it out against a barrage of misrepresentation from the party opposite and from their Press supporters who have not scrupled to use any means in order to try to disintegrate the popular will behind the programme.'[40] Including temporary 'prefabs', 284,230 houses were completed in 1948; 300,000 seemed attainable. This rate was not maintained, but that was not due to failures of Ministry of Health planning. As austerity bit further, Bevan received Cabinet instructions that annual completions should not exceed 200,000. Lee recalled his agonizing dilemma: 'Could you best help all you cared about by resigning, or would that merely hasten the collapse of the Government?'[41]

Bevan was right not to quit over this issue. In spite of the cutbacks, Labour succeeded in building three times as many houses in six years as was achieved in the equivalent period after the First World War – and with an egalitarian ethos that refused to see public housing as something that was just for society's poorest.[42] Other parts of government, beyond the Ministry of Health, contributed to the process of modernization. An Act of 1946 launched an ambitious programme of New Towns. Stevenage, the first of these to be designated, was quickly dubbed 'Silkingrad', after Lewis Silkin, the Minister of Town and Country Planning. Further legislation the following year created a national planning framework and attempted to control urban sprawl.[43]

As the youngest member of the Cabinet, Bevan remained outside the government's inner circle, and his early alliance with Shinwell soon dissipated. Shinwell came to see him as a 'sitter-on-the-fence' who judged issues by their effect on his personal prospects. Bevan reportedly described Shinwell – who came from a Jewish background – as 'just a Yiddish opportunist'.[44]

Bevan was not always an easy colleague. As was his right, he insisted on intervening in Cabinet across the full range of issues, and not merely those that concerned his own ministry. Wilkinson grumbled about 'the continual "Bevan monologue" which goes on whoever's department is discussed. [...] Talk about women talking, no woman has a look-in while Nye Bevan is around! – or anyone else.'[45] 'Sometimes Bevan's power over words was his undoing,' recalled Francis Williams. 'One could see him pause to taste an insult that had leapt to his mind and knew that nothing would stop him from the pleasure of uttering it, however much damage it might do him in the long run.'[46]

Bevan once told Attlee that he loved being the bugbear of the Tories. 'You can't be the bugbear of the Tories and be regarded as a statesman,' came the reply, but it is doubtful that, at least at this stage, Bevan much cared.[47] Barbara Castle, a passionate supporter, admitted it was unsurprising that her hero was loathed even by many on the Labour side.[48] 'I have often watched in despair as, carried away by the intoxication of his own power over words, he threw away the chance to influence more timid souls and strained the loyalty of his friends.' But she defended him as a pragmatist and a realist and emphasized the limits to his vanity: 'He was always uneasy among a crowd of Nyedolators who insisted in putting him on a pedestal.'[49]

In addition to hard-headedness, Bevan required all his charm, humour and patience in his battle with the medical profession over the creation of the NHS. He impressed his officials, including some who initially hesitated to work with a former wartime critic of Churchill, and rejected the comfy ministerial armchair that was provided for him. 'This won't do,' he said, 'it drains all the blood from the head and explains a lot about my predecessors.'[50] Yet, as his PPS Donald Bruce remembered, 'At first he had some difficulty in convincing his civil service chiefs that he was really determined to do what he said he would.'[51] The Permanent Secretary, Sir William Scott Douglas, tried to persuade him to stick with what had been proposed by the previous government, as it 'may be a pity to discard a plan which gives us much, if not all, of what we want, which is practically ready, and which would have a very large measure of agreement in its passage'.[52] But Bevan not only rejected the soft embrace of Whitehall continuity: he also turned much established Labour policy upside down.

To understand Bevan's position, it is necessary to appreciate both the complexities of existing healthcare provision and the proposals of previous reformers. Though the system had many bleak aspects, it is important not to draw the picture too dark. Concern about working-class health had grown from the late nineteenth century, boosted in particular by evidence of the poor health of the men who volunteered as recruits during the Boer War. From 1905, the first year that detailed statistics were kept, infant mortality fell substantially though not always on an even trend. Countries such as New Zealand and the Netherlands did better, and in spite of the all-round improvements there were disparities within and between UK regions. These were reflected in children's heights and weights.[53] Public spending on health as a percentage of Gross National Product increased from 1.1 per cent in 1921 to 1.8 per cent in 1937, though this was insufficient to tackle the scale of the problems at hand.[54] The number of hospital beds rose by 35,000 between 1921 and 1938, though provision for the poor remained stingy and inconsistent. A variety of reform endeavours, combined with charitable and mutualist efforts and the residue of the Poor Law, led to a situation in which public provision included centres of excellence as well as institutions where patients were confronted with appalling waiting times, neglect, and inedible hospital food.[55]

The growth of state involvement in the supply of healthcare pre-dated the First World War. The National Insurance Act (1911) was later extended to cover a larger proportion of the working population, though neglecting workers' dependants. By 1936, 50 per cent of British adults were served by 'panel doctors'. These were general practitioners (GPs) who earned a capitation fee for each patient they took on, but who normally handled private patients as well (and these could expect greater courtesy and better treatment). As panel doctors earned a fixed sum no matter what services they provided, they had an incentive to hand patients on to other agencies such as municipal hospitals and clinics.[56] Local authorities provided two out of three of the nation's hospital beds. The rest were provided by the ailing charity or voluntary sector; 'hospital flag days' (street collections) to fund them were an aspect of the system that Bevan found repugnant.[57]

The Local Government Act (1929), introduced by Neville Chamberlain as Minister of Health, permitted councils to take over Poor Law hospitals. In London, the LCC made vigorous use of this power, first of all under the Municipal Reform Party (in effect the Conservatives) and after 1934 under Labour. Morrison, of course, was the LCC leader at that point, and he always took pride in what the hospital service had achieved on his watch. The flaw of municipal provision, though, was that richer areas could afford better services: there would be no equality at the national level.[58]

During the 1930s, Labour developed coherent and distinctive health policies, under the influence of the Socialist Medical Association (SMA) and its first President, Dr Somerville Hastings. Born in 1878, Hastings was an Ear, Nose and Throat specialist, an unassuming and unambitious Christian Socialist, and a firm believer in preventive and holistic medicine. He sat in Parliament in 1924, from 1929 to 1931, and from 1945 to 1951. He was also a London councillor from 1932 to 1946 and chaired the LCC Hospital and Medical Services Committee for ten years after 1934. Edith Summerskill, another medical MP, wrote that 'The idea of a National Health Service germinated in the hospitable atmosphere of Somerville Hastings's Devonshire Street home [...] Although a teetotaller, he felt it his duty as a host to provide the type of refreshment which some of his less enlightened friends desired.'[59] 'There must be no economic barrier between the doctor and his patient,' Hastings insisted; no one should be deterred from seeking treatment by fear of the expense.[60] He played an important role in ensuring that the Labour Party committed itself to developing 'a State Health Service' separate from the National Insurance system.[61] Municipal hospitals remained fundamental to his vision.[62]

The 1943 official party statement *National Service for Health* likewise envisaged wide powers being left to local authorities. In line with SMA thinking, it proposed a system of health centres. As well as hosting groups of GPs, these would provide midwifery services, home helps, health visitors, social workers, and so forth.[63] This was no pipe dream: experiments on these lines in Bermondsey, Finsbury, Southwark and Woolwich had already sought to link preventive healthcare to improvements in the broader urban environment.[64] The (very sketchy) section on health in the 1945 manifesto stated that the new National Health should include 'health centres where the people may get the best that modern science can offer'. By this point, though, the landscape for reform had been further shaped by wartime developments.

In 1939 the government, anticipating large-scale casualties from bombing, established an Emergency Hospital Service (EHS). The expanded number of hospital beds were not only used for war-related cases but were made available to civilians in general. There was substantial modernization and the voluntary hospitals came to rely on the new Treasury subsidies.[65] The Beveridge Report, which was accepted in principle by the coalition, assumed that 'Medical treatment covering all requirements will be provided for all citizens by a national health service.'[66] Beveridge did not go into detail, however. A 1944 White Paper entitled *A National Health Service* offered a fudge, as Labour and the Conservatives were unable to reach agreement on some fundamental issues, but it was nonetheless denounced by the British Medical Association (BMA) as a sinister move towards bureaucratic state control of the medical profession. Henry Willink, the Tory Minister of Health, devised a set of proposals, making many concessions to the BMA, for example continuance of the lucrative private sale of GP practices. It was considered too risky to publish these plans before the general election.[67] Churchill's election manifesto did pledge 'a comprehensive health service', in which the voluntary hospitals would 'remain free' but 'play their part' in the new arrangements in partnership with municipal hospitals. These were the broad lines on which Douglas, the Permanent Secretary, wanted Bevan to continue. Bevan, for his part, believed that Willink 'ran away from so many vested interests that in the end he had no scheme at all'.[68]

As one of the NHS's leading historians has argued, it would be a mistake to see the emergence of the system simply as the logical outcome of previous developments. 'It was perhaps inevitable that the publicly-funded health services would continue to expand, but throughout the Second World War the scale and character of this reform remained an entirely unsettled question.'[69] On the basis of public opinion evidence, it has even been suggested that there was 'no great popular demand from the average man or woman in the street for radical or overarching change'.[70] (One might equally note that the critics' attacks on state control, red tape and 'regimentation' found purchase with parts of the press, but seemingly little with the bulk of the population.[71]) Bevan's achievement was to find a policy space in which dramatic change could be reconciled with the competing interests of the groups concerned. He can be seen simultaneously as an 'insurrectionist' (in the radicalism of his proposals) and as a pragmatic opportunist (in his willingness to cut deals with the profession).[72]

A key problem was that the voluntary hospitals were likely to resist any attempt to subject them to local authority control. The solution – apparently suggested to Bevan by a senior official, John Hawton – was to nationalize the hospitals in both sectors.[73] This would create a centralized system, governed by new regional boards, putting the old rivalries to bed. The plan was not merely plucked from the air: nationalization had already been extensively canvassed, notably in the columns of *The Economist*.[74] In a Cabinet memorandum of 5 October 1945, Bevan proposed this solution to his colleagues, arguing that it was needed to provide a uniform standard of care. There was no question, he wrote, 'that it would provoke an outcry from voluntary hospitals and from the local authorities' but he believed that doctors would plump for a nationalized service rather than a local government one.[75] His conversations with them led him to think that the plan would be welcomed by them and that it would reduce their opposition to the rest of the scheme.[76] Willink, Bevan's Tory predecessor, later gave him credit for this 'wise and important change from the scheme that was put forward by the Coalition Government [...] I do not think the Conservative party would have agreed to this.'[77]

As rumour vied with rumour about the government's intentions, Morrison challenged Bevan's reasoning in a counter-memo.[78] He argued that opposition to the move could delay the creation of the NHS as a whole, warned against weakening local government, and suggested that Labour had no mandate for the idea: 'there is nothing in "Let us face the Future" to suggest that we intended to do this'.[79] Bevan hit back. Morrison had only raised concerns about the political repercussions, he suggested, and did not 'dispute seriously my contention that the way to make these services efficient is to centralise responsibility for them'.[80] After a lengthy Cabinet discussion, Attlee summed up in favour of Bevan.[81] An attempt by Morrison to work up resistance from the LCC fell flat when Bevan met the relevant committee and charmed the socks off them.[82] Morrison never reconciled himself to the outcome.[83] The issue doubtless contributed to the Bevan–Morrison feud that in time threatened to eclipse even the Bevin–Morrison one.[84]

The conflict now moved to the public sphere. Bevan's battle with the medics has become the stuff of legend, in part due to the strident claims pushed by figures such as Charles Hill, 'the radio doctor'. It was alleged that the new system would destroy the trust and confidentiality of the doctor–patient relationship and that Bevan sought to set himself up as a dictator. Bevan did his best to charm the profession. He got on well with Lord Moran, President of the Royal College of Physicians (whose most famous patient, Winston Churchill, encouraged the relationship).[85] 'There is something disarming about the way in which the new Minister confesses his ignorance and his willingness to learn', noted the *British Medical Journal*. And yet: 'At the same time, behind this disarming front there is probably a very combative spirit.'[86]

Bevan maintained a public stance that he was not willing to negotiate with the profession the terms of his Bill, as this would be an affront to the authority of Parliament.[87] He was, however, quite willing to horse-trade on the terms on which professionals would join the new service. 'My trade union experience had taught me to distinguish between the atmosphere of the mass demonstration and the quite different mood of the negotiating table', he later wrote. 'I was therefore able to discount a great deal of what had been said from the rostrum.' It was easy for him to allow his opponents victories, he said, 'for they had usually worked themselves up into a fever of protest against proposals which had never been made'. Thus he conceded that doctors must 'never be made into civil servants'; as he had never meant that they should, he was able to allow the point without difficulty. There should be a 'free choice of doctor'; Bevan had never intended otherwise. 'And so it went on from one blown out slogan to another.'[88] Crucially, Bevan made it financially rewarding for doctors to join the system. Speaking of the consultants, who were allowed to continue with private practice alongside NHS work, he said: 'I stuffed their mouths with gold.'[89]

Jennie Lee's face operated as a barometer of her husband's progress. 'Jennie reminded me of the man who had labour pains during his wife's pregnancy,' Jean Mann recollected.[90] Though Bevan's Act received Royal Assent in November 1946, the opposition was by no means over. The doctors could still hold out the threat of refusing to join. But by the start of 1948, the government as a whole was recovering its position. Nationalization of the railways and of electricity came into effect in January and April respectively (though the government faced an epic parliamentary battle over gas).[91] A US embassy assessment noted that Attlee had come through the previous year's crisis with his reputation enhanced. He had appeased Bevan and other left-wingers who demanded immediate nationalization of the steel industry with the offer of a Bill to cut the powers of the House of Lords. He had transferred Shinwell, 'who was [a] major political liability', and had 'had a windfall' in the form of Dalton's resignation. Attlee had also 'backed Cripps' crisis measures in face of strong resistance from individual ministers whose programs had to be curtailed: i.e., education, housing, town and country development'. As the Cold War intensified, he had backed Bevin and seen almost the whole party united on foreign affairs. 'As [a] result of these manoeuvres, luck and this reassertion of his leadership, Attlee again heads a fairly well united Parliamentary Labour Party and Cabinet.'[92]

All this strengthened Bevan's hand in turn. He advised the Cabinet that, though the BMA as a body might oppose the system, doctors as individuals would probably not refuse the monetary incentives to sign up.[93] Though he threw out some last-minute concessions to weaken the resistance, he called the BMA's bluff by refusing to postpone the 'appointed day' when the NHS was to come into being. Three days after the crucial date, Russell-Smith noted that 'More doctors have joined the scheme than we thought existed.'[94] The National Health Service Act (1946) applied to England and Wales. The National Health Service (Scotland) Act (1947) came into effect at the same time – though its implementation was not smooth – as did the Health Services (Northern Ireland) Act (1948).[95] The Unionist leaders at Stormont had accommodated themselves to the expansion of social services and were gratified that, for its part, the government in London left the Irish border issue well alone.[96]

Though justly celebrated, the NHS was not without its flaws. The nationalization of the hospitals had come at the cost of a three-way division of the service: 'the community care (home nursing and other) services under the local authorities; the family doctor services regulated by central negotiation but administered by executive councils; and the hospital service under a battery of ad hoc and separate authorities'.[97] Although health centres were provided for in the Act, few were built, in part due to the impact of austerity on capital expenditure.[98] Bevan believed that private healthcare would wither away in the face of the excellence of the state system – this conviction proved unfounded. More broadly, it should be remembered that the development of the NHS and the welfare state occurred in a context in which Britain was writing down the wartime debts it owed to India and Pakistan, and was putting its own economic needs above those of its remaining colonies.[99] It is no surprise, then, that in the early years of the NHS (and of mass immigration by people of colour) the typical patients of this supposedly egalitarian system were consistently imagined and presented as white.[100]

For some socialists, like Harold Laski – who said he would have abolished private practice – the NHS system did not go far enough.[101] But it did succeed in improving poor people's access to healthcare, even if, in the long term, the better-off proved more successful at navigating the system to get higher-quality treatment. Doctors switched from opposition to being the most vociferous defenders of the NHS, which won enduring public affection. The institution has persisted in a form that Bevan would recognize, yet this has come at the cost of recurrent financial crises accompanied by a series of problematic reorganizations.[102] Expenditure ballooned immediately, in the face of unanticipated demand for eye tests, dental treatment, and even wigs. The number of prescriptions issued rose dramatically. Conservatives argued this all showed that patients were abusing the system, Labour countered it was proof that poverty had previously prevented people getting the help they needed.[103] Bevan cited 'numerous and shocking cases of people who have been wearing other people's spectacles (e.g., those of dead relatives) for sheer lack of means to get their own'.[104]

Within months, Bevan was having to tell his colleagues that the service was costing tens of millions more than had been expected. He was effective both at seeing off Tory attacks and at securing Cripps's support for extra funding. (Health thus fared better than housing when cuts had to be made.[105]) Though Cripps naturally wanted to keep spending under control, the 1940s version of austerity was less about squeezing the public sector than about keeping a lid on private consumption beyond the necessary minimum. In a landmark statement of his Chancellorship, Cripps said that so long as Britain remained in its impoverished condition, such consumption was bottom on the list of priorities. 'First were exports, second capital investment in industry, and last the needs, comforts and amenities of the family.'[106]

If anyone could sell this programme to the British people, it was him. Even some of Labour's critics thought 'that *all* thinking people now realise now that in Cripps we have a man who is capable not only of the clear thought that is necessary in a time such as this but also that he has the energy and belief necessary to translate his plans into action'.[107] They considered him an improvement on 'the Dirty Doctor' (Dalton) as he faced facts squarely, had the courage of his convictions, and did not court popularity with the different sections of his party.[108] His Stakhanovite work habits and wintry smile suggested a willingness to set an example of suffering. Attlee liked to tell how a visitor had turned up in Downing Street at 5 a.m. saying that he had a meeting with the Chancellor of the Exchequer. 'The policeman, assuming him to be a lunatic, played for time. But when the visitor insisted: "Sir Stafford Cripps asked me to come at this hour," the policeman replied: "Oh, him. Yes, please come in."'[109] Not that the teetotal Cripps insisted that everyone else followed his habits. When Francis Williams came round for an evening meeting, he insisted on offering him vodka from a bottle that he had acquired during his time as an ambassador to Moscow. 'The only thing is,' he said, 'we don't have any wine glasses. Would you mind drinking it out of an egg cup?'[110]

Having inherited Morrison's economic responsibilities, Cripps can be seen as 'the first minister to really carry out the role of economic manager', as opposed to being content with simply balancing the books.[111] Yet he did not achieve his initial ambition to make 'the "Planning Year" [...] the same as the "financial year"' by shifting the period covered by the annual Economic Surveys.[112] This signalled the final demise of planning as Labour had originally conceived it.

The 1948 Budget surplus was built on groundwork laid by Dalton – as the latter was keen to point out.[113] But Cripps used surpluses deliberately to regulate overall demand, to fight inflation and to determine the level of national investment. As the civil servant and economist Austin Robinson noted later, it was Cripps 'who first carried consciously into peacetime budgeting the concepts which Keynes had developed for war finance'.[114] Robert Hall, from his standpoint as the head of the Economic Section, put this down in part to Cripps's background as a barrister: 'once he was convinced he made much more of one's arguments than one could oneself [...] He did not really understand the basis of economic planning as we developed it under his regime, but he was entirely responsible for its development.'[115]

In his first Budget speech, Cripps laid out the resulting doctrine: 'The new task of the Chancellor of the Exchequer is not merely to balance the Budget; it is a much wider one – to match our resources against our needs so that the main features of our economy may be worked out for the benefit of the community as a whole.'[116] The government continued to publish a variety of production targets but these were quickly falsified and progressively abandoned. It should be noted that ministers remained committed to a range of physical controls. Still, the broadly Keynesian demand management policies that they now labelled 'planning' were, though effective, not quite the type of socialist economics that they had once had in mind.

By this point, Cripps had clearly reconciled himself to the persistence of private enterprise on a substantial scale within a mixed economy, albeit hedged with price controls, subsidies, and other types of state intervention.[117] The passage of Marshall Aid through Congress added to his briskness and confidence, but this required some obeisance to US private enterprise values.[118] (American pressure for increased productivity and 'efficiency' resonated to a fair extent with Cripps's own vision of socialist modernization.[119]) With limited tools of compulsion at his disposal, given Labour's established commitment to free collective wage bargaining, he continued to resort to exhortation, a technique that now reached its maximum level of success. A government *Statement on Personal Incomes, Costs and Prices* urged, in the context of growing inflationary pressure, 'that there should be no further general increase in the level of personal incomes without at least a corresponding increase in the volume of production'. There should be no rise 'in incomes from profits, rent, or other like sources'; wages or salaries should only go up in exceptional cases, where this was necessary to attract labour to understaffed industries. This required 'a general agreement by the people to act together upon sound and public spirited lines'.[120]

Though the TUC leaders were annoyed that they had not been consulted, they called a special conference, which gave qualified backing to wage restraint. The pill was sweetened by the fact that the Federation of British Industries (FBI) accepted voluntary limitations on dividends.[121] Cripps made it even easier to swallow by including in his Budget a 'special contribution' on investment income over £250 per annum, where the individual concerned had a total income of more than £2,000. This was, in effect, a capital tax, and thus counts as one of the most radical things that the Attlee government ever did.[122] Tory MP Chips Channon described Cripps's announcement in his diary: 'he was never offensive and always clear and logical, even when he announced his Capital Levy. It means that I must pay out more than I received last year. It is monstrous and a quite unnecessary piece of class legislation.'[123] To make it politically palatable Cripps went to lengths to emphasize that the move was a one-off. He avoided a major backlash and did something to win over the unions but did not make any further egalitarian assault on the problem of large fortunes.

As head of the Central Economic Planning Staff, Edwin Plowden was much happier under Cripps than he had been previously. 'As supreme co-ordinator of economic policy and Chancellor, Cripps was in a much more powerful position than Morrison had ever been,' he recalled.

> Unlike Morrison, he had full responsibility over economic and financial policy, but he was also lucky enough to have various political protégés in key departments who were alive to the need for firm action: Harold Wilson who took over from him as President of the Board of Trade, Nye Bevan at the Ministry of Health, Hugh Gaitskell at the Ministry of Fuel and Power, and Douglas Jay as Economic Secretary in the Treasury.[124]

Cripps held fortnightly dinners at which these and other ministers engaged freely in discussion and debate. After one of these occasions, Gaitskell wrote: 'I could not help feeling that Stafford was surveying his future Cabinet.' He also noted the Chancellor's surprisingly political acuity and anxiety to have Bevan as an ally.[125] Jay observed that 'Nye Bevan dominated the conversation during the Cripps dinners and not seldom poured forth a stream of mischievous gibes about most of his other senior colleagues.' But Bevan 'would always stop dead' when Cripps signalled he should be quiet: 'For nobody else other than Attlee in Cabinet would Bevan check the flow.'[126]

It should be stressed that, although the government was recovering its stride, the economic outlook remained threatening and the global situation alarmingly tense. The Cold War was intensifying, though Bevin (according to Christopher Mayhew) still held 'irrational hopes of a sudden settlement with [the] USSR'.[127] Bevin launched a proposal for 'Western Union', to include European nations and their colonies, under the auspices of Britain and France. He kept the details vague, but there were enough hints of 'Third Force' thinking to keep left-wing grumbles within bounds.[128] At the covert level, on the initiative of Mayhew, an aggressive campaign of anti-communist propaganda was carried out by the Information Research Department – a new, secret division of the Foreign Office.[129] There were still a few signs of backbench rebellion, as when 22 Labour MPs publicly backed the 'wrong' group of socialists (which supported closer links with the communists) at the time of the Italian elections. This became known as the 'Nenni telegram'. Most of the signatories agreed to recant when faced with the threat of party discipline.

Nineteen forty-eight also saw the start of the Soviet blockade of Berlin and the months-long airlift that, despite significant British doubts about its feasibility, successfully brought it to an end.[130] Meanwhile, the retreat from Empire continued. In the absence of any agreed solution, Britain simply withdrew from its mandate in Palestine, triggering the war that led to the creation of the state of Israel and the large-scale expulsion of Arabs. This was more than just a case of throwing in the towel in the face of economic problems and imperial exhaustion. Ministers decided to quit when Britain's presence in Palestine risked ruining relations with other countries in the region – withdrawal was intended to help maintain the UK's status and position in the Middle East as a whole.[131]

Forty-six per cent of voters approved of the government's handling of Palestine, against 33 per cent who disapproved. Forty-four per cent agreed with its foreign policy as a whole, versus 28 per cent who disagreed, though 62 per cent thought its policy towards the Soviets was not firm enough. However, very few voters saw the international situation as a priority; shortages and the cost of living were much greater concerns.[132] The latter were a particular concern for women, who were generally lumbered with the bulk of the queuing and the cooking.[133] The situation was undoubtedly frustrating, and some people resorted to the black market. As one historian has noted, 'Large-scale black market operations involving big sums of money and large quantities of controlled goods were few and far between, but petty transactions involving large numbers of people and little or no money were commonplace.' The initial post-war period saw a boom in illegality as shortages increased and controls persisted.[134] This was the age of the 'spiv', the flashy-suited supplier of dodgy goods, a figure who was comic and sinister at once.[135] The 1949 Ealing film comedy *Passport to Pimlico* exploited this background. When a medieval charter reveals a part of London to belong to the ancient kingdom of Burgundy, the inhabitants make use of their independence to create a black-market paradise, before a showdown with the British government that leads to order being restored.

The Conservatives were adept at suggesting that restrictions were the result of 'socialist mismanagement' rather than necessity. Discontent was also fomented by the British Housewives' League – which was alleged to be a front organization for the Tories, though the party refused to fund it. The attacks went down best with better-off women. The policy of 'fair shares for all' benefited the working classes, whereas high taxation, rising prices, rationing and labour shortages squeezed the perks that the middle classes had enjoyed pre-war.[136] The government countered the anti-austerity narrative with a fair degree of skill. Ministers did this partly by advancing persuasive arguments as to why controls were still needed and by challenging their opponents to say which ones they would abolish. They also removed the sting from the attacks by launching their own programme of progressive, albeit partial, decontrol. By 1948, only 12 per cent of consumer spending was covered by rationing.[137] But to convert such facts into political gain required publicity savvy. Nobody had more of this than the bumptious but brilliant Harold Wilson.

Born in Huddersfield during the First World War, the son of an industrial chemist and a former schoolteacher, Wilson was a precocious grammar-school boy who succeeded in winning an Oxford scholarship. Influenced by G. D. H. Cole, Wilson opted for an academic career, before putting his skills as an economist at the disposal of the civil service during the war. Elected for Ormskirk in 1945, he was immediately appointed as a junior minister. Encountering him just after Labour took office, Mayhew, an Oxford acquaintance from former times, was blown away by his intelligence. 'I watched his bulging cranium with anxiety as he talked, expecting the teeming, boiling brain within to burst out at any moment.'[138] When he entered the Cabinet, Wilson was just 31. 'Harold was a cherubic little man, inclined to be chubby, and his cheery approachability and Poirot-style moustache made it difficult to take him seriously,' recalled Barbara Castle. 'Nonetheless, we were all aware that he had a formidable mastery of statistics, a grasp of detail and an unrivalled memory for figures and dates.'[139] To those who disliked him he was 'short, fat, podgy & rather pushing'.[140]

Wilson's first 'Bonfire of Controls', timed just before Guy Fawkes Night 1948, ensured that the number of licences and permits issued each year would be reduced by around 200,000. This was the first of a series of dramatic announcements that took place over the following months. In his memoirs, Wilson wrote that he asked Scotland Yard about the black-market price of a ration coupon for clothing. He learned that it had fallen to a halfpenny, which implied a near match between supply and demand of the goods in question. 'I immediately abolished clothes rationing entirely and the press insisted on taking photographs of me tearing up my ration book. A further bonfire took place three days later, removing the requirement for 900,000 licences and permits and releasing a further 320 officials from my department.'[141] Yet this was really a media-friendly packaging of a mundane bureaucratic process that had been going on for over a year. Of the torn-up permits, 125,000 were for the manufacture of thermos flasks, and relatively little civil service effort was saved by the whole process.[142]

Though Wilson insisted the government would keep controls that were essential for economic recovery, for industrial efficiency or for full employment, he still attracted suspicion from the Left. Some of the criticisms were substantive, such as that the measures triggered the disappearance of cheap and basic 'utility' clothing from the shops.[143] There were also doubts about Wilson himself, who had seemed to show too much relish when sparking his inferno. 'What struck me was the glee with which he did it,' Ian Mikardo observed, 'the way he did it to seek the approval of the leader writers.'[144]

One Conservative argument against controls was that they created potential for criminality as people sought to evade them. This gained some credence when the government, and the Board of Trade in particular, was hit by scandal. Supposedly, ministers and officials had been paid large sums to circumvent the rules. The unfolding of the claims overlapped with Wilson's efforts to do away with unneeded red tape (he personally was untainted by the allegations). The key player was a conman called Sidney Stanley; he was Jewish, and much of the reporting had an anti-Semitic tinge. Stanley, a slightly ludicrous figure, told business acquaintances that, in return for large sums of money, he could secure licences and other favours. He boosted his credibility by boasting of his friendships in the circles of power, in particular with John Belcher, Parliamentary Secretary at the Board of Trade. But officials caught wind of the alleged misdeeds. When Attlee learned of the charges he moved quickly to appoint a Tribunal of Inquiry under High Court judge Sir George Lynskey. The hearings were widely reported, though the welter of accusations proved baffling to the public.[145]

'Sir Hartley, you are trying to trick me with the truth,' said Stanley during his lengthy cross-examination by Shawcross.[146] Though no evidence of rampant corruption was found, it transpired that, in return for gifts and hospitality, Belcher had provided favours, including dropping the prosecution of a company. He resigned as an MP and returned to his former employment as a railway clerk. Belcher's daughter has attested to the impact on her family. 'My mother, Louisa was cross-examined and forced to give details about her most private affairs. She was found to be transparently honest, but she collapsed after giving evidence and later suffered a series of nervous breakdowns, after which she never fully regained her mental health.'[147] Belcher gained the doubtful distinction of being the only one of Attlee's ministers who was forced to stand down due to personal wrongdoing.

To Cabinet Secretary Norman Brook the episode was damaging because it suggested that ministers 'had been hobnobbing with the scum of the Capitalist system while reviling the best elements in it'.[148] In fact, the government surmounted a threatening situation with its reputation largely intact. Attlee's deft handling of the matter signified not only his unimpeachable personal integrity but also his ability to react quickly to head off trouble. It could be said, in fact, that 1948 was the year that Labour truly came into its own as a governing party. Now, it was not merely passing ambitious bills, but navigating effectively with the messy realities of power. The shift towards Keynesianism and the (quite modest) conflagration of controls could be seen as a retreat from full-blown socialism. In reality, these were pragmatic adjustments that allowed Labour to pursue its goals in non-doctrinaire fashion – just as Bevan had used a combination of compromise and determination to secure the NHS. But Labour was soon to hit another crisis-point. At stake was a fundamental issue. Should the government pause and consolidate its gains, or power forward aggressively for fear that to hesitate was to be lost?

7

The Pound Thing

September 18th 1949. Around 9 p.m. The Treasury. Sir Stafford Cripps penned some final, previously secret, figures into his script and strode to 10 Downing Street. A BBC microphone had been set up for him in the Cabinet room.[1] It would have been hard to think of a better way to convey the seriousness of the situation 'than the sudden announcement of an important broadcast to be relayed on both Home and Light programmes on a Sunday evening'. 'They even faded out *Grand Hotel*,', observed one elderly charlady (referring to a popular music programme). '[S]o it must have been important, and I listened.'[2]

Attlee listened to the broadcast from Chequers, as Cripps delivered a disquisition on the functioning of exchange rates before finally dropping the bombshell. Sterling's value was to be slashed by just over 30 per cent. One pound would no longer be worth $4.03 but only $2.80. When the Chancellor turned to the impact on consumers, he was surprisingly optimistic. A 4½d loaf would now cost 6d, and a rise in the price of flour would follow. Apart from that 'there should not be any noticeable increase in other retail prices, at least for the time being'. There was therefore no justification for any rise in wages, he argued; the effort to earn dollars was to be redoubled. Here was 'another stage in the magnificent struggle of our people to overcome the crushing difficulties imposed upon them by their sacrifices in the world war'.[3]

One group of people who faced a struggle, magnificent or otherwise, were British travellers abroad, who immediately lacked the wherewithal to pay for their holidays. Consulates were besieged.[4] Herbert Morrison, relaxing with his wife in Nice, escaped the trap, because he had cashed in his traveller's cheques before Cripps's speech. A journalist wanted to know if he had had forewarning. 'You must not ask that,' Morrison replied.[5] He had not been at the Cabinet meeting where the crucial decision was formally taken, but the issue had been debated by ministers for many weeks in advance. He had taken part in the earlier discussions and had argued in favour of devaluation.[6]

Léon Blum, the former socialist premier of France, wrote in *Le Populaire* that the news was so surprising that at first he found it hard to believe. This was 'not on account of the categorical denials issued until zero hour by Sir Stafford Cripps', as he knew 'from bitter experience' that 'lying and dissimulation are the rule in such matters'. Rather, like many others, Blum had imagined that if the value of sterling was to be altered, this would be done as part of a coordinated realignment of other over-valued currencies.[7] Instead, a swathe of devaluations took place in an ad hoc way: 'like tenpins before the ball of a skilled bowler, many of the world's currencies fell in unison'.[8] Cripps, on his next visit to Paris, had to smooth things over with the UK's European allies.[9]

According to a Mass Observation survey, the British public's predominant reaction was one of shock, followed by 'relief tinged with resignation'. As Cripps had played down the extent of likely price rises, consumers were consoled that their pockets would not be hit too hard. 'I'm not a bit interested at all,' a lamp-lighter's wife was reported as saying. 'The poor person doesn't handle all that number of pounds.' A housewife from West London, when asked what she thought was the most important recent news item, supposed it was 'the pound thing'. But she had no strong feelings about it because she didn't know what it all meant.[10] *Picture Post*, which conducted its own poll, judged that the biggest surprise was that 30 per cent of respondents had no idea why the government had chosen to devalue. Arguably, the remarkable thing was that the rest thought they did know. Thirty-five per cent considered devaluation was inevitable because of the country's economic position, 23 per cent blamed US pressure, 4 per cent (but 10 per cent of Conservatives) fingered ministers' mismanagement, and the rest attributed it to unnamed other factors.[11] But having recently pulled roughly level with the Conservatives, the Labour Party now found itself 10 per cent behind in the Gallup poll.[12]

The relatively high levels of awareness around devaluation may be attributable to the government having improved its communications strategy since the dark days of 1947. MO found that among the public 'lip service at least is usually paid to the need for harder work and the spirit of shoulders to the wheel'.[13] The *Manchester Guardian*, carrying out vox-pop interviews in the north-west, found that 'It had to come' was a frequent response. Indeed, many people thought it should have come sooner. But industrialists realized that, even if some uncertainty was removed, devaluation was no panacea. The president of the Manchester Chamber of Commerce said: 'We shall only get two-thirds of the dollars for the present volume of goods going to the other side, and we must boost production, not only to get the other third but to get the extra at which we are aiming.' Among pottery firms, most were already selling as much as they could produce in the US market. They would only be able to boost exports if more skilled labour became available.[14] An embittered bus driver, holding forth to his passengers, observed: 'Cripps says that it will only affect us when we buy from America but where the hell does he think we are going to buy from? We buy all our zinc and copper from America, not to mention the oil and petrol we get. Not going to affect us, eh?'[15]

Unless there was tough action to hold down wages, the benefits of devaluation risked being cancelled. But as one American diplomat in London observed, the government had done nothing more than urge wage restraint. 'Exhortation in [the] past has had only [a] moderating effect on wage demands and will be even less effective in coming months.'[16] A National Union of Railwaymen official noted the disproportionate burden on the lower paid, who relied on bread as a staple food: 'It is ridiculous to talk of stabilising wages at 92s, 6d a week and the affront is greater when the talk comes from people with four-figure salaries.'[17] At a turbulent four-hour meeting the TUC General Council declined to give Cripps its endorsement, stating only that it was 'satisfied that the grave step to devalue would not have been taken by the Government without a careful assessment of all the factors involved'.[18]

The lightning bolt of devaluation had struck only ten days after the annual Trades Union Congress had endorsed continued wage restraint by 6,485,000 votes to 1,038,000.[19] Union leaders were divided over the shock move. Some blamed the USA's economic policies and sought a break with multilateralism; others accused the government of timidity and of failure to spread sacrifices equally between rich and poor.[20] Abe Moffat, President of the NUM's Scottish division, stressed that though the miners were second to none in their loyalty to the government, 'that in no way meant that they became a rubber stamp for everything they said and did'.[21]

Disguise it as he might, the entire episode was profoundly painful for Cripps. He had been forced into a position where he had no option but to lie about the government's intentions – and as a result had to face attacks upon his prized integrity. At the same time, the episode marked the moment that a group of the physically debilitated Chancellor's younger colleagues seized the initiative, in an unmistakable if unintended challenge to his authority. Douglas Jay later noted the paradoxical effects: 'The decision over devaluation in the summer of 1949 revived the country's fortunes and enabled the election of 1950 to be just won; but it also determined the succession to Cripps as Chancellor, gave rise indirectly to the so-called "Bevanite" schism and so eventually to the succession to Attlee as Leader also.'[22]

Not long before, Cripps had been at the height of his prestige. On New Year's Eve, 1948, he told an audience at Central Hall, Westminster, that the drain on Britain's financial reserves was being stemmed. Inflation was under control, though 'if prices and wages were to get out of hand all chance of further recovery would be destroyed'.[23] In April, an opinion poll found that 57 per cent of those asked thought he was doing a good job (and that he was now slightly more popular than the well-loved Bevin).[24] He was, however, at risk of physical burnout. Raymond Streat, Chairman of the Cotton Board, noted that 'The Cripps treadmill of duty was turning with its ceaseless revolutions, uninterruptedly, sixteen or eighteen hours a day.'[25]

'Bluntly, the way in which you've been working, for the last year at least, is lunacy,' Cripps's private secretary advised his boss. 'But there is nobody apart from yourself who can tackle your job, can make sense of it as you do, and can get the official machine to toil willingly and happily in spite of the very heavy weight of its burden.'[26] What is more, the economic and electoral outlook was darkening again. While doing his best to hold back expenditure on the NHS and on defence, Cripps delivered a Budget that put up income tax by 3d and increased telephone charges and the price of bread. Robert Hall wrote in his diary that 'the

Government benches disliked the very plain statements that we had to pay for our social services, while the Opposition applauded'.[27] Labour backbenchers blamed Cripps's 'psychologically disastrous' presentation of his proposals for that week's heavy losses in the local elections, though the Tories claimed the results merely confirmed a long-term trend in their favour.[28]

These tensions over tax and spending played out alongside three other concerns: capital punishment, the iron and steel industry, and the future of the House of Lords. These seemingly disparate issues were in fact interwoven. It was the Lords that linked the other two, because of the peers' power of obstruction. Under the Parliament Act of 1911, which removed their absolute power of veto, the Upper House could delay non-money bills for two years. During the latter part of a parliament, then, the Lords could effectively block controversial legislation. And the Conservatives had an enormous majority there. As of 1945, Labour had had only 16 peers, 'a tiny atoll in the vast ocean of Tory reaction'.[29] Under the leadership of Viscount Cranborne (from 1947 the Marquess of Salisbury), the Conservative peers played their hand skilfully. Under the 'Salisbury convention', they accepted that they could not legitimately reject laws for which the government had a clear electoral mandate, while reserving to themselves the right to decide which policies truly had the backing of the people and which did not.[30] This, of course, was a matter of self-preservation, given Labour's manifesto pledge that it would not tolerate obstruction by the Lords.

In the light of previous policy statements, it would have been reasonable to interpret the manifesto's wording as meaning that, if such obstruction occurred, Labour would either reform the composition of the second chamber or abolish it. But in the autumn of 1947, the Cabinet resolved to legislate simply to reduce the Lords' delaying powers. This offered some reassurance to those who were concerned that a bill to nationalize iron and steel had not yet been brought forward. It was also a move that could be justified in terms of increasing the efficiency of government (rather than being presented as part of a battle between Peers and People). Ministers were careful at this stage not to suggest that this was their last word and claimed still to believe in reform. But some of them, in particular Morrison, may have come to see an unreformed Lords as suiting their convenience. And here it was the question of hanging that was the key.[31]

The 1930s had seen a decline in the number of executions and the advent of the Labour government gave hope to those campaigning for abolition. A clear, even overwhelming, majority of the PLP supported the cause. The Cabinet was divided. Cripps insisted he could not vote in favour of prolonging the use of the gallows, and Bevan was on his side, but Attlee and Morrison were retentionists.[32] As Home Secretary during the war, the latter had been responsible for deciding whether people convicted of murder – for which the death penalty was mandatory – would be reprieved. He appears to have had no qualms about the exercise of his life-and-death powers, and even expressed the bizarre wish to see a female prisoner executed.[33] Friends and advisers tried, over many years, to change his mind but he was immovable. He said that 'he had never lost any sleep over a hanging. He believed all cases had been thoroughly examined and there was no chance of a mistake.'[34]

Chuter Ede was of a somewhat different stripe. Having started his career as a Liberal, as Labour chairman of the Tory-dominated Surrey County Council, he showed a knack for working with his political opponents and winning their respect.[35] Chosen as Home Secretary more for his earnestness and grasp of policy than for any inspirational qualities, he showed an unexpected dry humour as he went about his job 'studiously and unruffled'.[36] He had voted for abolition before the war but had changed his position. This was in the context of recent steep rises in murders and other violent crime, and in the face of public opinion that appeared strongly pro-hanging.[37] After leaving office, Ede regretted this shift, influenced by the discovery that Timothy Evans, whom he refused to reprieve in 1950, had been wrongfully executed.[38]

Ede did at least provide the abolitionists with an opportunity, in the form of his flagship Criminal Justice Bill. This was a revival of a measure that had been dropped on the outbreak of war and contained genuine humanitarian measures. It provided for the reform of prisons and probation and abolished the sentence of whipping (which was, however, to be kept as a punishment within prisons). Crucially, it could be amended to deal with capital punishment, and the backbencher Sydney Silverman, the leading parliamentary proponent of abolition, proposed suspending the operation of the death penalty for five years. Introducing his new clause in April 1948, Silverman thanked Ede for helping him ensure that it was free of drafting errors and that it would thus serve its intended purpose if passed.[39]

The government's official position, articulated by Ede, was to recommend that the amendment be rejected. Nevertheless, as the issue was regarded as a matter of conscience, MPs were allowed a free vote. Ministers were not allowed to oppose the government line, but they could abstain. Cripps, Bevan and Wilson did so; Attlee, Morrison, Bevin, Ede and five other Cabinet ministers voted for retention.[40] The clause passed by 245 to 222. According to the *Daily Mail*'s reporter, the government was taken aback by the result, and 'nobody was more surprised [...] than Mr. Herbert Morrison'.[41]

Anticipating that the Bill in its new form would become law, Ede decided, in the meantime, to grant mercy to all those sentenced to death. But the abolitionists' celebrations were premature. In June the House of Lords rejected Silverman's amendment. Ministers could have invoked the (1911) Parliament Act but did not. Given that they were simultaneously trying to pass a new Parliament Bill, it would be awkward to get into a fight on an issue where peers rather than MPs appeared to be in line with public opinion. Instead, the government proposed – with the consent of the PLP – a compromise that would distinguish between different classes of murder and retain capital punishment only for the most heinous.

The Commons passed the Bill in this form, yet, in July, the Lords rejected this too. The government backed down in order to save the legislation as a whole. Its only concession to the abolitionists was the creation of a Royal Commission on Capital Punishment – really a way of kicking the issue into the long grass. Executions resumed in November 1948.[42] There had been nineteen murders in the seven weeks before the hanging 'truce', twenty-five in the next seven weeks, seventeen in the seven weeks before executions resumed, and then twenty-eight in the next *six* weeks.[43] So much for the theory of deterrence.

In the midst of the controversy, the Lords threw out the Parliament Bill. The government then used the 1911 Act to push it through, meaning that the new law, cutting the delaying power to one year, would come into effect in 1949. Ministers never moved to change the Upper Chamber's other powers or to alter its composition. Morrison later explained that 'The Labour Government was not anxious for the rational reform or democratization of the Second Chamber, for this would have added to its authority and would have strengthened its position as against that of the House of Commons.'[44] But it is a fair surmise that he and his fellow retentionists had come to see the unreformed Lords as useful because of its capacity, as with capital punishment, to obstruct measures that could be seen as 'faddist' and electorally harmful.[45]

Morrison might not have been too displeased had their Lordships succeeded in blocking steel nationalization as well. The case for public ownership was less clear cut than in other industries mentioned in the manifesto. The sector was not wholly undynamic, as its contribution to the war effort showed. It was highly fragmented, comprising up to two and half thousand different firms, many of which were tiny. This made the task of nationalization complicated. The steel workers were, for the most part, not keen on nationalization themselves.[46] Union leader Lincoln Evans was privately opposed but kept quiet in order not to embarrass the government or alienate his own more militant members.[47] At the election, Labour had rested its case on the claim that the Iron and Steel Federation (ISF), the oligopolistic producers' organization, had kept up prices at the expense of consumers and 'allowed the industry to sink into a swamp of inefficiency'.[48]

Once in office, the government was caught between the Scylla of estranging powerful industrialists whose companies were essential to the export drive and the Charybdis of disaffecting its own supporters. John Wilmot, a Dalton protégé who was Minister of Supply, had responsibility for the issue. His initial proposal to proceed with nationalization met with opposition from his civil servants and from Morrison.[49] In the summer of 1947, Wilmot and Morrison put forward a halfway house solution, which won the consent of the ISF. This would involve the creation of an Iron and Steel Board with the power to take over underperforming firms. Bevan threatened to quit the Cabinet if a Bill for full public ownership was not brought forward in the next parliamentary session.[50] In his memoirs, Morrison claimed that Attlee had first asked him to devise a compromise, then silently backed away from the proposals when other ministers withheld their support. After the meeting Morrison told him privately, 'You know, Clem, as you started all this, you let me down badly.' The Prime Minister gave no clear explanation or reply.[51]

As part of the ministerial changes that accompanied Cripps's move to Economic Affairs, Wilmot was unceremoniously sacked. Attlee wanted Bevan (whom he also considered for the Board of Trade) to replace him. Bevan, caught up in his battle with the doctors, declined to move.[52] Instead, the task fell to the now forgotten figure of George Strauss. Strauss, who had served as Morrison's PPS in 1929–31, moved to the Left in the later 1930s yet stayed on good terms with his mentor. Due to his support for a Popular Front with communists and others, he was expelled from the Labour Party shortly before the war but was soon readmitted. Since then he had again moderated his views – sitting somewhere in the gap between Cripps and Bevan – but was tolerant of the enthusiasm of the younger generation. Strauss was also impressively wealthy, having inherited his father's metal business. According to the Labour MP Tam Dalyell, who knew him in old age, the fact that his family had done so well out of the Great War was 'the source of some guilt to him and one of the reasons why he fought so hard for a rational iron and steel industry'.[53]

In a Cabinet memorandum, Strauss acknowledged that the case for public ownership 'primarily rests on the need for taking this important basic industry out of the realm of private profit-making into public ownership rather than on grounds of any present inefficiency in the industry's management'.[54] Rejecting a more limited option, ministers decided to progress with the acquisition of all firms that in either 1946 or 1947 had produced more than 50,000 tons of iron ore or more than 20,000 tons of pig iron, ingot steel or re-rolled products.[55] In the autumn of 1948, the legislation was introduced in the Commons, and 'was enthusiastically welcomed by the Labour Party and execrated with equal passion by the Tories'.[56] Morrison, to his credit, gave it his strong support, though his personal relationship with Strauss became for a while 'very cool indeed'. Strauss piloted the Bill skilfully through the Commons, in the face of bitter opposition from the Tories, who 'were almost hysterical in their hatred and loathing' of it, and used all the tactics at their disposal to wear down government MPs.[57] By now it was clear, given the Lords' rejection of the Parliament Bill, that although steel nationalization would go through, there would not be time to implement it before the next election, which the Conservatives expected to win.[58]

By threatening the use of the delaying power, the Tories managed to extract a paper concession. Although the Act would go onto the Statute Book before the election, the government agreed not to appoint any member of the new Iron and Steel Corporation before 1 October 1950. By that point polling day would be months in the past. However, it would not have been practical to do so much earlier anyway, and in the meantime the government could take other preliminary steps. In this way, the Iron and Steel Act received Royal Assent in November 1949, *before* the new Parliament Act did a few weeks later.[59] At this point, the government could legitimately claim to have put into effect all of its major manifesto commitments.

This, of course, raised a new question: that of what to do next. Some answers could be found in *Labour Believes in Britain*, an 18,000-word policy statement issued in April 1949. At the previous year's party conference, Morrison, appearing to court the middle-class vote, had spoken of the need 'for the consolidation of existing achievements' and for 'proposals for tuning up the administrative organisation and the economic machine'.[60] The new programme could in some ways be seen as a victory for this vision of 'consolidation', and even as a foretaste of the revisionism of the 1950s. Reflecting contemporary concerns about excessive centralization and bureaucracy, the pamphlet also emphasized that material security was only a means to an end: 'the evolution of a people more kindly, intelligent, cooperative, enterprising and rich in culture'. It argued for nationalization where private enterprise was 'failing the nation' – which naturally implied that where private enterprise was efficient public ownership was not needed.[61] For some, like G. D. H. Cole, this raised worries that those who had drafted the proposals were 'minded to put off any further advance towards Socialism to a dateless future when the electorate will somehow mysteriously have become ready for it'.[62]

Yet even Cole recognized the need for pragmatic compromise and recognition of political reality. He acknowledged that there was real discontent in the nationalized sector and that its workers had not yet adopted a socialist mind-set. And in fact, *Labour Believes in Britain* was based on a wide Labour consensus on the party's basic principles: the achievement of equality, public ownership and planning as means to control economic power, the setting free of productive impulses that had been restricted under capitalism, and the congruence of socialism with the British parliamentary tradition.[63] The language was expansive – 'We seek freedom from the enslaving material bonds of Capitalism' – and plenty of the detail was appealing to the Left.[64] The programme seemed to promise a more flexible and responsive form of nationalization, which would allow parts of some industries to be taken under public control when they acted monopolistically or obstructed government planning.[65]

A list of specific candidates for future nationalization was included: the insurance industry, the cement industry, sugar manufacturing and refining, water supply, meat wholesaling and slaughterhouses, and unspecified 'suitable minerals'.[66] In *Tribune*, Mikardo praised the document's dynamism and contrasted it favourably with the discouraging 'philosophic background' of Cripps's recent Budget. 'The National Executive', he wrote, 'has markedly avoided repeating the cardinal error of its policy document of 1944, which, in talking about the transition to Socialism, put so much emphasis on the transition that it forgot about the Socialism.'[67]

Reactions to the programme should be read partly in the light of the signature earlier that month of an important new agreement, which committed the USA, the UK, Canada, France, and a number of other European countries to mutual defence. This was the basis of the North Atlantic Treaty Organization (NATO), which has been described as Bevin's greatest achievement. Left-wingers were wary of more Cold War confrontation and the accompanying costs.[68] The *New Statesman* found *Labour Believes in Britain* uninspiring yet conceded that a mixed economy that balanced welfare and consumer protection with the encouragement of private enterprise might be a credible possibility. 'But only on the assumption that we are not also seeking to maintain colossal armaments – which, in terms of 1949, means that the West must reach an accommodation with the USSR.'[69]

It is sometimes suggested that, by the end of its first five years, Labour was intellectually exhausted and unable to come up with more than a ragbag or shopping list of new proposals.[70] The pledges did include some important hostages to fortune. The sugar industry's highly effective campaign against nationalization was headed by a cartoon character, Mr Cube, who appeared on the Tate & Lyle packets found on the nation's breakfast tables.[71] Nevertheless, *Labour Believes in Britain* contained some worthwhile ideas. Nationalizing the insurance industry could be presented as the fulfilment of an as-yet-unimplemented part of the Beveridge Report, which had proposed taking industrial assurance under state control.[72] This was a type of life insurance used by working-class people to cover funeral expenses. Promoted by door-to-door canvassers, it was notoriously costly and subject to mis-selling.[73] There was also a proposal for a consumer advisory body – a brainchild of Michael Young – which would be included in the 1950 manifesto (although not that of 1951). A Gallup poll showed it to be the most popular of the manifesto proposals.[74] It was the germ of what became, as a private initiative, the Consumers' Association, famous for its magazine *Which?* It is interesting to ask what might have happened had Labour recognized its potential and embraced consumer politics more vigorously.

Labour was subtly shifting its emphasis at this point. The term 'welfare state' did not appear in *Labour Believes in Britain.* The phrase had been in circulation for a long time but was used mainly by academics. Then the Conservatives picked it up and applied it to the Attlee government's social policies as a term of abuse – with connotations of degeneracy, dependency and totalitarianism. At first Labour politicians resisted the tag, but in the period surrounding devaluation they came to embrace it *as a description of policies that they had already implemented under different labels.*[75] (James Griffiths defined it as applying 'to the nation as a family the code that we all feel it our duty to apply to our individual families'.[76]) They had long believed in social security but had regarded it as secondary to the task of building socialism via nationalization, and perhaps as something that would no longer be required when a more ideal society was reached. With public ownership not living up to all the hopes vested in it, it made sense to make more positive claims for what had already been gained. Bevan came to claim that the NHS 'was the most important socialist achievement' of the Labour government.[77] This may have been true, but it is doubtful that, at the point that he took office, he would have anticipated making this boast.

Far from running out of steam, then, Labour was achieving at least a tentative unity around plans for the future. It was laying claim to 'the welfare state' as a coherent and popular project, while deploying a rhetoric of responsibility that insisted that higher benefits could only be arrived at through greater production. But the growing crisis over sterling, and the fading strength of the party's older generation, put that unity in jeopardy. If devaluation had taken place a few months earlier than it did, it could have been presented as a planned and thought-through policy.[78] But it ended up looking like a panic response.

The pressure on sterling was produced in part by an American recession, which reduced US demand for goods from Britain and its colonies. In fact, the fall in dollar earnings was greater in other parts of the Sterling

Area than within the UK.[79] The fact that Britain's current account had reached an approximate balance by the end of 1948 threw into relief the reality that higher earnings in inconvertible currencies could not reduce the dollar deficit. Furthermore, in the USA, there was a strong current of opinion that held that generous social services were responsible for British economic fragility. And there were some in the British corridors of power, including Bank of England Governor Cameron Cobbold, who used the weakness of the pound to generate pressure for spending cuts and postponement of further nationalization. Washington opinion started to conclude that devaluation was inevitable.[80] As Gaitskell noted, 'Talk and expectation of devaluation' led all who could 'to delay converting dollars into sterling while converting sterling into dollars as fast as possible'.[81] By June, Cripps was warning ministers of the threat 'that, within twelve months, all our reserves will be gone. This time there will be nothing behind them, and there might well be "a complete collapse of sterling".'[82]

On 18 July Cripps left for Switzerland where he hoped to recover his fragile health. By this point no fundamental solution had been reached; and the question of whether and when to devalue was mixed up with the question about when to call the next general election. In the Chancellor's absence, Attlee took control of the Treasury, assisted by Wilson, Gaitskell and Jay. (Gaitskell was still Minister of Fuel and Power, outside the Cabinet; Jay was Economic Secretary to the Treasury, also a non-Cabinet role.) In his diary account, Gaitskell blamed Cripps's poor health for the lack of decision: 'It was quite clear from his vacillations that he was not really capable of thinking the problems out for himself; and the papers submitted were a hotchpotch of official views – themselves divided on some issues – tempered by what Stafford thought his colleagues would feel.'[83]

Jay and Gaitskell now agreed between themselves that devaluation was necessary. According to a harsh passage in Jay's memoirs, the two men then held a meeting with Wilson, who agreed (or so he and Gaitskell believed) to join with them in making the recommendation to Attlee and Morrison. But when it came to the point, Jay claimed, Wilson turned around and argued the opposite.[84] In an interview with Morrison's biographers, Jay was even franker. 'Harold Wilson simply told lies' and 'double-crossed people', he said. 'With one group of people he would be in favour of devaluation [...] and then at meetings with civil servants and other Ministers he would be against. [...] Wilson later leaked stories to *The Telegraph* and *Evening Standard* that it was *he* who had urged devaluation.' As a result, Attlee and Morrison came to distrust Wilson, which contributed to Gaitskell's rise. With respect to devaluation itself, 'Attlee and Herbert [Morrison] didn't understand the issue but they could see clearly that the reserves were going down and that something had to be done. They took the sensible course.'[85]

But first Cripps had to be won over. A letter to him from Attlee was drawn up, stating that ministers and officials were now agreed that sterling must be devalued, not least because it was clear that neither the USA nor Canada were likely to take action that would staunch the bleeding of dollars. Absolute secrecy was required. Wilson was due to attend a GATT meeting in Annecy, near the Swiss border, and to take a few days' holiday. Using this as cover, he could deliver the missive to Cripps in his Zürich sanatorium, the visit being presented as a purely personal call. Wilson did not expect his task to be easy, given that 'the Chancellor, a man of rigorously impeccable standards, had stated categorically earlier in the year, when sterling was under heavy speculative pressure, that it would not be devalued'. As Wilson detailed afterwards in a long manuscript letter to Attlee, Cripps initially seemed opposed to devaluation but came round to support it strongly, on condition that the timing was right. However, he argued that an election should take place beforehand. When Wilson's letter was handed to Attlee in Downing Street, 'He read it through standing in the secretary's office next to the Cabinet Room. When he came to the reference to a general election, he murmured, with his customary brevity, "Stafford – political goose".'[86]

Cripps was at best partially convinced, 'not flatly against devaluation but also very doubtful if it would do any good'.[87] On 19 August, by which time he had returned to the UK, he, Bevin, Wilson and Gaitskell visited Attlee at Chequers. Edward Bridges was also there in his role as Permanent Secretary to the Treasury. The men arrived at 5.30 and stayed until after dinner.[88] Like Cripps, Bridges 'saw devaluation as a dishonest, almost sordid action' but by this stage believed there was no alternative.[89] According to Gaitskell, the conclave was a disheartening experience: 'the argument rambled along; sometimes about devaluation itself; sometimes about the date'. Attlee sat silently doodling – a habit that was understandably irritating to his colleagues (but that psychologists have shown can be beneficial for maintaining attention). Cripps seemed 'quite out of touch'; Bevin 'swayed this way and that, and every now and then we were treated to a long monologue on some event of recent history, such as how he had handled the flour millers in 1924, and what he had said to Ramsay MacDonald in 1931, etc.'[90]

But the group did arrive at an agreement, even if, at the time, the decision did not look particularly firm. A date was set for devaluation, just shy of one month hence. This outcome would prevail unless Cripps and Bevin drew a different conclusion as a result of their conversations with the Americans and Canadians in upcoming talks in Washington.[91] When this proposal was put before the Cabinet it encountered only minor resistance. Bevan was supportive – but claimed: 'Our plight is [the] direct consequence of political manipulation by [the] USA.' His particular bugbear was the American insistence on non-discrimination in trade and payments. Bevin pointed out that this had been a condition of the 1945 loan agreement. 'Under duress,' replied Bevan. 'We must tell [the] US that this won't do. Unbearable for me to go on holding my tongue about this. [...] Our troubles [are] due to US and Canadian extortions.'[92]

Cripps and Bevin crossed a rough Atlantic on the *Mauretania*. Cripps generally woke by 5 a.m. and went to bed 12 hours later, when Bevin was getting up. It was only a few days into the trip, when Cripps consented to stay up a bit longer, that civil servants could speak to them both together. The question of the new exchange rate was not settled until the party reached the Washington Embassy. Officials concluded that it should lie between $2.80 and $3 to the pound – significantly lower than had been contemplated at Chequers. When Cripps asked Bevin's opinion, the latter asked in turn what the effect would be on the cost of a standard loaf. He was satisfied with the answer and the new parity was agreed.[93]

The British–American–Canadian talks took place alongside meetings of the Bretton Woods institutions. Dean Acheson, Truman's recently appointed Secretary of State, remembered that the first few days were 'a complete waste of time with rising exasperation among the conferees'. Marshall Plan administrator Paul Hoffman told the British they needed to cut wages and welfare to boost exports. Bevin fought back, saying that every time Britain's workers made sacrifices to boost competitiveness, 'the Congress set up a howl about cheap foreign labor and raised the tariff to new heights [...] He was not going home to flimflam the workers again.' (Bevan would have approved.) But the atmosphere warmed up as soon as Cripps and Bevin disclosed that they planned to devalue – a step that the Americans already favoured.[94] The scene was now set for Cripps's dramatic broadcast. Stepping out of a plane upon his return to London, he appeared ebullient: perhaps a clever act to quell the still-swirling sterling rumours.[95]

When put into effect, devaluation was 'more successful than even the most sanguine of its planners had predicted'.[96] In the year following the operation, the cost of living rose less than 3 per cent. This was partly because, after other countries had devalued too, the effective devaluation was below 10 per cent, once Britain's trading pattern was taken into account. By summer 1950, the reserves grew from around $1,300 million to over $2 billion. As the USA pulled out of recession British dollar exports boomed.[97] But at the moment of Cripps's original announcement, it was by no means certain that things would work out so well. A recurrence of the crisis seemed a real possibility; and the ghosts of 1931 were once again abroad.

The Bank of England wanted to raise interest rates. Civil servants pressed for cuts as a means of restoring confidence. Ministers were generally allergic both to 'dear money' and to the idea that there was a relationship between the level of public spending (especially on social services) and the country's external financial position. Cripps resisted the Bank's pressure on rates but asked his colleagues to find economies of £280 million. Some cuts were undoubtedly necessary as excess domestic demand could both put up inflation and stymie export capacity. Reaching agreement was a fraught process. Dalton recorded that Cripps and Bevan, 'supposedly in close alliance', clashed with one another, each hinting at quitting 'if the other succeeds in preventing him getting his way'. Bevan blocked the introduction of charges for hospital patients and for false teeth and glasses. Crucially, though, he accepted in principle that a small prescription charge might be introduced in the future. Although this had no immediate practical effect, the power to implement it was passed into law. The final package included some limited restraints on defence expenditure and cuts to the housing programme.[98]

Bevan initially seems to have been content with the economies in housing, because the reductions applied largely to private building.

According to the Cabinet Secretary's notebook, he suggested that Attlee's announcement 'must be made so as to draw fire on private licensing bldg. Put it as a class measure & get it criticised as such.' Scotland's housing programme, he said, was 'unbalanced' in favour of the private sector and 'ought to be cut'.[99] (When the reduction was later restored, Gaitskell appeared keener on the change than did the more radical Bevan.[100]) Nevertheless, Bevan quickly decided that the accompanying drop in defence spending was not large enough to justify the housing cuts.[101] Had the struggle between Cripps and Bevan come to an open split, Gaitskell would have backed the Chancellor.[102] But at this stage, though there were differences of temperament and perhaps a lack of mutual understanding, there was no enmity between Gaitskell and Bevan. In fact, after a dinnertime discussion of religion, which Bevan attacked on a rationalist rather than a Marxist basis, Gaitskell concluded that he was 'a more profound thinker than he is sometimes given credit for [...] very sympathetic to me'.[103] Morrison, however, felt that Cripps had shown weakness in not doing more to cap health spending: '"Nye is getting away with murder" was the general feeling of my colleagues.'[104]

The government handled the politics of devaluation less well than the economics. The decision of ministers not to call an early general election may have been wise. But Cripps – who continued to press for one – failed to take his advisers' suggestion that he should start his crucial broadcast 'by expressing regret that he had been forced by circumstances to agree to something he had wished to avoid'.[105] Cripps's sense of guilt, shame or dishonour made him haughty and defensive. The financial journalist Paul Einzig, with whom he had a difficult relationship, later acknowledged that the Chancellor's earlier protestations had been made in good faith. On those occasions when he said Britain would not devalue, it had seemed that there was a decent chance that it truly would not be necessary. However, at his post-devaluation press conference, 'Cripps was more provocative than ever before, insulting journalists right, left and centre.' Einzig judged: 'Presumably, having had to devalue in spite of his denials, he felt the need for trying to put up a bold face. Hence the behaviour which even for him was exceptionally arrogant.'[106]

In the Commons, Churchill launched 'a ninety minutes' fling against the Government and all its works'.[107] He admitted that Cripps's deception had been necessary but suggested that his reputation as a truth-telling Chancellor had been 'grievously crippled'.[108] Deeply wounded, Cripps refused to accept Churchill's assurances that he was not impugning his personal character. He declined to attend a ceremony at Bristol University where Churchill had been going to bestow an honorary degree upon him.

Perhaps surprisingly, Churchill's ruthless attempt to make political capital out of devaluation did not wholly pay off, the Tory opinion poll boost notwithstanding. By December, Attlee was said to be more cheerful than he had been for a long time, in spite of the results of the New Zealand election, which Labour had lost, to the dismay of other ministers. Guy Eden, lobby correspondent of the *Daily Express*, reported to his editor 'that the Cabinet and everybody around him are puzzled by his [Attlee's] "intense optimism and cheerfulness". There is [...] no apparent explanation, and when he is asked about it he makes evasive replies.'[109] Perhaps Attlee was anticipating the result of the Bradford South by-election, which his party won with only a slight fall in its share of the vote. Labour had not lost any of its own seats since 1945. Admittedly, vacancies had only occurred in seats where the party already had large majorities.[110] But the Conservatives had missed out on the 'glorious resurrection they had been looking for'.[111]

The Tories had made serious efforts at internal reform and policy renewal. These, however, had their limits. The *Industrial Charter* of 1947 was intended to show that the party had made a clean break with the interwar era of mass unemployment, but it was lacking in detail and made little impact on the public.[112] Churchill performed his duties as Leader of the Opposition only fitfully.[113] And he was determined to make only broad, declarative statements of future policy.[114] As R. A. Butler, then Chairman of the Conservative Research Department, later explained, Churchill's reluctance to propound 'positive policy' stemmed from 'a fear of "giving a hostage to fortune" by promising now what could not be performed later'.[115] Churchill did deign to provide a preface to the 1949 party programme *The Right Road for Britain*.[116] But even as he introduced it to the party faithful at Earl's Court, he emphasized that 'We are not going to try to get into office by offering bribes and promises of immediate material benefits to our people.'[117]

This strategy was frustrating to Churchill's younger colleagues. The lack of clear policy was open to mockery – the Tories might not know if they wanted more austerity or less, jibed Cripps, but 'They all support Lord Lyle the sugar king.'[118] It made a degree of sense, however, to avoid detail, at a time when Labour was struggling to repeat the success of *Let Us Face the Future*. In attacking controls and rationing, the Tories had an effective negative appeal, which was targeted especially at women voters.[119] (Labour countered that shortages were due to the fact that, thanks to full employment, people could now afford to buy the food they needed, driving demand beyond available supply.[120]) But if floating voters could be persuaded that nationalization was simply a case of 'jobs for the boys', it was hard for the Conservatives to shed their image as the party of big business.[121] In these circumstances, Labour could play a decent if uninspiring defensive game. When Attlee wound up the devaluation debate in the Commons, Chips Channon concluded that his 'anodyne speech is deliberately subtle camouflage to lull the middle classes and perhaps woo them back to his party. It is a wolf in mouse's clothing.'[122]

Another factor in the electoral mix was the Representation of the People Act (1948). Relative to previous reforms of the franchise this has received little scholarly attention, perhaps because it generated less controversy at the time, but its significance should not be overlooked. The remaining double-member constituencies (including that of the City of London) were done away with. So too were the university seats. Plural voting, which benefited graduates and owners of business premises, was abolished. The government thereby implemented the principle of 'one person, one vote' for the first time.[123]

Some of the above measures were to Labour's electoral benefit, but they were accompanied by a redistribution of seats, which was not. Ede, when introducing the Bill, proposed following the recommendations of the recently established Boundary Commissioners, which would mean the majority of constituencies being redrawn. Dalton, at that point out of the Cabinet, objected that not enough had been done to equalize the number of voters in different seats, and that the plan contained 'a much too heavy bias against large cities, against blitzed cities in particular, and against industrial areas generally'.[124] He also took the view that redistribution could reasonably have been left until the population had settled down after wartime and post-war dislocation. Though there was little love lost between the Home Secretary and the ex-Chancellor, Ede did make some concessions. Yet had the next election been fought on the old boundaries, Labour might have won an additional 25 seats or more. Dalton was scornful, writing in his memoirs that 'this Bill, so conscientiously fabricated by Ede, was a gravedigger's spade'.[125]

Certainly, the government could not be accused of gerrymandering, and there is a case that it was morally obliged to act as it did. More questionable was Cripps's insistence that the government go to the country before he launched his next Budget. He had decided that were his plans to be announced prior to the election they would constitute an ethically unacceptable 'election budget' (designed to win votes rather than for the good of the country). This was the case even though the tough proposals he was developing could scarcely be considered electoral bribery. His conscience impelled him to demand that Britain go to the polls before he set out his plans – or he would resign. The election was thus set for February 1950. It may be that Churchill's devaluation attack had so stung him that he resolved to prove his rectitude beyond all doubt. This was unfortunate for Labour's prospects. Had the vote been delayed until May – by which time petrol rationing had been abolished and the party's opinion poll lead had widened – the results could have been significantly different.[126]

However, from the trend of the polls during the campaign itself, it is clear that Labour was able to exploit its strengths. One of these was organization – in spite of the fact that General Secretary Morgan Phillips, though energetic, was drunken and ineffectual.[127] For the first time, the party put up candidates in all constituencies, excepting that of the Speaker, in England, Scotland and Wales. (It did not enter any contests in Northern Ireland, although its sister party, the Northern Ireland Labour Party, fought five seats there, albeit as in 1945 without hope of success.[128]) Party membership was booming. The election saw high turnout although, paradoxically, the campaign seemed quiet, even dull.[129] Nevertheless, Attlee attracted large audiences on his national election tour. On the first day, he addressed two thousand people in Coventry: 'after the Prime Minister and Mrs Attlee had taken their seats a miners' choir from the nearby colliery of Binley sang the "Miners' Song" while two ranks of miners in their pit clothes marched into the Hall wearing their helmets surmounted by lighted electric lamps and formed a guard of honour on the platform'.[130]

Bevin, briefly burying the hatchet with Morrison, spoke on the latter's behalf at Lewisham.[131] Cripps seemed 'much more violent and "socialist"' than he had been for years.[132] When Churchill said that Cripps favoured 'equality for all (except of course members of the Government and those who enjoy their favour)' Cripps took this as an allegation of personal corruption.[133] He replied by lamenting that a man whose war leadership he had admired and whose friendship he had appreciated 'should sink to quite this level of guttersnipe politics'.[134]

Churchill's biting barbs were part of a broader narrative alleging socialist incompetence. Strikingly, 'the pound thing' did not become a major theme of the election (though Bevan was greeted with boos and catcalls when he claimed that sterling was the most stable currency in the world).[135] As prices remained under control, Tories were deprived of strong attack lines. And Labour had little incentive to summon memories of the crisis, even though their policy was working. Foreign affairs, by contrast, took an unexpected prominence, in response to Churchill's call (in the same speech in which he attacked Cripps) for 'a parley at the summit' with Stalin. Of course, had such a meeting been likely to show results, Attlee and Bevin would already have tried it, but the initiative may have taken the edge off Churchill's reputation as a warmonger.[136] Labour dismissed the idea as an irresponsible stunt. 'This is hardly a time for soap-box diplomacy,' Morrison observed.[137]

There were undoubtedly problems with Labour's programme. Though some party propaganda emphasized 'The People's Needs Before Private Profits' – the broad theme that had proved effective in 1945 – this was not backed up by an easily saleable set of policies.[138] Barbara Castle complained in her memoirs that the party's manifesto, *Let Us Win Through Together*, was an uninspiring document 'which revealed that our reforming drive had petered out'. It paid lip service to the need to extend public ownership but 'the list of proposed takeovers – chiefly sugar, cement and "mutualization of industrial assurance" – appeared to have been picked out of a hat'.[139] There is a case that mutual ownership of the insurance companies in place of private shareholders was a genuinely radical idea, though it could be seen as a watering down of the previous proposal for conventional public ownership. Yet even Michael Young, who devised the concept, admitted it was 'not good politics' even if it was better in that respect than straightforward nationalization would have been.[140] A survey carried out after the election showed that voters had a poor grasp of the plan and that it was widely disliked.[141] But if the manifesto was a mishmash, it is not clear (on the evidence of the Keep Left group's contemporaneous proposals) that the radical wing of the party had anything more compelling to offer.[142]

Nevertheless, manifestos are not the be-all and end-all of campaigning. One internal party assessment suggested that 'Few people in the recent election appeared to be influenced by individual items of party programmes [...] Citizens who vote Labour do so because they have a "feeling" that Labour will look after the interests of their sort; others feel the same way about the Tory Party.' Such feelings, the report argued, developed slowly and were rarely impacted on permanently by a single event, like devaluation, or by a single proposal, such as the nationalization of sugar.[143] Well in advance of the election, Labour had made effective use of fear tactics, pointing to the interwar dole queues and warning that they would recur if the Tories returned to power.[144] After the ballots were counted, a Conservative Party post-mortem concluded that undecided voters had mobilized in unexpected numbers and that they had broken decisively in favour of Labour. Many of them had worried that if they sent Churchill back to No. 10, the new government would side with the employers, there would be more unemployment, and a greater likelihood of war. According to Conservative Central Office, 'It seems evident that [...] unremitting Socialist propaganda over a long period had struck home.'[145]

Polling took place on 23 February with a continuation of the foul, wet, blustery weather that afflicted the entire campaign. 'It rained throughout the day and we were all wet through more than once,' remembered Callaghan.[146] As the results started to come in, an election that had previously seemed uninspiring went down to a nail-biting finish. The BBC provided its first TV results programme and stayed on air until around 2 a.m.[147] His Limehouse constituency having been abolished, Attlee was fighting a different seat, Walthamstow West. After attending the count he and Vi went to Labour's Transport House HQ 'before returning to No. 10 in the not so very early morning'.[148] It was not until the evening of the 24th that it was clear that Labour had secured a small majority. This settled at six, after one result (delayed due to the death of a candidate) came in on 9 March.[149] Yet Morrison and Attlee were said to have increased their authority.[150] When Parliament reassembled the PLP seemed in good heart.[151] As Attlee entered the Commons chamber, 'Labour members rose together, cheered, and clapped their hands. [...] There was no "Red Flag" this time – no singing at all – but streams of cheerful taunts flowed from side to side of the House.'[152]

In retrospect, the result of the election can be presented as the beginning of the end. Clearly, the Attlee government's most confident and powerful phase was now over. Not only did it have less room for parliamentary manoeuvre, but there was also a risk that some anticipated event could trigger the downfall of the government or a new election. These factors also heightened the risk that ideological strains could develop into splits. But Labour had secured the largest vote in its history and delivered the Tories a second demoralizing defeat. It was unclear if the Conservatives, under the ailing Churchill, could perform better in a repeat engagement. They certainly didn't want to force another contest quickly.[153] As Attlee's reshuffled ministers got to work on their red boxes, it wasn't again the glad, confident morning of 1945. But the politics of the second half of the twentieth century was yet to be determined, and there was much, if not everything, to play for.

The Unravelling

The evening of 2 November 1950. Unity House, St George, Bristol. The General Committee of the Bristol South-East Labour Party was meeting to select its candidate for the by-election triggered by the retirement of Sir Stafford Cripps. Three nominees were present to make their respective cases. There was the front-runner and former Colonial Secretary Arthur Creech Jones, who had lost his seat at the recent election. There was the former MP for Bradford North, Muriel Nichol, who had likewise been defeated. And there a public-school-educated BBC producer, who had previously been an RAF pilot and President of the Oxford Union (in that order). This *ingénue* – 'he is twenty-five and looks much younger' – had stepped into the city for the first time that day.[1] He was the Hon. Anthony Wedgwood Benn – Tony to his friends.

As Benn stood forward to make his speech he believed he had no hope of winning. There was, after all, the matter of that pesky title. The Bristol delegates do not seem to have suffered from inverted snobbery – but there was a practical issue. Benn's father Viscount Stansgate, the former William Wedgwood Benn, had accepted a peerage during the war, to help boost Labour's representation in the Lords. (He then served as Attlee's Secretary of State for Air from 1945 to 1946.) Stansgate was now 73, and, such time as he died, Tony would inherit the peerage and be automatically excluded from the Commons. Fortunately for him, the selection committee was not too bothered about this, nor about the fact that he did not intend to live in the constituency. Benn recalled: 'What I did not know was that having had a Cabinet minister as their

MP for five years, Bristol South East desperately wanted some young candidate who would work with the constituency and not be siphoned off into high office.'[2]

Benn was also unaware of the forces working on his behalf behind the scenes. The constituency party was a rebellious one, having backed Cripps when he was expelled from Labour in 1939, and did not much care for Transport House's efforts to foist Creech Jones upon it. Benn sealed the deal with a brilliant speech ('From my opening sentence I felt I had them') and won the selection decisively.[3] The breathless nominee dashed downstairs to break the news to his beloved American wife Caroline, who was waiting in the couple's car. She got out and jumped for joy in the centre of the street. 'I'm so excited,' she said. 'I come from a wonderful country but the only thing we haven't got is the Labour Party.'[4]

Benn's reputation in the 1970s and 1980s was that of a firebrand. That was not the case at this earlier stage. During the short by-election campaign that followed he left no doubt as to the depth of his socialist convictions, but he was most concerned to present himself as the natural heir to the locally admired Cripps.[5] The Times thought that the terms of his election address were 'certainly unusual', in part because Benn used it to stress that he had benefited from 'a radical Christian upbringing'.[6] In his letter of support, Cripps praised Benn as 'one who is as true a Socialist and who is as keen a Christian as I am myself'.[7] Benn won the by-election decisively, albeit with a reduced majority on a low turnout. On 30 November, when polling took place, the candidate was inevitably too busy to listen to the news. It was only later that he learned of the 'devastating threat' that had emerged from Washington: 'that day President Truman said, almost casually, that he might use an atomic bomb in the Korean War'.[8]

The foreign affairs picture had long been gloomy, of course. But it had deteriorated further, first with the successful Soviet nuclear test of 1949 and then with the triumph of the communists in the Chinese civil war a few months later. The British government quickly and pragmatically recognized the new People's Republic of China (PRC), but the Americans refused to do so. In January 1950, Truman announced that the USA would pursue the development of the hydrogen bomb or 'superbomb' (in the knowledge that espionage had probably given the Soviets the secret of how to build one). During the general election campaign, Bevin made a broadcast in which he acknowledged that efforts to establish a nuclear control and inspection regime had failed.[9] According to Conservative Party research, 'Mr. Bevin's wireless speech caused great disappointment, and many electors of all opinions regarded it with concern as a confession of failure.'[10] This assessment cannot be dismissed simply as the product of Tory bias. The *New Statesman* argued that 'Mr. Bevin's lamentable broadcast amounted to no more than a pathetic appeal to put him back in office because he had failed in the past.'[11]

One person observing Bevin at close quarters was Kenneth Younger, an able former barrister and MI5 officer who had been elected for Grimsby in 1945. Now, following a few years in a junior position at the Home Office, he was Minister of State at the FO. Given Bevin's ill health Younger had a great deal of work but little power to get things done. He started keeping a diary, in which he noted the Foreign Secretary's own comment, made after a spell in hospital, that he was 'only half alive'. According to Younger, Bevin's doctors gave him so many drugs that he sometimes had trouble staying awake in meetings. 'At other times he has been quite all right, and in fact very good.' Younger also noted hints of foreign policy dissent coming from Nye Bevan: 'He thinks the country passionately wants some new initiative to be made for an agreement with the Soviet Union. I think this is so, but at the moment I can see no basis for thinking that the Soviet Union is thinking in terms of genuine agreement.' Bevan disputed this: 'He feels the Soviet empire is already overstretched and would be glad of a détente.'[12]

One of Younger's first major tasks was to speak in a foreign affairs debate initiated by the Opposition. Churchill's speech was made in the context of the recent foundation of the German Federal Republic (West Germany) and the creation of the German Democratic Republic (East Germany).[13] He made a plea for Franco-German reconciliation within a united Europe as the best hope of preserving peace. He called for the (West) Germans to make a contribution to Western defence, though he denied favouring German rearmament or the recreation of the German army.[14] Younger thought that Bevin's winding-up effort was fairly successful: 'he rose unsteadily, & said a number of very sound things, speaking in a low weak voice'. However, 'he also said some things which will discourage progressive forces in Germany, especially the Social Democrats'.[15] Bevin dismissed talk of arming Germany. 'All of us are against it,' he declared, though the less than unanimous cheers from the Labour benches suggested that this wasn't quite true. The Nazi revolution, he insisted, 'did not change the German character very much. It expressed it.'[16] In Bonn, the press service of the governing Christian Democrats said that Bevin had 'forgotten nothing and in his own words does not intend to forget anything. His inflexibility has macabre features for reawakening Europe.'[17]

This Churchill–Bevin clash reflected broader tensions over the question of European integration. Speaking in Zürich in 1946, Churchill had launched a visionary campaign for a 'United States of Europe'. He was deliberately ambiguous about the role that Britain would play in such an organization. At first, in private, he appeared to countenance British membership, but he later said, also behind closed doors, that he did not favour taking his country 'into a binding federation with the other states of Western Europe'.[18] Churchill did obtain some cross-party support but the Attlee government demonstrated little enthusiasm. Ministers understood his quest was not purely idealistic; he wanted to seize the political initiative on the Continent to make up for his exclusion from power at home. Indeed, the proposed new European human rights regime, which he supported, could be seen as a way of constraining socialist governments from carrying out 'tyrannical' policies such as nationalization, which Conservatives believed assaulted property rights.[19] Labour responded by insinuating that the Tories were seeking to entangle Britain in major commitments without first putting such proposals before the electorate.[20] Federalism had attracted a fair measure of popular support before the outbreak of war in 1939, but suspicion of it was now growing.[21]

For decades, much scholarship (and political discourse) on Britain's relationship with Europe emphasized 'missed chances'.[22] The claim was that governments of both complexions had failed to respond constructively to early opportunities to pursue integration and that the UK therefore ended up as a late and resentful supplicant at the European table. Labour, it is true, did suffer from a fair degree of insularity and (in some quarters) from outright Germanophobia. Just as was true for the Tories, there was a reluctance to prejudice the position of the Empire-Commonwealth. As one observer later put it, the government's hesitation over integration was 'strengthened by a desire to preserve world-wide links and, in particular, to maintain a special position vis-à-vis the United States, despite the clear existence of a very strong

American trend to encourage European integration with (and in some American minds only with) the inclusion of Britain'.[23] However, after Gaitskell – who was appointed Minister of Economic Affairs following the 1950 election – overcame his strong initial doubts in the face of US pressure, Britain did help found the European Payments Union (EPU). There is widespread agreement that this, in combination with the liberalization of intra-European trade, helped spark the boom of the 1950s and 60s, laying the foundations for the birth of the Common Market in 1958.[24]

The genuine misgivings of Attlee and his colleagues about integration need to be put in the perspective of the complex relationship between the UK, the USA and Western Europe. From early in the government's life, Bevin had championed 'Western Union', which was to involve not only military and political cooperation within Europe but economic and cultural collaboration too.[25] In retrospect, the Western Union idea may look simply like an initial step towards NATO and British subordination within the Anglo-American alliance. In fact, it represented a sincere attempt (mixed up with continuing imperialist assumptions) to develop a power bloc that could compete with the USSR and the USA (albeit in the expectation of friendly support from the latter).[26] Britain's developing Atlantic orientation was a product of circumstance as much as of choice.

At the same time, the government did engage seriously, if defensively, with the new Council of Europe. This was an organization that was institutionally separate from the European Economic Community (EEC) as it eventually developed and had a more limited sphere of competence. Labour's delegation to the first meeting of the Council's Assembly in Strasbourg, in 1949, was led by Morrison, with Dalton as his deputy. Morrison, Dalton recalled a little too gleefully, was at sea. 'Unfortunately he knew no French and was also quite unused to international conferences. [...] He showed no aptitude at all for handling foreigners, or for showing conventional civilities or performing simple functions such as fall to all political leaders.'[27] Resenting the press attention that Churchill got as head of the Conservative delegation, Morrison left early.[28] In the early years, the Labour representatives resisted what they saw as the impractical and overly theoretical ideas of the European federal enthusiasts. But despite the doubts of Cripps and others, who felt that it might hinder governments from economic planning, the UK did sign the European Convention on Human Rights (ECHR) and became the first country to ratify it. Though this can be seen partly as a concession to ward off more ambitious projects, the government wanted to limit, control and channel moves towards European unity, not to block them entirely.[29]

In the late spring of 1950, the issue shot up the political agenda. This came on top of a crisis triggered by the government's scandalous treatment of Seretse Khama, paramount chief of the Ngwato people in Britain's Bechuanaland protectorate. After he married a white British woman, Ruth Williams, ministers succumbed to pressure from South Africa, deposing Khama and forcing him into exile. Patrick Gordon Walker, Secretary of State for Commonwealth Relations, lied in the Commons, saying there had been no communication with the Apartheid authorities over the issue. There was a storm of protest, triggering a lengthy campaign for justice.[30] (After many years, these efforts resulted in success, and in 1966 Khama was elected the first President of independent Botswana.) The distinguished Caribbean-born economist W. Arthur Lewis denounced the government's behaviour as dishonest, cowardly, insulting, and 'certain to cause the disintegration of the Empire'. He resigned his appointment to the Colonial Economic and Development Council in disgust.[31]

But although parts of the public were genuinely angered by the affair, colonial matters, however embarrassing, tended to be treated as of second-order significance. And the Conservatives agreed with the government about Khama (confirming his exile after they returned to power). By contrast, with respect to Europe, they intended to make political capital. They got their chance when, on 9 May, French foreign minister Robert Schuman held a remarkable press conference. Drawing on the ideas of Jean Monnet, the head of the French planning commission, he put forward a plan to 'place Franco-German production of coal and steel as a whole under a common higher authority', which would be open to other counties to join. 'The pooling of coal and steel production should immediately provide for the setting up of common foundations for economic development as a first step in the federation of Europe,' he argued.[32] Soviet propagandists declared it an American plot for 'the creation of an industrial basis for their aggressive plans in Europe'.[33]

As an American journalist had previously noted, Bevin was 'certainly no enemy of a United Europe. Indeed it was he who first publicly proclaimed the related concept of Western Union.'[34] But he was informed of the proposed new scheme by the French Ambassador only shortly before Schuman's announcement and soon discovered that the US government knew more about it than he did. According to Edwin Plowden, 'Bevin saw what he thought was a Franco-American plot, hatched behind his back, to force the pace on European integration.' When Schuman and Dean Acheson arrived in London for tripartite talks, 'it took all Acheson's diplomatic skills to stop Bevin from immediately issuing a statement condemning Schuman's announcement'. Morrison took the view that 'we cannot do it, the Durham miners won't wear it'. Yet, though the Foreign Office was more supportive than the economic departments, the government certainly did not dismiss the plan out of hand. Cripps even went so far as to tell Monnet that he thought Britain should negotiate on the basis proposed by the French, provided certain points were cleared up. He did not want a 'capitalist cartel', but though 'he realised that the proposal might lead to political federation' he thought that was a problem for the future. In the Commons, Attlee gave the plan a lukewarm welcome.[35]

However, the French insisted on terms that proved a fatal barrier to British participation. They proposed holding a conference, requiring all participants to make an advance commitment to pooling coal and steel production under an international authority with powers of compulsion over governments. This was to be done before the practical details were discussed. Younger, notionally in charge of the Foreign Office as Bevin started a long hospital stay, noted: 'The object of this very rigid attitude apparently was to bind the Germans & prevent them from subsequently putting forward conditions; it was also designed to prevent us or anyone else from going back on the idea of a binding international authority.'[36] On 1 June, the French delivered an ultimatum, insisting on acceptance of the principle of the binding high authority by 8 p.m. the following day or face being cut out of the negotiations. The British demurred, though they said that they were still 'anxious to do their best to see whether a workable scheme could be produced'.[37]

France, Germany, Italy, Belgium and the Benelux countries went ahead without the UK. They soon created the European Coal and Steel Community (ECSC), a forerunner of the EEC. Douglas Jay, at this point Financial Secretary to the Treasury, was convinced that France had plotted to put the blame on the UK: 'the whole operation had been so devised that the British Government was bound initially to decline'.[38] It is fairer to say that Schuman and Monnet would have been happy for the British to participate, but only on their own terms, which they felt were necessary to safeguard France's position with respect to Germany.[39] They feared a watering down of the proposals if the UK was involved at the start, as had happened with the Council of Europe, and were willing to proceed with their own ideas in the belief that Britain might join later.[40]

Though the Conservatives deplored a missed opportunity, it is doubtful that any other government would have proceeded on the French conditions. But the reasoned and regretful British refusal turned into a PR calamity when a Labour Party pamphlet called *European Unity* was published, on 12 June, the day before Attlee was due to make a Commons statement on the Schuman Plan. According to one French commentator, the publication threw 'a formidable paving stone into the stagnant waters of European union and federalism'.[41]

The document had been in the works a long time and had received formal (if inattentive) approval from Attlee and Bevin.[42] Denis Healey recollected: 'Though I had written the first draft [...] Dalton got the National Executive to insert a number of passages which overemphasised the obstacles which the supranational approach would present to the economic programmes of a Labour Government.'[43] Worse still, Dalton held a launch at which 'he was so rude to all the foreign journalists that they went away determined to make trouble for him'.[44] The pamphlet paid lip service to the importance of European cooperation but, on the basis of opposition to private enterprise, was strongly negative in its attitude to existing federalist ideas:

> There has recently been much enthusiasm for an economic Union based on dismantling all internal barriers to trade, such as customs duties, exchange controls and quotas. Most supporters of this policy believe that the free play of economic forces within the Continental market so created would produce a better distribution of manpower and resources. The Labour Party fundamentally rejects this theory. Market forces by themselves could operate only at the cost of economic disturbances and political tensions which would throw Europe open to Communism.

Ironically, references to the Schuman scheme (which had been inserted at a late stage) were relatively upbeat. Though there was a danger that capitalists would 'pervert the Schuman proposals for their own selfish and monopolistic ends', Schuman's 'historic proposal' created the chance 'to fill the greatest gap in European economic co-operation'. If European countries would plan their economies in the same way that Britain did, there was an opportunity for them to work together to plan internationally, guaranteeing full employment and welfare across the board. 'The decisive part in co-ordinating Europe's basic industries must be played by the governments, as trustees for their peoples.'[45]

This approach laid ministers open to the accusation that, being only willing to collaborate with other socialist governments, they were in practice ruling out cooperation with much of Europe. In the Commons, Attlee resorted to claiming that the pamphlet was merely Labour Party policy, not government policy.[46] Tory MPs detected a rift between him and Bevin on the one hand and Bevan and Dalton on the other.[47] In Washington, politicians on both sides of the aisle were 'hopping mad'. Paul Hoffman, who saw integration as a key to the success of the Marshall Plan, described *European Unity* as 'deplorable isolationism in the worst possible form'.[48] The US ambassador to London was disturbed by the inept way in which the matter had been handled but did not think it would have a profound influence on Anglo-American relations. According to him, the pamphlet in two respects signified a positive advance. 'First, [the] idea of a united Europe as [a] neutral force between USA and Russia is attacked with great vehemence. Second, [the] pamphlet pays tribute to [the] progressive domestic and foreign program of [the] present US administration. This shows how far British socialist thought has shifted in [the] past five years.'[49]

Yet, within the Labour Party, there remained a strand of opinion that was profoundly suspicious of the USA. And although Attlee and Bevin wanted to keep in step with the Truman administration, they were no slavish adherents of American policy. The outbreak of the Korean War pushed the Schuman Plan down the scale of concerns but brought these other tensions to the fore. In 1945, the USA and USSR had split Korea (at the 38th parallel) into two occupation zones. In 1948 these became sovereign states: in the North, the communist totalitarian Democratic People's Republic of Korea (DPRK) under Kim Il-sung, and in the South, an American client regime, the Republic of Korea, led by Syngman Rhee. On 25 June 1950, the North invaded the South, probably with the approval of Stalin and Mao.[50] Fears that the conflict might develop into a third world war were very real. One Tory MP, Peter Roberts, immediately suggested use of the atomic bomb.[51]

Seeing comparisons with the 1930s, the Americans intervened in Korea at once. As Barbara Castle recalled, this was something mainstream British socialists could approve. Not only was the North in obvious breach of international law but the UN passed a resolution in support of the South. This was possible because the Soviets were boycotting the Security Council at the time. 'When, therefore, America sent in forces to drive back the invader and Attlee announced Britain's support for the war, there was no murmuring in the party – or in the Cabinet.'[52] Castle, however, was a backbencher and did not know the full truth. Ministers had real differences but these did not become widely known. Gordon Walker recorded the 'very hostile and critical view' taken by Cripps and Bevan, who regarded the American action as a declaration of war on the Soviets. 'Both thought we should support them in Korea, which was covered by [the] UN resolution: but we should dissociate ourselves elsewhere.' The majority view, held powerfully in particular by Shinwell as Minister of Defence, was for 'full and unconditional support of America'.[53] Over forty thousand British servicemen were deployed throughout the course of the conflict, and National Service was extended from eighteen months to two years.[54]

Cripps and Bevan were not themselves at one. With the US pressing its NATO allies to step up their defence commitments, the former proposed a £1,100 million increase over the course of four years. In Cabinet, Bevan expressed 'grave misgivings'. The government's foreign policy, he argued, had previously been based on the idea that 'the best method of defence against Russian imperialism' was to improve economic and social conditions of countries threatened by communism. 'The United States Government now seemed to be abandoning this social and political defence in favour of a military defence.' Though he did not question the fundamentals of the Anglo-American alliance, Bevan suggested that the US approach was ill-advised. Britain might be able to cope with the increased spending, but he doubted if this was true of France and some other Western European nations. What was more, if Cripps's plans were endorsed, 'he foresaw very great difficulties for the Ministers responsible for the social services. They would be forced to accept reductions in the Government's civil programmes; their only freedom would be to decide which of those programmes should suffer first or most.'[55] Bevan was overruled, but the issue would soon rear its head again.

Bevin, who started to take back the reins of the Foreign Office in early July, had concerns about aspects of US strategy. In addition to providing military support for the South Koreans, Truman ordered the 7th Fleet to prevent any attack from mainland China on Formosa (Taiwan), the last stronghold of the defeated Nationalists.[56] Bevin thought it dangerous to conflate the two issues. 'Before we know where we are we'll be in a World War for the sake of Chiang Kai-shek,' he said. 'Why can't they keep it to Korea?'[57] (The British, who wanted to 'keep a foot in the door' for their trading interests on the mainland, took the view that Mao's regime should be admitted to the Security Council, a view that was anathema to the Americans.[58]) When Bevin conveyed his concerns via the Washington Embassy, Acheson sent a strongly worded reply. This was meant to leave Bevin 'in no doubt' that there could be implications for 'our whole future relationship' if the British persisted in this vein.[59] One US diplomat concluded that Bevin was dreaming of a great act of East–West *détente*. 'He sees himself as almost at the end of his career and life, and he is dramatizing the possibility that he, as his final act, can engineer a settlement with Russia, that will bring peace.'[60]

The British did not change their opinion about China. They were justifiably nervous about the influence of the US military on policy: the erratic General Douglas MacArthur, the American head of the UN forces in Korea, was increasingly beyond Truman's control. But ministers were cautious about pressing their differences with the Americans.[61] At the same time, the Labour Party was floundering. A post-election policy conference had done little to achieve renewal. ('General ideals were still too low,' said Attlee, blandly. 'We must strive to raise them.'[62]) The war in Korea started to drive up inflation, as demand for raw materials boomed. In the autumn, the TUC unexpectedly rejected a motion, which the General Council had supported, to continue wage restraint. Cripps's policy of high-minded exhortation had run out of road.

There was press talk of a Cabinet split, with Bevan (who had been bandying the threat of resignation) pitched against Morrison.[63] The tensions were said to range across a swathe of policy areas; the nationalization of the water industry, which had been delayed, was a particular point of tension. Left-wingers alleged that Attlee and Morrison were quite content with their small majority, as 'they can continually appeal to the Left not to be so rough and bring the Government into disrepute'.[64] This was unfair. Attlee found it unpleasant 'to have Members coming from hospital at the risk of their lives to prevent a defeat in the House'.[65] At the party's autumn gathering, both he and Morrison made an ostentatious show of applause when Bevan spoke. 'Mr. Bevan, with equal ostentation, did not join in the applause for Mr. Morrison.'[66]

Arriving in the conference hall in Margate, a frail-looking Bevin was greeted with a chorus of 'For He's a Jolly Good Fellow'. He gave a robust defence of the government's Korean policy – though at one point he had to pause to swallow a tablet – and easily overcame the limited opposition that he faced.[67] As Richard Crossman noted, the debate throughout the week was *vin ordinaire* rather than vintage. There had been a little-observed change within the government, he suggested. 'The Prime Minister has become something much more important than the Chairman of a difficult cabinet, wielding the balance of power between jostling personalities greater than his own. With Cripps and Bevin so much away and Bevan self-sent into the corner, there is no power to balance.' Attlee, Crossman judged, was now the Supreme Commander, with Morrison as Chief-of-Staff; the rest were merely staff officers.[68]

The truth was a little more complicated; or at least, the situation that Crossman described was not as advantageous as it might sound. Attlee still commanded a great deal of respect from across the party; he would never again face a 1947-style challenge. But the weakening and departure of the older generation presented him with a problem, as the younger hands started a struggle for the succession. In October, Cripps's ill-health finally got the better of him. 'We talked for more than an hour,' he reported of his final meeting with Attlee. 'It was the first real conversation I ever had with him.'[69]

Cripps resigned, not only as Chancellor, but from Parliament (thus paving the way for Benn to acquire his seat). Gaitskell was on government business in New York when he received a message from Attlee asking him to take Cripps's place. The cartoonist Leslie Illingworth portrayed him as a glamorous actress being welcomed by theatre manager Attlee to the role of leading lady. As 'Gorgeous Gaitskell' entered the stage door, his disappointed rivals looked on resentfully.[70]

Bevan – one of those pictured – was certainly angry. The fact that it was his former ally Cripps who had recommended Gaitskell probably made it harder to bear.[71] His friend and biographer Michael Foot made the plausible case that, although he had not necessarily expected to get the job himself, he believed that Gaitskell, whom he saw as 'a quintessential bourgeois intellectual', lacked the necessary roots in the Labour movement. Bevan wrote to the Prime Minister of his 'consternation and astonishment'.[72] He buttonholed Jay in the House of Commons 'and began to pour forth with uncontrolled passion a torrent of vitriolic abuse on the head of Attlee for daring to make such an appointment'.[73] Bevan and Gaitskell's relations had not been improved by their joint service on a Cabinet committee charged with keeping health spending under control. Gaitskell, in his own words, acted as 'Treasury Prosecutor against the Minister of Health', and on one occasion Bevan nearly stormed out before Attlee rescued the situation.[74] John Strachey once asked Bevan why he seemed to be going out of his way to alienate Gaitskell, one of the most considerable members of the government. '*Considerable!*' replied Bevan. 'But he's nothing, nothing, nothing!' Strachey tried to explain that, on the contrary, Gaitskell had 'a will like a dividing spear', but he was wasting his breath.[75]

Gaitskell's reputation as Chancellor, as it developed during the 1950s and after, was as one half of 'Mr. Butskell'. Supposedly he and his Conservative successor, R. A. Butler, shared a bipartisan commitment to moderate Keynesian policies, neither doing much more than tinker with the level of demand.[76] In fact, Gaitskell retained his conviction that the use of direct physical controls was 'the distinguishing feature of British socialist planning' and that it would be wrong to rely entirely on monetary and budgetary policy.[77] This was a point on which he and Morrison could find shared ground with Bevan and others on the Left. However, plans to use a 'Full Employment Bill' were ultimately dropped due to the Korean situation, which required a different set of powers to be put in place on an emergency basis.[78] Gaitskell was no less sincere a socialist than Bevan, and if he was less openly passionate about his beliefs, he nonetheless felt matters deeply. As Roy Jenkins, a junior colleague and genuine admirer, later admitted: 'He was stubborn, rash, and could in a paradoxical way become too emotionally committed to an over-rational position which, once he had thought it rigorously through, he believed must be the final answer.'[79] Another sympathetic critic, Jim Griffiths, judged that 'if he had been more calculating he might have saved himself from the personal attacks which caused him deep anguish'.[80]

During the autumn of 1950, further groundwork was laid for the final Gaitskell–Bevan clash. The *New York Times* reported that Bevan, Strachey and Strauss wanted to reject US financial help for Britain's rearmament programme and to scale defence spending back.[81] The paper did not name Bevan, but it transpired that the article was based on remarks he had made, off the record, over lunch, to four American journalists. Bevan issued a statement: 'I share the fullest responsibility for the rearmament policy with my colleagues, and it has my complete support.'[82] His denial of the story was unconvincing, and the Kremlin exploited it 'with extreme enthusiasm' as evidence of a growing rift between the USA and its allies.[83] Moreover, his public statement of support for rearmament narrowed his options.

Then came a frightening new development. Military success at the Battle of Inchon, which was followed by the recapture of Seoul, seemed to vindicate MacArthur's judgement. But he then decided to press on into North Korea, a move that prompted intervention by the PRC. In November, China's second-wave offensive – which involved 300,000 soldiers lying in ambush – caught UN forces by surprise.[84] Just days after he had announced a 'Home by Christmas' offensive, MacArthur cabled Washington: 'The Chinese military forces are committed in North Korea in great and ever increasing strength. [...] We face an entirely new war.'[85] The panic this induced was the backdrop for the notorious presidential press conference that followed.[86] Truman stated: 'We will take whatever steps are necessary to meet the military situation, just as we always have.' Asked if this included use of the atomic bomb, he replied: 'That includes every weapon that we have.' Asked further if its use was under 'active consideration', he answered: 'Always has been. It is one of our weapons.' Pressed further, he suggested that MacArthur had the power to deploy the bomb: 'The military commander in the field will have charge of the use of the weapons, as he always has.'[87]

The White House quickly rowed back, stressing that the very possession of any weapon implied consideration of its use; that only the President had the legal power to authorize use of the bomb; and that no such authorization had been given.[88] Yet this was cold comfort, given that Truman himself had authorized the destruction of Hiroshima and

Nagasaki five years before. Although the effects of the weapons were known to be terrible (as Truman acknowledged) a nuclear war remained thinkable. The concept of 'Mutual Assured Destruction' had not yet been coined and the 'nuclear winter' phenomenon was still to be modelled.[89] Furthermore, the weapons, which were designed for delivery by aircraft rather than missiles, were less numerous and less powerful than those of today. One physicist told a meeting of the Birmingham Peace Council that it was 'just nonsense' to suggest that atomic bombs could destroy the entire world. 'Even if America and Russia devoted their resources to this one end it would take about 20,000 years.' Nevertheless, Britain itself was very vulnerable, he suggested, and 'British civilisation could disappear completely in an atomic war.'[90]

US bombers stationed on British soil meant that the country was a prime target. And Moscow's recent treaty with the PRC raised the spectre of Soviet involvement in Korea.[91] It was possible to imagine, then, that the spread of the war in Asia could lead to a nuclear conflict that the superpowers would withstand but that would destroy the UK's infrastructure (though perhaps not all human life). Civil defence preparations continued on the assumption that such a war would be survivable. The first time Benn returned to his constituency after the by-election he found Bristol 'in the middle of a full-scale atomic bomb exercise'. The centre of the city, 'laid flat by the air raids in the last war, was full of military and police searching for "radio-activity"'. Benn noted wryly, however, that 'the traditional British imperturbability was well demonstrated by the fact that all the high-ups lunched in comfort at the Grand Hotel where we were staying'.[92]

Following Truman's comments, and in the face of alarm among MPs, the Cabinet determined that Attlee should immediately travel stateside for consultations.[93] Truman quickly accepted his proposal for a visit, and the Prime Minister's party touched down in a BOAC Stratocruiser at 9.40 a.m. Washington time on 4 December after a bumpy descent.[94] As the Americans realized, the British resented being treated as a junior partner in the alliance; Attlee's overarching objective was to secure status in line with the UK's global spread of interests.[95] Bevin, not well enough to travel, was absent from the talks. Acheson found Attlee's personality depressing but reckoned him a wily negotiator.[96] Attlee reported to Bevin that both sides agreed on the need to avoid a major war with the PRC, 'and I think that we have at least shaken the American Service Chiefs by impressing upon them the dangers of limited war with China'.[97]

Much of his effort was fruitless, however. He argued for a ceasefire in Korea in order to help hold the line against communism in Europe – 'we must not get so involved in the East as to lay ourselves open to attack in the West' – but this met with a cool response from the Americans.[98] On the nuclear issue, he extracted a verbal pledge from Truman 'that the Governments of the United Kingdom and Canada were partners with the United States in this weapon and that the United States Government would not consider its use without consulting the United Kingdom and Canada'.[99] But this had little practical value, and the Americans refused to put it in the final communiqué.[100] On his return to London, Attlee could only tell the Commons, without going into details, that he was 'completely satisfied by my talk on this question with the President'.[101] Overall, the discussions were a public relations success, as they seemed to show that the British were being consulted and taken seriously. And the UK government was not entirely without sway. In the New Year, against the wishes of the Americans, it succeeded in modifying a UN resolution targeting the PRC.[102]

Influence, or the appearance of it, came with a price. In Washington, Attlee came under pressure to boost Britain's rearmament effort.[103] On his return, the Cabinet decided to make public the government's determination to accelerate defence preparation, while resisting US pressure to name a spending figure before a detailed scheme could be worked out.[104] In January 1951, it further committed itself to a plan that would cost in the region of £4,700 million. There was a caveat: 'it would be inexpedient for the Government to commit themselves publicly to achieving the programme in full within a specified term of years'.[105] Troubles brewed throughout the winter. Oliver Franks, the ambassador to Washington, described how the wettest weather in eight decades had overlapped with a severe flu epidemic: 'the Government had been under unceasing fire and had had to cope with crises about once a week, which they had barely pulled through; everyone was tired; the Foreign Office had been practically leaderless'.[106]

There were, moreover, emergent signs of dissent. Strauss, who as Minister of Supply would be charged with procuring the required equipment, recalled telling his colleagues 'that to do this [rearmament] on the suggested scale and in the proposed three-year time-table would have grave economic consequences'.[107] This is borne out by the cabinet Secretary's notebook, though it also shows that Strauss agreed that the proposals were technically feasible. Wilson, with some foresight, cast doubt on the latter notion: 'Economic possibility. Believe sights are set too high. [...] Capacity: may aim too high on certain items & as result get less.' Bevan also raised objections, saying that the programme was 'over-accelerated'. The impact, he claimed, would be excessive. 'Moral[e] will be undermined. Nothg. in internatl sitn to call for increase on that scale.'[108] At the same time, he stopped well short of a full-scale attack. Gaitskell noted:

> It was expected that Bevan would put up a lot more resistance. I never thought so myself for the simple reason that once the programme had been put forward it was difficult to see what we could do other than accept it. We were committed to some acceleration – we could hardly start arguing with the Chiefs of Staff about what was essential and what was not essential.[109]

Furthermore, when the plans were debated in the Commons, Bevan defended them in a vigorous *tour de force*. He was praised in the *Manchester Guardian* for 'bringing the whole House into enthusiastic agreement with him on a definition of the main objects of our foreign policy and rearmament programme'.[110] As one Labour MP described it, 'Bevan attempted to relate the problems of the present to the whole philosophical conflict between Communism and democratic Socialism – and succeeded brilliantly.'[111] Even the *Daily Telegraph* found him 'pleasantly unvituperative'.[112]

Bevan argued that 'armed preparedness' was needed 'to bring about not appeasement but the pacification of the tensions of the world'.[113] He did caution that too rapid rearmament brought with it the danger of McCarthyite hysteria, and it is thus possible to read the speech as a coded warning that the Soviets needed to be fought with ideas (and improved living standards) rather than with weapons.[114] But whereas Attlee and Gaitskell made sure to state that the physical limits on production might make it impossible to spend all the money, Bevan did not offer any such warning.[115] Instead, he concluded with a firm suggestion that the rearmament project would be put through in its entirety: 'We shall carry it out; we shall fulfil our obligations to our friends and Allies, and at the same time we shall try to prevent such an exacerbation of the world atmosphere as makes it impossible for the nations to come together in peace and harmony and give mankind another breathing space.'[116]

Bevan was speaking in a new role, that of Minister of Labour and National Service. Attlee had at last persuaded him to switch from the Ministry of Health. (Dalton became Minister of Town and Country Planning, taking over responsibility for Housing.) The change could have been considered a mere sideways move. But in conditions of war – and threatening world war – it was arguably something more substantive. Bevan was the successor not merely to the ineffectual George Isaacs, who went to the Ministry of Pensions, but to Bevin in his great wartime days. This was not enough to satisfy Bevan's ambition, though. Might he replace Bevin at the Foreign Office? It was clear that things could not go on as they were. 'My impression of Ernie has been lamentable,' noted Younger at the start of the year. 'Sometimes he seems very unwell, sometimes not so bad; but every time I have seen him so far he has seemed to me to be morally a broken man.'[117]

Finally, in March, Attlee bit the bullet and moved Bevin to the job of Lord Privy Seal. That role was essentially a sinecure. The bitterness of the blow was intensified by an unfortunate coincidence. When the Prime Minister rang Bevin to tell him that the change had to be announced, the call reached him while he was at a party organized by civil servants to celebrate his seventieth birthday. 'I thought it was a dreadful thing to do,' remembered Bevin's wife, Florence. 'I could have murdered Attlee and all of them.'[118] In a 1962 interview Attlee defended his approach to Cabinet reshuffles ('It's a dirty job and a Prime Minister has to get on with it') but denied any brutality in Bevin's case. Given the state of his health, Bevin's 'only hope of survival was to take a less fatiguing job' and the two men had discussed his resignation for some time.[119] Putting a brave face on it, Bevin wrote to Acheson that he had stuck at the job as long as he could. 'I think the understanding that has grown up between the United States and ourselves is most encouraging, but unfortunately I could not stay the course.'[120] He continued to take part in government business. In the Commons, Chips Channon observed him on the Treasury bench, 'sallow and shrunken', looking 'as if he had been kissed by death'.[121]

When it came to choosing the new Foreign Secretary, Attlee passed over Bevan, though, as he recalled, he asked him (among others) whom he thought would be a good candidate. 'I can't remember what he said, but he certainly did not ask for the job himself; and he did not indicate that he wanted it.'[122] This was naïve. According to Dalton, Bevan was 'deeply disappointed and angry to have missed, in the space of five months, both the Treasury and the Foreign Office', and it is hard not to read his subsequent behaviour in this light.[123] But though Attlee might have done more to soothe his ego, Bevan was certainly not the safe pair of hands the Prime Minister was looking for. Neither, unfortunately, was Morrison, the man he finally chose, who was the most heavyweight figure remaining in the government. Retrospectively, Attlee put the blame on Morrison for campaigning for the job, and on the press for supporting him. 'He brought every possible influence to bear. He turned down every other suggestion. A great mistake on his part.'[124]

Gordon Walker's diary tells a different story, in which Attlee asked Morrison who should succeed Bevin. Morrison ran through some possibilities before saying that he favoured Hartley Shawcross. 'Attlee thought he couldn't do it and had said to Morrison "I suppose there's no one but you" – which M described as pretty cool.'[125] There is evidence that Morrison himself was reluctant to take the job, partly for fear of his predecessor breathing down his neck. Isaacs 'felt that Herbert had to take the Foreign Office or get out. Attlee gave him this choice to show who was the boss.'[126]

Chuter Ede took over Morrison's role as Leader of the House of Commons and Lord Addison his responsibilities as Lord President of the Council. US intelligence reached an assessment that proved flawed but that looked reasonable on the facts available at the time. Morrison's appointment, it suggested, would end the 'domestic irritation' over the lack of a physically fit Foreign Secretary and would make for continuity of policy. 'Although inexperienced in the handling of foreign affairs, Morrison's success as a party manager will facilitate his task of winning the support of the Parliamentary Labor Party for his policies.' Furthermore: 'On balance, Attlee seems to have strengthened his Government, and incidentally, to have greatly enhanced Morrison's political chances in the latter's potential rivalry with Aneurin Bevan for the future leadership of the Labor Party.'[127]

Though it would be unfair to call Morrison's short spell as Foreign Secretary disastrous, it was certainly unfortunate. One might say that he was unlucky with his timing – he quickly had to deal with the scandal of the escaped Soviet spies, Burgess and Maclean – but in truth there had scarcely been a crisis-free moment since 1945. He certainly suffered from following Bevin, who had been so loved by his officials, and he had many distractions to deal with. These included his pet project, the Festival of Britain – a five-month-long London-based extravaganza that attracted eight million visitors, and that was intended to promote a positive image of the nation and boost the economy.[128] Whether because his mind was not on the task, or because of the effects of age, Morrison failed to master his new brief. 'I had no idea he was so ignorant,' said Attlee later.[129] MPs 'squirmed in agony' when he 'called the Euphrates the "You Frates", in two separate words'.[130] Perhaps his critics on this occasion were being snooty, but as somebody who knew both men said: 'Ernie can't pronounce the names either. But he does know where the places are.'[131]

William Strang, Morrison's Permanent Secretary, noted a further contrast. Morrison always grumbled that the British army was not large enough, whereas Bevin, knowing that a strong economy was the basis for a sound foreign policy, was habitually worried about coal exports. Strang recalled that the first thing Morrison did on taking over was to ask for a biography of Lord Palmerston, the quintessential exponent of gunboat diplomacy. Soon afterwards, he summoned senior officials to his House of Commons room and 'attacked them for not being militant enough in the defence of British interests'.[132] Lord (William) Henderson, one of his junior ministers, thought Morrison was good at delegating but 'displayed very doubtful judgement' and was too belligerent.[133] This was all of a piece with Morrison's fondness for the Empire, though it had been some years since he had issued one of his most notorious remarks: 'It would be sheer nonsense – ignorant, dangerous nonsense – to talk about grants of full self-government to many of the dependent territories for some time to come. In those instances it would be like giving a child of ten a latch-key, a bank account, and a shotgun.'[134]

An addition to Morrison's burdens came when, on 21 March, Attlee entered St Mary's Hospital, Paddington, for an extended stay. It was an NHS institution, but Attlee was treated in the private Lindo Wing; this drew no criticism at the time. He was suffering from a duodenal ulcer.

According to the *Manchester Guardian*, which noted his recent 'ease of manner' and seeming good health, 'This is an illness of nervous strain and sometimes it is the price paid for an appearance of placidity.' His engagements were kept to a minimum, though at one point he returned briefly to Downing Street to deliver a Party Political Broadcast.[135] As Deputy Prime Minister, Morrison took over the running of the government, though Attlee continued to be consulted in the developing row between Gaitskell and Bevan over health service charges, in advance of the upcoming Budget. 'It was unfortunate that I was ill just then,' Attlee recalled. 'It oughtn't to have gone so far, but both sides dug their feet in and took up positions and wouldn't budge.'[136]

However, it is far from certain that Attlee's presence would have led to a different outcome. And though the gulf between the principals was ultimately unbridgeable, both Gaitskell and Bevan showed at least a tactical willingness to compromise. But Bevan's relationship with his colleagues was 'increasingly tetchy' and many of them, in turn, regarded him as a prima donna.[137] He pursued his goals in a way that was querulous and ultimately quixotic, whereas Gaitskell's ability to remain calm under pressure helped him draw others into his camp.

At stake was the question of how the rearmament package, as agreed in February, should be financed. Tax rises were inevitable, but Gaitskell wanted to increase old-age pensions. He concluded that, to pay for the latter while keeping social spending under control, economies in the health service would be needed. As efficiency savings would not be enough, small-scale NHS charges would have to make good the difference. The new Health Minister, Hilary Marquand, devised a plan for dental and optical fees, as well as for a shilling payment for prescriptions. The discussions played out in committees and in full Cabinet. Bevin, in his last significant act, tried to broker a compromise. A ceiling of £400 million would be set to health spending and the prescription charges would be dropped (but the eye and teeth charges retained). Gaitskell agreed to this, whereas Bevan (albeit at the last minute) said he was willing to accept the prescription charges but not the other ones. As we have seen, he had accepted the principle of prescription charges in 1949, but there was no clear logic to his claim that these conformed to the principle of a free health service whereas fees for dentures and spectacles did not. At a mass meeting on 3 April – perhaps as an unplanned comment in response to heckling – he declared that he would 'never be a member of a Government which makes charges on the National Health Service for the patient'.[138]

The showdown took place on 9 April, the very eve of the Budget. After one Cabinet meeting failed to reach a conclusion, Morrison and William Whiteley, the powerful Chief Whip, went to see Attlee in hospital. When the Cabinet met again that same evening they conveyed the Prime Minister's message, which gave firm support to Gaitskell. 'The Chancellor of the Exchequer had particular responsibility for the national finances; and no other Minister ought to claim that any particular estimate should be treated as sacrosanct.' Furthermore, it would be 'stark folly for any Minister to provoke a political crisis at the present time'. If Labour had to fight an election under such conditions, 'they would inevitably wear the appearance of being incompetent to govern', and the party would face a long period out of office. Bevan nevertheless indicated he would resign unless the charges were revoked, as did Wilson, but they received support only from education minister George Tomlinson.[139] The next day, Attlee was visited by Bevan and Wilson, and then, separately, by Gaitskell, who insisted that his position would be impossible unless the charges were put through. 'Finally,' Gaitskell recorded, the Prime Minister 'murmured what I took to be "Very well, you will have to go." In a split second I realised he had said, "I am afraid *they* will have to go."'[140]

That same afternoon, Gaitskell, 'fresh as paint' and wearing a red carnation, delivered his Budget. As yet, there had been no resignations, but Bevan stayed away from the front bench. He was visibly deflated when Labour MPs heard the proposals for health charges without protest; only Jennie Lee was heard to let out a cry of 'Shame!'[141] Benn, witnessing events as a novice MP, thought Gaitskell had given 'a brilliant exposition, there is no doubt that speech made his reputation secure'. The following morning, the PLP met in good spirits, buoyed by the news that Truman had dismissed the unstable MacArthur. Gaitskell spoke, followed by Bevan who, though 'pale and angry', said that he would not resign. But this seemed to be contingent on the Budget being modified. Then Benn got a chance to speak. He described the 'principle' of a free health service as 'nonsense'. The question of health charges was purely a practical one. Only a single test could be applied: 'with what we have and can get by way of revenue, how can we lay it to the best advantage of those who need help most?' Pensioners deserved better treatment.

While Benn was speaking, Bevin, 'flabby and pale and motionless, and half-asleep, woke up, looked up and asked, "Who is that boy?"' When given the answer he replied, 'Nice boy, nice boy.'[142] Three days later, Bevin died. He fell back on his pillow while still trying to work on his despatch box; the key had to be prised out of his hands.[143] A 'great familiar landmark' had vanished from the skyline.[144]

Bevan still hung on, yet continued to maintain his opposition to the charges. Finally, Attlee demanded to know where he stood. In response, Bevan sent a letter of resignation, which argued that the Budget was 'based upon a scale of military expenditure, in the coming year, which is physically unattainable'. Attlee's reply accused him of extending the field of disagreement beyond the question that had appeared to be at stake. 'I had certainly gathered that if the proposal for imposing charges on dentures and spectacles were dropped, you would have been satisfied.'[145] Wilson resigned too, as did John Freeman, a highly able junior minister who went on to have a distinguished career outside politics.[146] Bevan's Commons resignation speech was a dud. Castle, who felt that his fundamental arguments were indisputable, described how 'his emotions ran away with him and he lapsed into attacks on Gaitskell which sounded embarrassingly like personal pique'. She was appalled by his bitterness. 'I realized then that we backroom boys and girls of the Keep Left Group had acquired a leader who would put us on the political map, but at a heavy price.'[147]

Who, though, was right about the substantive questions? On rearmament, Bevan was correct to argue that the programme was too ambitious to be wholly achieved. He received some vindication when the Tories were obliged to pare it down after their return to office. However, Gaitskell had never staked his reputation on it being fulfilled to the last penny – he had been clear that there were many uncertainties.[148] If Attlee's suggestion that he raised the issue merely as 'an afterthought' was somewhat unfair, it is certainly true that Bevan had not raised his genuine concerns as the major issue during the Cabinet battle.[149] If he had wanted to make this the grounds of the fight, he should have resigned earlier rather than backing the plan in public. On the question of the charges, there is an argument that they were inessential to the well-being of the economy, and that Gaitskell was gratuitously provocative and pedantic. The fees were expected to bring in only £23 million each financial year, a mere bagatelle in the context of a budget of £4,000 million, so why continue to press them in the knowledge that Bevan considered them a resigning matter?[150] But the argument also cut the other way. As Attlee put it in retirement: 'If you really think that putting a charge for medicine [*sic*] entitles a man to wreck the whole party – if you have a sense of proportion you don't.'[151]

Bevan asserted that the charges represented a pebble that would launch an avalanche – but although prescription charges were soon introduced under the Conservatives, he was wrong to claim that the NHS was now at risk of being dismembered.[152] Gaitskell had delivered an egalitarian Budget that skilfully balanced reliefs and impositions and that delivered a better deal for the elderly. His insistence on the charges was an insistence on his authority as Chancellor – that he should not be obliged to treat any particular class of expenditure as untouchable. The struggle, then, had not been merely a simple clash of wills between two stubborn men, but rather a dispute over how government itself was to be conducted. Bevan seemed to regard the NHS as his personal fiefdom, and this, to Gaitskell, was a threat to the principle of collective responsibility: 'It was an impossible and uncivilized procedure if one minister, and one minister alone, exercised a veto on majority decisions by threatening to create a crisis whenever he wished.'[153]

Just as these events were playing out, ministers were dealing with another overseas crisis. The government held a majority stake in the Anglo-Iranian Oil Company (AIOC); the firm's refinery at Abadan was the biggest in the world and represented the UK's most sizeable investment abroad.[154] The concession agreement, which determined how much revenue the Iranians received, was grossly exploitative. If AIOC had increased its dividend, Iran would have benefited, but the British Treasury opposed this, as it would have undermined the case for wage restraint at home.[155] After long negotiations had failed to produce a better deal, the new government of Mohammed Mossadeq passed a law nationalizing the company's local assets. If this succeeded, it would raise the threat that other nationalist governments in the Middle East would be encouraged to eradicate foreign influences. There was already talk in the Egyptian press of nationalizing the Suez Canal.[156] But it was obviously difficult for a British socialist government to try to deny another country the right to nationalize a key industry.

The nationalization legislation went into effect at the start of May. Younger felt that Morrison, who favoured the use of force to restore

Britain's position, handled things poorly. 'He was slow in conceding the principle of nationalisation. Then he hankered after strong-arm methods though it was pretty clear that they couldn't be adopted.' He came across as a party politician, unstatesmanlike and out of his depth.[157] This low opinion was shared by Acheson, who felt that both sides in the dispute 'were pressing their luck to the point of suicide in this game of Russian roulette'.[158] The Americans, though sceptical of Mossadeq, saw Iranian nationalism as a lesser evil than communism – and they did not want to be seen to be backing British imperial adventures. When negotiations proved abortive, Morrison told the US ambassador that 'If they had backed us all along, the whole situation would now be very different [...] we were tired of being lectured by the United States.'[159]

Morrison seemed to want 'to send gunboats to Abadan' but Attlee realized that military intervention without US support was too big a risk.[160] Whether he would have agreed to such a venture if Washington had smiled on it remains an open question, but in retrospect he could present the decision to hold back as a principled refusal to 'revert to old form'.[161] On 26 September, Iran demanded that AIOC's remaining staff withdraw from Abadan. The British quickly complied. Within days Egypt denounced its 1936 treaty with Britain, lending force to the Conservative charge that the government was scuttling from its responsibilities and enfeebling Britain's position in the region.[162] But that sword was double-edged, as the Tory approach to the Iran crisis reinforced the party's die-hard image.[163] At Labour's autumn conference, Bevan, back on form, told the delegates: 'I do not think that Winston Churchill wants war, no sane man wants war, but the trouble with him is that he does not know how to avoid it.'[164]

By this point, Attlee had already called a general election. Though he had been considering an autumn poll for some while, the exact timing was influenced by the King, who was planning a lengthy Commonwealth tour and wanted the political situation resolved before he left the country.[165] The decision to call an election may seem strange, given that there was no strict necessity for one and that the government was likely to do badly. But Attlee was troubled by the fact that his small majority put pressure on sick MPs and, if Labour were to lose, it was best to pick a moment when the damage could be minimized. And in fact, given the split in its ranks, Labour performed surprisingly well during the campaign (with help from the *Daily Mirror*, which pressed the warmonger charge on Churchill). The emerging Bevanite faction had performed strongly in voting for the NEC, but Bevan himself was co-opted onto the committee that drew up the party's manifesto, creating an appearance of harmony.[166] In addition to peace and full employment, the document promised to keep prices and rents under control, and to maintain food subsidies, which it claimed were worth 12 shillings a week to the average family. It also appealed to the party's record:

> To-day, after six years of Labour rule and in spite of post-war difficulties, the standard of living of the vast majority of our people is higher than ever it was in the days of Tory rule. Never have the old folk been better cared for. Never had we so happy and healthy a young generation as we see in Britain to-day.[167]

On polling day, Thursday 25 October, Attlee left No. 10 with his family at 8.10 a.m. After recording their votes at Caxton Hall they returned for breakfast, and after the Prime Minister saw 'the only telegram of importance', they left for his Walthamstow constituency. Attlee and his wife stayed there until his result was announced in the early hours and then went to Transport House. They journeyed back to Downing Street at 4.15 a.m. The following day, Attlee worked in the Cabinet room, spoke on the phone to Morrison at 3.30 p.m., and listened to the election results. A little before 5 p.m. it became clear that the Conservatives had secured a majority. Attlee then had an audience with the King, tendering his resignation, 'which His Majesty was graciously pleased to accept'. After dinner the Attlees went down to Chequers for the weekend, finally vacating 10 Downing Street on 1 November for their new home, Cherry Cottage, Prestwood, Buckinghamshire.[168] Vi Attlee hurried down the stairs carrying the last pile of books as the new Cabinet was already meeting.[169] Asked later how he felt about his defeat, her husband's reply was characteristically low key. 'I don't know,' he said. 'Just one of those things.'[170]

Arguing About Attlee

Attlee, 'gay and optimistic' in his new role as Leader of the Opposition, took the election result complacently. He told the PLP that the new government would last six months to a year, that the King's Speech was devoid of content, 'and made the usual fun of Tory high birth and schooling'. According to the *Manchester Guardian*'s political correspondent, Labour MPs were bright and breezy. 'The result of the election is exactly what some of them hoped for – strength enough to be a powerful element in the political scene, but no responsibility for the application of difficult and painful policies.'[1] 'The election results are wonderful', wrote Dalton in his diary. 'We are out just at the right moment, and our casualties are wonderfully light.'[2]

There were some true grounds for optimism. The party had at one stage looked like it was heading for a landslide defeat, but its campaigning had held Churchill to a majority of only 17. Remarkably, Labour had won slightly more votes than the Conservatives (piling up big wins in safe seats and losing out in marginals). Its defeat could be attributed in part to the ongoing tribulations of the shattered Liberal Party, which fielded only 109 candidates; its would-be voters split disproportionately in favour of the Tories. According to the *New Statesman*, 'Instead of proving that the country is sick of Socialism and giving Mr. Churchill a mandate to dismantle it, the election has shown that just under half the British people, despite the grievous failures of Labour leadership in the last twelve months, believe tenaciously in the Welfare State whose foundations have been laid since 1945.' It would now be the turn of Labour 'to profit in Opposition from all those misfortunes and discomforts to which the British people are subjected'.[3]

The mood did not last. Labour was quickly riven by new bouts of infighting, as the fault line between Bevan's and Gaitskell's supporters widened further. According to Douglas Jay, Bevanism became an example of what Thucydides called 'stasis': 'faction for faction's sake in which the protagonists know which side they are on, but usually cannot remember why it all started'.[4] Richard Crossman, by contrast, scorned 'the extraordinary bitterness' he detected among Gaitskell's followers. 'They have convinced themselves that we [Bevanites] are demagogues who are deliberately exploiting the simple-mindedness of the rank and file for our own ends.'[5] Meanwhile, according to Woodrow Wyatt, Attlee 'avoided exacerbation and often pretended not to notice there was a row on'.[6]

Labour's disunity was the product, as much as the cause, of its wider problems. That is to say, the two sides might have sunk their differences if the outlook for long-term electoral success had been more propitious. But the hope that the new Conservative ministers would be tortured on the rack of economic crisis proved vain. This was in part because the Attlee administration had been so successful. In the words of the civil servant and economist Alec Cairncross, that government 'pointed the economy in the right direction, rode out the various crises that the years of transition almost inevitably gave rise to, and by 1951 had brought the economy near to eventual balance'.[7] In office, Labour had pursued 'fair shares' in a way that shored up support in its heartlands at the expense of middle-class votes in the south-east. Though plenty of problems persisted, the Tories were perfectly placed to profit from the probity of their predecessors, especially after the fighting ended in Korea in 1953. They were able to present the end of food rationing the following year as a triumph for 'Conservative freedom' and brandish the threat that restrictions would return if 'the Socialists' got back into power.[8] And as mass prosperity proliferated – yet while poverty did not disappear – Labour struggled to adjust to the new age of affluence. The party had little to offer to voters who wanted, not uplifting exhortations to greater effort and community, but cars, TVs and washing-machines bought 'on the never-never'.[9]

The Tories, for their part, proved skilled at maintaining those parts of the Attlee legacy that were popular or uncontroversial and jettisoning those that were not. The nationalization of water fell victim to Labour's election defeat. Iron and steel were denationalized, as was road haulage, which had been taken into public ownership alongside the railways.[10] The other nationalized industries were kept in public hands. The NHS and the wider welfare state were maintained, albeit with some trimming and tinkering. The Conservatives hit their eye-catching target of 300,000 houses a year, though on a reduced set of building standards.[11]

Whether through deliberate policy or as a product of beneficent global conditions, full employment continued. Ministers dropped Operation ROBOT, a secret plan to float the pound, in the face of fears about a return to the dole queues. Nor did they take on the unions, preferring generous negotiated settlements to the disruption caused by strikes. There was substantial continuity in foreign policy; the 1956 invasion of Egypt was a disastrous but short-lived aberration. Though progress on decolonization initially halted, and imperial 'dirty wars' did not, the early 1960s saw a sharp acceleration of moves towards independence in Africa. Labour, in office, had altered the political landscape, but it was its opponents who dominated the new terrain.

For decades, scholars have debated whether the policy overlap between the two main parties amounted to a 'post-war consensus'. These arguments have been about the Attlee government and its successors but have also concerned the long-term meaning and influence of the Churchill coalition. They have not been purely academic, because they have been influenced by, and have spilled over into, political contests over the legacy and symbolism of the war. In other words, the consequences of 1945 included battles over whom should be considered the true heirs and custodians of the British people's wartime achievements and sacrifices. The question of the Attlee period and its relation to 'consensus', then, has not been an issue of mere historic interest but a part of active political controversy. For consensus can be evaluated in different ways – either as a desirable, progressive coalescence of competing forces, or as a deadening constraint on genuine radicalism (of either Left or Right).

This is not to say that the idea of consensus was a retrospective invention, nostalgic or otherwise. During the lifetime of the Attlee government the term 'consensus' did not gain traction, but similar concepts did. The idea of 'the middle way', for example, was frequently linked with claims about national identity and the supposed English genius for compromise. Many politicians sought to define and colonize the middle ground and exclude their opponents from it. Labour and Tory partisans were eager to claim *both* that their respective parties had something distinct to offer *and* that they occupied an ideological space that represented a national accord (but did not include the other party). However, consensus was suspect on each of the two main parties' radical wings. Consequently, after 1951, Gaitskell resented being bracketed with his Tory opposite number (the other half of 'Mr. Butskell'). He complained of Left 'attempts to identify me with Mr. Butler on every possible occasion. [...] It is hard to believe that this is not a deliberate attempt to "smear" me in the eyes of Labour people.'[12]

There is a version of history in which the achievements of the Attlee government were not properly recognized in its immediate aftermath and were even unjustly disdained. Supposedly, 'it was routinely attacked on the left for not trying hard enough to form a Socialist state as a bulwark against capitalism'.[13] True, there was some ridicule of complacent ex-ministers who seemed to regard their own tenure as a golden age.[14] But the Bevanites could scarcely denigrate the government wholesale, given that their own hero's reputation was mixed up in it. Bevan naturally defended his own ministerial record. In his 1952 book *In Place of Fear* – often described as his political testament – he rejected the criticisms made by foreign visitors during the government's life who had dwelt on the dull, grey quality of austerity Britain. 'If they had looked closer they would have seen the roses in the cheeks of the children, and the pride and self-confidence of the young mothers', he wrote. 'They would have found that more was being done for working people than in any other part of the world at that time.'[15]

Attlee stayed on as leader, some thought, in order to scupper Morrison's hopes of succeeding him. He may have been a steadying influence on his party but – turning 70 in 1953 – he was scarcely a dynamic force. In 1955, Churchill retired from Downing Street, and was replaced by the camera-friendly Eden, who quickly went to the polls. Labour's manifesto, drafted by Crossman and his fellow Bevanite MP Tom Driberg, placed much emphasis on the Attlee government's record.[16] It had 'earned the confidence of the colonial peoples'; it 'did not shirk the heavy burden of rearmament'; it had increased exports and protected consumers; it had begun 'to abolish the fear of old age, sickness and disablement which haunted working-class life before the war'.[17] After Eden won with an increased majority, one Tory official noted:

> It is often said that a Government which fights an election on its record is bound to lose. Curiously enough in 1955 it was the Labour Party who chose to fight on their record, 1945–51, compared sometimes with before the war or sometimes with 1951–55. This meant that the Conservatives were able to put over their programme, such as it was, without too great competition.[18]

At the end of the year, Attlee finally stood down. When Labour MPs chose his replacement, Gaitskell won, with 157 votes. Bevan received 70. Morrison, who trailed in with 40, never recovered from the humiliation.

Afterwards, a somewhat mellowed Bevan reached accommodation with Gaitskell, taking his side against those within the party who favoured unilateral nuclear disarmament. Labour nonetheless suffered a landslide defeat at the hands of Harold Macmillan in 1959, and though Gaitskell hung on as leader, he failed in his attempt to rethink nationalization by revising Clause 4. Bevan perished of cancer in 1960. Three years later, Gaitskell died early too. His successor was Wilson, who had never been a fully committed Bevanite but had still preserved a reputation as a man of the Left. At the 1963 party conference, flushed from delivering his famous 'white heat of technology' speech, he moved across the platform to present Attlee with a pipe, in honour of his eightieth birthday. The journalist Alan Moorehead reflected on their differences: 'The one man lean, spare and self-effacing; the other a chubby figure with a handsome head of hair and an apt and pungent manner.' Wilson was known to hold similar views to Attlee, Moorehead wrote, yet this was not obvious on the surface. Attlee's 'principles might have been anathema to a great number of the electorate, but one was never left in doubt about them for two minutes'.[19]

In December 1955, Attlee was elevated to the peerage. As an active member of the Lords, he remained in the public eye. He was an advocate of world government, and an opponent of Britain's (first, failed) application to join the EEC. ('I find growing opposition & I don't see how Macmillan can have the effrontery to try to put it through.'[20])

Though mourning the recent death of his wife, he campaigned vigorously in the 1964 election. He used a speech in Hemel Hempstead to mock the Tories for producing policies as electoral bait: 'Wonderful plans for education – after 13 years. Great plans for a lot of new universities – after 13 years. That's their record. Always going to do things.'[21] Douglas Jay recalled seeing him speak in Battersea: 'He was lifted onto the platform amid a tumultuous meeting and said merely this: "I am a very old man. I have lived through two great wars and many General Elections. I shall not live much longer. But if I live till Friday, and my side wins, I shall die happy."'[22] He got his wish, though Wilson scraped in with only a wafer-thin majority. Attlee used an *Observer* article to explain why sometimes a Prime Minister had to be 'cruel' in order to keep Cabinet business moving: 'If somebody starts to ramble, a quick "Are you objecting? You're not? Right. Next business," and the Cabinet can move on.'[23]

Attlee made efforts to curate his reputation and shape interpretations of his government. On the face of it, he was much less successful at this than Churchill, whose war memoirs were produced with the help of a dedicated team and which became a global media sensation.[24] Attlee published his autobiography in 1954 (receiving £10,000 for the copyright) while still Leader of the Opposition.[25] It immediately 'sunk without trace', overshadowed by the arrival of Churchill's final volume of *The Second World War*.[26] Though some insights can be extracted from the book, Attlee's terse style was no match for Churchill's orotund prose; even his title, *As it Happened*, was pedestrian. The *New Statesman & Nation* set a competition that challenged readers to provide an episode from Churchill's life as described by Attlee, or vice versa. 'The Yalta Conference reminded me of our own Labour Party conferences, except that it was considerably warmer', began one of the winning entries.[27]

A TV interview conducted by Francis Williams in 1959 was much livelier – though when Attlee followed up with a transatlantic joint appearance with Truman, his diction was hard to follow, 'especially when he spoke with a pipe clenched between his teeth'.[28] 'It seems I do better in this kind of thing than when I write myself when I am apt to be too laconic,' he noted.[29] Accordingly, he collaborated with Williams on a further series of conversations, which were published as *A Prime Minister Remembers* in 1961.[30] More such exercises followed.[31] Taken together with the many book reviews and other articles he published, which often combined his recollections with pungent judgements, it added up to a significant quantity of autobiographical reflection. He helped researchers almost up until his death, though he continued to dish out reprimands: 'When I was young it was considered good manners if one wanted information from anyone to enclose a stamped and addressed envelope for reply, but *autres temps autres moeurs*'.[32]

It is worth noting that most cabinet ministers, let alone most MPs, did not publish memoirs. This led to some significant gaps in historical memory. In 1952, Cripps had died in Zürich of cancer, just short of his sixty-third birthday. He was not shy of self-promotion, having previously collaborated with sympathetic biographers, but we cannot know if he would have written his memoirs had he survived longer.[33] It is a reasonable guess that Bevin, for his part, would not have done so. In the 1930s he had turned down the opportunity to work with a ghost-writer (and, perhaps being sensitive about his humble origins, he was wary of biographical attention).[34] Bevan was a prolific writer of *Tribune* articles, and *In Place of Fear* contains some autobiographical detail, but he never published a proper memoir. Ede stayed in the Commons until 1964 (the year before his death) and apparently felt no inclination to go into print. The diaries of Gaitskell, Younger and Gordon Walker were not published until long after their respective deaths – and the People's Party produced no brilliant backbench chronicler in this era. A fair number of retrospective accounts did appear, sometimes decades after the events they described, but the best-written were by Castle, Benn and Healey, who had only been junior figures in 1945–51.

This meant that those who published early on had a good chance of permeating the early drafts of history. This was, however, contingent not only on literary skill but on willingness to deploy candour, or at least the appearance of it. Morrison failed these tests. He and his ghost-writer, F. G. Kay, had a miserable relationship. Kay, who had earlier worked on Shinwell's memoirs, later described Morrison 'as a man of consuming ambition, vanity, meanness, a snob, pompous, a lonely, pathetic little man, very secretive and very childish'. Morrison would not include personal information in the book, nor would he let Kay access his papers.[35] No wonder that the book fell flat. Attlee called it 'a fine work of fiction. All to the glory of Herbert.'[36] He might have been even harsher had he known that (according to Kay) Morrison regarded him as 'a nasty little solicitor who went slumming with Oxford graduates in the East End'.[37]

Ironically, it was Dalton who emerged as the most influential memoirist of the Attlee era, in spite of his famous career blow-up and his considerable number of enemies. It was published in three volumes, and the final book, which covered the post-1945 period, hit the bookstalls in February 1962, just days before its author's death in a geriatric ward.[38] Reviewing it, the political scientist Robert McKenzie confessed to having previously disliked Dalton, but now admitted him to be 'an able, exuberant (if somewhat domineering) extrovert who has unswervingly, and even unselfishly, devoted himself to certain causes in which he believes'. The book itself was 'the most important contribution to an understanding of the post-war political scene so far made by any of those who played a part in it'.[39]

Not that it was universally well received. Jennie Lee, one of the custodians of Bevan's memory, denounced it as 'a frenzied, sustained hymn of hate' directed against the Left. It would have been better for the Labour Party if it had not been published, she said. 'The gossip, the intrigues, the unworthy motives attributed to others are bound to spread poison and lead to further controversy.'[40] Yet all these things – recorded in Dalton's catty diary, which was (selectively) reproduced in the memoirs – gave the book a living quality that so many others lacked. And as the academic (and future Labour MP) David Marquand observed, 'History, especially the history of the working-class movement, has a built-in bias in favour of the literate intellectual, and against the inarticulate, the ill-educated, or the shy.' Thus, 'there may be a danger that Lord Dalton may be given an even more prominent place in history than he deserves, simply because his memoirs are so much franker, more attractive, and more readable than Lord Attlee's or Lord Morrison's'.[41]

Morrison died in 1965. Attlee outlived him by two years, entering hospital for the last time in September 1967. He died in his sleep a month later, and 'the knowledge that his friends were thinking of him so much gave those last weeks a particular happiness of their own'.[42] In the light of his subsequent standing, it is tempting to dwell with wry amusement on those obituaries that declared him an able Prime Minister but not a great one.[43] But if he was somewhat underrated, most commentary, including from the Right, strove to be fair, and to address the contradiction between his downbeat personality and the remarkable record of his government.[44] When *The Economist* described him as 'a sound and conscientious political leader of the second rank', it was deliberately going against the grain.[45] In contrast to Baldwin, a once-loved leader whose prestige crashed soon after his retirement, Attlee's elder statesman years had boosted his popularity beyond what it had been when he left No. 10.[46] As a *Times* editorial noted, it was now common 'to relish his dry and matter-of-fact manner, his inability to dramatize his leadership, and to compare these attributes favourably with the flamboyance of his opponent and the studied television personalities of his successors'.[47]

Attlee's personal reputation remained at least stable over subsequent decades and was likely enhanced further. (Surveys of experts in 2004, 2010, 2016 and 2021 all rated him the best post-1945 Prime Minister, though of course the attitude of the wider public may have been different.[48]) How he was viewed as an individual, however, was separate from the question of how his government was regarded. And there was a broader issue still: whether or not that government's policy solutions remained in favour. That was wrapped up in turn with public perceptions of institutions such as the nationalized industries and the NHS, as well as with wider societal change. These things were all influenced by complex interactions between popular and academic history, the world of archives, the media, think-tanks, and the political/ rhetorical exploitation of the past. Though the memory of Attlee as an individual never proved to be strikingly divisive, the ideological wrangles that accompanied the breakdown of the post-war settlement certainly were.

As the 1960s progressed, industrial troubles mounted and inflation started to rise, apparent certainties about the capacity of Keynesianism to maintain growth and employment looked increasingly shaky. It seemed plausible to think that historical study could teach lessons in the present about how to avoid the errors of the past. The roots of the discipline we now call 'contemporary history' – which developed in parallel with social history and new social science approaches to politics – can be traced back at least as far as the 1940s.[49] In the decade of The Beatles, it took off further. The Public Records Act of 1967 reduced the closure period for government documents to 30 years, meaning that those concerning the Second World War became available in the early

1970s and those relating to the Attlee government by the early 1980s. On top of this, the private papers of some key individuals were made accessible to researchers.

As much as with memoirs, decisions surrounding politicians' own archives had an effect, not only on how they personally were regarded but also on their more general ability to influence the writing of history from beyond the grave. Dalton ensured his voice would remain heard by bequeathing his diary and other documents to the LSE. Morrison, probably to his own detriment, burned most of his papers when moving house a few years before his death.[50] Many researchers active during this period deserve credit for their efforts to track down written material and to gather oral recollections, as do archivists and other 'memory entrepreneurs' who collected and preserved material that might otherwise have been lost. Yet these processes were necessarily imperfect, and the haphazard dimension of archival survival continues to shape narratives through to the present day.

The major historical debates over the Attlee government, and about Labour's record more generally, took place within the Left of British politics, rather than between socialists and Conservatives. In 1961, the Marxist academic Ralph Miliband, a former student of Harold Laski, published *Parliamentary Socialism*, in which he excoriated the party for its timid, incrementalist 'labourism'. Despite their protestations of socialist belief, Attlee and his ministers had never truly challenged capitalist economic power, he argued. This line of criticism gained increased resonance due to the disappointments of the Wilson years, but it was far from hegemonic. A panoply of historians and biographers with moderate, social democratic views presented the 1945 government as a commendable if imperfect exercise in practical reform. These included Alan Bullock on Bevin (1960–83), Bernard Donoughue and G. W. Jones on Morrison (1973), Philip M. Williams on Gaitskell (1979), Kenneth Harris on Attlee (1982) and Ben Pimlott on Dalton (1985). Michael Foot on Bevan (1962–73) had a very clear view of who the hero of the tale was – but the picture he painted of the Attlee government was one of promise incompletely fulfilled rather than one of out-and-out betrayal.

Such works often carried a current-day agenda, if less openly than did the critiques offered by the New Left.[51] This was certainly true of *The Road to 1945* (1975), which its author, Paul Addison, described as 'a tough political property which could be very timely from the point of view of current debates'.[52] Addison had graduated with a First from Pembroke College, Oxford, in 1964. He then started as a research student at Nuffield College. He recalled: 'When I began my research, Harold Wilson, who had of course acted as secretary to the Beveridge report, was campaigning for office on a platform which, had I realised it at the time, was a re-run of wartime social reconstruction, demanding efficiency on the one hand and better social service on the other.'[53]

Addison found a friend and ally in Angus Calder, whose researches on the wartime party Common Wealth were intended to 'add a new dimension to the assessment of Labour's performance in office'.[54] Though it is normal to cite *The Road* as the starting point for the 'post-war consensus debate', Calder's book *The People's War* used the term six years earlier; indeed it appeared on the book's dustjacket.[55] This is not to say that Calder coined the concept, which Addison credited to unspecified social scientists.[56] The question of who originated the form of words is less important than what it signified. Although the two men exchanged ideas freely, their respective works (which were aimed at a mass market) had different emphases. 'We both regarded it as axiomatic that the drawing up of post-war plans was an elitist exercise in the creation of "blueprints from above",' Addison recalled. 'But whereas Dr Calder regarded the consensus as a victory for the forces of privilege and bureaucracy over the "participatory democracy" of 1940–42, I regarded it as "positive and purposeful": the basis of a more enlightened and humane society.'[57] Or as he put it at the time: 'Angus appears to judge the political system by reference to a popular social revolutionary alternative which did not exist for the public, or even in the minds of the leading left-wingers of the day: a New Left view projected on to the past.'[58]

From the early 1960s, discussion of the UK's (relative) economic decline had intensified. As the era of 'stagflation' dawned, the mood sometimes verged on the apocalyptic. Addison later noted, '*The Road to 1945* was written during the latter half of the Heath government of 1972–4, and the first year or so of the Labour governments of 1974–9. That problems were mounting was obvious: the "post-war consensus" was under pressure.'[59] Early in 1975, Margaret Thatcher displaced Heath as Tory leader. Unbeknown to Addison, a few months before publication of his book, her Shadow Cabinet debated the post-war consensus vigorously.[60] Ideologically divided, they differed among themselves over its nature, extent and desirability. None of them, though, seemed to doubt it existed. That should not be taken as proof that it did – the point is that the concept was a salient one in politics and not just in academia.[61]

Meanwhile, and now in his final term as Prime Minister, Wilson presented Labour's plans for extending public ownership as a modernized version of Keynesian doctrine, 'an updating of what we all agreed in the 1944 White Paper'. But although this cross-party agreement had once existed, he suggested, the Conservatives had now reneged on it, and were opposing the government's policy out of ideological obstinacy.[62] In truth, Wilson didn't much care for the policy he was defending but was now facing a left-wing grass-roots insurgency led by Tony Benn. Benn found himself on the losing side of the 1975 referendum on EEC membership but hung on as a troublesome though marginalized Cabinet member. Playing to the gallery at the party conference, he made clear that he thought the government was too cautious. Studiously avoiding looking at Wilson, Benn quoted Attlee as saying that public ownership was the only solution for the evils of capitalism.[63] 'We have not heard that sort of language for over a generation,' he said, 'but we have not had a slump of these proportions for at least as long.'[64]

Once Wilson retired, and was replaced by Jim Callaghan, Benn returned to the charge, advocating a return to the principles of the 1945 manifesto.[65] After Benn had again reiterated these arguments, the *Guardian* used the release of the paperback of *The Road to 1945* as an opportunity to editorialize against them. 'What Dr. Addison shows is that the Attlee platform, spectacular though it looked by the standards of earlier government programmes, succeeded as it did because it commanded the support not just of confirmed socialists but of people of all parties and none.' In the conditions of 1977, the paper suggested, there was little evidence of popular support for the course favoured by Benn and Labour's Left-dominated NEC. To pursue radical policies without the backing of the mass of the people would be a gamble, the probable outcome of which 'would be a government headed by Mrs. Margaret Thatcher'.[66]

After the defeat of 1979, which was followed by internal Labour battles and a swing to the Left, Benn subtly shifted his position, at a time when Thatcher's actions were driving unemployment higher.

In conversation with the historian Eric Hobsbawm, he presented the Attlee government as the product of wartime consensus rather than of thorough-going socialism. The consensus solutions succeeded in their time, but only as a product of conditions that would not recur: 'more recently we have seen the slump and the collapse of that consensus as an option'.[67] In 1981, Denis Healey – who won a knife-edge victory over Benn for the Deputy Leadership a few months later – weighed into the party's history wars. 'You cannot expect the electorate to support a movement in which important members are saying it does not deserve trust [...] and that every Labour Government since Attlee has been a fraud.'[68]

That same year, former Foreign Secretary David Owen, gearing up for the formation of the breakaway Social Democratic Party (SDP), published an attack on bureaucratic socialism and demands for unilateral nuclear disarmament and withdrawal from the EEC. His choice of title, *Face the Future*, was a clear attempt to seize the mantle of the 1945 government but his original hope of creating a new democratic socialist party was not one shared by Roy Jenkins and the other founders of the new party.[69] Benn, with a quotation handy for every occasion, compared the SDP to Ramsay MacDonald, and observed that Attlee had once compared MacDonald to Hitler and Mussolini.[70]

Callaghan stayed on for a year as party leader after the general election, using his final conference speech to issue a pitiful plea for party unity. He noted wryly that Attlee was 'being quoted by all and sundry [...] I must say it only goes to show what happens to us after we are dead.'[71] Callaghan's successor, Michael Foot, made use of his own association with Bevan – including the fact that he had inherited his constituency – in his struggles with the Left. He cited him in opposition to the view that party conference decisions should be binding on MPs, and contrasted the open dissent offered by Bevan and Cripps in the 1930s with the secretive methods of the present-day Militant Tendency. Such reference points were of some use when conducting internal party arguments but were of declining relevance to new generations of voters. Given Labour's wider difficulties, defeat in the 1983 general election was doubtless inevitable, but it did not help that Foot often seemed to be fighting the battles of the past.[72]

Thatcher's triumphant Tories had their own story to tell about the meaning of post-war history. At the time of the 1945 election, Thatcher was a student at Oxford. She remembered hearing Churchill's Gestapo broadcast and thinking, 'He's gone too far.' She approved of the principles of the Beveridge Report but thought that Labour implemented them too swiftly and too generously. As a young Conservative candidate at the start of the 1950s she offered standard criticisms of the waste and muddle supposedly perpetrated by the Labour government.[73] Over the next decades she beat a path to prominence by presenting herself as a champion of the middle classes against an Establishment consensus that threatened to defeat the bourgeois virtues of enterprise and thrift.[74] Yet, as Leader of the Opposition and Prime Minister she made no special habit of assaulting Attlee's record. From the Thatcherite perspective, his government's role in the foundation of NATO, and the birth of the British nuclear weapons programme, was positively commendable.[75] In fact, it was convenient for Thatcher to portray him as a representative of Labour's comparatively virtuous past, from which, by the 1980s, it had supposedly gone astray. Playing the more-in-sorrow-than-in-anger card, she asserted: 'the Labour Party we face now are totally different from the Labour Party of Gaitskell, Attlee and even of Harold Wilson and Jim Callaghan'.[76]

Thatcher was more concerned to attack the 'fraudulent' consensus in its entirety than to discredit in detail the actions of its founders.[77] The memory of the 'winter of discontent' of 1978–9 was more immediately politically useful than attacking Attlee. Moreover, in the opinion of her and her acolytes, Conservative governments were as much to blame as Labour ones for the malaise that had afflicted Britain.[78] But of course, historical attacks on the Attlee government were not unwelcome to her. In 1986, Correlli Barnett published *The Audit of War*, the second in his series of books on the decline of British power. Barnett had made his name as a military historian with a controversial attack on the cult of Montgomery. He now found another sacred cow to slay in the form of the welfare state. In his view, the vision of a New Jerusalem had been successfully pressed 'on the British people between 1940 and 1945, with far-reaching effects on Britain's post-war chances as an industrial power struggling for survival and prosperity'.[79] Yet, as Paul Addison pointed out, Barnett was 'no Thatcherite: he does not suppose that a return to *laissez-faire* in 1945 would have wrought an economic miracle'. Rather, he believed in the necessity of a state-led industrial strategy.[80] Nevertheless, Thatcher's education minister (and ideological mentor) Keith Joseph regarded the book as essential reading.[81] Barnett's 1995 follow-up, which dealt with the 1945–50 period, was distributed to each member of John Major's Cabinet by Deputy Prime Minister Michael Heseltine.[82]

Barnett's work probably appealed to Conservatives less for its detailed policy implications than for its general message – that past errors had led to British decline, which nonetheless, through determined action, could be reversed. But it was not only the (real or alleged) decline of Britain that needed explaining. In 1984, the year of Thatcher's epic battle with the miners, Kenneth O. Morgan published *Labour in Power 1945–1951*. An Oxford-based historian, and later a Labour peer, Morgan had previously written distinguished works on Lloyd George, Keir Hardie, and the politics of his native Wales. He was motivated to write the book in part as 'a response to intense public interest in the Labour Party in power during its heyday after 1945, at a time when the troubled and divided Party of the early 1980s seemed cast into perhaps irreparable decay and decline'. The work gained in interest from the fact that it drew on newly available sources. The moderate Morgan's view of the government's record was essentially positive, but he believed that the freshly revealed Cabinet records showed Bevan to have been justified in his great battle with Gaitskell over rearmament. 'In writing a careful account based on the national archive,' he recalled, 'I had also vindicated a great socialist hero.'[83]

Not all of Morgan's readers accepted this, but in general the book was warmly received. One academic reviewer noted that Attlee had 'become almost a cult-figure; and the agency of his government in shaping post-war Britain is universally acknowledged, whether in celebration or reproach'.[84] The future Labour MP and minister Denis MacShane wrote that the Attlee government served as 'a bottomless source of inspiration and argument' that could be invoked in support of a broad range of Left positions.[85] E. P. Thompson, the renowned historian of the English working-class, was strongly critical of Morgan's book, which in his view underestimated the radicalism of the popular mood of 1945. This had been betrayed, he thought, by the government's acceptance of the logic of the Cold War, 'which led the nation into a waste land of the spirit'. Nevertheless, he argued, Attlee and his ministers deserved credit for creating the NHS (as well as for conceding Indian independence).[86] The merit of a free health service was one of the few things that everyone in the Labour Party could agree upon; the fact that a Marxist scholar could do so too was no trivial fact in this fractious time.

It is worth noting that the legacy of 1945 was now invoked in support of the left-wing version of Scottish nationalism – even though the Attlee government had been resistant to devolution in Scotland and Wales.[87] The NHS, moreover, had become an emblem of UK national identity, albeit one that was always the subject of controversy.[88] During her first term, Thatcher embraced a monetarist agenda at the cost of mass unemployment, but radical proposals to replace the NHS with private health insurance were shelved after a Cabinet revolt.[89] During her second, the pace of privatization accelerated but the health service remained exempt. However, it was not untouched by reform, and complaints about underfunding grew. In 1988, a year after the third Tory election victory in a row, the NHS celebrated its fortieth anniversary. 'I was somewhat surprised to be woken up the other morning by the Secretary of State informing us on the radio that it was not Bevan who formed the NHS in 1948 but Churchill in 1944,' Shadow Health Secretary Robin Cook remarked in the Commons. 'There is, of course, one inconvenient historical fact in that reconstruction of history, which is that every Conservative Member voted against the creation of the NHS on the Third Reading of the Bill.'[90]

Claiming to have served as stewards of the health service during most of its life, the Conservatives did not abolish the broad principle of care free at the point of use. They did, however, whittle away at it, introducing charges for eye tests and dental checks. Of course, in explaining the survival of the NHS in recognizable form, one should not place too much weight on Labour's invocation of the bad old days of charity hospitals dependent on flag days. The fact that the vast majority of patients were satisfied with their care was surely more important than the folk memory of past battles.[91] Nevertheless, Bevan, in particular, remained a name to conjure with. Like Foot, his predecessor, Labour leader Neil Kinnock could claim some measure of affinity with him, 'my fellow countryman, my fellow townsman, my inspiration'.[92] Though he had met Bevan only twice, briefly, as a boy, the young Kinnock was inspired by his writings and oratory. Identified with the 'soft Left' when he took over the leadership, Kinnock wanted to position his party as a moderate, modernizing force. Therefore, he liked to cite, not the rebellious early Bevan, but the more reflective later one.[93] He quoted *In Place of Fear* to challenge those who would be content with nothing less than a complete victory for socialism: 'They are purists and therefore barren.'[94]

After Labour's devastating 1992 defeat, Kinnock was replaced by John Smith, who considered Attlee 'a formidable figure' and shared his low-key style and commitment to full employment.[95] But two years later Smith was killed by a heart attack. Into his shoes stepped Tony Blair, a fresh-faced modernizer who seemed to have blasted in from another planet. His radical revamp of the party under the New Labour banner inaugurated voter-friendly policies and the replacement of Clause 4. It also initiated a new phase of discussion of Labour's traditions, in which debates concerning the Attlee government took a prominent place. Past leaders had often fought the Left, but Blair faced intensified suspicion, partly because he did not seem to 'belong' in the movement. In these conditions, and with considerable initial success, he had to work much harder than his predecessors to legitimize his place in Labour's history. If New Labour's methods were different, he argued, the party's commitment to fairness and justice continued, albeit now liberated from outdated dogma and applied to the modern world.

This was a period in which the scholarship on the Attlee years was developing in complex ways, and one in which historians were themselves trying to work out where Blair fitted into Labour's longer history. There had always been a division between optimists and pessimists; that is, between those who thought that the 1945 government had done a good job in tough conditions, and those who believed that it had squandered its moment. There had been some measure of agreement, though, on Labour's fundamental pragmatism, commendable or otherwise. Now, in addition to new gender and cultural approaches, there were moves to take Labour's socialist ideas more seriously, even if they were judged problematic in many ways.[96] It was suggested, for example, that Labour had *over*rated the radicalism of the populace – that there was a disjuncture between its high-minded hopes for new forms of living and the more individualistic, everyday aspirations of the ordinary citizen.[97] Blair was not, of course, following the academic literature – but this latter argument would have been music to his ears. It implied that Labour needed to drop its own obsessions and get back in touch with the needs and desires of the people.

Moreover, Blair's own arguments did contain significant references to serious historical works. (Though left-wing critics like to describe him as ignorant of Labour's history, what they really meant was that he did not share their interpretation of it, or, more importantly still, their broader values.) Especially striking was his speech given on the fiftieth anniversary of the election that brought Attlee to power. In this he drew on David Marquand's 1991 book *The Progressive Dilemma*. According to Marquand, the central failure of the Labour Party's history was its inability 'to construct an enduring Labour-led equivalent of the heterogeneous, ramshackle, but extraordinarily successful progressive coalition which the Liberals led before the First World War'.[98] Blair used this theme as the basis of his explanation of 1945. 'It was a government that was willing to draw on the resources of the whole progressive tradition,' he said. 'The ideas of Keynes and Beveridge were the cornerstone of reform.' By playing up the contribution of famous Liberals, and subtly downplaying that of Attlee and Bevan, he sought to vindicate his present ambition – the building of a 'big tent' left-of-centre coalition freed from what he regarded as the inconvenient baggage of the past.[99]

Here we see Blair navigating a tricky rhetorical dilemma with considerable skill. He needed, on the one hand, to reassure floating voters, and, on the other, his own party activists. His approach to the Attlee government was part and parcel of a broader agenda, whereby he and his allies distanced themselves aggressively from certain periods and aspects of Labour's history, while asserting that their 'core values' remained those that had motivated the party throughout its life. This meant wrapping themselves in the warm glow of the 1945 victory and its contribution to the welfare state and simultaneously side-lining politically inconvenient aspects of the government's record as outmoded or marginal to its true purposes.

It could thus be admitted that nationalization of industry had been appropriate in its time – even if it was no longer relevant in changed conditions. As Blair's communications guru Peter Mandelson put it in a co-authored book, 'The all-embracing commitment to nationalisation in the infamous Clause IV of Labour's 1918 constitution gave the unfortunate impression that Labour favoured public ownership on principle. The truth is that old Labour's approach to nationalisation was always pragmatic and considered case by case.'[100] At the same time Mandelson tried to blunt some of the hatred targeted at him personally from the party's Left by playing up his own Old Labour connections. His mother was the daughter of Herbert Morrison, and though in truth the two had had little contact, Mandelson claimed that 'from a very early age, I quickly became my grandfather's grandson'.[101] Morrison was, he wrote, 'a consistent moderniser throughout his political career. [...] Of all Labour's leaders in the 1945 government, he understood best the need for political parties constantly to renew their policies and appeal.'[102]

Such arguments would never win over the die-hard opponents of the New Labour project, who could claim that Attlee personified the opposite of Mandelsonian 'spin'. They might, however, blunt left-wing attacks. Just as importantly, they could reassure traditionalists who wanted to believe that Blair really shared their views and was only holding back from saying so due to electoral caution. 'Recently, I spoke to some Party members and said I would spend as high a proportion of our national income in the public sector as Attlee', Blair noted wryly in a 1996 *Observer* article. 'There were murmurs of surprise and relief amongst some of the older members. The young ones thought I had finally lost my bottle.'[103]

Labour's newfound popularity – the product both of its positive appeal and of Tory mismanagement and scandal – helped assuage the doubters. John Major's government received a tiny flicker of encouragement when Attlee's grandson, the third Earl Attlee, announced that he was leaving the cross-benches and joining the Conservatives.[104] But when election day finally came on 1 May 1997, Labour secured a staggering 179 majority – outdoing the 146-seat one it had obtained in 1945. Meantime, Stephen Churchett's play *Tom and Clem* was playing at the Aldwych Theatre. It portrayed an invented meeting between the MP and journalist Tom Driberg and Clement Attlee at Potsdam, just after Labour's victory. In this imagining, Driberg made the case for socialist radicalism and ideological purity; Attlee that for caution and compromise. When another character declared that the Tories had been in power much too long, the audience broke out in applause.[105]

Once in Downing Street, Blair continued to advance and contest historically based arguments, which took on a new dimension as he confronted a series of foreign policy challenges. In a 1998 lecture, Tony Benn – still an MP, though well past the peak of his influence

– drew attention to Attlee's belief in the UN and efforts to restrain Truman over Korea. 'By contrast, a few days ago another Labour Prime Minister flew to Washington to pledge his full support for President Clinton, in launching air strikes against Iraq, in clear contravention of the United Nations Charter.'[106] In the wake of the following year's NATO intervention against Serbia, Blair turned the argument around. He asked delegates at Labour's autumn conference, 'wouldn't Clem Attlee and Ernie Bevin have applauded when in Kosovo, faced with racial genocide in Europe for the first time since they fought fascism in the Second World War, it was Britain and this Government that helped defeat it and set one million people free back to their homeland?'[107]

New Labour's second landslide, in June 2001, was quickly followed by the attacks of 9/11. The launch of the 'War on Terror', the battle against the Taliban, and above all Blair's decision to commit troops to the US invasion of Iraq, derailed what until that point had been a fairly successful administration. In the summer of 2003, as he faced mounting criticism, Blair surpassed Attlee as the longest continuously serving Labour Prime Minister. In anticipation of the moment, he reminded his party that his esteemed predecessor had not always been universally admired. Addressing a Fabian Society audience, he began by quoting a 1954 *New Statesman* profile of Attlee. It was, he said, notable for the lack of any reference to the creation of the NHS and for its judgement on the 1945 government. He offered a quotation: 'it was the only event of its kind in history which contributed almost nothing new or imaginative to the pool of ideas with which men seek to illuminate human nature and its environment'. In fact, the article had also said that Labour's programme had been 'perfectly fitted' to the problems of post-war adjustment; and to suggest that the period had not generated new *ideas* was at any rate not unfair. But this single example gave Blair the opportunity to argue that Labour was now repeating its history of ingratitude: 'Once more the left's laudable restlessness is mingling with what seems to be the equally strong impulse to decry.'[108]

Although he achieved an historic third election victory in 2005, on a reduced share of the vote, Blair never recovered his momentum. His long-standing rival Gordon Brown took over two years later and soon faced the challenge of a global financial crisis. As he and his advisers crafted a successful emergency response, the talk in the media was of Keynes more than Attlee, but after Labour's 2010 defeat there was a

resurgence of discussion of the legacy of 1945. Under the Cameron–
Clegg coalition, the UK faced a new era of austerity. This was not
a time of physical controls and rationing driven by global shortages.
Rather, it was one of brutal and unnecessary public spending cuts
driven by a combination of free market ideology and astute political
calculus. In a sign of the developing culture wars, the government even
pressured director Danny Boyle to cut a sequence paying tribute to the
NHS from the opening ceremony of the 2012 London Olympics. He
stood firm.[109]

Labour's new leader, Ed Miliband, provided an analysis very different
to that given by his father Ralph in *Parliamentary Socialism*. The younger
Miliband was influenced by Blue Labour, a ginger group that wanted
to combine conservative social values with left-wing economics. Jon
Cruddas MP, one of its leading lights, portrayed Attlee, not as a statist
centralizer but as a romantic utopian in the ILP tradition. Cruddas
highlighted his 'democratic patriotism' and his 'leadership built on the
notions of duty, responsibility, loyalty and courage – and to a party
respectful of ordinary, parochial culture, not elite and remote'.[110]

This interpretation fitted Miliband's agenda. He wanted to present
Labour as patriotic without being nationalist, and radical without
being irresponsible. In his 2012 conference speech, he tried to channel
Disraeli and Attlee simultaneously, an awkward pairing placed in service
of the short-lived theme of 'One Nation Labour'.[111] The following year,
Miliband tried to assuage supporters concerned about his decision to
accept some of the coalition's planned limits on spending. He said that
he admired the Attlee government because of its willingness to take
tough decisions. Though it was remembered for creating the NHS, it
had also run a budget surplus, he pointed out. 'This is a government
that banned the import of sardines because they were worried about
the balance of payments. It shows a government can be remembered in
difficult times for doing great things.'[112]

These attempts to claim Attlee for the Centre were matched by
others to secure him for the Left. The 2013 documentary *The Spirit of
'45* was directed by Ken Loach, who was known for powerful dramas
such as *Cathy Come Home* and *The Wind that Shakes the Barley*. It drew
praise for its powerful combination of archival and interview footage,
for its humanity, and for its 'rousing and saddening' reminder of post-
war progress and what had been subsequently lost.[113] But it was also

criticized, including by some Labour sympathizers, for its superficial and nostalgic quality. The political scientist and historian Steven Fielding wrote: 'it peddles a fantasy, albeit one that provides comfort during these hard times for some on the left'.[114] Philip French, the veteran *Observer* critic, described it as 'an over-extended party political broadcast for a phantom old Labour party that is forever waiting in the wings' and as 'a thin, misleading and sentimental account of history'.[115]

Yet the film repays close attention. On the one hand, though there was no narrator or single authorial voice, Loach was undoubtedly pushing a betrayal narrative and a critique of the current Labour leadership. 'Miliband is talking about this socially responsible capitalism,' remarked one interviewee. 'It's a bit like the Arabian phoenix, isn't it? Everyone's heard about it, nobody's ever seen one.'[116] On the other hand, actual criticism of the Attlee government itself was muted. There was some comment on the failure to develop a system of workers' control in the nationalized industries. Yet Labour's very mixed colonial record, its approach to the Cold War, and even the Bevan–Gaitskell dispute, were entirely ignored. There was no mention of or explanation for the 1951 defeat, but merely a disconcerting cut from the Festival of Britain to Thatcher on the steps of Downing Street quoting St Francis of Assisi.

Nor – in contrast, for example, to E. P. Thompson's 1980s comments – did the film assert that the British people had been burning with socialist belief in 1945. In a promotional interview, Loach highlighted the mood of 'never again' and the desire to use wartime methods to win the peace: 'Not that the people were filled with an ideological conviction, not at all, it was a matter of common sense.'[117] Thus, though many of the contributors had Far Left backgrounds, the film gave a feel-good portrayal of the Attlee government in place of the radical analysis that might have been expected. It was better to own Attlee than to attack him for breach of promise. The documentary contributed to the atmosphere in which, following Labour's further defeat in 2015, Jeremy Corbyn won the party leadership. 'Corbynites were right to believe it was advantageous to claim Labour's 1945 moment as their own', Fielding notes. 'It legitimized their resetting of the party's direction amongst members most of whom regarded the period positively if hazily.'[118]

The Corbynist interpretation of 1940s history was, of course, contested. A weighty contribution came from John Bew, Professor in History and Foreign Policy at King's College London, author of a study of Lord Castlereagh and an expert on *realpolitik*. Bew was not a tribal Labour figure: he later served as foreign policy adviser to Johnson, Truss and Sunak. In writing a hefty new biography, he was inspired by Cruddas's distinction between the 'orthodox' interpretation of Attlee and the 'unorthodox' one. Whereas the orthodox figure was simply an efficient and pragmatic chairman, the unorthodox one was a committed idealist and patriot inspired by nineteenth-century utopianism. Published in 2016, Bew's book *Citizen Clem* won multiple prizes and became a bestseller. It poked fun at Corbyn supporters who had taken to wearing T-shirts bearing the legend 'What Would Clement Do?' and argued that Corbyn himself marked 'a distinct break from the political tradition in which Attlee stood'.[119]

Following the loss of the 2019 general election and the accession of Keir Starmer as leader, Labour faced the problem of trying to win back northern 'Red Wall' seats that had fallen to the Tories. One of the challenges was to re-establish the party's patriotic credentials, which had been called into question during the Corbyn years. The Cruddas/Bew version of Attlee might have been invoked to this end, but perhaps Starmer recalled the pitfalls suffered by Miliband and others. Rather than attempt complex arguments that might run counter to Labour members' strongly held feelings about 1945, it was perhaps wiser to keep things simple. In 2021, as the Covid pandemic ebbed, Starmer urged a rethink of free market orthodoxy, and urged a call to arms, 'like the Beveridge Report was in the 1940s'.[120] This raised the question of how radical he was really intending to be.[121] But he could rely on the press to suggest that he was emulating Attlee without having to mention him at every turn.[122] As the Tories began to implode under the weight of their own incompetence, Starmer could also depend on many commentators to make the stock comparison between his restrained personality and that of his downbeat but distinguished predecessor. One *FT* journalist even paired Starmer and Joe Biden as the new Attlee and Truman – underestimated men with unspectacular reputations that belied the weight of evidence.[123]

Starmer's decision not to discuss the historical parallels explicitly or in depth was one that made considerable sense. Cultural memory of the Second World War remains powerful, even though most people who experienced the conflict are now dead, but debates about the 1945 government have always been of more interest to Labour audiences than to national ones. As far back as the 1980s, the party's pollsters had spotted that Attlee references were increasingly lost on younger voters.[124] In contrast to Churchill, Attlee has avoided the extremes of posthumous glorification and vilification. His reputation has benefited from an expert consensus on his virtues, and he remains a touchstone for media commentators, but he does not function as a lightning conductor for British collective feeling. Rather, it is the institutions of the welfare state, and the NHS in particular, that command popular enthusiasm (and if one individual is taken to represent these it is Bevan rather than Attlee). However, when it comes to sheer electoral achievement, it is still 1945, rather than other landmarks such as 1924, 1964 and 1997, that carries the greatest emotional charge. And even if Starmer gains a victory that exceeds it in statistical terms, his government will inevitably have to battle under the weight of the symbolism of an event that took place almost four-score years ago. In that sense, the myth and memory of the Attlee years are not just Labour's legacy but also its burden.

Conclusion

In 1995, in the foreword to a new edition of his superb biography of Hugh Dalton, Professor Ben Pimlott reflected on the origins of the book, which had first appeared ten years earlier. It had been researched and written as Thatcherism triumphed and the Labour Party tore itself apart. Pimlott, himself a Labour candidate in the 1970s, was a moderate, but in spite of the excesses of the Bennite Left he was not tempted to join the SDP. 'Writing about Dalton became a refuge from much that was sterile in the present,' Pimlott acknowledged later.

> In an ideological decade of political saints and villains, I remember hoping that the contradictions of Dalton's personality would puzzle and befuddle Labour's rival tribalists. At the same time, I wanted to remind defectors of the rich traditions they were deserting; and to suggest that expectations of Labour's imminent demise [...] did not take account of deep and multifarious roots.[1]

Though not all scholars of the Labour Party have shared Pimlott's sense of missionary zeal, none of us can wholly extract ourselves from the preoccupations of our own time. That is true for this book as much as any, and though I have not been conscious of writing for any direct purpose in the present, I cannot claim that my historical assessments have been uninfluenced by my own politics. Readers will have deduced that I am dismayed, for example, by the Attlee government's failure to abolish hanging, and also by the Seretse Khama affair, which was symbolic of a distinctly mixed imperial record. I have found much to admire, on the other hand, in the government's conduct of domestic and international economic matters. And I am forced to concede that, in the field of foreign policy, it is hard to identify a credible alternative to the rather uninspiring course that Bevin established. In terms of prescriptions for today, laying down 'lessons from the past' is always risky. But how on earth can one learn, if not from things that have previously happened?

To offer detailed policy recommendations to today's Labour Party would be to court immediate irrelevance. Instead, here, I content myself with offering three broad conclusions with potential applicability, not only for the UK, but also for progressive parties elsewhere. Taken together, they might offer inspiration for those undertaking the hardest of political tasks: not merely kindling a mood of optimism in advance of an election but sustaining it in office after victory is won.

First, leadership. Attlee's model was not perfect. One can understand the frustration of those who felt let down when he bowed to the feeling of a meeting rather than fight for a proposal to which he had previously appeared sympathetic. But on balance his reliance on collective decision-making rather than self-assertion was a strength, and his methods helped ensure that government business progressed efficiently, rather than getting stuck in the mire of endless debate. And although his personal interactions with colleagues could be awkward, his incomparable knowledge of his own MPs is something any leader should aspire to emulate. Knowing what each of your supporters will want in any given situation is valuable. Knowing that the one you need to contact can be found at that exact moment eating kippers in the Commons tearoom is priceless.[2]

Moreover, Attlee's placid demeanour – often compared to that of a schoolmaster or bank manager – was an important element of his success. While he was in office, the Conservatives sharpened their rhetoric against the workers and claimed that the government was acting only in the interests of this single class.[3] In an obituary piece, Woodrow Wyatt told readers that it was due to Attlee 'that Labour's social revolution was accepted by the middle classes'. Nationalization, the NHS and Indian independence might not have seemed like much to *New Statesman* readers in 1967,

but it was a hell of a packet then. If it had been accompanied by provocative language, by jeering at middle-class conventions, there could have been upheaval. But Attlee made it sound so respectable, if not dull, that he soothed his opponents and even made his followers, frequently to their irritation, think nothing was happening.[4]

A progressive party should at any rate aspire to govern in the interests of the entire nation, and to present itself as doing so is no sell-out. On the contrary, it can be a potent political weapon that can sometimes achieve what more overt radicalism cannot.

Second, public ownership. Nationalization has had a bad press, sometimes because of developments that occurred decades after Attlee had left No. 10. There was merit in the argument that the Morrisonian model did not do enough to involve or energize the workers, but perhaps Morrison himself should have been listened to more as well. Though his concept of 'consolidation' was politically unsexy, making sure that state industries worked better across the board might have given public ownership a more viable future. For although we can now see that there are many sectors where private ownership is indeed the right solution, there are others where privatization has failed spectacularly. Gas companies blatantly exploit customers while making billions in profits; water companies spew raw sewage into the sea. In fact, since the onset of the global financial crisis, governments of both complexions have undertaken nationalizations, albeit usually in a shamefaced way as an emergency or temporary solution. This has mainly applied to failing banks and to parts of the railway system; though the probation service was taken back into public hands in 2021 after a disastrous privatization. Nationalization should not be a dogma but rather a pragmatic policy response in cases where it is necessary – as Labour's leaders believed in 1945.

Third, the framing of the debate. Faced with choosing between 'the free market' and 'socialism', most people will opt for the former. But the choice is a false one. As the economist James K. Galbraith has pointed out, we do 'not actually live under the benign sovereignty of the "free market"'.[5] Instead we live in an economy dominated by price-fixing and cartels and, increasingly, one of cronyism and corruption. This is not to say that all private firms are guilty of abuses. It is important to avoid the mistake, which the Attlee government arguably committed, of appearing hostile to business in general. But the truth is that the free market does not exist, that it possibly never has existed, and that perhaps it never can exist (at least not in the form that its advocates would have us believe). Indeed, intelligent state regulation is needed to secure the very advantages that supposedly belong to the free market (as the history of the EU single market demonstrates). The problem must therefore be reframed – as in 1945 – as one of 'public control' in the interests of the many versus private control in the interests of the few. Put that way, the case becomes emotionally as well as intellectually compelling.

Finally, it may seem that the current moment is a poor one for launching a new radical project. The UK is struggling with the consequences of Brexit, of the Covid pandemic, of climate change, and of the ongoing war in Ukraine. But if Thomas Piketty is correct that the destruction of the world wars paved the way for decades of greater equality, then today's crises may have a silver lining too. Though it would not be without its trials, perhaps a new Age of Hope is just around the corner.

Notes

INTRODUCTION

1. Adele Toye, 'Why Churchill Was Defeated', *Middletown Press*, 4 Sept. 1945.
2. Adele Toye, 'War Diary', *Middletown Press*, 29 Oct. 1938.
3. Adele Toye, 'Why Churchill Was Defeated'.
4. Ibid.
5. These debates are discussed in depth in the final chapter.
6. A classic statement of this view can be found in Ralph Miliband, *Parliamentary Socialism: A Study in the Politics of Labour*, Allen & Unwin, London, 1961.
7. Teddy Brett, Steve Gilliatt and Andrew Pople, 'Planned Trade, Labour Party Policy and US Intervention: The Successes and Failures of Post-War Reconstruction', *History Workshop*, 13 (spring, 1982), pp. 130–42.
8. Steven Fielding, 'What Did "the People" Want? The Meaning of the 1945 General Election', *Historical Journal*, 35 (1992), pp. 623–39; Steven Fielding, Peter Thompson and Nick Tiratsoo, *'England Arise!' The Labour Party and Popular Politics in 1940s Britain*, Manchester University Press, Manchester, 1995.
9. Lawrence Black, *The Political Culture of the Left in Britain, 1951–64: Old Labour, New Britain?*, Palgrave Macmillan, Basingstoke, 2002.
10. The texts of all manifestos cited can be found in F. W. S. Craig (ed.), *British General Election Manifestos, 1900–1974*, The Macmillan Press Ltd, London and Basingstoke, 1975.
11. *Speaker's Handbook 1945*, Labour Party, London, 1945, p. 48.
12. Gerald Crompton, '"Good Business for the Nation": The Railway Nationalisation Issue, 1921–47', *Journal of Transport History*, 20 (1999), pp. 141–59; Geoffrey William Buttle, 'A Signal Failure? The Organisation and Management of British Railways 1948–1964', PhD thesis, Durham University, 2008; Jeremy Hartill, 'British Railway Shipping 1948–1984: A Nationalised Success Story', MA research thesis, University of York, 2014; Andrew Jenkins, 'Government Intervention in the British Gas Industry, 1948 to 1970', *Business History*, 46 (2004), pp. 57–78.
13. Ina Zweiniger-Bargielowska, *Austerity in Britain: Rationing, Controls, and Consumption, 1939–1955*, Oxford University Press, Oxford, 2000.

14 Thomas Piketty, *Capital in the Twenty-First Century*, The Belknap Press, Cambridge, MA, 2014, p. 20.

15 Paul Gilroy, *Postcolonial Melancholia*, Columbia University Press, New York, 2005, Chapter 3.

16 David Edgerton, 'The Nationalisation of British History: Historians, Nationalism and the Myths of 1940', *English Historical Review*, 136 (2021), pp. 950–85; Sean Dettman and Richard Toye, 'The Discourse of "The people's war" in Britain and the USA during World War II: A Reply to David Edgerton', *English Historical Review*, forthcoming. Though Dettman and I dissent from Edgerton's claim that the term 'people's war' was little used during the war itself, we agree with him that it gained renewed currency during the 1960s.

17 Cummings, 'I Predict', *Daily Express*, 8 Aug. 1958.

18 Richard Jobson, *Nostalgia and the Post-War Labour Party: Prisoners of the Past*, Manchester University Press, Manchester, 2018.

19 Shirley Williams, *Climbing the Bookshelves*, Virago Press, London, 2009, p. 387.

20 Evelyn Waugh, 'Aspirations of a Mugwump', *The Spectator*, 2 Oct. 1959.

21 Ernest Bevin to Seymour Cocks, 5 Jan. 1946, Bevin Papers, Churchill Archives Centre (henceforward CAC), BEVN II 6/2. For an earlier precedent, see Julie Gottlieb, 'An Epidemic of Nervous Breakdowns and the Crisis Suicides: Britain's War of Nerves, 1938–1940', forthcoming.

22 Douglas Jay, 'Attlee: A Memorial', *The House Magazine*, 15 Apr. 1963, copy in Jay Papers, MS.6745/140.

23 Roy Jenkins, *Mr. Attlee: An Interim Biography*, William Heinemann Ltd, London, 1948; Kenneth Harris, *Attlee*, Weidenfeld & Nicolson, London, 1982. Both books were written with Attlee's cooperation. Jenkins's took the story only as far as 1945. Harris's was reissued in a new edition in 1995, and it is this version that is cited in subsequent references.

24 Trevor Burridge, *Clement Attlee: A Political Biography*, Jonathan Cape, London, 1985; Jerry H. Brookshire, *Clement Attlee*, Manchester University Press, Manchester, 1995; Francis Beckett, *Clem Attlee*, Richard Cohen Books, London, 1997; David Howell, *Attlee*, Haus, London, 2006; John Bew, *Citizen Clem: A Biography of Attlee*, Riverrun, London, 2016; Nicklaus Thomas-Symonds, *Attlee: A Life in Politics*, I.B. Tauris, London, 2010; Leo McKinstry, *Attlee and Churchill: Allies in War, Adversaries in Peace*, Atlantic Books, London, 2019. See also Geoffrey Dellar (ed.), *Attlee as I Knew Him*, Tower Hamlets Library Service, London, 1983.

25 Stephen Hart, *James Chuter Ede: Humane Reformer and Politician*, Pen & Sword, Barnsley, 2021; D. Ben Rees, *Jim: The Life and Work of the Rt. Hon. James Griffiths*, Modern Welsh Publications, Allerton, Liverpool, 2021.

26 Nevertheless, sterling work has been done on the lesser-known figures of this and other periods by contributors to the *Dictionary of Labour Biography*. The most recent instalment is Keith Gildart and David Howell (eds), *Dictionary of Labour Biography; Vol. XV*, Palgrave Macmillan, London, 2019.

27 Kenneth O. Morgan, *Labour In Power 1945–1951*, Clarendon Press, Oxford, 1984; Peter Hennessy, *Never Again: Britain, 1945–51*, Jonathan Cape, London, 1992; David Kynaston, *Austerity Britain, 1945–51*, Bloomsbury, London, 2007.

28 Stuart Ward, *Untied Kingdom: A Global History of the End of Britain*, Cambridge University Press, Cambridge, 2023, pp. 103–4.

29 Ben Pimlott (ed.), *The Political Diary of Hugh Dalton: 1918–40, 1945–60*, Jonathan Cape, London, 1986, p. 472 (entry for 28 Feb. 1950).

30 Felicity Harwood, 'Clem: Father and Politician', Attlee Memorial lecture, 20 Feb. 1985, https://attleefoundation.org/wp-content/uploads/2022/12/Attlee-Foundation -Lecture-1985-Lady-Felicity-Harwood.pdf (consulted 15 Feb. 2023). There have been three separate series of Attlee memorial lectures. The Attlee Memorial Foundation, founded in 1967, established its series in 1983. Harwood's lecture was part of it. University College Oxford launched its own in 2011. Haileybury College has a series too.

31 Keith Gildart, 'Séance Sitters, Ghost Hunters, Spiritualists, and Theosophists: Esoteric Belief and Practice in the British Parliamentary Labour Party, c. 1929–51', *Twentieth Century British History*, 29 (2018), pp. 357–87.

32 'Spiritualist MP takes his seat in Beyond', *Spiritualist News*, 5 March 1983; Parliamentary Debates, House of Commons, Fifth Series, Vol. 481, 1 Dec. 1950, cols 1464–6; Marc David Collinson and Keith Gildart, 'Rogers, George Henry Roland (1906–1983)', in Gildart and Howell, *Dictionary of Labour Biography; Vol. XV*, pp. 209–20.

33 To give but one example, my request to see closed extracts (IND/49/10, 12 and 19) from the UK National Archives file FO 800/470 was denied under Section 27(1) subsections (a)(c)(d) of the Freedom of Information Act. These exempt information that, if it was released, could put at risk relations between the UK and any other state, the interests of the UK abroad, or the UK's ability to promote or protect its interests. It is clear that the suppressed information relates to India and/or Pakistan in 1949, but beyond that one can only speculate.

34 Adele Toye, 'The Launching', in ACCO, *Child Care 1949–1970: ACCO – A Souvenir Portrait 1949–1970*, Association of Child Care Officers, London, 1970, pp. 63–6, at 65.

CHAPTER I

1 Stuart Ball (ed.), *Parliament and Politics in the Age of Churchill and Attlee: The Headlam Diaries 1935–1951*, Cambridge University Press for the Royal Historical Society, London, 1999, pp. 472–3 (entry for 1 Aug. 1945).

2 Geoffrey de Freitas and Helen de Freitas, *The Slighter Side of a Long Public Life*, privately published, 1985, p. 62.

3 'The Curtain Rises on the New Parliament', *Manchester Guardian*, 2 Aug. 1945; Hugh Dalton, *The Fateful Years: Memoirs 1931–1945*, Frederick Muller Ltd, London, 1957, p. 479; Lord Morrison, *Herbert Morrison: An Autobiography*, Odhams Press Ltd, London, 1960, p. 251.

4 'The London Letter', *Aberdeen Journal*, 2 Aug. 1945.

5 Morrison, *Autobiography*, p. 251.

6 Parliamentary Debates, House of Commons, Fifth Series, Vol. 413, 1 Aug. 1945, col. 7.

7 'Janus' [Wilson Harris], 'A Spectator's Notebook', *The Spectator*, 3 Aug. 1945.

8 Dean Acheson, *Present at the Creation: My Years in the State Department*, W. W. Norton & Co., New York, 1969, p. 301.

9 Jennie Lee, 'As I Please', *Tribune*, 10 Aug. 1945.

10 Paul Ward, *Red Flag and Union Jack: Englishness, Patriotism, and the British Left, 1881–1924*, Boydell Press for the Royal Historical Society, Woodbridge, 1998, p. 202.

11 Jason Whittaker, *Jerusalem: Blake, Parry, and the Fight for Englishness*, Oxford University Press, Oxford, 2022, p. 123.

12 Kingsley Martin, 'The Webbs in retirement', in Margaret Cole (ed.), *The Webbs and Their Work*, Frederick Muller Ltd, London, 1949, pp. 285–301, at 287.

13 Ben Pimlott, *Hugh Dalton*, Jonathan Cape, London, 1985, p. 74.

14 C. R. Attlee, *As It Happened*, William Heinemann Ltd, London, 1954, p. 4.

15 Harold Wilson, *A Prime Minister on Prime Ministers*, Book Club Associates, London, 1977, p. 128.

16 Clement Attlee to Janet Shipton, 7 Jan. 1964, Attlee Papers (Bodleian), MS.CRA.3.

17 Bew, *Citizen Clem*, pp. 21–3, 97–105.

18 Morrison, *Autobiography*, p. 24.

19 'Profile – Ernest Bevin', *Observer*, 23 May 1948.

20 Alan Bullock, *Ernest Bevin: Foreign Secretary*, Heinemann, London, 1983, p. 82.

21 Eric Estorick, *Stafford Cripps*, William Heinemann Ltd, London, 1949, p. 21.

22 Stafford Cripps diary, 5 Oct. 1918, Cripps Papers, MS. 9661/1.

23 Richard Stafford Cripps, *Towards Christian Democracy*, The Philosophical Library, New York, 1946, p. 2.

24 Bernard Donoughue and G. W. Jones, *Herbert Morrison: Portrait of a Politician*, Weidenfeld & Nicolson, London, 1973, pp. 51, 60.

25 W. W. Knox, 'Religion and the Scottish Labour Movement c. 1900–39', *Journal of Contemporary History*, 23 (1988), pp. 609–30, at 610.

26 Mark Bevir, 'The Labour Church Movement, 1891–1902', *Journal of British Studies*, 38 (1999), pp. 217–45.

27 Gildart, 'Séance Sitters, Ghost Hunters, Spiritualists, and Theosophists', pp. 357–87.

28 For this distinction, see H. M. Drucker, *Doctrine and Ethos in the Labour Party*, George Allen & Unwin Ltd, London, 1979.

29 Beatrice Webb to Mary Playne, Sept. 1908, Norman MacKenzie (ed.), *Letters of Sidney and Beatrice Webb; Vol. II: Partnership 1892–1912*, Cambridge University Press, Cambridge, 1978, p. 316.

30 The quotation is from Cripps, *Towards Christian Democracy*, p. 19. Morrison would have chosen a recording of 'Jerusalem' as one of his *Desert Island Discs* selections, had he been invited to appear. Donoughue and Jones, *Herbert Morrison*, p. 559.

31 Attlee to Roy Jenkins, 20 Jan. 1947, Jenkins Papers, MSS. Jenkins 359.

32 Harris, *Attlee*, p. 564.

33 Janice Norwood, 'The performance of protest: The 1889 dock strike on and off the stage', in Peter Yeandle, Katherine Newey and Jeffrey Richards (eds), *Politics, Performance and Popular Culture: Theatre and Society in Nineteenth-Century Britain*, Manchester University Press, Manchester, 2016, pp. 237–58.

34 'Our London Correspondence' and 'Mr. James Connell', *Manchester Guardian*, 11 Feb. 1929.

35 Andrew Boyd, *Jim Connell: Author of the Red Flag*, Donaldson Archives/Socialist History Society Occasional Papers No. 13, p. 11. For a contrasting account, see Tom Smallwood to the editor of the *Daily Herald*, published 13 Feb. 1929.

36 George Bernard Shaw, 'The Superior Person at the Labor Conference', *The Clarion*, 5 Feb. 1909.

37 Bevir, 'Labour Church Movement', p. 217.

38 See Frank Trentmann, *Free Trade Nation: Commerce, Consumption, and Civil Society in Modern Britain*, Oxford University Press, Oxford, 2008.

39 T. Dundas Pillans to the editor of the *Observer*, published 1 March 1914.

40 Transcript of interview for 'Lord Attlee Remembers', BBC Home Service, 21 Apr. 1963, Attlee Papers (Bodleian), MS.CRA.11.

41 'Morel, the War and the Peace', *Dundee Courier*, 13 Nov. 1922.

42 Hugh Dalton, *With British Guns in Italy: A Tribute to Italian Achievement*, Methuen & Co. Ltd, London, 1919.

43 'Election Campaign in the West', *Western Daily Press*, 7 Dec. 1918.

44 Duncan Tanner, 'The Parliamentary Electoral System, the "Fourth" Reform Act and the Rise of Labour in England and Wales', *Historical Research*, 56 (1983), pp. 205–19; Peter Clarke, 'In Memoriam: Duncan Tanner', *Twentieth Century British History*, 21 (2010), pp. 137–40; David Jarvis, 'British Conservatism and Class Politics in the 1920s', *English Historical Review*, CXI (1996), pp. 59–84.

45 *Daily News*, 29 July 1921, quoted in 'The Failure of the Opposition', *The Lloyd George Liberal Magazine*, Aug. 1921.

46 See, notably, Sidney and Beatrice Longman's & Co. Webb, *A Constitution for the Socialist Commonwealth of Great Britain*, London, 1920.

47 G. D. H. Cole, *Guild Socialism*, Fabian Society, London, 1920, p. 6.

48 John Stephen Enderby, 'The English Radical Tradition and the British Left 1885–1945', PhD thesis, Sheffield Hallam University, 2019, p. 16.

49 Attlee, *As It Happened*, p. 53.

50 Quoted in G. D. H. Cole, *History of the Labour Party from 1914*, Routledge & Kegan Paul, London, 1948, p. 104.

51 Alan Bullock, *The Life and Times of Ernest Bevin; Volume 1: Trade Union Leader 1881–1940*, Heinemann, London, 1960, p. 134. Contrary to legend, it is unlikely that the episode had an impact on government policy: Norman Davies, 'Lloyd George and Poland, 1919–20', *Journal of Contemporary History*, 6 (1971), pp. 132–54.

52 See, for example, David Englander, 'The National Union of Ex-Servicemen and the Labour Movement, 1918–1920', *History*, 76 (1991), pp. 24–42, at 38.

53 'Labour Party Medley', *Daily Mail*, 28 Oct. 1922.

54 L. MacNeill Weir, *The Tragedy of Ramsay MacDonald: A Political Biography*, Secker & Warburg, London, 1938, pp. 110–11.

55 Attlee, *As It Happened*, p. 58.

56 Transcript of interview with Vi Attlee in 'Lord Attlee Remembers'.

57 Parliamentary Debates, House of Commons, Fifth Series, Vol. 159, 23 Nov. 1922, cols 94–6.

58 Attlee, *As It Happened*, pp. 58–9.

59 Emrys Hughes, 'Attlee', n.d. but post-1955, Hughes Papers, Dep.176/18.

60 Transcript of interview for 'Lord Attlee Remembers'.

61 'The Debate', *Daily Herald*, 24 Nov. 1922; 'What Will They Do With It?', *Daily Herald*, 25 Nov. 1922.

62 'Frightfulness in Parliament', *Morning Post*, 25 Nov. 1922.

63 Robert S. Angus, 'The New House', *The Man In the Street*, May 1925. Privately, though, some Conservatives thought that the media was exaggerating. Earl Winterton wrote in his diary for 24 November 1922: 'The press is making a lot of the "new spirit" infused by the Labour Phalanx, but all that they say might be a rehash of what they said [about the Liberal election victory] in 1906 and I think this is a smaller bouleversement than that.' Winterton Papers, 30.

64 David Kirkwood to the editor of *The New Leader*, dated 26 March 1923 and published in the issue of 30 March.

65 'Politics & Work', *New Leader*, 15 Dec. 1922.

66 'Uproar In the Commons', *The Times*, 12 Apr. 1923.

67 David Howell, *MacDonald's Party: Labour Identities and Crisis 1922–1931*, Oxford University Press, Oxford, 2002, pp. 29, 37; Henry Snell, *Daily Life in Parliament*, G. Routledge & Sons, London, 1930, p. 50; 'The Man in the House', 'Inside the House', *The Man In the Street*, Feb. 1926.

68 F. John Sherwood, 'If Socialists Ruled', *The Popular View*, May 1923.

69 'That Reminds Me, By R.W.A.', *Lloyd George Liberal Magazine*, May 1923.

70 'Hymns V. "Red Flag"', *Aberdeen Journal*, 5 Oct. 1922.

71 Hugh Dalton, *Call Back Yesterday: Memoirs 1887–1931*, Frederick Muller Ltd, London, 1953, p. 143; Ralph Miliband, *Parliamentary Socialism: A Study in the Politics of Labour* (2nd edn), Merlin Press, London, 1972, p. 95, n. 1.

72 'London Letter', *Exeter and Plymouth Gazette*, 9 Jan. 1924.

73 Stanley Baldwin to George V, 17 Jan. 1924, Baldwin Papers, Vol. 60; Arthur Ponsonby, 'On the Eve of Historic Change', *New Leader*, 18 Jan. 1924.

74 William Wedgwood Benn diary, 21 Jan. 1924, Stansgate Papers, ST/66. Benn – whose son Tony was to eclipse him in fame – was to serve as a Cabinet minister under both MacDonald and Attlee. He was exactly the kind of convert that MacDonald wanted to woo, though many other Liberal defectors were less fortunate and struggled to adjust to Labour's union-dominated culture. See Alun Wyburn-Powell, *Defectors and the Liberal Party 1910–2010: A Study of Inter-Party Relationships*, Manchester University Press, Manchester, 2012.

75 David Marquand, *Ramsay MacDonald*, Jonathan Cape, London, 1977, p. 304.

76 '"The Red Flag"', *The Times*, 22 Jan. 1924.

77 Jack Lawson, *A Man's Life*, Hodder & Stoughton, London, 1944, p. 167.

78 Ramsay MacDonald diary, 2 March 1924, PRO 30/69/1753, The National Archives, Kew, London (henceforward TNA). Anyone wishing to refer to these diaries is obliged to explain that MacDonald meant them simply 'as notes to guide and revive memory' and did not intend them to be published.

79 John Shepherd and Keith Laybourn, *Britain's First Labour Government*, Palgrave Macmillan, Houndmills, Basingstoke, 2006, p. 199.

80 Attlee, *As It Happened*, pp. 60–1.

81 Ian Wood, *John Wheatley*, Manchester University Press, Manchester, 1990, p. 142.

82 'Mr. Bevin', *Daily Mail*, 28 March 1924.

83 Francis Williams, *Ernest Bevin: Portrait of a Great Englishman*, Hutchinson, London, 1952, p. 122; 'Mr. Bevin Urges Acceptance of the Terms', *Manchester Guardian*, 31 March 1924.

84 Roland Atkinson, 'Our Paris Letter', *Sunday Times*, 7 Sept. 1924.

85 Labour Party Manifesto, 1924.

86 Attlee, *As It Happened*, pp. 60–1.

87 Parliamentary Debates, House of Commons, Fifth Series, Vol. 171, 17 March 1924, col. 125.

88 Harris, *Attlee*, p. 64.

89 Lucian M. Ashworth, 'Rethinking a Socialist Foreign Policy: The British Labour Party and International Relations Experts, 1918 to 1931', *International Labor and Working-Class History*, 75 (2009), pp. 30–48.

90 Howell, *MacDonald's Party*, Chapter 22.

91 'Red Army Strength', *Daily Telegraph*, 5 July 1924.

92 W. P. Coates and Zelda K. Coates, *A History of Anglo-Soviet Relations*, Lawrence & Wishart and the Pilot Press, London, 1945, pp. 577–8; Paul Corthorn, 'Labour, the Left, and the Stalinist Purges of the Late 1930s', *Historical Journal*, 48 (2005), pp. 179–207.

93 C. R. Attlee, 'Labour Party and Labour Government', *New Leader*, 3 Oct. 1924.

94 'Civil War Plot By Socialists' Masters', *Daily Mail*, 25 Oct. 1924.

95 Gill Bennett, *The Zinoviev Letter: The Conspiracy That Never Dies*, Oxford University Press, Oxford, 2018, p. 253.

96 Dalton, *Call Back Yesterday*, p. 155.

97 Laura Beers, 'A Model MP? Ellen Wilkinson, Gender, Politics and Celebrity Culture in Interwar Britain', *Cultural and Social History*, 10 (2013), pp. 231–50.

98 'The "Red Flag" a Ditty', *Sunday Times*, 10 May 1925.

99 Boyd, *Jim Connell*, pp. 33–4; '"Red Flag" Triumphs', *Daily Herald*, 5 Nov. 1925.

100 'The Red Flag', *Halifax Daily Courier*, 12 May 1925.

101 Malcolm Petrie, '"Contests of vital importance": By-elections, the Labour Party, and the Reshaping of British Radicalism, 1924–1929', *Historical Journal*, 60 (2017), pp. 121–48, at pp. 121, 125, 145.

102 *Labour and the Nation*, revised edition, Labour Party, London, n.d. but 1928, pp. 13–14.

103 'Farewell to Jim Connell', *Daily Herald*, 15 Feb. 1929.

104 Adrian Bingham, '"Stop the Flapper Vote Folly": Lord Rothermere, the *Daily Mail*, and the Equalization of the Franchise 1927–28', *Twentieth Century British History*, 13 (2002), pp. 17–37.

105 Philip Williamson, '"Safety First": Baldwin, the Conservative Party, and the 1929 General Election', *Historical Journal*, 25 (1982), pp. 385–409; 'Red Flag Bogy', *Daily Herald*, 27 May 1929.

106 'Labour's Final Town Hall Rally', *Dover Express*, 31 May 1929.

107 John Campbell, *Lloyd George: The Goat in the Wilderness, 1922–1931*, Jonathan Cape, London, 1977, Chapter 8; Michael Dawson, 'Liberalism in Devon and Cornwall, 1910–1931: "The Old-Time Religion"', *Historical Journal*, 38 (1995), pp. 425–37, at 430.

108 Donoughue and Jones, *Herbert Morrison*, p. 144.

109 Parliamentary Debates, House of Commons, Fifth Series, Vol. 230, 6 July 1929, col. 341.

110 Neil Riddell, *Labour in Crisis: The Second Labour Government, 1929–1931*, Manchester University Press, Manchester, 1999.

111 Robert Skidelsky, *Politicians and the Slump: The Labour Government of 1929–1931* (2nd edn), PaperMac, London, 1994; Ross McKibbin, 'The Economic Policy of the Second Labour Government 1929–1931', *Past & Present*, 68 (1975), pp. 95–123; Peter Clarke, *The Keynesian Revolution in the Making, 1924–1936*, Clarendon Press, Oxford, 1988; Duncan Tanner, 'Political leadership, intellectual debate and economic policy during the second Labour government, 1929–1931', in E. H. H. Green and D. M. Tanner (eds), *The Strange Survival of Liberal England: Political Leaders, Moral Values and the Reception of Economic Debate*, Cambridge University Press, Cambridge, 2007, pp. 113–50.

112 Aneurin Bevan, E. J. Strachey and George Strauss, *What We Saw in Russia*, Hogarth Press, London, 1931; 'Ebbw Vale MP's View of Russia', *Western Mail*, 30 Sept. 1930.

113 'The Mosley Manifesto', *Observer*, 7 Dec. 1930.

114 Aneurin Bevan, W. J. Brown, John Strachey and Allan Young, *A National Policy: An Account of the Emergency Programme advanced by Sir Oswald Mosley*, Macmillan, London, 1931.

115 Matthew Worley, *Oswald Mosley and the New Party*, Palgrave Macmillan, London, 2010, p. 7.

116 Morrison, *Autobiography*, p. 131.

117 Andrew Thorpe, *The British General Election of 1931*, Clarendon Press, Oxford, 1991, p. 256.

118 Peter Clarke, *The Cripps Version: The Life of Sir Stafford Cripps, 1889–1952*, Allen Lane, London, 2002, p. 62.

119 Harris, *Attlee*, p. 103.

120 Attlee, *As It Happened*, pp. 77–8.

121 J. M. Keynes, 'The Monetary Policy of the Labour Party – I', *New Statesman & Nation*, 17 Sept. 1932.

122 R. H. Tawney, *The Attack and Other Papers*, George Allen & Unwin, London, 1953, p. 60.

123 Elizabeth Durbin, *New Jerusalems: The Labour Party and the Economics of Democratic Socialism*, Routledge, London, 1985; Alan Booth, 'How Long are Light Years in British Politics? The Labour Party's Economic Ideas in the 1930s', *Twentieth Century British History*, 7 (1996), pp. 1–26.

124 Ben Pimlott, 'The Road from 1945', *Guardian*, 27 July 1985; Gary Love, 'The Periodical Press and the Intellectual Culture of Conservatism in Interwar Britain', *Historical Journal*, 57 (2014), pp. 1027–56; Clarisse Berthezène, *Training Minds for the War of Ideas: Ashridge College, the Conservative Party and the Cultural Politics of Britain, 1929–54*, Manchester University Press, Manchester, 2015; Dean Blackburn, *Penguin Books and Political Change: Britain's Meritocratic Moment, 1937–1988*, Manchester University Press, Manchester, 2020.

125 Clare V. J. Griffiths, *Labour and the Countryside: The Politics of Rural Britain 1918–1939*, Oxford University Press, Oxford, 2007; Owen Sellers, 'Labour in the South East: A Regional Study of Political Culture & Practices circa 1931–1945', DPhil thesis, University of Oxford, 2021.

126 Hugh Dalton USSR diary, entry for 19 July 1932, Dalton Papers, I/53.

127 C. R. Attlee, *The Labour Party In Perspective*, Victor Gollancz Ltd, London, 1937, pp. 59–60.

128 C. R. Attlee and Stafford Cripps, 'The Joint Stock Banks', Jan. 1933, Dalton Papers, 2/1.

129 Ben Pimlott, *Labour and the Left in the 1930s*, Cambridge University Press, Cambridge, 1977, pp. 50–3; William Frame, '"Sir Stafford Cripps and His Friends": The Socialist League, the National Government and the Reform of the House of Lords 1931–1935', *Parliamentary History*, 24 (2005), pp. 316–31.

130 Stafford Cripps, 'Can socialism come by constitutional methods?', in Christopher Addison et al., *Problems of a Socialist Government*, Victor Gollancz Ltd, London, 1933, pp. 35–66, at 39.

131 Pimlott (ed.), *Political Diary of Hugh Dalton*, p. 181 (entry for 19 Jan. 1934).

132 *Labour Party Annual Conference Report* (henceforward LPACR), 1935, p. 157.

133 'General Election Battle', 31 Oct. 1935, available at www.britishpathe.com (consulted 19 March 2023).

134 Ivor Brown, 'Questions of Class', *Manchester Guardian*, 23 Nov. 1935.

135 Pimlott, *Political Diary of Hugh Dalton*, p. 192 (entry for 26 Nov. 1935).

136 'Opposition Parties Choose their Leaders', *Manchester Guardian*, 27 Nov. 1935.

137 Laura Beers, *Your Britain: Media and the Making of the Labour Party*, Harvard University Press, Cambridge, MA, 2010, Chapter 8.

138 John Callaghan, 'British Labour's Turn to Socialism in 1931', *Journal of Political Ideologies*, 14 (2009), pp. 115–32.

139 Dalton, *Fateful Years*, p. 99; Report on Ilford by-election, 1937, Topic Collection 46, Mass Observation Archive.

140 'Britain's Name "Dragged in the Mud"', *Manchester Guardian*, 29 May 1939.

141 He added: 'No doubt this situation has its dangers for the Labour Party, but for the Tories it is rank poison.' Aneurin Bevan, 'This is How Fascism is Born', *Tribune*, 1 July 1938.

CHAPTER 2

1 'Peace Principles', *The Times*, 2 March 1940.

2 Norman and Jeanne MacKenzie (eds), *The Diary of Beatrice Webb; Vol. IV: 1924–1943, 'The Wheel of Life'*, Belknap Press, Cambridge, MA, 1985, p. 447. Although Webb dated this entry 29 February, newspaper accounts place Attlee's lecture on 1 March.

3 Report by Sumner Welles on his mission to Europe, entry for 12 March 1940, *Foreign Relations of the United States, Diplomatic Papers, General, 1940; Vol. I*, Government Printing Office, Washington, 1959, p. 81.

4 Kingsley Martin, *Editor: A Second Volume of Autobiography, 1931–45*, Hutchinson, London, 1968, p. 10.

5 David Edgerton, *The Rise and Fall of the British Nation: A Twentieth-Century History*, Allen Lane, London, 2018, p. 34.

6 Geraint Thomas, *Popular Conservatism and the Culture of National Government in Inter-War Britain*, Cambridge University Press, Cambridge, 2020, p. 235.

7 Andrew Thorpe, 'Reconstructing Conservative Party Membership in World War II Britain', *Parliamentary Affairs*, 62 (2009), pp. 227–41.

8 Attlee, *The Labour Party In Perspective*, p. 101.

9 Hugh Dalton, *Practical Socialism for Britain*, George Routledge & Sons, London, 1935, pp. 45–6.

10 Andrew Thorpe, *A History of the British Labour Party* (4th edn), Palgrave, London, 2015, p. 109.

11 Pimlott (ed.), *Political Diary of Hugh Dalton* , p. 297 (entry for 6 Sept. 1939).

12 Andrew Thorpe, *Parties at War: Political Organization in Second World War Britain*, Oxford University Press, Oxford, 2009, p. 283.

13 Paul Ward, 'Preparing for the People's War: Labour and Patriotism in the 1930s', *Labour History Review*, 7 (2002), pp. 171–85.

14 'Parliament', *The Times*, 4 Sept. 1939.

15 See, for example, 'Gracchus', *Your MP*, Victor Gollancz, London, 1944.

16 Robert Crowcroft, *Attlee's War: World War II and the Making of a Labour Leader*, I.B. Tauris, London, 2011, Chapter 1.

17 C. R. Attlee, *Labour's Peace Aims*, Labour Party, London, 1939, p. 11.

18 Fabian Society, *Labour's Next Step: A Wartime Strategy*, Fabian Society, London, 1940, pp. 9–10.

19 'Political Notes', *The Times*, 3 Nov. 1939.

20 'Mr. Attlee on Soviet Aggression', *Manchester Guardian*, 18 Dec. 1939.

21 'Appeals to Workers for Sacrifices', *Manchester Guardian*, 5 Feb. 1940.

22 Nick Smart, 'Four Days in May: The Norway Debates and the Downfall of Neville Chamberlain', *Parliamentary History*, 17 (1998), pp. 215–43.

23 Pimlott, *Political Diary of Hugh Dalton*, p. 345 (entry for 10 May 1940).

24 Transcript of interview for 'Lord Attlee Remembers', BBC Home Service, 21 Apr. 1963, Attlee Papers (Bodleian), MS.CRA.11.

25 Winston Churchill to Neville Chamberlain, 11 May 1940, Chamberlain Papers, NC/7/9/81.

26 Betty D. Vernon, *Ellen Wilkinson*, Croom Helm, London, 1982, p. 184.

27 Recollection of Thelma Cazalet Keir, in 'Miss Ellen Wilkinson: Tributes of Three Women', *Observer*, 9 Feb. 1947.

28 Emanuel Shinwell, *Conflict Without Malice*, Odhams Press Ltd, London, 1955, pp. 146–7.

29 Jennie Lee, *My Life With Nye*, Jonathan Cape, London, 1980, p. 139.

30 Kingsley Martin, *Harold Laski, 1893–1950: A Biographical Memoir*, Victor Gollancz, London, 1953, p. 158.

31 Weekly Report, 18 May 1943, INF 1/292, TNA.

32 Ernest Bevin, *Labor's Achievement and the Goal* (speech of 18 Aug. 1941), British Library of Information, New York, 1941, p. 1. The original text uses the American spelling ('Minister of Labor'), but I have used the British spelling above.

33 Williams, *Ernest Bevin*, p. 7.

34 Parliamentary Debates, House of Commons, Fifth Series, Vol. 411, 4 June 1945, col. 579.

35 Miliband, *Parliamentary Socialism*; Paul Addison, *The Road to 1945: British Politics and the Second World War*, Jonathan Cape, London, 1975; Maurice Cowling, *The Impact of Hitler: British Politics and British Policy 1933–1940*, Cambridge University Press, Cambridge, 1975.

36 Robert Blake, 'The Road to Coalition', *Times Literary Supplement*, 25 July 1975 (review of Cowling, *Impact of Hitler*).

37 William Armstrong (ed.), *With Malice Toward None: A War Diary by Cecil H. King*, Sidgwick & Jackson, London, 1970, pp. 44–6 (entry for 6 June 1940); Neville Chamberlain to Ida Chamberlain, 8 June 1940, Robert Self (ed.), *The Neville Chamberlain Diary Letters; Vol. IV: The Downing Street Years, 1934–1940*, Ashgate, Aldershot, 2005, p. 538.

38 S. S. Silverman, 'When the House Cheers', *Tribune*, 21 June 1940.

39 Scott Kelly, '"The Ghost of Neville Chamberlain": Guilty Men and the 1945 election', *Conservative History Journal*, 5 (autumn 2005), pp. 18–24.

40 Maurice Webb (Bradford Central) election address, 1945, National Liberal Club collection, DM 668/2.

41 Parliamentary Debates, House of Commons, Fifth Series, Vol. 261, 22 May 1940, col. 155.

42 W. Ivor Jennings, 'The Emergency Powers (Defence) (No. 2) Act, 1940', *Modern Law Review*, 4 (1940), pp. 132–6.

43 Neil Rollings, 'Whitehall and the Control of Prices and Profits in a Major War, 1919–1939', *Historical Journal*, 44 (2001). pp. 517–40.

44 Neil Rollings, '"The Reichstag method of governing"? The Attlee Governments and Permanent Economic Controls', Helen Mercer, Neil Rollings, and Jim Tomlinson (eds), *Labour Governments and Private Industry: The Experience of 1945–1951*, Edinburgh University Press, Edinburgh, 1992, pp. 15–36.

45 Ernest Bevin to Winston Churchill, 13 May 1940, Churchill Papers, CHAR 20/11/59–60.

46 Alan Bullock, *The Life and Times of Ernest Bevin; Vol. II: Minister of Labour 1940–1945*, Heinemann, London, 1967, pp. 36–49.

47 Kevin Jefferys, *The Churchill Coalition and Wartime Politics*, Manchester University Press, Manchester, 1991, p. 74.

48 John Parker, 'After a Year of Coalition', *Fabian Quarterly*, XXX (summer 1941), pp. 5–9.

49 Kevin Jefferys (ed.), *Labour and the Wartime Coalition: From the Diary of James Chuter Ede, 1941–1945*, Historian's Press, London, 1987, p. 26 (entry for 3 Dec. 1941).

50 Aneurin Bevan, 'Conscription: Why MPs Revolted', *Tribune*, 5 Dec. 1941.

51 Nigel Nicolson (ed.), *Harold Nicolson: Diaries and Letters 1939–1945*, Collins, London, 1967, p. 192 (entry for 4 Dec. 1941).

52 Stephen Brooke, *Labour's War: The Labour Party and the Second World War*, Oxford University Press, Oxford, 1992, p. 330.

53 Sonya O. Rose, *Which People's War? National Identity and Citizenship in Britain 1939–1945*, Oxford University Press, Oxford, 2003.

54 Fielding, 'What Did "The People" Want?', pp. 623–39.

55 Peter Calvocoressi, 'The General Election 1945', 4 Aug. 1945, Beveridge Papers, 6/18. Author identified through internal evidence.

56 Henry Pelling, 'The 1945 General Election Reconsidered', *Historical Journal*, 23 (1980), pp. 399–414, at 411.

57 'Mr. Attlee on the "Irresponsibles"', *Manchester Guardian*, 15 May 1944. Johnston was Secretary of State for Scotland from 1941 to 1945.

58 Weekly Report, 18 Feb. 1942, INF 1/292, TNA.

59 'Home-made Socialism', 24 March 1942, INF 1/292, TNA.

60 'The Movement Away From Party', *Tribune*, 3 Apr. 1942; Steven Fielding, 'The Second World War and Popular Radicalism: The Significance of the "Movement away from Party"', *History*, 80 (1995), pp. 38–58.

61 Clarke, *Cripps Version*, pp. 257–75.

62 Tom Harrisson, 'Sir Stafford Cripps', File Report 1166, 23 March 1942, Mass Observation Archive.

63 'Summary Report on Prestige of Government Leaders', File Report 1207, 16 Apr. 1942, Mass Observation Archive.

64 A. J. Sylvester to David Lloyd George, 19 March 1942, Lloyd George Papers, LG/G/25/1.

65 *Common Wealth Manifesto*, Common Wealth, London, 1943, copy in Union of Women Teachers Archive, UWT/D/46/17.

66 Thorpe, *Parties At War*, pp. 277–8.

67 Andrew Thorpe, 'Locking out the Communists: The Labour Party and the Communist Party, 1939–46', *Twentieth Century British History*, 25 (2014), pp. 221–50.

68 Dean Blackburn, 'Reassessing Britain's "Post-war consensus": The Politics of Reason 1945–1979', *British Politics*, 13 (2018), pp. 195–214.

69 'Nation and Party', *The Times*, 25 May 1942.

70 Parliamentary Debates, House of Lords, Fifth Series, Vol. 123, 2 June 1942, col. 19.

71 Barbara Castle, *Fighting All the Way*, Macmillan, London, 1993, p. 114.

72 Clement Attlee to Winston Churchill, n.d., 1942–3, Attlee Papers (Cambridge), ATLE 2/2, ff. 7–9.

73 Winston Churchill to Lord Croft, 17 March 1945, Croft Papers, CRFT 1/8.

74 Jefferys, *Labour and the Wartime Coalition*, p. 122 (entry for 17 Feb. 1943).

75 Cabinet Secretary's notebook, WM (43) 43rd Meeting, 19 March 1943, CAB 195/2, TNA.

76 Anthony King (ed.), *British Political Opinion 1937–2000: The Gallup Polls*, Politico's, London, 2001, p. 2.

77 Kevin Jefferys, 'R.A. Butler, The Board of Education, and the 1944 Education Act', *History*, 69 (1984), pp. 415–31, at 428.

78 Booth, 'How Long are Light Years in British Politics?', pp. 1–26.

79 Hugh Dalton to Herbert Morrison, 24 Jan. 1943, Dalton Papers, 8/1.

80 Labour Party, *Full Employment and Financial Policy*, Labour Party, London, 1944, p. 4; Stephen Brooke, 'The Labour Party and the Second World War', in Anthony Gorst, Lewis Johnman and W. Scott Lucas (eds), *Contemporary British History, 1931–1961: Politics and the Limits of Policy*, Pinter, London, 1991, pp. 1–16, at 9–10.

81 Note the contrast in interpretations in Angus Calder, *The People's War*, Jonathan Cape, London, 1969, and Addison, *The Road to 1945*.

82 'Celticus' (Aneurin Bevan), *Why Not Trust the Tories?*, Victor Gollancz, London, 1944, pp. 48–9.

83 'Back to Politics', *The Economist*, 14 Oct. 1944; Ben Pimlott (ed.), *The Second World War Diary of Hugh Dalton, 1940–45*, Jonathan Cape, London, 1986, p. 800 (entry for 29 Oct. 1944).

84 'Labour Party Faces Election Problems', *Observer*, 29 Oct. 1944.

85 'The "Impending" Election: Liberal Decision Independent Fight on Own Programme', *Manchester Guardian*, 6 Oct. 1944.

86 Policy Committee minutes 12 Sept. 1944 and appendix to NEC minutes 30 Oct. 1944, LPA.

87 Pimlott, *Hugh Dalton*, p. 238; Morgan, *Labour in Power*, p. 95.

88 LPACR 1944, p. 163.

89 Ian Mikardo, *Back-Bencher*, Weidenfeld & Nicolson, London, 1988, p. 77.

90 Lewis Minkin, *The Labour Party Conference*, Manchester University Press, Manchester, 1980, pp. 18–21; Jon Lawrence, 'Labour – the myths it has lived by', in Duncan Tanner, Pat Thane and Nick Tiratsoo (eds), *Labour's First Century*, Cambridge University Press, Cambridge, 2000, pp. 341–66; Hugh Dalton, *The Fateful Years: Memoirs 1931–1945*, Frederick Muller Ltd, London, 1957, pp. 432–3; Stephen Brooke, 'The Labour Party and the 1945 General Election', *Contemporary Record*, 9 (1995), pp. 1–21, at 13.

91 Brooke, 'The Labour Party and the 1945 General Election', p. 13.

92 Michael Young, '1945', in Giles Radice (ed.), *What Needs to Change: New Visions For Britain*, HarperCollins, London, 1996, pp. 249–56, at 249; Paul Thompson, interview with Young for the National Life Story Collection, 12 May 1990, Young Papers, YUNG 10/002.

93 Interview for the 1994 Channel 4 programme 'What Has Become Of Us?', quoted in Peter Hennessy, 'Michael Young and the Labour Party', *Contemporary British History*, 19 (2005), pp. 281–4, at p. 282.

94 Labour Party manifesto, 1945.

95 'A Note on the Health Service Question', June 1945, BF/1945/3, LPA.

96 See David Thackeray and Richard Toye, *Age of Promises: Electoral Pledges in Twentieth Century Britain*, Oxford University Press, Oxford, 2021, esp. Chapter 3.

97 Labour Party manifesto, 1945.

98 'Into Battle', *Tribune*, 27 Apr. 1945.

99 LPACR 1945, pp. 91–2.

100 'Notes of the Week', *The Economist*, 28 Apr. 1945.

101 *Daily Mail*, 21 Apr. 1945.

102 *General Election 1945: Notes for Speakers and Workers*, Conservative Central Office, London, 1945, p. 297.

103 'General Election, July, 1945: report on campaign publicity services', 23 July 1945, 1945 election file, LPA.

104 John Gorman, 'The Labour Party's Election Posters in 1945', *Labour History Review*, 61 (1996), pp. 299–308, at 303.

105 Harris, *Attlee*, pp. 250–2.

106 Martin Francis, 'Tears, Tantrums, and Bared Teeth: The Emotional Economy of Three Conservative Prime Ministers, 1951–1963', *Journal of British Studies*, 41 (2002), pp. 354–87.

107 Jon Lawrence, *Electing Our Masters: The Hustings in British Politics from Hogarth to Blair*, Oxford University Press, Oxford, 2009, Chapter 5.

108 Austin Mitchell, *Election '45: Reflections on the Revolution in Britain*, Bellew Publishing, London, 1995, p. 42.

109 Beers, *Your Britain*, p. 178.

110 Sam Manning, *Cinemas and Cinema-Going in the United Kingdom: Decades of Decline, 1945–65*, University of London Press, London, 2020, p. 1.

111 Geoffrey Lloyd to Ralph Assheton, 29 May 1945, Churchill Papers CHAR 2/556/19. Attlee filmed at least two speeches: 'The Parties Speak No. 4: The Rt. Hon. C. R. Attlee: Labour Party', Pathé Gazette, 18 June 1945, and the Gaumont newsreel 'A Message From Mr. C.R. Attlee – War Time Deputy Prime Minister and Labour Party Leader Speaks to Britain', Gaumont, 25 June 1945. Both are available at www.britishpathe.com (consulted 15 July 2021).

112 Lawrence, *Electing Our Masters*, p. 133.

113 R. A. Rendall, 'The Election Broadcasts of 1945: Overseas Coverage', 3 Aug. 1945, BBC Written Archives, R44/189/1, General Election File 1.

114 Broadcast of 4 June 1945. Unless otherwise stated, all of Churchill's broadcasts and speeches cited were found in Robert Rhodes James (ed.), *Winston S. Churchill: His Complete Speeches, 1897–1963*, 8 vols, Chelsea House Publishers, New York, 1974.

115 Joanne Reilly, *Belsen: The Liberation of a Concentration Camp*, Routledge, London, 1998, esp. Chapter 2.

116 *Daily Herald*, 5 June 1945.

117 Attlee, *As It Happened*, pp. 141–2.

118 'Labour Case for Socialism', *The Times*, 6 June 1945.

119 'Cripps Answers Churchill', *Forward*, 16 June 1945.

120 'July Election Nearer', *The Times*, 22 May 1945.

121 *Speaker's Handbook 1945*, p. 3.

122 Isaac Kramnick and Barry Sheerman, *Harold Laski: A Life on the Left*, Hamish Hamilton Ltd, London, 1993, pp. 483–9.

123 For example, Trevor Evans, 'This Man Laski', *Daily Express*, 20 June 1945.

124 Gary McCulloch, 'Labour, the Left, and the British General Election of 1945', *Journal of British Studies*, 24 (1985), pp. 465–89, at 484–6.

125 'Attlee tells Churchill: You Underrate the Common Man', *News Chronicle*, 4 July 1945; J. T. Baxter to Labour candidates, 4 July 1945, BF/1945/3, LPA; Attlee, *As It Happened*, p. 145.

126 Lord Moran, *Winston Churchill: The Struggle for Survival, 1940–1965*, Houghton Mifflin, Boston, 1966, p. 273.

127 Anthony Beevor, interviewed for the BBC2 documentary *Churchill: When Britain Said No*, broadcast 25 May 2015.

128 Paul Addison, *Churchill on the Home Front, 1900–1955*, Jonathan Cape, London, 1992.

129 Conservative Party manifesto, 1945.

130 Harriet Jones, 'The Conservative Party and the Welfare State 1942–1955', PhD thesis, University of London, 1992, pp. 93–7.

131 A. V. Alexander election address 1945, Alexander Papers, AVAR 8/1, CAC. Emphasis in original.

132 *Ernest Bevin's Work in Wartime, 1940–1945*, Labour Party, London, 1945.

133 R. B. McCallum and Alison Readman, *The British General Election of 1945*, Oxford University Press, London, 1947, p. 199.

134 'Housing a National Emergency', *Manchester Guardian*, 18 June 1945.

135 'Bevin Answers Steel Ring: "New Scheme to Fix Prices"', *Daily Mirror*, 12 June 1945.

136 Bullock, *Ernest Bevin; Vol. II: Minister of Labour*, pp. 381–5.

137 'Bevin "You Decide Future"', *Daily Mail*, 23 June 1945. See also Ernest Bevin, 'The Case for Labour', *Observer*, 24 June 1945.

138 Albert Hird diary, 19 June 1945.

139 Jefferys, *Labour and the Wartime Coalition*, p. 226 (entry for 26 July 1945).

140 Kit Kowol, '"I weep with shame and grief": The Feeling of the 1945 General Election in Letters to Winston Churchill', unpublished manuscript, 2023.

141 Castle, *Fighting All the Way*, p. 125.

142 Laura Beers, 'Labour's Britain, Fight for It Now!', *Historical Journal*, 52 (2009), pp. 667–95, at 667–8.

143 Nicolson, *Diaries and Letters 1939–1945*, p. 477 (entry for 24 July 1945).

144 Beverley Baxter, 'London Letter – Will Britain Swing Left?', *Maclean's Magazine*, 15 Apr. 1945.

145 'Mr. Churchill Develops the Laski "Scare"', *Manchester Guardian*, 3 July 1945.

146 'Record polling, say the experts', *Daily Mail*, 6 July 1945. For Morrison's private uncertainty, see Donoughue and Jones, *Herbert Morrison*, p. 338.

147 'The Liberals', *Manchester Guardian*, 4 July 1945.

148 Hird diary, 27 June 1945.

149 'Polling Today in the "Little Election"', *Manchester Guardian*, 12 July 1945; 'Britain's Revulsion Against Tory Rule', *Manchester Guardian*, 27 July 1945.

150 Jefferys, *Labour and the Wartime Coalition*, p. 224 (entry for 2 July 1945).

151 Transcript of interview for 'Lord Attlee Remembers'.

152 John W. Wheeler-Bennett, *King George VI: His Life and Reign*, St Martin's Press, New York, 1958, p. 635.

153 Pimlott, *Political Diary of Hugh Dalton*, p. 360 (entry for July 1945).

154 J. A. Crang, 'Politics on Parade: Army Education and the 1945 General Election', *History*, 81 (1996), pp. 215–27.

155 'Help him finish the job', n.d. but 1945, Macmillan Papers, MS.Macmillan dep.c.249, f.16.

156 Charles Hilditch election address, 1945, quoted in Matthew Johnson, '"A fighting man to fight for you": The armed forces, ex-servicemen, and British electoral politics in the aftermath of the two world wars', in David Thackeray and Richard Toye (eds), *Electoral Pledges in Britain since 1918: The Politics of Promises*, Palgrave Macmillan, Cham, Switzerland, 2020, pp. 71–93, at 91.

157 *'Give Labour Power': An Appeal to the People by the Rt. Hon. C.R. Attlee*, 23 June 1945, BF/1945/3, LPA.

158 McCallum and Readman, *The British General Election of 1945*, p. 181.
159 Martin Pugh, 'The Daily Mirror and the Revival of Labour 1935–1945', *Twentieth Century British History*, 9 (1998), pp. 420–38; Fielding, 'The Second World War and Popular Radicalism', p. 40.
160 'A Report on the General Election, June–July 1945', File report 2270A, Oct. 1945, Mass Observation Archive.
161 Clare Griffiths, 'Broken promises and the remaking of political trust: Debating reconstruction in Britain during the Second World War', in Thackeray and Toye, *Electoral Pledges in Britain*, pp. 95–115.
162 'A Report on the General Election, June–July 1945'.
163 D. J. Richards to Paul Addison, 23 May 1994, Addison Papers.
164 Daniel Weinbren (ed.), *Generating Socialism, Recollections of Life in the Labour Party*, Sutton Publishing, Stroud, 1997, p. 201.

CHAPTER 3

1 Parliamentary Debates, House of Commons, Fifth Series, Vol. 421, 2 Apr. 1946, cols 1213–14.
2 *Desert Island Discs*, BBC Radio 4, 7 July 1991, https://www.bbc.co.uk/sounds/play/p0093z01 (consulted 19 March 2023).
3 Hugh Dalton, *High Tide and After: Memoirs 1945–1960*, Frederick Muller Ltd, London, 1962, p. 31.
4 'Disputes Bill Battle', *Manchester Guardian*, 27 Feb. 1946.
5 Stanley Bishop, 'Shawcross, KC, Attorney-General', *Daily Herald*, 10 Sept. 1945.
6 Hartley Shawcross, *Life Sentence: The Memoirs of Lord Shawcross*, Constable, London, 1995, p. 142.
7 'News From All Parts', *Daily Mail*, 17 March 1948.
8 Colm Brogan, *Our New Masters*, Hollis and Carter, London, 1948; Margaret Thatcher, *The Path to Power*, HarperCollins, New York, 1995, pp. 51–2.
9 Shawcross, *Life Sentence*, p. 142.
10 John Durston, 'Attlee Pledges Early Battle for Labor Reforms', *New York Herald Tribune*, 29 July 1945.
11 Herbert Morrison to Clement Attlee, 24 July 1945, Attlee Papers (Bodleian) MS Attlee dep. 18, f. 50.
12 John Parker, unpublished memoirs, Parker Papers, 1/9.
13 Interview with James Griffiths, 12 Jan. 1968, Morrison Papers (LSE), 6/2; Harris, *Attlee*, pp. 262–3.
14 Peter Hennessy, *The Prime Minister: The Office and Its Holders Since 1945*, Allen Lane, London, 2000, p. 149.
15 'Mr. Attlee Declares: We Can Carry It Through', *Daily Telegraph*, 27 July 1945.
16 Ian Mikardo diary, 27 July 1945, Mikardo Papers, P/Rich/1/4.
17 Donoughue and Jones, *Herbert Morrison*, p. 342.
18 Francis Williams, *A Prime Minister Remembers: The War and Post-War Memoirs of the Rt. Hon. Earl Attlee*, William Heinemann Ltd, London, 1961, p. 4.
19 Attlee Chronology, 26 July 1945, Attlee Papers (Bodleian), MS.CRA.20.
20 Vi Attlee memoir, n.d., Attlee Papers (Bodleian), MS.CRA.1.

21   Russell Rees, *Labour and the Northern Ireland Problem 1945–1951: The Missed Opportunity*, Irish Academic Press, Dublin, 2009, pp. 34–5.
22   H. G. Nicholas (ed.), *Washington Despatches, 1941–1945: Weekly Political Reports from the British Embassy*, University of Chicago Press, Chicago, 1981, p. 597. Attlee later wrote that it would have been better if Truman had become President six months earlier. 'Attlee on Moran's Churchill Diary', *Forum World Features*, week of 14 May 1966, Attlee Papers (Bodleian), MS.CRA.32.
23   Arthur Krock, 'Labor Party's Sweep Raises Problems Here', *New York Times*, 29 July 1945.
24   W. L. Mackenzie King diary, 26 July 1945, https://www.bac-lac.gc.ca/eng/discover/politics-government/prime-ministers/william-lyon-mackenzie-king/Pages/diaries-william-lyon-mackenzie-king.aspx (consulted 7 Jan. 2022).
25   Labour Party manifesto, 1945.
26   Moscow in English, 23.00, 26 July 1945, commentary by Mihail Mihailov, *Daily Digest of World Broadcasts*, 27 July 1945, BBC Written Archives.
27   Francis Williams, *A Prime Minister Remembers*, p. 71.
28   *Foreign Relations of the United States: Diplomatic Papers: The Conference of Berlin (The Potsdam Conference), 1945; Vol. II*, United States Government Printing Office, Washington DC, 1960, p. 601.
29   C. L. Sulzberger, *A Long Row of Candles: Memoirs and Diaries, 1934–1954*, The Macmillan Company, Toronto, 1969, p. 264 (entry for 28 July 1948).
30   Stephen King-Hall, 'Some Colleagues 1939–45', n.d., King-Hall Papers, STKH 1/7.
31   Edward Hulton, 'A Welcome to a New World', *Picture Post*, 18 Aug. 1945.
32   Rees, *Labour and the Northern Irish Problem*, p. 34.
33   John Wheeler-Bennett, *King George VI: His Life and Reign*, St Martin's Press, New York, 1958, p. 638.
34   Duff Hart-Davis (ed.), *King's Counsellor: Abdication and War – The Diaries of Sir Alan Lascelles*, Weidenfeld & Nicolson, London, 2006, p. 385 (entry for 3 Feb. 1946).
35   Francis Williams, *A Prime Minister Remembers*, p. 71.
36   Attlee, autobiographical notes, n.d. but 1950 or 1951, Attlee Papers (CAC), ATLE/1; Douglas Jay, *Change and Fortune: A Political Record*, Hutchinson & Co., London, 1980, p. 129.
37   James Chuter Ede, undated diary entry, March 1946, Chuter Ede Papers, 390/2/11.
38   Francis Williams, *A Prime Minister Remembers*, pp. 80–1.
39   W. J. Brown, 'Why Attlee is Safe in His Job', *Evening Standard*, 19 March 1946.
40   Edward Tull-Warnock to the editor of *Tribune*, published 18 Oct. 1940; Campbell, *Nye Bevan*, p. 149.
41   Aneurin Bevan, 'Next Steps to a New Society', *Tribune*, 25 Oct. 1940.
42   Emanuel Shinwell, 'The Rise of Clement Attlee', *Sunday Times*, 18 Sept. 1960.
43   Christopher Mayhew, *Time To Explain: An Autobiography*, Hutchinson, London, 1987, p. 95
44   C. R. Attlee, *As It Happened*, William Heinemann Ltd, London, 1954, p. 156.
45   Chuter Ede diary, 6 Jan. 1948, Ede Papers, 390/2/12.
46   Attlee took the Minister of Defence role himself until the end of the war with Japan.

47 Peter Hennessy, *Whitehall*, Fontana Press, London, 1989, p. 131; Miles Taylor, 'Labour and the constitution', in Tanner, Thane and Tiratsoo (eds), *Labour's First Century*, pp. 151–80, at 164.

48 Kevin Theakston, 'Brook, Norman Craven, Baron Normanbrook (1902–1967), civil servant', *Oxford Dictionary of National Biography*. Retrieved 23 Mar. 2022 from https://www.oxforddnb.com/view/10.1093/ref:odnb/9780198614128.001.0001/odnb-9780198614128-e-32089; 'Normanbrook, Man of a Million Secrets', *Daily Mail*, 16 June 1967.

49 Jean Mann, *Woman in Parliament*, Odham's Press Ltd, London, 1962, p. 13.

50 Clement Attlee, undated memorandum, Attlee Papers (CAC), ATLE/2. Attlee reviewed it and added a note on 7 June 1948: 'It is not without interest in view of modern developments.'

51 George Strauss, unpublished memoirs, p. 99, Strauss Papers, STRS1/2.

52 Woodrow Wyatt, 'The Secret of Clement Attlee', *New Statesman*, 13 Oct. 1967.

53 G. W. Jones, interview with Kingsley Martin, 1 Feb. 1968, Morrison Papers (LSE), 6/3.

54 Evan Durbin, 'CRA', n.d. but c. 1946, Durbin Papers, 3/9. Emphasis in original.

55 Attlee to Francis Williams, 27 Sept. 1945, Williams Papers, FRWS 8/1; Francis Williams, *Nothing So Strange: An Autobiography*, Cassell, London, 1970, pp. 215, 219.

56 James Margach, *The Abuse of Power: The War between Downing Street and the Media from Lloyd George to James Callaghan*, W. H. Allen, London, 1978, p. 91.

57 Jay, *Change and Fortune*, pp. 131–2.

58 John Kenneth Galbraith, *A Life In Our Times: Memoirs*, Andre Deutsch, London, 1981, p. 168.

59 Hugh Dalton diary, 27 June 1947, Dalton Papers I/35. See also Dalton, *High Tide and After*, p. 256, where Dalton gives an edited version of this diary entry, misdated 28 July 1947.

60 R. F. Harrod, *The Life of John Maynard Keynes*, Macmillan, London, 1954, pp. 593–4.

61 Mayhew, *Time To Explain*, p. 88; Allen Drury, *A Senate Journal 1943–1945*, McGraw Hill Book Company, New York, 1963, pp. 247, 438 (entries for 16 Aug. 1944 and 30 May 1945).

62 Nicholas (ed.), *Washington Despatches*, p. 597.

63 C. R. Attlee, *Clem Attlee: The Granada Historical Records Interview*, Panther Books, London, 1967, p. 35.

64 Clement Attlee, 'The Hiroshima Choice', *Observer*, 6 Sept. 1959.

65 'Lend-Lease Halts: Allies' Needs Put on Purchase Basis', *New York Times*, 22 Aug. 1945.

66 Cadogan diary, 20 Aug. 1945, Cadogan Papers, ACAD 1/15; Lord Keynes, 'Our Overseas Financial Prospects', 13 Aug. 1945, CP (45) 112, CAB 129/1/12, TNA.

67 Robert Skidelsky, *John Maynard Keynes; Vol. 3: Fighting For Britain 1937–1946*, Macmillan, London, 2000, p. 322; Peter Clarke, *The Last Thousand Days of the British Empire*, Allen Lane, London, 2007, p. 372; Truman Library oral history interviews with Emilio Collado, 7 July 1971, and Joseph D. Coppock, 29 July 1974.

68 Harry S. Truman, *Year of Decisions*, Doubleday, New York, 1955, pp. 227–8.

69 Richard N. Gardner, *Sterling-Dollar Diplomacy: The Origins and the Prospects of our International Economic Order*, McGraw Hill, New York, 1980, pp. 184–7; Philip Gannon, 'The Special Relationship and the 1945 Anglo-American Loan', *Journal of Transatlantic Studies*, 11 (2014), pp. 1–17.

70 Michael F. Hopkins (ed.), *British Financial Diplomacy With North America 1944–1946: The Diary of Fredric Harmer and the Washington Reports of Robert Brand*, Cambridge University Press, Cambridge, 2021, p. 67 (Harmer diary entry for 20 Sept. 1945).

71 'The Dining Room Is Closed', *Chicago Tribune*, 25 Aug. 1945.

72 'Note of a meeting held at 6.30 p.m. on 20 August in the Foreign Secretary's room at the House of Commons', Rohan Butler and M. E. Pelly (eds), *Documents on British Policy Overseas, 1945; Vol. III*, London, HMSO, 1986, pp. 55–9.

73 Hopkins, *British Financial Diplomacy*, p. 14.

74 L. S. Pressnell, *External Economic Policy Since the War; Vol. I: The Post-war Financial Settlement*, HMSO, London, 1986, p. 262.

75 'Note of a Meeting held in the Secretary of State's Room on 21 August at 10 a.m.', Butler and Pelly, *Documents on British Policy Overseas, 1945; Vol. III*, pp. 59–64.

76 Keynes, 'Our Overseas Financial Prospects'.

77 Harrod, *Life*, p. 596.

78 Lord Halifax diary, 24 Nov. 1945, York Digital Library.

79 Susan Howson and Donald Moggridge (eds), *The Wartime Diaries of Lionel Robbins and James Meade, 1943–45*, Palgrave Macmillan, Basingstoke, 1990, p. 224 (Robbins diary entry for 29 Sept. 1945).

80 Dalton, *High Tide and After*, pp. 74–5.

81 Richard Wevill, *Britain and America After World War II: Bilateral Relations and the Beginnings of the Cold War*, I.B. Tauris, London, 2012, Chapter 2; Pimlott (ed.), *Political Diary of Hugh Dalton*, p. 365 (entry for 7 Dec. 1945).

82 Jay, *Change and Fortune*, p. 137.

83 R. W. B. Clarke diary, 12 Feb. 1946, Clarke Papers, CLRK 4/4/4.

84 Pimlott, *Hugh Dalton*, pp. 461–5.

85 Parliamentary Debates, House of Commons, Fifth Series, Vol. 414, 23 Oct. 1945, col. 1902.

86 Dalton, *High Tide and After*, p. 25.

87 Dalton diary, 1 Nov. 1945, Dalton Papers, I/33.

88 *Daily Mirror*, 24 Oct. 1945; '2,000,000 Freed from Tax', *Daily Mail*, 24 Oct. 1945.

89 Margaret G. Myers, 'The Nationalization of Banks in France', *Political Science Quarterly*, 64 (1949), pp. 189–210.

90 Philip Williamson, 'A "Bankers' Ramp"? Financiers and the British Political Crisis of August 1931', *English Historical Review*, XCIX (1984), pp. 770–806.

91 'A Spiritless Tory Attack', *Manchester Guardian*, 30 Oct. 1945.

92 James Callaghan, *Time and Chance*, William Collins Sons & Co. Ltd, Glasgow, 1987, p. 68.

93 Castle, *Fighting All the Way*, p. 128.

94 John Fforde, *The Bank of England and Public Policy, 1941–1958*, Cambridge University Press, Cambridge, 1992, Chapter 1; Jim Tomlinson, *Democratic*

Socialism and Economic Policy: The Attlee Years, 1945–1951, Cambridge University Press, Cambridge, 1996, pp. 148–50.

95 Labour Party manifesto, 1945.

96 Tomlinson, *Democratic Socialism*, p. 163.

97 Herbert Morrison, *Prospects and Policies*, Alfred A. Knopf, New York, 1944, p. 3.

98 Ben Shephard, *The Long Road Home: The Aftermath of the Second World War*, Alfred A. Knopf, New York, 2011, pp. 133–5; 'Economic State of Europe', *The Times*, 26 Oct. 1945.

99 Peter Stanford, *The Outcast's Outcast: A Biography of Lord Longford*, Sutton Publishing, Stroud, 2003, p. 161.

100 'Mr. Morrison in New York', *The Times*, 12 Jan. 1946.

101 Hugh Pemberton, 'Isaacs, George Alfred (1883–1979), trade unionist and politician', *Oxford Dictionary of National Biography*. Retrieved 11 Mar. 2022 from https://www.oxforddnb.com/view/10.1093/ref:odnb/9780198614128.001.0001/odnb-9780198614128-e-31275.

102 Bullock, *Ernest Bevin: Foreign Secretary*, pp. 126–7.

103 Garry Allighan, 'The Big "Demob." Muddle', *Daily Mail*, 23 Aug. 1945. In 1947, Allighan published an article revealing that politicians leaked inside information to the press in return for drinks or money. The affronted MPs came down on him like a ton of bricks. Using the excuse that Allighan himself had been such a source, they expelled him from the Commons and he never returned. Matthew Parris and Kevin Maguire, *Great Parliamentary Scandals: Five Centuries of Calumny, Smear and Innuendo*, Robson Books, London, 2004, pp. 122–4.

104 Cabinet minutes 30 Aug. 1945, CM (45) 26th conclusions, CAB 128/1/9, TNA; Cabinet Secretary's notebook, 30 Aug. 1945, CAB 195/3/8, TNA. Emphasis in original.

105 Emrys Hughes, 'Mr. Attlee and the Demob', *Forward*, 8 Sept. 1945.

106 Parliamentary Debates, House of Commons, Fifth Series, Vol. 414, 22 Oct 1945, col. 1688.

107 Ernest Bevin to Attlee, 15 Nov. 1945, FO 800/473, TNA.

108 Bullock, *Ernest Bevin: Foreign Secretary*, p. 127.

109 Correlli Barnett, *The Lost Victory: British Dreams, British Realities, 1945–1950*, Macmillan, London, 1995.

110 Jim Tomlinson, 'Correlli Barnett's History: The Case of Marshall Aid', *Twentieth Century British History*, 8 (1997), pp. 222–38.

111 David Edgerton, *Warfare State: Britain, 1920–1970*, Cambridge University Press, Cambridge, 2006, p. 5.

112 Jay, *Change and Fortune*, p. 152.

113 William Crofts, *Coercion or Persuasion? Propaganda in Britain after 1945*, Routledge, London, 1989; Richard Williams-Thompson, *Was I Really Necessary?*, World's Press News Publishing Co., London, 1951.

114 Ben Jackson, *The Case for Scottish Independence: A History of Nationalist Political Thought in Modern Scotland*, Cambridge University Press, Cambridge, 2020, p. 25.

115 Henry Pelling, *A History of British Trade Unionism*, Macmillan, London, 1963, p. 224; Richard Toye, *The Labour Party and the Planned Economy, 1931–1951*, Boydell and Brewer for the Royal Historical Society, Woodbridge, 2003, p. 121.

116 'Evershed Report on Dockers' Wages', *Manchester Guardian*, 11 Dec. 1945.

117 Pimlott, *Political Diary of Hugh Dalton*, p. 363 (entry for 17 Oct. 1945).

118 George Orwell, 'You and the Atom Bomb', *Tribune*, 19 Oct. 1945.

119 Nicholas, *Washington Despatches*, p. 603.

120 Clement Attlee, 'The Atomic Bomb', GEN 75/1, 28 Aug. 1945, CAB 130/3, TNA; Attlee to Harry S. Truman, 25 Sept. 1945, in Margaret Gowing, *Independence and Deterrence: Britain and Atomic Energy, 1945–1952; Volume 1: Policy Making*, Macmillan, Basingstoke, 1974, pp. 78–81.

121 James L. Gormly, 'The Washington Declaration and the "Poor Relation": Anglo-American Atomic Diplomacy, 1945–6', *Diplomatic History*, 8 (1984), pp. 125–44, at 131.

122 Robert H. Ferrell (ed.), *Truman in the White House: The Diary of Eben A. Ayers*, University of Missouri Press, Columbia, MO, 1991, p. 95 (entry for 1–3 Nov. 1945).

123 Arthur Sears Henning, 'Attlee's Goal: 5 Billions and A-Bomb Facts', *Chicago Tribune*, 5 Nov. 1945.

124 Harris, *Attlee*, p. 284.

125 Geoffrey Skinner, 'The Development of Military Nuclear Strategy and Anglo-American Relations, 1939–1958', PhD thesis, University of Exeter, 2018, p. 203.

126 Parliamentary Debates, House of Commons, Fifth Series, Vol. 416, 6 Dec. 1945, col. 2552.

127 'Tories' Censure Motion Ends in Fiasco', *Daily Herald*, 7 Dec. 1945.

128 *Financial Agreement Between the Governments of the United States and the United Kingdom*, Cmd. 6708, 6 Dec. 1945; *Proposals for Consideration by an International Conference on Trade and Employment*, Cmd. 6709, 6 Dec. 1945; Gardner, *Sterling-Dollar Diplomacy*, Chapter 11.

129 Francine McKenzie, 'Renegotiating a Special Relationship: The Commonwealth and Anglo-American Economic Discussions, September–December 1945', *Journal of Imperial and Commonwealth History*, 26 (1998), pp. 71–93.

130 James Byrnes to J. G. Winant, 31 Oct. 1945, *Foreign Relations of the United States: Diplomatic Papers, 1945; Vol. VI: The British Commonwealth, the Far East*, United States Government Printing Office, Washington DC, 1969, p. 152; Parliamentary Debates House of Commons Fifth Series, Vol. 416, 6 Dec. 1945, col. 2668.

131 Although it has not proved possible to locate a copy of this statement in either the US or the UK National Archives, in July 1947 Will Clayton reminded the British in detail of what had occurred. They did not dissent from the account that he gave. 'Memorandum of Conversation: United States and United Kingdom Tariff Offers (continued)', 14 July 1947, RG 43, International Trade Files Box 83, United States National Archives.

132 Parliamentary Debates, House of Commons, 5th Series, Vol. 417, 12 Dec. 1945, col. 468.

133 Brett, Gilliatt and Pople, 'Planned Trade, Labour Party Policy and US Intervention', pp. 130–42.

134 'Party meeting, 12.12.45', Castle Papers, MS Castle 225.

135 Dalton, *High Tide and After*, p. 85.

136 John Gerard Ruggie, 'International Regimes, Transactions, and Change: Embedded Liberalism in the Post-war Economic Order', *International Organization*, 36 (1982), pp. 379–415.

137 See, for example, Leo Amery diary, 9 March 1946, Amery Papers, AMEL 7/40.

138 Cabinet Secretary's notebook, 29 Nov. 1945, CAB 195/3/75, TNA.

139 Castle, *Fighting All the Way*, p. 139.

140 PLP minutes, 12 Dec. 1945, LPA.

141 Callaghan, *Time and Chance*, p. 74.

142 The Earl of Birkenhead, *Halifax: The Life of Lord Halifax*, Hamish Hamilton, London, 1965, pp. 556–7.

143 Parliamentary Debates, House of Commons, 5th Series, Vol. 417, 13 Dec. 1945, col. 727. For the more colourful details, see telegram from J. G. Winant to the President and Secretaries of State and Treasury, 14 Dec. 1945, Vinson Papers, Box 149.

144 Clarke diary, 3 March 1946, Clarke Papers, CLRK 4/4/4.

145 Rees, *Labour and the Northern Ireland Problem 1945–1951*, p. 58.

146 Parliamentary Debates, House of Commons, Fifth Series, Vol. 420, 9 Apr. 1946, col. 1807.

147 Mann, *Woman in Parliament*, p. 12.

CHAPTER 4

1 'Conference by the Sea', *Newsweek*, 9 June 1947.

2 'Praise – and Blame – for Mr. Bevin', *Nottingham Evening Post*, 29 May 1947.

3 R. H. S. Crossman et al., *Keep Left*, New Statesman, London, 1947, p. 35.

4 Martin Ceadel, 'British political parties and the European crisis of the late 1940s', in Josef Becker and Franz Knipping (eds), *Power in Europe? Great Britain, France, Italy and Germany in a Post-war World, 1945–50*, De Gruyter, New York, 1986, pp. 137–59, at 145.

5 Andrew Defty, *Britain, America and Anti-Communist Propaganda 1945–53: The Information Research Department*, Routledge, London, 2013, p. 50; Parliamentary Debates, House of Commons, Fifth Series, Vol. 415, 7 Nov. 1945, col. 1337; *Cards on the Table: An Interpretation of Labour's Foreign Policy*, Labour Party, London, n.d. but 1947.

6 Daily Summary, 27 Jan. 1947, CREST database, https://www.cia.gov/readingroom/document/02996864 (consulted 20 May 2022).

7 'An Eye on Margate', *Manchester Guardian*, 23 May 1947; 'Margate', *Manchester Guardian*, 24 May 1947; 'What They Are Saying', *The Listener*, 29 May 1947.

8 Denis Healey, *The Time of My Life*, Michael Joseph, London, 1989, pp. 103–4.

9 'Notes of the Week', *The Economist*, 7 June 1947.

10 'Mr. Bevin Addresses Party Conference', Gaumont-British News, released 2 June 1947, Britishpathe.com (consulted 16 May 2022). The official conference report captured the sense of this but corrected the grammar and rendered the words in a slightly different way.

11 Pimlott (ed.), *Political Diary of Hugh Dalton*, p. 393 (entry for 24–29 March 1947).

12   "'Ernest Bevin": A Radio Portrait by Christopher Mayhew', West of England Home Service, broadcast 24 Apr. 1957, Citrine Papers, 10/3. Emphasis in original.

13   Kenneth O. Morgan, *Michael Foot: A Life*, HarperCollins, London, 2007, p. 122.

14   Michael Foot, 'The Unanswered Questions', *Tribune*, 6 June 1947.

15   'Mr. Bevin's Demand', *The Times*, 30 May 1947. Emphasis in original. However, the official conference report did not record this remark.

16   Crossman et al., *Keep Left*, p. 43.

17   Gladwyn Jebb, '"Keep Left"', 5 May 1947, FO 800/493, TNA.

18   PLP minutes, 15 Aug. 1945, LPA.

19   'Labour Meeting at Saltaire', *Shipley Times & Express*, 13 June 1945. The reporting of the speech was somewhat fragmentary. According to the *Daily Worker* ('Socialism Was Basis of Vast Soviet War Effort', 13 June 1945), Bevin stated: 'Left can speak to Left in comradeship and confidence.' This phrase – which was certainly consistent with the broad sentiments that he expressed – was quoted against him later by Conservatives.

20   'Lord Back-Door', *Daily Express*, 13 June 1945. The 'buddy' phrase was Beaverbrook's.

21   Parliamentary Debates, House of Commons, Fifth Series, Vol. 413, 20 Aug. 1945, col. 287.

22   Pierson Dixon diary, 20 Aug. 1945, quoted in Piers Dixon, *Double Diploma: The Life of Sir Pierson Dixon, Don and Diplomat*, Hutchinson, London, 1968, p. 182.

23   Richard Crossman diary, 24 Aug. 1945, Crossman Papers, MSS.154/3/AV/130.

24   'French Press Gives Little Space to Mr. Bevin's Speech' and 'US Liberal Opinion Upset By Mr. Bevin's Speech', *Manchester Guardian*, 23 Aug. 1945.

25   '*Pravda* and Spain', *The Scotsman*, 27 Aug. 1945.

26   Soviet European Service in English, 11 Sept. 1945, Daily Report: Foreign Radio Broadcasts, 12 Sept. 1945, FBIS-FRB-45-219.

27   'What They Are Saying', *The Listener*, 30 Aug. 1945.

28   'Socialists Talk of Mr. Bevin', *Daily Telegraph*, 23 Aug. 1945. A hint of the dissent can be read between the lines of the bland PLP minutes, 22 Aug. 1945, LPA.

29   'Britain and World Socialism', *Tribune*, 7 June 1946.

30   Lord Sherfield, 'Making Our World: Lord Gladwyn', *Guardian*, 26 Oct. 1996; Kenneth Younger, review of *The Memoirs of Lord Gladwyn*, *International Affairs*, 48 (1972), pp. 637–8.

31   Ben Pimlott (ed.), *The Second World War Diary of Hugh Dalton, 1940–45*, Jonathan Cape, London, 1986, p. 7 (entry for 16 May 1940).

32   Mayhew, *Time To Explain*, p. 99.

33   Gladwyn Jebb, *The Memoirs of Lord Gladwyn*, Weybright and Talley, New York, 1972, pp. 175–6, 228; John Julius Norwich (ed.), *The Duff Cooper Diaries, 1915–1951*, Weidenfeld & Nicolson, London, 2005, p. 389 (entry for 30 Sept. 1945).

34   R. H. Bruce Lockhart, *Comes the Reckoning*, Putnam, London, 1947, p. 371.

35   'UNO: Great Commoner', *Time*, 18 Feb. 1946.

36   'No Circulation Record', 11 Feb. 1946', FO 800/463, TNA.

37   Lord Killearn to Lord Mountbatten, 14 Feb. 1946, FO 371/54017, TNA; Nicholas Tarling, 'Some Rather Nebulous Capacity: Lord Killearn's Appointment in Southeast Asia', *Modern Asian Studies*, 20 (1986), pp. 559–600.

38 LPACR 1947, p. 179. On one occasion Bevin asked an official why the FO took so many public schoolboys and was apparently satisfied with the explanation that 'We take only the best, whatever their background.' Peter Leslie, *Chapman-Andrews and the Emperor*, Pen & Sword, Barnsley, 2005, p. 140.

39 Anthony Adamthwaite, 'Britain and the world, 1945–9: The view from the Foreign Office', *International Affairs*, 61 (1985), pp. 223–35, at 225.

40 Cabinet minutes, 11 March 1946, CM (46) (23rd), CAB 128/5/23, TNA.

41 Adam Richardson, 'Orme Sargent, Ernest Bevin and British Policy Towards Europe, 1946–1949', *International History Review*, 41 (2019), pp. 891–908.

42 Valentine Lawford, 'Three Ministers', *Cornhill Magazine*, No. 1010, winter 1956/7.

43 Duff Cooper, *Old Men Forget*, E. P. Dutton & Co., New York, 1954, p. 361.

44 Nigel Nicolson (ed.), *Harold Nicolson: Diaries and Letters 1945–1962*, Collins, London, 1968, p. 31 (entry for 8 Aug. 1945).

45 Alexander Cadogan to Theodosia Cadogan, 31 July 1945, David Dilks (ed.), *The Diaries of Sir Alexander Cadogan, 1938–1945*, Cassell, London, 1971, p. 778.

46 'Ernest Bevin', 1947 (unused footage), Britishpathe.com (consulted 25 May 2022).

47 Lord Strang, *Home and Abroad*, Andre Deutsch, London, 1956, p. 294.

48 Lawford, 'Three Ministers'.

49 Strang, *Home and Abroad*, p. 294.

50 Mayhew, *Time To Explain*, p. 122. The most common version of the story involves 'Hugh and Nye' (Gaitskell and Bevan) but here Mayhew quotes from a letter Attlee sent him.

51 Roderick Barclay, *Ernest Bevin and the Foreign Office 1939–1969*, published by the author, London, 1975, p. 39.

52 Bullock, *Ernest Bevin: Foreign Secretary*, p. 77; Dalton, *High Tide and After*, p. 129.

53 Donoughue and Jones, *Herbert Morrison*, p. 346.

54 Clement Attlee, 'A Man of Power', *Observer*, 20 March 1960, in Frank Field (ed.), *Attlee's Great Contemporaries: The Politics of Character*, Continuum, London, 2009, p. 129.

55 Pimlott, *Hugh Dalton*, pp. 498–500.

56 Pimlott, *Political Diary of Hugh Dalton*, p. 397 (entry for 26 July 1947).

57 George Brown, *In My Way: The Political Memoirs of Lord George-Brown*, Victor Gollancz, London, 1971, p. 50.

58 Attlee, 'A man of power', in Field, *Attlee's Great Contemporaries*, pp. 123, 129–30.

59 Norwich, *Duff Cooper Diaries*, pp. 384–5 (entry for 11 Sept. 1945).

60 Jebb, *Memoirs of Lord Gladwyn*, p. 170.

61 O. G. Sargent, 'Foreign Office Circular No. 130: Correspondence from No. 10', 25 Nov. 1946, FO 800/463, TNA.

62 Francis Williams, *Nothing So Strange*, p. 218.

63 Pimlott, *Political Diary of Hugh Dalton*, p. 369 (entry for 22 March 1946).

64 John Kent, 'The Egyptian Base and the Defence of the Middle East, 1945–54', *Journal of Imperial and Commonwealth History*, 21 (1993), pp. 45–65; Saul Kelly, *Cold War in the Desert: Britain, the United States and the Italian Colonies, 1945–52*, Palgrave Macmillan, London, 2000, pp. 43–4; Christopher Mayhew diary, 26 May 1947 (copy), Mayhew Papers, 5/2.

65 Penderel Moon (ed.), *Wavell: The Viceroy's Journal*, Oxford University Press, London, 1973, p. 399 (entry for 24 Dec. 1946); Cabinet Secretary's notebook, 31 Dec. 1946, CM 108 (46), CAB 195/4, TNA; Bevin to Attlee, 1 Jan. 1947, FO 800/470, TNA.

66 Attlee to Bevin, 2 Jan. 1947, FO 800/470, TNA.

67 H. Kumarasingham (ed.), *The Rise of Labour and the Fall of Empire: The Memoirs of William Hare, Fifth Earl of Listowel*, Cambridge University Press, Cambridge, 2019, p. 122.

68 Francis Williams, *A Prime Minister Remembers*, p. 149.

69 Emrys Hughes, 'Mr. Bevin and Moscow', *Forward*, 5 Jan. 1945.

70 Emrys Hughes, 'Attlee', n.d. but post 1955, Hughes Papers, Dep.176/18.

71 Labour Party manifesto, 1945.

72 Stuart Ward, 'The European Provenance of Decolonization', *Past & Present*, 230 (2016), pp. 227–60.

73 Wm. Roger Louis, 'The dissolution of the British Empire', in Judith Brown and Wm. Roger Louis (eds), *The Oxford History of the British Empire; Vol. IV: The Twentieth Century*, Oxford University Press, Oxford, 1999, pp. 329–56.

74 Cabinet minutes, 31 Dec. 1946, CM (46) 108th Conclusions: Confidential Annex, Cab 128/8/8, TNA.

75 Partha Sarathi Gupta, *Imperialism and the British Labour Movement, 1914–1964*, Holmes & Meier Publishers, New York, 1975, Chapters 9 and 10. For Labour's later claims about its record see, for example, the party's 1955 manifesto.

76 Geoffrey Warner, 'The Study of Cold War Origins', *Diplomacy and Statecraft*, 1 (1990), pp. 13–26.

77 John Lewis Gaddis, *The Cold War: A New History*, The Penguin Press, New York, 2005, pp. 94–5.

78 Daniel W. B. Lomas, *Intelligence, Security and the Attlee Governments, 1945–51*, Manchester University Press, Manchester, 2017, p. 86.

79 John Kent, 'Bevin's imperialism and the idea of Euro-Africa, 1945–49', in Michael Dockrill and J. W. Young (eds), *British Foreign Policy, 1945–56*, Macmillan, London, 1989, pp. 47–76.

80 Castle, *Fighting All the Way*, pp. 128, 154.

81 Odd Arne Westad, *The Cold War: A World History*, Penguin Books, London, 2017, p. 64.

82 Healey, *Time of My Life*, p. 104.

83 Alexander Cadogan diary, 23 Sept. 1945, Cadogan Papers, ACAD 1/15.

84 'Dominion Prime Ministers: Extract from PMM (46) 1st meeting', 23 Apr. 1946, CAB 121/165, TNA.

85 Martin H. Folly, '"The impression is growing ... that the United States is hard when dealing with us": Ernest Bevin and Anglo-American Relations at the Dawn of the Cold War', *Journal of Transatlantic Studies*, 10 (2012), pp. 150–66.

86 Dixon diary, 30 July 1945, quoted in Dixon, *Double Diploma*, p. 170.

87 Ferrell (ed.), *The Diary of Eben A. Ayers*, , p. 60 (entry for 8 Aug. 1945).

88 James F. Byrnes, *Speaking Frankly*, William Heinemann Ltd, London, 1947, p. 79; Walter Millis (ed.), *The Forrestal Diaries: The Inner History of the Cold War*, Cassell & Company Ltd, London, 1952, p. 139 (entry for 8 Feb. 1946).

89 Archibald Clark Kerr to Bevin, 24 Nov. 1945, and 'Record of a Teletype Conversation Between the Foreign Secretary and Mr. Byrnes on November 27th, 1945', FO 800/446, TNA; 'Memorandum of Conversation, by the Secretary of State', 4 Dec. 1945, *Foreign Relations of the United States: Diplomatic Papers 1945; Vol. II: General: Political and Economic Matters*, United States Government Printing Office, Washington DC, 1967, pp. 593–5.

90 John Balfour (Washington Embassy) to Foreign Office, 27 Feb. 1946, FO 800/470, TNA.

91 Bullock, *Ernest Bevin: Foreign Secretary*, p. 416.

92 Jennifer Luff, 'Covert and Overt Operations: Interwar Political Policing in the United States and the United Kingdom', *American Historical Review*, 122 (2017), pp. 727–57; K. D. Ewing, Joan Mahoney and Andrew Moretta, *MI5, The Cold War, and the Rule of Law*, Oxford University Press, Oxford, 2020.

93 Thorpe, 'Locking out the Communists', pp. 221–50.

94 Parliamentary Debates, House of Commons, Fifth Series, Vol. 415, 7 Nov. 1945, col. 1342.

95 E. T. Bradford (on behalf of Yiwesley and West Drayton Labour Party) to Bevin, 27 Nov. 1945, and Bevin to Bradford, 5 Dec. 1945, FO 800/491, TNA.

96 Valentine Lawford diary (copy), 19 Dec. 1945, Lawford Papers, LWFD 2/8.

97 Frank Costigliola (ed.), *The Kennan Diaries*, W. W. Norton & Company, New York, 2014, pp. 192–3 (entry for 19 Dec. 1945).

98 Francis Williams, *Nothing So Strange*, p. 200.

99 David Robertson, *Sly and Able: A Political Biography of James F. Byrnes*, W. W. Norton & Company, New York, 1994, p. 452.

100 Alin-Victor Matei, 'Secretary of State Byrnes, the US East European Policy and the Moscow Conference of December 1945', *Romanian Journal of History and International Studies*, 2 (2015), pp. 7–22; Vasil Paraskevov, 'Conflict and Necessity: British–Bulgarian Relations, 1944–56', *Cold War History*, 11 (2011), pp. 241–68; Mihaela Sitariu, 'The British–Romanian Relations during the Cold War', *Studia Politica: Romanian Political Science Review*, 6 (2006), pp. 959–72.

101 'British Diplomatic Correspondents Press Conference', 1 Jan. 1946, FO 800/498, TNA.

102 'UNO: Great Commoner', *Time*, 18 Feb. 1946.

103 Louise Fawcett, 'Revisiting the Iranian Crisis of 1946: How Much More Do We Know?', *Iranian Studies*, 47 (2014), pp. 379–99.

104 Jebb, *Memoirs*, p. 183.

105 Healey, *Time of My Life*, p. 101.

106 Churchill, speech of 5 March 1946.

107 Cabinet Secretary's notebook, 11 March 1946, CM 23(46), CAB 195/4, TNA.

108 Parliamentary Debates, House of Commons, Fifth Series, Vol. 420, 11 March 1946, col. 760.

109 Attlee to W. L. Mackenzie King (draft telegram, n.d. but March 1946), FO 800/443, TNA. Note, though, that this was an officially drafted telegram in reply to one from King to Bevin, which Bevin himself had not considered worth answering.

110 Gardner, *Sterling-Dollar Diplomacy in Current Perspective*, pp. 238–9, 249; J. A. Hudson, 'Mr. Churchill and the Loan', 14 Mar 1946, PREM 8/197, TNA.

111 Duff Cooper to P. J. Dixon, 29 Sept. 1946, FO 800/464, TNA.

112 Millis, *Forrestal Diaries*, p. 150 (entry for 10 March 1946).

113 Anthony Eden, *The Reckoning*, Houghton Mifflin Company, Boston, 1965, p. 585.

114 Anthony Eden, *Full Circle*, Cassell, London, 1960, p. 5.

115 There is a vast literature on this topic. A landmark text is Addison, *The Road to 1945*. For discussion of how the debate developed see Chapter 9 below.

116 Arthur H. Vandenberg Jr (ed.), *The Private Papers of Senator Vandenberg*, Houghton Mifflin Company, Boston, p. 276 (entry for 6 May 1946).

117 United States delegation record, Council of Foreign Ministers, 6 May 1946, *Foreign Relations of the United States, 1946, Council of Foreign Ministers; Vol. II*, United States Government Printing Office, Washington DC, 1970, pp. 255–6.

118 Bullock, *Ernest Bevin: Foreign Secretary*, pp. 287–8; 'Mr. Bevin Must Rest for Week', *Sunday Times*, 28 July 1946.

119 'Mild Russian Reaction To Mr. Bevin', *Observer*, 27 Oct. 1946.

120 'A Policy Wanted', *Daily Mail*, 23 Oct. 1946.

121 'New Approach to Germany?', *New Statesman & Nation*, 26 Oct. 1946.

122 'Mr. Bevin's Labour Critics', *Manchester Guardian*, 25 Oct. 1946.

123 Cecil Bloom, 'The British Labour Party and Palestine, 1917–1948', *Jewish Historical Studies*, 36 (1999), pp. 141–71.

124 'Jew Gang Sent Letter-Bombs', *Aberdeen Journal*, 6 June 1947.

125 Harry S. Truman, *Memoirs; Vol. II: Years of Trial and Hope*, Doubleday and Company Inc., New York, 1956, pp. 153–4; LPACR 1946, p. 165.

126 Raphael Langham, 'The Bevin Enigma: What Motivated Ernest Bevin's Opposition to the Establishment of a Jewish State in Palestine', *Jewish Historical Studies*, 44 (2012), pp. 165–78.

127 Mayhew, *Time To Explain*, p. 119.

128 Crossman et al., *Keep Left*, p. 44.

129 Castle, *Fighting All the Way*, p. 155.

130 Victoria Honeyman, *Richard Crossman: A Reforming Radical of the Labour Party*, I.B. Tauris, London, 2007, p. 72.

131 R. H. S. Crossman, *A Nation Reborn: The Israel of Weizmann, Bevin, and Ben-Gurion*, Hamish Hamilton, London, 1960, p. 80.

132 Jay, *Change and Fortune*, p. 133.

133 Tam Dalyell, *Dick Crossman: A Portrait*, Weidenfeld & Nicolson, London, 1989, p. 20.

134 Barbara Ayrton Gould et al. to Attlee, 29 Oct. 1946, Levy Papers, LEV/18.

135 Jonathan Schneer, 'Hopes Deferred or Shattered: The British Labour Left and the Third Force Movement, 1945–49', *Journal of Modern History*, 56 (1984), pp. 197–226, at 206.

136 Mayhew diary (copy), 13 Nov. 1946, Mayhew Papers, 5/2.

137 'The Prime Minister Talks to Picture Post', *Picture Post*, 27 July 1946. The interview was by Barbara Castle.

138 Parliamentary Debates, House of Commons, Fifth Series, Vol. 430, 18 Nov. 1946, col. 538.

139 Foreign Office to Washington Embassy, 25 Nov. 1946, FO 371/51640, TNA.

140 Lord Inverchapel to the Foreign Office, 20 Nov. 1946, FO 371/51640, TNA.

141 Castle, *Fighting All the Way*, p. 157.

142 Jay, *Change and Fortune*, p. 160.

143 Denise M. Bostdorff, *Proclaiming the Truman Doctrine: The Cold War Call to Arms*, Texas A & M University Press, College Station, 2008, p. 51.

144 Harry S. Truman, 'Special Message to the Congress on Greece and Turkey: The Truman Doctrine', 12 March 1947, *Public Papers of the Presidents of the United States: Harry S. Truman: 1947*, United States Government Printing Office, Washington DC, 1963, pp. 178–9.

145 Lord Montgomery, *The Memoirs of Field-Marshal Montgomery*, Collins, London, 1958, p. 436.

146 Bullock, *Ernest Bevin: Foreign Secretary*, pp. 348–52.

147 Peter Hennessy, 'How Bevin Saved Britain's Bomb', *The Times*, 30 Sept. 1982.

148 R. H. S. Crossman to the editor of the *New Statesman*, published 31 May 1963.

149 G. R. Strauss to the editor of the *New Statesman*, published 10 May 1963; Strauss, unpublished memoirs, p. 126, Strauss Papers, STRS1/2. The debate had been triggered by comments Crossman made in his introduction to a new edition of Walter Bagehot's *The English Constitution*, which marked the start of a long-running academic debate about the nature of prime ministerial power.

150 Attlee, 'Near Eastern Policy', 5 Jan. 1947, FO 800/476, TNA.

151 Mayhew diary, 26 May 1947, Mayhew Papers, 52.

152 Pimlott, *Political Diary of Hugh Dalton*, p. 391 (entry for 24 Feb. 1947).

153 John Julius Norwich (ed.), *Darling Monster: The Letters of Lady Diana Cooper to Her Son John Julius Norwich, 1939–1952*, Overlook Press, New York, 2014, p. 210 (letter of 10 Feb. 1947).

154 Kathleen Paul, '"British Subjects" and "British Stock": Labour's Post-war Imperialism', *Journal of British Studies*, 34 (1995), pp. 233–76.

155 LPACR 1950, p. 147.

156 Richard Taylor, *English Radicalism in the Twentieth Century: A Distinctive Politics?*, Manchester University Press, Manchester, 2020, p. 125.

CHAPTER 5

1 Stafford Cripps, 'Wages Policy', CP (47) 303, 11 Nov. 1947, CAB 129/22/13, TNA.

2 Philip M. Williams (ed.), *The Diary of Hugh Gaitskell, 1945–1956*, Jonathan Cape, London, 1983, p. 45 (entry for 14 Nov. 1947); Cabinet minutes, CM (47) 37th Conclusions, 13 Nov. 1947, CAB 128/10/38, and Cabinet Secretary's notebook, CM 37 (47), 13 Nov. 1947, CAB 195/5, TNA.

3 *Daily Mail*, 14 Nov. 1947. The article was by Wilson Broadbent.

4 'London Letter', *Belfast News-Letter*, 14 Nov. 1947.

5 Mikardo, *Back-Bencher*, pp. 127–8; Jay, *Change and Fortune*, p. 177.

6 Barbara Castle, 'Only an Idealist?' (review of *The Life of Richard Stafford Cripps* by Colin Cooke), *New Statesman & Nation*, 2 March 1957. Castle's official biographer mistakenly suggests that this article was published in *Tribune*. Anne Perkins, *Red Queen: The Authorized Biography of Barbara Castle*, Macmillan, London, 2003, p. 85.

7   Michael Foot, *Aneurin Bevan: A Biography; Vol. II: 1945–1960*, Davis-Poynter, London, 1973, p. 35; Paul Einzig, *In the Centre of Things: The Autobiography of Paul Einzig*, Hutchinson, London, 1960, p. 262.

8   Hugh Dalton, 'Note on a Difference of Opinion', 20 Jan. 1947, Attlee Papers (Bodleian), MS Attlee dep. 49, ff. 86–91. Much of this document is reproduced in Dalton, *High Tide and After*, pp. 194–8.

9   Tomlinson, *Democratic Socialism*, p. 58.

10 Pimlott, *Hugh Dalton*, pp. 475, 489.

11 Dalton, *High Tide and After*, p. 6.

12 Jim Tomlinson, 'Welfare and the Economy: The Economic Impact of the Welfare State, 1945–1951', *Twentieth Century British History*, 6 (1995), pp. 194–219, and 'Correlli Barnett's History: The Case of Marshall Aid', *Twentieth Century British History*, 8 (1997), pp. 222–38.

13 Einzig, *In the Centre of Things*, p. 263.

14 Parliamentary Debates, House of Commons, Fifth Series, Vol. 430, 18 Nov. 1946, col. 580; Herbert Morrison, 'Full Employment in the Soviet Union', CP (46) 35, 24 Sept. 1946, CAB 129/13/5, TNA.

15 Speech of 17 Oct. 1946 in Herbert Morrison, *The Peaceful Revolution*, George Allen & Unwin Ltd, London, 1949, p. 17.

16 Susan Howson and D. E. Moggridge (eds), *The Collected Papers of James Meade; Vol. IV: The Cabinet Office Diary, 1944–1946*, Unwin Hyman, London, 1990, p. 202 (entry for 27 Jan. 1946); Edward Bridges to James Meade, 22 Aug. 1945, T230/18, TNA.

17 Hugh Dalton, 'Our financial plan', in Herbert Morrison et al., *Forward From Victory! Labour's Plan*, Victor Gollancz Ltd, London, 1946, pp. 38–51, at 47.

18 Howson and Moggridge, *Cabinet Office Diary*, p. 283 (entry for 30 June 1946).

19 Dalton to Morrison, 17 Jan. 1947, CAB 124/898, TNA.

20 R. W. B. Clarke diary, 5 Feb. 1946, Clarke Papers, CLRK 4/4/4.

21 Richard Acland et al., *Keeping Left: Labour's First Five Years and the Problems Ahead*, New Statesman, London, 1950, p. 29. The revisionist Tony Crosland drew attention to this passage with a certain amount of relish. C. A. R. Crosland, *The Future of Socialism*, The Macmillan Company, New York, 1957 (first published 1956), p. 476.

22 Robert Millward, 'Industrial organisation and economic factors in nationalisation', in Robert Millward and John Singleton (eds), *The Political Economy of Nationalisation in Britain 1920–1950*, Cambridge University Press, Cambridge, 1995, pp. 3–12.

23 Broadcast by A. V. Alexander, 11 June 1945, quoted in 'Bevin Gives Ultimatum to Building Combines', *Daily Herald*, 12 June 1945.

24 Henry Usborne, 'The Spirit of Competition', *The Town Crier* (Birmingham), 23 June 1945. Usborne won the seat of Acock's Green for Labour.

25 Andrew J. Taylor, 'The Miners and Nationalisation, 1931–36', *International Review of Social History*, 28 (1983), pp. 176–99; Barry Supple, *The History of the British Coal Industry; Vol. 4, 1914–1946: The Political Economy of Decline*, Clarendon Press, Oxford, 1987, p. 667.

26 Emanuel Shinwell, *Conflict Without Malice*, Odhams Press Ltd, London, 1955, pp. 172–3.

27 Hugh Chevins, 'State Takes Over Coal Mines', *Daily Telegraph*, 2 Jan. 1947.

28 'Too Big for Them', *Daily Mail*, 2 July 1947.
29 Roy Church and Quentin Outram, *Strikes and Solidarity: Coalfield Conflict in Britain, 1889–1966*, Cambridge University Press, Cambridge, 1998, pp. 260–1.
30 Peter Ackers and Jonathan Payne, 'Before the Storm: The Experience of Nationalization and the Prospects for Industrial Relations Partnership in the British Coal Industry, 1947–1972 – Rethinking the Militant Narrative', *Social History*, 27 (2002), pp. 184–209.
31 Jim Phillips, 'Deindustrialization and the Moral Economy of the Scottish Coalfields, 1947 to 1991', *International Labor and Working-Class History*, 84 (2013), pp. 99–115.
32 Neil Evans and Dot Jones, '"A Blessing for the Miner's Wife": The Campaign for Pithead Baths in the South Wales Coalfield, 1908–1950', *Llafur*, 6 (1994), pp. 5–28.
33 David Greasley, 'The coal industry: images and realities on the road to nationalisation', in Millward and Singleton, *Political Economy of Nationalisation*, pp. 37–64.
34 Pimlott, *Hugh Dalton*, pp. 351–5.
35 C. A. Jones, S. J. Davies and N. Macdonald, 'Examining the Social Consequences of Extreme Weather: The Outcomes of the 1946/1947 Winter in Upland Wales, UK', *Climatic Change*, 113 (2012), pp. 35–53, at 37.
36 Simon Burgess, *Stafford Cripps: A Political Life*, Victor Gollancz, London, 1999, p. 226.
37 Anon, *The Scottish Socialists: A Gallery of Contemporary Portraits*, Faber and Faber, London, 1931, p. 157.
38 'Mr. Shinwell Claims to Have Tact', *Sunday Times*, 14 July 1946.
39 Parliamentary Debates, House of Commons, Fifth Series, Vol. 426, 24 July 1946, col. 45.
40 '"Improvements" to Coal Bill', *Financial Times*, 11 Apr. 1946.
41 Jay, *Change and Fortune*, p. 152.
42 Shinwell, *Conflict Without Malice*, p. 182.
43 Jay, *Change and Fortune*, pp. 142–52.
44 Emanuel Shinwell, 'Output, Recruitment and Conditions of Employment in the Coal-Mining Industry', CP (46) 232, 17 June 1946, CAB 129/10/32, TNA; Parliamentary Debates, House of Commons, Fifth Series, Vol. 426, 24 July 1946, col. 68.
45 '"No Crisis in Coal"', *The Times*, 25 Oct. 1946.
46 Shinwell, *Conflict Without Malice*, p. 182.
47 Williams, *Diary of Hugh Gaitskell*, p. 30 (entry for 12 Aug. 1947).
48 Herbert Morrison, 'Economic Survey for 1947', CP (47) 20, 7 Jan. 1947, CAB 129/16/20, TNA.
49 'Economic Survey for 1947: Report from the Ministerial Committee on Economic Planning', CP (47) 25, CAB 129/16/25, TNA.
50 Cabinet minutes, CM (47) 7th conclusions, 16 Jan. 1947, CM (47) 8th conclusions, 16 Jan. 1947, CM (47) 9th conclusions, 17 Jan. 1947, CAB 128/9/7-9.
51 Dalton, 'Note on a Difference of Opinion'; Dalton diary, 27 Jan. 1947, Dalton Papers, I/35.
52 Dalton diary, 7 Feb. 1947, in Dalton, *High Tide and After*, p. 203.

53 Morgan, *Labour in Power*, p. 333; Hugh Chevins, 'Ban on Electric and Gas Fires', *Daily Telegraph*, 25 Apr. 1947.

54 Richard Farmer, 'All Work and No Play: British Leisure Culture and the 1947 Fuel Crisis', *Contemporary British History*, 27 (2013), pp. 22–43, and 'Suspension Or Suppression? The British Periodical Press and the 1947 Fuel Crisis', *Media History*, 19 (2013), pp. 153–68.

55 Anthony King (ed.), *British Political Opinion 1937–2000: The Gallup Polls*, Politico's, London, 2001, p. 2.

56 Francis Williams, *A Prime Minister Remembers*, p. 221.

57 *Economic Survey for 1947*, Cmd. 7046, Feb. 1947.

58 Alec Cairncross, *Years of Recovery: British Economic Policy 1945–51*, Methuen & Co. Ltd, London, 1985, p. 309.

59 'The Language of Leadership' (File Report 2462), 20 March 1947, Mass Observation Archive.

60 Fenner Brockway, *Inside the Left: Thirty Years of Platform, Press, Prison and Parliament*, George Allen & Unwin Ltd, London, 1942, p. 137.

61 Margaret Cole, 'Ellen Wilkinson', *Tribune*, 6 Nov. 1964; Alice Davidson, 'For Humanity – She Directs British Education', *New York Post*, 14 Aug. 1945, copy in Wilkinson Papers, LP/WI/5-6.

62 Beers, 'A Model MP?', pp. 231–50.

63 Jennie Lee, 'Ellen Wilkinson', *Tribune*, 14 Feb. 1947; Laura Beers, *Red Ellen: The Life of Ellen Wilkinson, Socialist, Feminist, Internationalist*, Harvard University Press, Cambridge, MA, 2016, pp. 386–7.

64 Mary Agnes Hamilton, 'Miss Wilkinson', *Spectator*, 24 Aug. 1945; Kingsley Martin, 'Ellen Wilkinson', *New Statesman & Nation*, 15 Feb. 1947; Fenner Brockway, 'The Tireless Activism of Ellen Wilkinson' (review of *Ellen Wilkinson* by Betty D. Vernon), *Tribune*, 19 Feb. 1982.

65 Matt Perry, *'Red Ellen' Wilkinson: Her Ideas, Movements and World*, Manchester University Press, Manchester, 2014, p. 374

66 'Education Has New Plan For Commerce', *Sheffield Telegraph*, 17 July 1946, copy in Wilkinson Papers, LP/WI/5-6.

67 Ellen Wilkinson, 'Ellen Wilkinson', in the Countess of Oxford and Asquith (ed.), *Myself When Young, by Famous Women of Today*, Frederick Muller Ltd, London, 1938, pp. 319–416, at 403–4.

68 'Accidental Overdose of Drugs', *The Times*, 1 March 1947.

69 Paddington and Westminster fell under the jurisdiction of the coroner for the County of London Western district in 1947. The London Metropolitan Archives holds only a 10 per cent sample of surviving coroners' inquests. Sadly, the papers of the Wilkinson inquest are not among the papers that have survived. Though the inquest was reported in the press, such material might have cast additional light on what occurred.

70 Donoughue and Jones, *Herbert Morrison*, p. 392.

71 'London', 10 Feb. 1947, britishpathe.com (consulted 28 June 2022).

72 In 1950 Edith Summerskill became Minister of National Insurance but without a Cabinet seat. Two other women served briefly as junior ministers: Jennie Adamson and Margaret (Peggy) Herbison.

73 Mann, *Woman in Parliament*, p. 40.

74 Lord Tedder, J. H. D. Cunningham and Lord Montgomery, 'The Defence of the Commonwealth', DC (47) 23, 7 March 1947, FO 800/451, TNA.

75 Moon (ed.), *Wavell: The Viceroy's Journal,* , pp. 274, 310 (entry for 20 May 1946 and retrospect of March to June 1946).

76 Clarke, *Cripps Version*, pp. 435–6.

77 Anwesha Roy, *Making Peace, Making Riots: Communalism and Communal Violence, Bengal 1940–1947*, Cambridge University Press, Cambridge, 2018, p. 148.

78 Y. Krishnan, 'Mountbatten and the Partition of India', *History*, 68 (1983), pp. 22–38.

79 Earl Mountbatten, 'Reflections on the transfer of power and Jawaharlal Nehru', in Lord Butler et al., *The Jawaharlal Nehru Memorial Lectures: Being the four lectures given in the years between 1966 and 1971*, The Jawaharlal Nehru Memorial Trust, London, 1973, pp. 17–36, at 20.

80 Philip Ziegler, *Mountbatten*, Alfred A. Knopf, New York, 1985, pp. 335–6.

81 'Full Power For Indians By June, 1948', *The Times*, 21 Feb. 1947.

82 Leading articles of, respectively, the *Hindustan Times* and *Dawn*, 21 Feb. 1947, both reproduced in Nicholas Mansergh and Penderel Moon (eds), *The Transfer of Power 1942–47; Vol. IX: The Fixing of a Time Limit 4 November 1946–22 March 1947*, HMSO, London, 1980, pp. 775–8.

83 'Mr. Attlee's Statement', *The Hitavada* (Nagpur), 22 Feb. 1947, text in Records of the State Department, Central File: Decimal File 845.00, National Archives (USA).

84 Nicholas Owen, 'The Conservative Party and Indian Independence, 1945–1947', *Historical Journal*, 46 (2003), pp. 403–36.

85 'Two New Dominions', *Daily Mail*, 15 Aug. 1947.

86 Lewis Douglas to George C. Marshall, 2 June 1947, *Foreign Relations of the United States, 1947; Vol. III: The British Commonwealth; Europe*, United States Government Printing Office, Washington DC, 1972, pp. 155–6.

87 Yasmin Khan, *The Great Partition: The Making of India and Pakistan*, Yale University Press, New Haven, CT, 2017, p. 6.

88 Speech of 6 Dec. 1947.

89 Ronald Hyam, 'Africa and the Labour Government, 1945–1951', *Journal of Imperial and Commonwealth History*, 16 (1988), pp. 148–72, at 169.

90 Huw Bennett, '"A very salutary effect": The Counter-Terror Strategy in the Early Malayan Emergency, June 1948 to December 1949', *Journal of Strategic Studies*, 32 (2009), pp. 415–44.

91 Tomlinson, *Democratic Socialism*, p. 65; D. K. Fieldhouse, 'The Labour governments and the Empire Commonwealth 1945–51', in Ritchie Ovendale (ed.), *The Foreign Policy of the British Labour Governments 1945–51*, Leicester University Press, Leicester, 1984, pp. 83–118.

92 Nathan Jumba Anyonge, 'British Groundnut Scheme in East Africa: Labour Government's Dilemma', MA thesis, Kansas State University, 1966; Edgerton, *The Rise and Fall of the British Nation*, p. 100; Nicholas Westcott, *Imperialism and Development: The East African Groundnut Scheme and Its Legacy*, James Currey, Woodbridge, Suffolk, 2020.

93 George C. Marshall, speech of 5 June 1947, https://www.marshallfoundation.org/the-marshall-plan/speech/ (consulted 4 July 2022).

94 Leonard Miall, 'How the Marshall Plan Started', *The Listener*, 4 May 1961.

95 Francis Williams, *Ernest Bevin*, p. 265; Strang, *Home and Abroad*, p. 289.

96 Charles E. Bohlen, *Witness to History 1929–1969*, W. W. Norton & Company Inc., New York, 1973, p. 264.

97 'Ce discours serait le prolongement logique de la doctrine du président Truman', *Le Monde*, 6 June 1947.

98 Henry Pelling, *Britain and the Marshall Plan*, St Martin's Press, New York, 1988, pp. 8–9.

99 Acheson, *Present at the Creation*, p. 234.

100 'Text of Bevin's Speech on the Atlantic Pact', *New York Times*, 2 Apr. 1949.

101 Bullock, *Ernest Bevin: Foreign Secretary*, p. 404.

102 Larry I. Bland and Joellen K. Bland (eds), *George C. Marshall: Interviews and Reminiscences for Forrest C. Pogue*, George C. Marshall Research Foundation, Lexington, VA, 1991, p. 560.

103 Diane B. Kunz, 'The Marshall Plan Reconsidered: A Complex of Motives', *Foreign Affairs*, 76 (1997), pp. 162–70, at 168.

104 Jim Tomlinson, 'Marshall Aid and the "Shortage Economy" in Britain in the 1940s', *Contemporary European History*, 9 (2000), pp. 137–55, at 140.

105 Gardner, *Sterling-Dollar Diplomacy In Current Perspective*, pp. 312, 319.

106 Cabinet minutes, CM (47) 65th conclusions, 29 July 1947, CAB 128/10/16, TNA.

107 Pimlott, *Hugh Dalton*, pp. 483–4, 499–500. On coalition rumours see, for example, 'Coalition Rumours', *The Economist*, 2 Aug. 1947; Albert Hird diary, 14 Aug. 1947; Lord Beaverbrook to Brendan Bracken, 13 Aug. 1947, in Richard Cockett (ed.), *My Dear Max: The Letters of Brendan Bracken to Lord Beaverbrook, 1925–1958*, The Historians' Press, London, 1990, p. 73.

108 Edwin Plowden, *An Industrialist in the Treasury: The Post-War Years*, Andre Deutsch, London, 1989, p. 13.

109 Pimlott (ed.), *Political Diary of Hugh Dalton*, pp. 405–7 (entries for 31 July and 8 Aug. 1947); Dalton, *High Tide and After*, p. 259 (diary entry for early August 1947).

110 Williams, *Diary of Hugh Gaitskell*, p. 24 (entry for 12 Aug. 1947).

111 Gardner, *Sterling-Dollar Diplomacy*, pp. 323–5.

112 Christopher Mayhew diary, 17 Aug. 1947 (copy), Mayhew Papers 5/2.

113 *Daily Mail*, 20 Aug. 1947.

114 *Minutes of Evidence Taken Before the Royal Commission on the Press, 29th April 1948*, Cmd. 7480, July 1948, p. 303.

115 Pearce, *Patrick Gordon Walker Diaries*, p. 169, n. 6.

116 Brown, *In My Way*, pp. 50–1.

117 Parliamentary Debates, House of Commons, Fifth Series, Vol. 441, 7 Aug. 1947, col. 1766.

118 Jay, *Change and Fortune*, p. 165.

119 Mikardo, *Back-Bencher*, p. 128.

120 Dalton diary, entries for 5–9 Sept. 1947, Dalton Papers I/35 (Dalton paraphrased these entries closely in *High Tide and After*, pp. 240–6); Herbert Morrison to Stafford Cripps, 8 Sept. 1947 (copy), and Cripps to Morrison, 8 Sept. 1947,

Morrison Papers (Nuffield), E35–36; Pearce, *Patrick Gordon Walker Diaries*, p. 167 (entry for 8 Sept. 1947).

121 Mikardo, *Back-Bencher*, p. 93.

122 Harris, *Attlee*, p. 349. Emphasis added.

123 George W. Jones, interview with Philip Noel-Baker, 20 March 1969, Morrison Papers (LSE), 6/1.

124 Mayhew, *Time To Explain*, p. 104, quoting diary entries for 29 July and 17 Aug. 1947. The original of Mayhew's diary does not appear to have survived, though a transcript of another part of the August entry is in the Mayhew Papers, 5/2.

125 Speech by Cripps at the opening of the Geneva conference, 11 Apr. 1947, Robinson Papers, ROBN 6/6/3.

126 Speech by Wilson in Geneva on 23 Aug. 1947, Wilson Papers, MS Wilson c. 1096.

127 William L. Clayton to Robert A. Lovett, 11 Aug. 1947, RG 59 560.AL/8-1147, National Archives (USA).

128 'Note by President [of the Board of Trade]', 22 Sept. 1947, BT 11/3647, TNA.

129 Telegram from Foreign Office to UK delegation in Geneva, 27 Sept. 1947, BT 64/2346, TNA.

130 Winthrop G. Brown oral history, 25 May 1973, Truman Library.

131 Francine McKenzie, *GATT and Global Order in the Post-war Era*, Cambridge University Press, Cambridge, 2020, Chapter 1.

132 Ian Mikardo, 'Sir Stafford Takes Over', *Tribune*, 10 Oct. 1947.

133 Alec Cairncross (ed.), *The Robert Hall Diaries 1947–1953*, Unwin Hyman, London, 1989, p. 8 (entry for 30 Sept. 1947).

134 'Report from the Select Committee on the Budget Disclosure', HMSO, London, 1947.

135 Dalton, *High Tide and After*, pp. 276–8.

136 Pimlott, *Hugh Dalton*, p. 540.

137 Francis Williams, *Nothing So Strange*, p. 226.

CHAPTER 6

1 'Mr. Bevan's Bitter Attack on Conservatives', *Manchester Guardian*, 5 July 1948; 'Bevan says: "The Tories Are Lower Than Vermin"', *Northern Whig*, 5 July 1948.

2 'The Vermin Club', *Belfast Telegraph*, 12 July 1948; 'Bevan's "Vermin" Form a National Club', *Aberdeen Journal*, 7 Aug. 1948.

3 '"Vermin" Painted on Bevan's Home', *Derby Daily Telegraph*, 10 July 1948.

4 'Bevan Explains "Vermin"', *Leicester Evening Mail*, 24 July 1948.

5 'Good Men Doing Bad Things', *Manchester Guardian*, 7 July 1952.

6 Vincent Brome, *Aneurin Bevan: A Biography*, Longmans, Green and Co., London, 1953, p. 82.

7 Foot, *Aneurin Bevan: Vol. II:*, , p. 241.

8 Campbell, *Nye Bevan*, p. 178.

9 'Mr. Bevan', *Manchester Guardian*, 12 July 1948

10 Martin Francis, 'Tears, Tantrums, and Bared Teeth: The Emotional Economy of Three Conservative Prime Ministers, 1951–1963', *Journal of British Studies*, 41 (2002), pp. 354–87.

11 'Churchill to Attlee: "Disavow Bevan"', *Observer*, 11 July 1948.

12 'Conservative Reply to Mr. Bevan', *Yorkshire Post*, 10 July 1948.

13 F. E. Sibbons to the editor of the *Chelmsford Chronicle*, published 16 July 1948.

14 Brian Rees-Williams to Morgan Phillips, 29 Jan. 1951, General Secretary's Papers, LP/GS/BCST/167–169, LPA.

15 'Behaviour', *Observer*, 11 July 1948.

16 Nikolaus Coupland, 'Aneurin Bevan, class wars and the styling of political antagonism', in Peter Auer (ed.), *Style and Social Identities Alternative Approaches to Linguistic Heterogeneity*, Mouton de Gruyter, Berlin, 2007, pp. 213–45.

17 Aneurin Bevan to Morgan Phillips, 15 Sept. 1948, General Secretary's Papers, LP/GS/HEA/106–110, LPA.

18 Beverley Baxter, 'London Letter: The Pit Boy Who Never Forgets', *Maclean's Magazine*, 1 July 1951.

19 James Griffiths, '"The Enigma" (Nye Bevan)', 9 Oct. 1973, Griffiths Papers, E1/41; Mann, *Woman in Parliament*, p. 108.

20 Noel Thompson, 'To See Ourselves: The Rhetorical Construction of an Ideal Citizenry in the Perorations of Twentieth-Century Budget Speeches', *British Politics*, 12 (2017), pp. 90–114, at 103–4.

21 'Celticus' (Aneurin Bevan), *Why Not Trust the Tories?*, Victor Gollancz, London, 1944, Chapter 5.

22 Peter Malpass, 'The Wobbly Pillar? Housing and the British Post-war Welfare State', *Journal of Social Policy*, 32 (2003), pp. 589–606.

23 Kevin Morgan, 'The Problem of the Epoch? Labour and Housing, 1918–51', *Twentieth Century British History*, 16 (2005), pp. 227–55.

24 Dalton, *High Tide and After*, p. 358.

25 Enid Russell-Smith to R. A. Russell-Smith, 22 Aug. 1945 (letter started on 19 August), Russell-Smith Papers, RUSM 1/5.

26 Lee, *My Life with Nye*, p. 158.

27 Parliamentary Debates, House of Commons, Fifth Series, Vol. 395, 15 Dec. 1943, col. 1617.

28 Aneurin Bevan, 'Housing', CP (45) 208, 6 Oct. 1945, CAB 129/3/8, TNA. The 'super area' of a property includes its share of common areas and balconies, terraces, etc.

29 Dalton, *High Tide and After*, p. 358.

30 Harriet Jones, '"This is magnificent!": 300,000 Houses a Year and the Tory Revival after 1945', *Contemporary British History*, 14 (2000), pp. 99–121. Jones points out that the move to lower standards began in the last year of the Labour government, when Dalton rather than Bevan was in charge.

31 Parliamentary Debates, House of Commons, Fifth Series, Vol. 494, 4 Dec. 1951, col. 2255.

32 John A. Chenier, 'The Development and Implementation of Post-war Housing Policy Under the Labour Government', DPhil thesis, University of Oxford, 1984; Nicholas Timmins, *The Five Giants: A Biography of the Welfare State*, HarperCollins, London, 1995, Chapter 8.

33 James Hinton, 'Self-help and Socialism: The Squatters' Movement of 1946', *History Workshop Journal*, 25 (1988), pp. 100–126; Jo Guldi, 'World Neoliberalism as

Rebellion From Below? British Squatters and the Global Interpretation of Poverty, 1946–1974', *Humanity*, 10 (2019), pp. 29–57; Cabinet minutes, CM (46) 30th conclusions, 9 Sept. 1946, CAB 126/6/18 and Cabinet Secretary's notebook 9 Sept. 1946, CM 80 (46), CAB 195/4/59, TNA.

34 '"Mounties" Foil Squat Crowds', *Daily Mail*, 13 Sept. 1946.

35 'Squatters and Squatted Against', *Picture Post*, 28 Sept. 1946.

36 'It's Anarchy, Says Ellen', *Daily Mail*, 13 Sept. 1946.

37 'Squatters Will Have To Get Out', *Sunday Post*, 8 Sept. 1946; 'Squatters Upset Housing Plans, Bevan Complains', *Dundee Courier*, 19 Sept. 1946.

38 B. B. Dickinson, 'Communist Meeting' 19 Sept. 1946, KV 2/994, TNA. The speaker was Fred Parkes.

39 Hinton, 'Self-help and Socialism', pp. 114–16.

40 Parliamentary Debates, House of Commons, Fifth Series, Vol. 453, 14 July 1948, cols 1317–18.

41 Lee, *My Life With Nye*, p. 179.

42 John Robert Temple, 'A Radical and Progressive Legacy: Labour's Housing Record, 1945 to 1951', *Labour History Review*, 87 (2022), pp. 65–89.

43 Guy Ortolano, *Thatcher's Progress: From Social Democracy to Market Liberalism through an English New Town*, Cambridge University Press, Cambridge, 2019, p. 12.

44 Arthur Christiansen to Lord Beaverbrook, 28 May 1948, Beaverbrook Papers, BBK H/127.

45 Ellen Wilkinson to Ernest Bevin, ?30 Sept. 1945, FO 800/491, TNA.

46 Francis Williams, *Nothing So Strange*, pp. 226–7.

47 Clement Attlee, 'Bevan as Hero', *Observer*, 21 Oct. 1962, in Field (ed.), *Attlee's Great Contemporaries*, p. 138. Field misdates the article to 6 Nov. 1960.

48 Castle, *Fighting All the Way*, p. 108.

49 Barbara Castle, 'A passionate defiance', in Geoffrey Goodman (ed.), *The State of the Nation: The Political Legacy of Aneurin Bevan*, Victor Gollancz, London, 1997, pp. 36–67, at 36.

50 Foot, *Bevan; Vol. II*, p. 40.

51 Donald Bruce, 'Nye', in Goodman, *State of the Nation*, pp. 130–55, at 133.

52 William Scott Douglas to Aneurin Bevan, 22 Sept. 1945, MH 80/29, TNA; Charles Webster, *The National Health Service: A Political History* (2nd edn), Oxford University Press, Oxford, 2002, p. 14.

53 J. M. Winter, 'The Impact of the First World War on Civilian Health in Britain', *Economic History Review*, 30 (1977), pp. 487–507; J. M. Winter, 'Infant Mortality, Maternal Mortality and Public Health in Britain in the 1930s', *Journal of European Economic History*, 8 (1979), pp. 439–62; Timothy J. Hatton, 'Infant Mortality and the Health of Survivors: Britain, 1910–50', *Economic History Review*, 64 (2011), pp. 951–72; Steven David Thompson, 'A Social History of Health in Interwar South Wales', PhD thesis, Aberystwyth University, 2001, p. 355.

54 Charles Webster, 'Conflict and Consensus: Explaining the British Health Service', *Twentieth Century British History*, 1 (1990), pp. 115–51, at 142.

55 Alysa Levene, 'Between Less Eligibility and the NHS: The Changing Place of Poor Law Hospitals in England and Wales, 1929–39', *Twentieth Century British History*, 20 (2009), pp. 322–45; Nick Hayes, 'Did We Really Want a National Health

Service? Hospitals, Patients and Public Opinions before 1948', *English Historical Review*, CXXVII (2012), pp. 625–61.

56 Anne Digby and Nick Bosanquet, 'Doctors and Patients in an Era of National Health Insurance and Private Practice, 1913–1938', *Economic History Review*, 41 (1988), pp. 74–94.

57 Martin Gorsky and John Mohan, 'London's Voluntary Hospitals in the Interwar Period: Growth, Transformation, or Crisis?', *Non-profit and Voluntary Sector Quarterly*, 30 (2001), pp. 247–75, at 248, 271.

58 John Stewart, '"The Finest Municipal Hospital Service in the World"? Contemporary Perceptions of the London County Council's Hospital Provision, 1929–39', *Urban History*, 32 (2005), pp. 327–44.

59 Note by Edith Summerskill appended to 'Somerville Hastings', *British Medical Journal*, 15 July 1967.

60 Somerville Hastings, *The People's Health*, Labour Party, London, 1932, p. 4.

61 *For Socialism and Peace*, Labour Party, London, 1934, p. 23; John Stewart, 'Hastings, Somerville (1878–1967), surgeon and politician', *Oxford Dictionary of National Biography*. Retrieved 10 Aug. 2022 from https://www.oxforddnb.com/view/10.1093/ref:odnb/9780198614128.001.0001/odnb-9780198614128-e-50372.

62 John Stewart, 'Socialist Proposals for Health Reform in Inter-War Britain: The Case of Somerville Hastings', *Medical History*, 39 (1995), pp. 338–57, at 344.

63 *National Service For Health*, Labour Party, London, 1943.

64 Esyllt Jones, 'Nothing Too Good for the People: Local Labour and London's Interwar Health Centre Movement', *Social History of Medicine*, 25 (2012), pp. 84–102.

65 Charles Webster, *Problems of Health Care: The National Health Service Before 1957*, HMSO, London, 1988, pp. 22–4.

66 William Beveridge, *Social Insurance and Allied Services*, HMSO, London, 1942, p. 8.

67 Webster, *Problems of Health Care*, pp. 50–75; Harriet Jones, 'The Conservative Party and the Welfare State 1942–1955', pp. 95–7.

68 Foot, *Bevan; Vol. II*, p. 131.

69 Webster, *National Health Service*, p. 3.

70 Hayes, 'Did We Really Want a National Health Service?', p. 661.

71 For a round-up of the main lines of newspaper views, see 'Public Opinion: The Press and the Bill', *British Medical Journal*, 6 Apr. 1946.

72 Ian Greener and Martin Powell, 'Beveridge, Bevan and Institutional Change in the UK Welfare State', *Social Policy & Administration*, 56 (2022), pp. 271–83.

73 John E. Pater, *The Making of the National Health Service*, King's Fund, London, 1981, p. 178.

74 Charles Webster, 'Birth of the dream', in Goodman, *State of the Nation*, pp. 106–29.

75 Aneurin Bevan, 'National Health Service: The Future of Hospital Services', CP (45) 205, 5 Oct. 1945, CAB 129/3/5, TNA

76 Cabinet Secretary's notebook, CM 40 (45), 11 Oct. 1945, CAB 195/3/61, TNA.

77 Henry Willink, unpublished autobiography, 1968, p. 81, Willink Papers, WILL 9.

78 'Mr. Bevan's Plans', *The Lancet*, 24 Nov. 1945.

79 Herbert Morrison, 'National Health Service: The Future of Hospital Services', CP (45) 227, 12 Oct. 1945, CAB 129/3/27, TNA.

80 Aneurin Bevan, 'National Health Service: The Hospital Services', CP (45) 231, 16 Oct. 1945, CAB 129/3/31, TNA.

81 Cabinet minutes, CM (45) 43rd, 18 Oct. 1945, CAB 128/1/26, TNA.

82 John Parker, unpublished memoirs, Parker Papers, 1/9.

83 Herbert Morrison, *Government and Parliament: A Survey From the Inside*, Oxford University Press, London, 1954, p. 284.

84 Pimlott (ed.), *Political Diary of Hugh Dalton*, p. 448 (entry for 24 May 1949).

85 Lord Moran, *Churchill: Taken From the Diaries of Lord Moran: The Struggle for Survival, 1940–1965*, Houghton Mifflin Company, Boston, 1966, p. 333.

86 'Heard At Headquarters', *Supplement to the British Medical Journal*, 1 Dec. 1945.

87 Parliamentary Debates, House of Commons, Fifth Series, Vol. 422, 30 Apr. 1946, col. 60.

88 Aneurin Bevan, *In Place of Fear*, William Heinemann Ltd, London, 1952, p. 87.

89 Brian Abel-Smith, *The Hospitals 1800–1948: A Study in Social Administration in England and Wales*, Heinemann Educational Books, Ltd, London, 1964, p. 480. Abel-Smith reports that Bevan said this to a friend but does not give a source.

90 Mann, *Woman in Parliament*, p. 107.

91 Philip M. Williams, *Hugh Gaitskell*, Jonathan Cape, London, 1979, pp. 153–5.

92 Waldemar J. Gallman to George C. Marshall, 30 Jan. 1946, *Foreign Relations of the United States, 1948; Vol. III: Western Europe 1948*, United States Government Printing Office, Washington DC, 1974, pp. 1075–6.

93 Aneurin Bevan, 'National Health Service: Attitude of the Medical Profession', CP (48) 23, 19 Jan. 1948, CAB 129/23/23, TNA.

94 Enid Russell-Smith, 'Inside View: Recordings of a Civil Servant's Work 1925–1963', Russell-Smith Papers 2/1 f.45.

95 Leigh Ann Merrick, '"In need of care and attention": Local authorities and the Implementation of the Scottish NHS Act, 1948–1960', *Family & Community History*, 12 (2009), pp. 130–45; A. T. Elder, 'Health Services of Northern Ireland', *British Journal of Preventive and Social Medicine*, 7 (1953), pp. 105–11.

96 Rees, *Labour and the Northern Ireland Problem 1945–1951*, pp. 152–5.

97 Brian Abel-Smith, 'Hospital Planning and the Structure of the Hospital Service', *Medical Care*, 2 (1964), pp. 47–51, at 47.

98 Michael Ryan, 'Health Centre Policy in England and Wales', *British Journal of Sociology*, 19 (1968), pp. 34–46.

99 Gurminder K. Bhambra, 'Relations of Extraction, Relations of Redistribution: Empire, Nation, and the Construction of the British Welfare State', *British Journal of Sociology*, 73 (2022), pp. 4–15.

100 Roberta Bivins, 'Picturing Race in the British National Health Service, 1948–1988', *Twentieth Century British History*, 28 (2017), pp. 83–109.

101 'Laski & Health Scheme', *Daily Telegraph*, 25 March 1946.

102 Rudolf Klein, 'The National Health Service (NHS) at 70: Bevan's Double-edged Legacy', *Health Economics, Policy and Law*, 14 (2019), pp. 1–10.

103 'Progress of the Health Service', *The Economist*, 4 Sept. 1948

104 Aneurin Bevan, 'The National Health Service', CP (48) 302, 13 Dec. 1948, CAB 129/31/32, TNA.

105 Campbell, *Nye Bevan*, pp. 180–2.

106 'Warning Against Wage Claims', *The Times*, 10 Jan. 1949.

107 Albert Hird diary, 18 Feb. 1948. Emphasis in original.

108 Ball (ed.), *Parliament and Politics in the Age of Churchill and Attlee*, pp. 541, 551 (entries for 29 Jan. and 7 Apr. 1948).

109 Jay, *Change and Fortune*, p. 177.

110 Williams, *Nothing So Strange*, p. 224.

111 Interview with Max Nicholson, 11 Oct. 1968, Morrison Papers (LSE), 6.

112 Comments by Cripps of 2 Jan. 1948 on 'Draft Paper by Chancellor of the Exchequer: The Economic Survey for 1948', 1 Jan. 1948, T229/46, TNA.

113 Nicholas Davenport, *Memoirs of a City Radical*, Weidenfeld & Nicolson, London, 1974, p. 177.

114 E. A. G. Robinson, *Economic Planning in the United Kingdom: Some Lessons*, Cambridge University Press, Cambridge, 1967, p. 21.

115 Cairncross (ed.), *The Robert Hall Diaries*, p. 222 (entry for 29 Apr. 1952).

116 Parliamentary Debates, House of Commons, Fifth Series, Vol. 449, 06 April 1948, col. 37.

117 Martin Daunton, *Just Taxes: The Politics of Taxation in Britain, 1914–1979*, Cambridge University Press, Cambridge, 2002, p. 216.

118 'Cripps and Soda', *Time*, 19 Apr. 1948; Anthony Carew, 'The Anglo-American Council on Productivity (1948–52): The Ideological Roots of the Post-War Debate on Productivity in Britain', *Journal of Contemporary History*, 26 (1991), pp. 49–69.

119 Rhiannon Vickers, *Manipulating Hegemony: State Power, Labour and the Marshall Plan in Britain*, Macmillan Press Ltd, Houndmills, Basingstoke, 2000, Chapter 7.

120 *Statement on Personal Incomes, Costs and Prices*, Cmd. 7231, Feb. 1948, pp. 2–4.

121 Russell Jones, *Wages and Employment Policy 1936–1985*, Allen & Unwin, London, 1987, p. 37.

122 Richard Whiting, *The Labour Party and Taxation: Party Identity and Political Purpose in Twentieth-Century Britain*, Cambridge University Press, Cambridge, 2001, pp. 77–82.

123 Simon Heffer (ed.), *Henry 'Chips' Channon: The Diaries 1943–57*, Hutchinson, London, 2022, p. 442 (entry for 6 Apr. 1948).

124 Plowden, *Industrialist*, p. 22.

125 Philip M. Williams (ed.), *The Diary of Hugh Gaitskell*, pp. 61–2 (entry for 23 Apr. 1948).

126 Jay, *Change and Fortune*, p. 179.

127 Mayhew diary, 24 Apr. 1948, Mayhew Papers, 5/2.

128 Bullock, *Ernest Bevin: Foreign Secretary*, pp. 520–1.

129 Lyn Smith, 'Covert British Propaganda: The Information Research Department: 1947–77', *Millennium*, 9 (1980), pp. 67–83.

130 Emma Peplow, 'The Role of Britain in the Berlin Airlift', *History*, 95 (2010), pp. 207–24.

131 Ellen Jenny Ravndal, 'Exit Britain: British Withdrawal From the Palestine Mandate in the Early Cold War, 1947–1948', *Diplomacy & Statecraft*, 21 (2010), pp. 416–33.

132 George H. Gallup, *The Gallup International Opinion Polls: Great Britain 1937–1975; Vol. I: 1937–1964*, Random House, New York, 1976, pp. 173, 181. Questions about Palestine and foreign policy asked in April 1948; question about voters' priorities asked in August 1948.

133 Zweiniger-Bargielowska, *Austerity in Britain*, p. 63.

134 Mark Roodhouse, *Black Market Britain: 1939–1955*, Oxford University Press, Oxford, 2013, p. 48.

135 Chris Ritchie, '"Only Mugs Work": The spiv in British comedy', *Comedy Studies*, 2 (2011), pp. 13–20.

136 Ina Zweiniger-Bargielowska, 'Rationing, Austerity and the Conservative Party Recovery after 1945', *Historical Journal*, 37 (1994), pp. 173–97; James Hinton, 'Militant Housewives: The British Housewives' League and the Attlee Government', *History Workshop Journal*, 38 (1994), pp. 129–56.

137 Cairncross, *Years of Recovery*, p. 348.

138 Christopher Mayhew to his family, 8 Aug. 1945, Mayhew Papers, 1/3.

139 Castle, *Fighting All the Way*, p. 162.

140 Mark Pottle (ed.), *Daring to Hope: The Diaries and Letters of Violet Bonham Carter, 1946–1969*, Weidenfeld & Nicolson, London, 2000, p. 65 (entry for 15 March 1949).

141 Harold Wilson, *Memoirs: The Making of a Prime Minister, 1916–64*, Weidenfeld & Nicolson and Michael Joseph, London, 1986, p. 104.

142 Henry Irving, 'The Birth of a Politician: Harold Wilson and the Bonfires of Controls, 1948–9', *Twentieth Century British History*, 25 (2014), pp. 87–107.

143 'The Bonfire Scorches', *Tribune*, 21 Apr. 1950.

144 Ben Pimlott, *Harold Wilson*, HarperCollins, London, 1992, p. 128.

145 *Report of the Tribunal appointed to inquire into Allegations reflecting on the Official Conduct of Ministers of the Crown and other Public Servants*, Cmd. 7616, Jan. 1949; John Gross, 'The Lynskey Tribunal', in Philip French and Michael Sissons (eds), *Age of Austerity*, Hodder & Stoughton, London, 1963, pp. 257–75; Mark Roodhouse, 'The 1948 Belcher Affair and Lynskey Tribunal', *Twentieth Century British History*, 13 (2002), pp. 384–411.

146 Shawcross, *Life Sentence*, p. 174.

147 Parris and Maguire, *Great Parliamentary Scandals*, p. 134.

148 Cairncross, *Robert Hall Diaries*, p. 46 (entry for 1 Dec. 1948).

CHAPTER 7

1 'Cripps Devalues £', *Daily Express*, 19 Sept. 1949.

2 '"The Pound Thing"', File Report 3163, 28 Sept. 1949, Mass Observation Archive.

3 'Sir S. Cripps's Explanation', *The Times*, 19 Sept. 1949; Attlee chronology 18 Sept. 1949, Attlee papers (Bodleian), MS.CRA.21.

4 'Britons Stranded By Slash In Pound', *New York Times*, 20 Sept. 1949

5 'Mr. Morrison's Travel Cheques', *Daily Telegraph*, 22 Sept. 1949.

6 Donoughue and Jones, *Herbert Morrison*, pp. 437–8.

7 Quoted in 'Press Reacts to Devaluation', French Home Service, 19 Sept. 1949, FBIS Daily Report 20 Sept. 1949, FBIS-FRB-49-181.

8 R. C. Leffingwell, 'Devaluation and European Recovery', *Foreign Affairs*, Jan. 1950, pp. 203–30, at 203.

9 Henry Pelling, *Britain and the Marshall Plan*, Palgrave Macmillan, Macmillan Press, Houndmills, Basingstoke, 1988, p. 87.

10 '"The Pound Thing"'.

11 'Public Opinion Survey Number Six', *Picture Post*, 12 Nov. 1949.

12 A. J. Cummings, 'Tories will win the Election on present trends', *News Chronicle*, 29 Nov. 1949.

13 '"The Pound Thing"'.

14 'A Help But Not a Solution', *Manchester Guardian*, 20 Sept. 1949.

15 '"The Pound Thing"'.

16 Julius C. Holmes to Dean Acheson, 20 Sept. 1949, *Foreign Relations of the United States 1949; Vol. IV: Western Europe*, United States Government Printing Office, Washington DC, 1975, p. 840.

17 'A Help But Not a Solution'.

18 TUC General Council minutes, 20 Sept. 1949, TUC Archive; Leslie Randall, 'Approval on £ is Withheld', *Daily Mail*, 21 Sept. 1949.

19 *Report of Proceedings at the 81st Annual Trades Union Congress*, 1949, TUC, London, 1949, p. 460.

20 Holmes telegram of 21 Sept. 1949, paraphrased in *Foreign Relations of the United States 1949; Vol. IV*, p. 840n; 'TUC in Travail', *The Economist*, 29 Oct. 1949.

21 'Scots Miners Against Devaluation', *Dundee Evening Telegraph*, 30 Sept. 1949.

22 Jay, *Change and Fortune*, p. 185.

23 'Chancellor on the Next Stage of the Recovery Programme', *Manchester Guardian*, 1 Jan. 1949.

24 Gallup, *The Gallup International Opinion Polls: Vol. I*, pp. 196–7.

25 Marguerite Dupree (ed.), *Lancashire and Whitehall: The Diary of Sir Raymond Streat: Vol. II: 1939–57*, Manchester University Press, Manchester, 1987, p. 473 (entry for 14 Nov. 1948).

26 Burke Trend to Stafford Cripps, 16 Feb. 1949, quoted in Clarke, *Cripps Version*, pp. 512–13.

27 Cairncross (ed.), *The Robert Hall Diaries*, p. 55 (entry for 6 Apr. 1949).

28 'Socialist MPs Blame Budget', *Daily Telegraph*, 9 Apr. 1949.

29 *Speaker's Handbook 1945*, p. 209; Lord Addison, 'It's Hard Work For the Labour Peers', *Forward*, 27 July 1946.

30 Glenn Dymond, 'The Salisbury Doctrine', House of Lords Library Note (LLN 2006/006), 2006.

31 Kevin Manton, 'Labour and the 1949 Parliament Act', *Contemporary British History*, 26 (2012), pp. 149–72; Cabinet Secretary's notebook, CM 81 (47), 20 Oct. 1947, CAB 195/5, TNA.

32 Cabinet Secretary's notebook, CM 89 (47), 18 Nov. 1947, CAB 195/5, TNA.

33 Donoughue and Jones, *Herbert Morrison*, p. 309.

34 Interview with Max Nicholson, 11 Oct. 1968, and with S. A. and J. Melman, 21 March 1968, both in Morrison Papers 6/3.

35 Francis Williams, 'Chuter Ede', *The Spectator*, 1 Oct. 1948.

36 Trevor Evans, 'Attlee's First Year', *Maclean's Magazine*, 15 July 1946.

37 Hart, *James Chuter Ede*, p. 203; Claire Langhamer, '"The Live Dynamic Whole of Feeling and Behavior": Capital Punishment and the Politics of Emotion, 1945–1957', *Journal of British Studies*, 51 (2012), pp. 416–41.

38 Evans was convicted for the murder of his wife and baby daughter. In 1953, it became clear that his neighbour John Christie, whom Evans had accused at his trial, had been responsible and had also killed other women. Ede continued to insist that his original decision was the right one on the information before him at the time but campaigned for official recognition of Evans's innocence. Cyril de Gruchy, 'Life Peerage Would Be A Fitting Tribute To Chuter Ede', *Shields Gazette*, 25 Sept. 1964, copy in Ede Papers, 390/10/3.

39 Parliamentary Debates, House of Commons, Fifth Series, Vol. 449, 14 Apr. 1948, col. 980.

40 Two other Cabinet members were abroad and two more (who favoured retention) were in the Lords. For a detailed breakdown, see Victor Bailey, 'The Shadow of the Gallows: The Death Penalty and the British Labour Government, 1945–51', *Law and History Review*, 18 (2000), pp. 305–49, at 334.

41 Wilson Broadbent, 'What Can Mr Ede Do Now?', *Daily Mail*, 15 Apr. 1948.

42 Bailey, 'The Shadow of the Gallows'.

43 Howard League for Penal Reform, Sub-Committee on the Death Penalty, Bulletin No. 28, Stansgate Papers, ST/121.

44 Herbert Morrison, *Government and Parliament: A Survey From the Inside*, Oxford University Press, London, 1954, p. 194.

45 Manton, 'Labour and the 1949 Parliament Act'.

46 Ruggero Ranieri, 'Partners and enemies: The government's decision to nationalise steel 1944–8', in Robert Millward and John Singleton (eds), *The Political Economy of Nationalisation in Britain 1920–1950*, Cambridge University Press, Cambridge, 1995, pp. 275–305.

47 Strauss, unpublished memoirs, p. 115, Strauss Papers, STRS 1/2.

48 *Speakers' Handbook 1945*, Labour Party, London, 1945, p. 43.

49 Ben Pimlott, 'Wilmot, John Charles, Baron Wilmot of Selmeston (1893–1964), politician', *Oxford Dictionary of National Biography*. Retrieved 13 Oct. 2022 from https://www.oxforddnb.com/view/10.1093/ref:odnb/9780198614128.001.0001/odnb-9780198614128-e-36941.

50 Dalton, *High Tide and After*, 1962, p. 250.

51 Lord Morrison, *Herbert Morrison: An Autobiography*, Odhams Press Ltd, London, 1960, p. 296.

52 Clement Attlee to Herbert Morrison, 15 Sept. 1947, Morrison Papers (LSE), 8/3; Foot, *Aneurin Bevan: Vol. II*, p. 226.

53 Tam Dalyell, obituary of Lord Strauss, *Independent*, 9 June 1993.

54 George Strauss, 'The Iron and Steel Bill', CP (48) 145, 10 June 1948, CAB 129/27, TNA.

55 Cabinet minutes, CM (48) 39th conclusions, 14 June 1948, CAB 128/12, TNA.

56 Strauss, unpublished memoirs, p. 116.

57 Alan Thompson, *The Day Before Yesterday: An illustrated history of Britain from Attlee to Macmillan*, Granada Publishing Limited, London, 1971, p. 58.

58 Arthur Christiansen to Lord Beaverbrook, 11 June 1948, Beaverbrook Papers, BBK/H/127.

59 Strauss, unpublished memoirs, p. 117; Cabinet minutes, CM (48) 65th conclusions, 10 Nov. 1949, CAB 128/16, TNA.

60 LPACR 1948, p. 122.

61 *Labour Believes in Britain*, Labour Party, London, 1949, pp. 3, 12; Brooke, *Labour's War*, p. 340; Mark Tookey, 'The Labour party and nationalisation from Attlee to Wilson, 1945–1968: Beyond the commanding heights', PhD thesis, University of Durham, 2000, p. 90; Vernon Bogdanor, 'Britain in the 20th Century: The Attempt to Construct a Socialist Commonwealth, 1945–1951', lecture at Gresham College, 15 Nov. 2011, https://www.gresham.ac.uk/watch-now/britain-20th-century-attempt -construct-socialist-commonwealth (consulted 17 Oct. 2022).

62 G. D. H. Cole, *Labour's Second Term: A Comment on the Draft: 'Labour Believes in Britain'*, Fabian Publications Ltd and Victor Gollancz Ltd, London, 1949, p. 8.

63 Martin Francis, '"Not reformed capitalism, but … democratic socialism": The ideology of the Labour Leadership, 1945–1951', in Harriet Jones and Michael Kandiah (eds), *The Myth of Consensus New Views on British History, 1945–64*, Macmillan Press, Ltd, Basingstoke, 1996, pp. 40–57, at 42.

64 *Labour Believes in Britain*, p. 3.

65 Richard Acland et al., *Keeping Left: Labour's First Five Years and the Problems Ahead*, New Statesman & Nation, London, 1950, p. 29.

66 *Labour Believes in Britain*, p. 15.

67 Ian Mikardo, 'Another Man's Budget', *Tribune*, 22 Apr. 1949.

68 John Baylis, *The Diplomacy of Pragmatism: Britain and the Formation of NATO, 1942–1949*, Kent State University Press, Kent, Ohio, 1993, p. 7.

69 'Jubilee Manifesto', *New Statesman & Nation*, 16 Apr. 1949.

70 See, for example, Dimitri Batrouni, *The Battle of Ideas in the Labour Party: From Attlee to Corbyn and Brexit*, Policy Press, Bristol, 2021, pp. 14–15.

71 Ron Noon, 'Goodbye, Mr Cube', *History Today*, Oct. 2001.

72 Herbert Morrison, 'Labour's New Statement of Policy', *The Listener*, 28 Apr. 1949.

73 Jose Harris, *William Beveridge: A Biography*, Clarendon Press, Oxford, 1997, p. 366.

74 Joyce Epstein, interview with Michael Young, 22 Oct. 1984, Young Papers, YUNG 10/001.

75 David Garland, 'The emergence of the idea of "the welfare state" in British political discourse', *History of the Human Sciences*, 35 (2022), pp. 132–57.

76 *Report of Proceedings at the 81st Annual Trades Union Congress, Bridlington, 1949*, TUC, London, 1950, p. 301.

77 Aneurin Bevan, *Democratic Values*, Fabian Publications Ltd and Victor Gollancz Ltd, London, 1950, p. 14. This lecture was given on 13 October 1950.

78 J. C. R. Dow, *The Management of the British Economy 1945–60*, Cambridge University Press, Cambridge, 1970, p. 41.

79 Douglas Jay, 'Dollar Situation', 5 July 1949, Gaitskell Papers, C/26.

80 Cairncross, *Years of Recovery*, pp. 168, 172; Tomlinson, *Democratic Socialism*, p. 37.

81 Hugh Gaitskell, 'British Economic Policy', 18 Aug. 1949, in Philip M. Williams (ed.), *The Diary of Hugh Gaitskell*, p. 143.

82 Pimlott (ed.), *Political Diary of Hugh Dalton*, p. 450 (entry for 15 June 1949).

83 Philip M. Williams, *The Diary of Hugh Gaitskell*, p. 126 (entry for 3 Aug. 1949).

84 Jay, *Change and Fortune*, p. 187.

85 Interview with Douglas Jay, 28 Oct. 1968, Morrison Papers (LSE), 6/2. Emphasis in original.

86 Harold Wilson to Clement Attlee, 8 Aug. 1949, PREM 8/1178, TNA; Wilson, *Memoirs*, pp. 107–8. According to Wilson, the letter was written by Cripps, but his recollection was clearly mistaken.

87 Cairncross, *The Robert Hall Diaries*, p. 70 (entry for 26 Aug. 1949).

88 Attlee chronology, 19 Aug. 1949, Attlee Papers (Bodleian), MS.CRA.21.

89 Plowden, *Industrialist*, p. 57.

90 Philip M. Williams, *Diary of Hugh Gaitskell*, p. 137 (entry for 21 Sept. 1949); Jackie Andrade, 'What does doodling do?', *Applied Cognitive Psychology*, 24 (2010), pp. 100–106.

91 Note of a meeting of ministers held at Chequers on 19 Aug. 1949, CAB 128/21/1, TNA.

92 Cabinet Secretary's notebook, 29 Aug. 1949, CM 53 (49), CAB 195/7/49, TNA.

93 Plowden, *Industrialist*, pp. 62–4.

94 Acheson, *Present At the Creation*, pp. 324–5.

95 Raymond Daniell, 'Cripps, Optimistic, Arrives in Britain', *New York Times*, 18 Sept. 1949.

96 Douglas Jay, *Sterling: Its Use and Misuse: A Plea for Moderation*, Sidgwick & Jackson, London, 1985, p. 123.

97 John Fforde, *The Bank of England and Public Policy 1941–1958*, Cambridge University Press, Cambridge, 1992, pp. 301–2.

98 Pimlott, *Political Diary of Hugh Dalton*, p. 460 (entry for 12 Oct. 1949); Cairncross, *Years of Recovery*, pp. 194–5; Foot, *Aneurin Bevan: Vol. II*, p. 293; Cabinet minutes, CM (49) 61st, CAB 128/16/18, TNA.

99 Cabinet Secretary's notebook, CM 61 (49), 21 Oct. 1949, CAB 195/7/55, TNA.

100 Douglas Jay, 'Civil servant and minister', in W. T. Rodgers (ed.), *Hugh Gaitskell 1906–1963*, Thames and Hudson, London, 1964, pp. 77–103, at 96.

101 Bevan to Attlee, 21 Oct. 1949, Alexander Papers, AVAR/5/14, ff. 18–19.

102 Pimlott, *Political Diary of Hugh Dalton*, p. 460 (entry for 12 Oct. 1949).

103 Philip M. Williams, *Diary of Hugh Gaitskell*, p. 158 (entry for 21 Nov. 1949).

104 Morrison, *Autobiography*, p. 267.

105 Burgess, *Stafford Cripps*, p. 298; Plowden, *Industrialist*, p. 21.

106 Einzig, *In the Centre of Things*, p. 272.

107 '90-Minute Assault By Mr. Churchill', *Manchester Guardian*, 29 Sept. 1949.

108 Parliamentary Debates, House of Commons, Fifth Series, Vol. 468, 28 Sept. 1949, col. 168.

109 Arthur Christiansen to Lord Beaverbrook, 2 Dec. 1949, Beaverbrook Papers, BBK H/134.

110 'Socialists Hold Bradford', *Evening Standard*, 9 Dec. 1949.

111 Christiansen to Beaverbrook, 13 Dec. 1949, Beaverbrook Papers, BBK JH/135.

112 Andrew Taylor, 'Speaking to democracy: The Conservative Party and mass opinion from the 1920s to the 1950s', in Stuart Ball and Ian Holliday (eds), *Mass Conservatism: The Conservatives and the Public since the 1880s* (London: Routledge, 2002), pp. 78–99, at 85–8.

113 'Attlee on Moran's Churchill Diary', *Forum World Features*, 14 May 1966, Attlee Papers (Bodleian), MS.CRA.32.

114 John Ramsden, *The Age of Churchill and Eden, 1940–1957*, Longman, London, 1995, Chapter 4.

115 R. A. Butler, *The Art of the Possible: The Memoirs of Lord Butler K.G., C.H.*, Hamish Hamilton, London, 1971, p. 133.

116 *The Right Road for Britain: The Conservative Party's Statement of Policy*, Conservative and Unionist Central Office, London, 1949, p. 5.

117 Churchill, speech of 14 October 1949.

118 Stafford Cripps, speech at High Wycombe, 18 Jan. 1950, Cripps Papers, MS.9661/163.

119 Zweiniger-Bargielowska, *Austerity in Britain*, Chapter 5.

120 *Speakers' Handbook 1949–50*, Labour Party, London, 1949, p. 217.

121 Albert Hird diary, 8 Jan. 1950.

122 Heffer (ed.), *Henry 'Chips' Channon*, p. 585 (entry for 25 Oct. 1950).

123 Hart, *James Chuter Ede*, pp. 194–8; Ivor Jennings, *The British Constitution*, Cambridge University Press, Cambridge, 1958, p. 199.

124 Parliamentary Debates, House of Commons, Fifth Series, Vol. 447, 16 Feb. 1948, col. 939.

125 H. G. Nicholas, *The British General Election of 1950*, Macmillan & Co. Ltd, London, 1951, p. 4; Dalton, *High Tide and After*, pp. 297–9. Quotation at 299.

126 Jay, *Change and Fortune*, pp. 192–3.

127 Michael Young diary, 9 Feb. 1950, Young Papers, YUNG 4/3.

128 R. T. Windle, 'General Election 1950: National Agent's Report', 22 March 1950, LPA, B/F1950/1.

129 Lawrence, *Electing Our Masters*, pp. 137–43.

130 Attlee chronology, 8 Feb. 1945, Attlee Papers (Bodleian), MS.CRA.21.

131 'The World and Lewisham', *Manchester Guardian*, 23 Feb. 1950.

132 Young diary, 20 Jan. 1950, Young Papers, YUNG 4/3.

133 Churchill, speech of 14 Feb. 1950.

134 '"Guttersnipe Politics"', *The Times*, 16 Feb. 1950

135 Public Opinion Research Department, 'Public Opinion Report No. 26', 15 Feb. 1950, Conservative Party Archive, CCO 4/3/250.

136 'Public Opinion Summary No. 14', March 1950, Conservative Party Archive, CCO 4/3/249.

137 'Don't Let Churchill Talk to Stalin', *Daily Mail*, 17 Feb. 1950.

138 John Hynd (MP for Sheffield Attercliffe), 1950 election address, Hynd Papers, HYND 2/7.

139 Castle, *Fighting All the Way*, p. 177.

140 Young diary, 20 Jan. 1950, Young Papers, YUNG 4/3.

141 'Survey of Public Opinion on "Mutualisation" of Industrial Assurance', May 1950, Abrams Papers, ABMS 3/26.

142 Acland et al., *Keeping Left*.

143 'General Election 1950: Notes on the Findings of the Public Opinion Polls', RD 350, Apr. 1950, LPA, B/F1950/1.

144 Public Opinion Research Department, 'Confidential Supplement to Public Opinion Summary No. 5', May 1949, Conservative Party Archive, CCO 4/3/249.

145 'Public Opinion Summary No. 14'.

146 Callaghan, *Time and Chance*, p. 99.

147 Grace Wyndham Goldie, *Facing the Nation: Television and Politics 1936–1976*, The Bodley Head, London, 1977, p. 66.

148 Attlee chronology, 23 Feb. 1950, Attlee Papers (Bodleian), MS.CRA.21.

149 Nicholas, *British General Election*, pp. 286–7.

150 'Tories Differ On Quick Challenge', *Observer*, 5 March 1950.

151 J. P. W. Mallalieu, 'Westminster Commentary', *Tribune*, 10 March 1950.

152 'Parliament Starts Off In Jovial Mood', *Manchester Guardian*, 2 March 1950.

153 Heffer (ed.), *Henry 'Chips' Channon*, p. 602 (entry for 9 March).

CHAPTER 8

1 Pendennis, 'Table Talk', *Observer*, 5 Nov. 1950.

2 Tony Benn, *Dare to be a Daniel: Then and Now*, Hutchinson, London, 2004, p. 154.

3 Pimlott (ed.), *Political Diary of Hugh Dalton*, p. 491 (entry for 2 Nov. 1950).

4 'Surprise in Bristol SE', *Western Daily Press*, 2 Nov. 1950.

5 '3 Candidates on the Platform', *Daily Telegraph*, 27 Nov. 1950.

6 'Labour Query in SE Bristol', *The Times*, 24 Nov. 1950.

7 *Bristol Evening World*, 17 Nov. 1950, quoted in Jad Adams, *Tony Benn*, Macmillan, London, 1992, p. 67.

8 Benn, *Dare to be a Daniel*, p. 155.

9 'Work For Atomic Agreement Through UN', *Manchester Guardian*, 16 Feb. 1950.

10 'Public Opinion Summary No. 14', March 1950, Conservative Party Archive, CCO 4/3/249.

11 'The Hustings and the H-Bomb', *New Statesman & Nation*, 25 Feb. 1950.

12 Geoffrey Warner (ed.), *In the Midst of Events: The Foreign Office Diaries and Papers of Kenneth Younger*, February 1950–October 1951, Routledge, London, 2005, pp. 12, 14 (entry for 12 March 1950).

13 'London Day By Day', *Daily Telegraph*, 29 March 1950; 'Mr. Churchill Urges Europe To Bury Past Feuds', *Manchester Guardian*, 29 March 1950.

14 Parliamentary Debates, House of Commons, Fifth Series, Vol. 473, 28 March 1950, cols 189–207.

15 Warner, *In the Midst of Events*, p. 11 (entry for 8 Apr. 1950).

16 Parliamentary Debates, House of Commons, Fifth Series, Vol. 473, 28 March 1950, cols 323–4; Geoffrey Wakeford, 'Churchill: Let Germans Aid Defence', *Daily Mail*, 29 March 1950.

17 'German Comment on Mr. Bevin', *Manchester Guardian*, 30 March 1950.

18 Felix Klos, *Churchill's Last Stand: The Struggle to Unite Europe*, I.B. Tauris, London, 2017, p. 83; A. H. Bradford to Arthur Hays Sulzberger, 29 March 1949, New York Times Company Records: Arthur Hays Sulzberger Papers, Series I b. 12.

19 Marco Duranti, *The Conservative Human Rights Revolution: European Identity, Transnational Politics, and the Origins of the European Convention*, Oxford University Press, Oxford, 2017.

20 See Morrison's speech reported in 'Council of Europe and West Germany', *Financial Times*, 18 Aug. 1949.

21 Taru Haapala and Teemu Häkkinen, 'Debating Federal Europe in the British Parliament, c. 1940–49', *European Review of History: Revue européenne d'histoire*, 24 (2017), pp. 801–16.

22 A critique of this idea can be found in J. W. Young, 'Churchill's "No" to Europe: The "Rejection" of European Union by Churchill's Post-War Government, 1951–1952', *Historical Journal*, 28 (1985), pp. 923–37.

23 Eric Roll, *Crowded Hours: An Autobiography*, Faber and Faber, London, 1985, p. 83.

24 Till Geiger and Richard Toye, 'Britain, America and the Origins of the European Payments Union: A Reassessment', Working Paper, 2008, https://ore.exeter.ac.uk/repository/handle/10036/31032.

25 Parliamentary Debates, House of Commons, Fifth Series, Vol. 446, 22 January 1948, col. 419.

26 John Kent and John W. Young, 'The "Western Union" Concept and British Defence Policy, 1947–8', in Richard J. Aldrich (ed.), *British Intelligence, Strategy and the Cold War, 1945–51*, Routledge, London, 1992, pp. 166–92.

27 Dalton, *High Tide and After*, , p. 323.

28 Callaghan, *Time and Chance*, p. 82.

29 Duranti, *Conservative Human Rights Revolution*, pp. 248–52.

30 Neil Parsons, 'The Impact of Seretse Khama on British Public Opinion 1948–56 and 1978', *Immigrants & Minorities*, 12 (1993), pp. 195–219.

31 W. Arthur Lewis to the editor of the *Manchester Guardian*, 9 March 1950, published 11 March.

32 The Schuman Declaration, Paris, 9 May 1950, text available https://www.cvce.eu/en/recherche/unit-content/-/unit/5cc6b004-33b7-4e44-b6db-f5f9e6c01023/141a459f-ccc8-4472-8055-4222724eb1b6/Resources#9cc6ac38-32f5-4c0a-a337-9a8ae4d5740f_en&overlay (consulted 19 March 2023).

33 'West Allies at Odds Over Schuman Plan', Moscow, Soviet European Service, in Slovak, 5 June 1950, Daily Report, Foreign Radio Broadcasts, 7 June 1950, FBIS-FRB-50-110.

34 Max Ways, 'London Dispatch', 8 May 1948, Time Inc. Records, Box 1102, F6, MS 3009: RG 13.

35 Plowden, *Industrialist*, pp. 86–7; Donoughue and Jones, *Herbert Morrison*, p. 481; Cairncross (ed.), *The Robert Hall Diaries*, p. 112 (entry for 12 May 1950).

36 Warner, *In the Midst of Events*, p. 20 (entry for 12 June 1950).

37 UK memorandum of 2 June 1950, *Anglo-French Discussions regarding French proposals for the Western European Coal, Iron and Steel Industries, May–June, 1950*, Cmd. 7970, 1950, p. 293.

38 Jay, *Change and Fortune*, p. 199.

39 Alan S. Milward, *The Rise and Fall of a National Strategy: The UK and the European Community; Vol. 1*, Routledge, London, 2002, pp. 49–50.

40 Piers Ludlow, 'The Schuman Plan and the Start of Supranational European Integration', *Oxford Research Encyclopedia of Politics*, Oxford University Press, Oxford, 2019, https://oxfordre.com/politics/view/10.1093/acrefore/9780190228637.001.0001/acrefore-9780190228637-e-111.

41 Albert Mousset in *L'Epoque*, quoted in 'Paris Sees Hope in Attlee's Statement', Paris, in French to the Antilles and Guiana, 14 June 1950, Daily Report, Foreign Radio Broadcasts, 15 June 1950, FBIS-FRB-50-116.

42 Pimlott, *Hugh Dalton*, pp. 580–1.

43 Healey, *Time of My Life*, pp. 116–17.

44 Warner, *In the Midst of Events*, p. 25 (entry for 6 July 1950).

45 Labour Party, *European Unity: A Statement by the National Executive Committee of the British Labour Party*, Labour Party, London, 1950. Text available at https://www.cvce.eu/content/publication/2005/4/8/626bf849-0be2-499c-a924-d768c9f05feb/publishable_en.pdf (consulted 19 March 2023).

46 Parliamentary Debates, House of Commons, Fifth Series, Vol. 476, 13 June 1950, col. 38.

47 Wilson Broadbent and Geoffrey Wakeford, 'Dalton on the Carpet', *Daily Mail*, 16 June 1950.

48 'British Labour's European Unity Programme Turns Americans Hopping Mad', *Economic Weekly*, 1 July 1950.

49 Lewis W. Douglas to Dean Acheson, 15 June 1950, *Foreign Relations of the United States 1950: Western Europe; Vol. III*, United States Government Printing Office, Washington DC, 1977, pp. 1648–51.

50 Steven Hugh Lee, 'The Korean War in History and Historiography', *Journal of American-East Asian Relations*, 21 (2014), pp. 185–206.

51 Parliamentary Debates, House of Commons, Fifth Series, Vol. 476, 26 June 1950, col. 1906.

52 Castle, *Fighting All the Way*, p. 184.

53 Robert Pearce (ed.), *Patrick Gordon Walker Diaries*, p. 189 (entry for 30 June 1950).

54 Grace Huxford, *The Korean War in Britain: Citizenship, Selfhood and Forgetting*, Manchester University Press, Manchester, 2018, p. 2; L. V. Scott, *Conscription and the Attlee Governments: The Politics and Policy of National Service 1945–1951*, Oxford University Press, Oxford, 1993, Chapter 9.

55 Cabinet minutes, 1 Aug. 1950, CM (50) 52nd Conclusions, CAB 128/18/12, TNA.

56 'Statement by the President on the Situation in Korea', 27 June 1950, *Public Papers of the Presidents of the United States: Harry S. Truman: 1950*, United States Government Printing Office, Washington DC, 1965, p. 492.

57 Interview with Kenneth Younger by Richard Rose, 1961, quoted in Warner, *In the Midst of Events*, p. 26.

58 Foreign Office to the Washington Embassy, 30 July 1949, FO 800/462, TNA.

59 Acheson to Douglas, 8 July 1950, *Foreign Relations of the United States, 1950; Vol. VII: Korea*, United States Government Printing Office, Washington DC, 1976, p. 352.

60 J. C. Holmes to the Acting Secretary of State, 11 Sept. 1950, *Foreign Relations of the United States, 1950; Vol. III: Western Europe*, United States Government Printing Office, Washington DC, 1977, p. 1187.

61 Rosemary J. Foot, 'Anglo-American Relations in the Korean Crisis: The British Effort to Avert an Expanded War, December 1950–January 1951', *Diplomatic History*, 10 (1986), pp. 43–57.

62 'Conference at Beatrice Webb House, Dorking, 20–21 May 1950', General Secretaries' Papers, GS/DORK/47, LPA.

63 Pearce, *Patrick Gordon Walker Diaries*, pp. 190 (entry for 12 Oct. 1950).

64 'Cabinet Threatened With Split', *Observer*, 24 Sept. 1950.

65 C. R. Attlee, *As It Happened*, William Heinemann Ltd, London, 1954, p. 206.

66 'Bevin the Cabinet King-Maker', *Observer*, 8 Oct. 1950.

67 'Labour Party And Korea', *The Times*, 6 Oct. 1950; Hugh Chevins, 'Mr. Bevin's Challenge and Offer to Russia', *Daily Telegraph*, 6 Oct., 1950.

68 R. H. S. Crossman, 'At Margate', *New Statesman & Nation*, 7 Oct. 1950.

69 Woodrow Wyatt, *Confessions of an Optimist*, Collins, London, 1985, p. 118.

70 Illingworth, 'Stealing the Limelight', *Daily Mail*, 23 Oct. 1950.

71 James Griffiths, '"The Enigma" (Nye Bevan)', 9 Oct. 1973, Griffiths Papers, E1/41.

72 Foot, *Aneurin Bevan:; Vol. II*, Davis-Poynter, London, 1973, pp. 299–300; Roy Jenkins, *A Life at the Centre*, Macmillan, London, 1991, p. 112.

73 Jay, *Change and Fortune*, p. 202.

74 Philip M. Williams (ed.), *The Diary of Hugh Gaitskell*, p. 193 (entry for 11 Aug. 1950).

75 John Strachey, 'The Unreaped Harvest', *Sunday Times*, 20 Jan. 1963. Emphasis in original.

76 For the original coinage, see 'Mr. Butskell's Dilemma', *The Economist*, 13 Feb. 1954.

77 Hugh Gaitskell, 'Economic Planning and Liberalisation', EPC (50) 9, 7 Jan. 1950, CAB 134/225/11, TNA.

78 Rollings, '"The Reichstag method of governing"?', pp. 15–36.

79 Jenkins, *A Life at the Centre*, p. 148.

80 James Griffiths, *Pages From Memory*, J. M. Dent & Sons Ltd, London, 1969, p. 135.

81 Raymond Daniell, 'Attlee Aides Seek Curb On Rearming', *New York Times*, 19 Nov. 1950.

82 'Mr. Bevan and Rearmament', *Manchester Guardian*, 23 Nov. 1950; 'Reporter Disavows Error on Bevan Talk', *New York Times*, 29 Nov. 1950.

83 Edward Crankshaw, 'Moscow Trying To Split the West', *Observer*, 3 Dec. 1950.

84 Brandon E. Pasko, *The Role of the Operational Artist: General MacArthur in the Korean War from June 1950 to April 1951*, US Army Command and General Staff College Fort Leavenworth, KS, 2019, p. 36.

85 Douglas MacArthur to the Joint Chiefs of Staff, 28 Nov. 1950, *Foreign Relations of the United States, 1950; Vol. VII*, p. 1237.

86 Steven Casey, *Selling the Korean War: Propaganda, Politics, and Public Opinion in the United States, 1950–1953*, Oxford University Press, New York, 2008, Chapter 5.

87 'The President's News Conference', 30 Nov. 1950, *Public Papers of the Presidents 1950*, p. 727.

88 White House press release, 30 Nov. 1950, ibid., p. 727, n. 3.

89 'Assured Destruction' was an official US doctrine in the 1960s; the analyst Donald Brennan added the word 'Mutual' to create the acronym 'MAD'. The nuclear winter effect was only modelled in the 1980s. See Alan Robock, 'Nuclear Winter', *WIREs Climate Change*, 1 (2010), pp. 418–27.

90 'Scale of Atomic Warfare', *The Scotsman*, 20 Nov. 1950.

91 Matthew Jones, 'Great Britain, the United States, and Consultation Over Use of the Atomic Bomb, 1950–1954', *Historical Journal*, 54 (2011), pp. 797–828.

92 Tony Benn, *Years of Hope: Diaries, Letters, and Papers, 1940–1962*, Hutchinson, London, 1994, p. 139 (entry for 11 Feb. 1951).

93 Cabinet minutes, 30 Nov. 1950, CM (50) 80th conclusions, CAB 128/18/40, TNA.

94 Ian McDougall, 'Attlee Arrival', 4 Dec. 1950, Attlee Papers (Bodleian), MS.CRA.5.

95 Holmes to Acheson, 3 Dec. 1950, *Foreign Relations of the United States 1950: Western Europe; Vol. III*, pp. 1698–703.

96 Acheson, *Present At the Creation*, pp. 478–85.

97 Clement Attlee to Ernest Bevin, 10 Dec. 1950, FO 800/517, TNA.

98 'United States Minutes, Truman–Attlee Conversations, First Meeting, The White House, Washington, December 4, 1950, 4:00–5:35 pm', Foreign Relations of the United States 1950: Western Europe; Vol. III, p. 1711.

99 Oliver Franks to the Foreign Office, 7 Dec. 1950, FO 800/457.

100 Jones, 'Great Britain', p. 804.

101 Parliamentary Debates, House of Commons, Fifth Series, Vol. 482, 12 Dec. 1950, col. 984.

102 Rosemary Foot, 'Anglo-American Relations', pp. 53–6.

103 Roger Makins, 'Record of Conversation held at Mr. [Averell] Harriman's House on December 7th 1950', 8 Dec. 1950, FO 800/517, TNA.

104 Cabinet minutes, 18 Dec. 1950, CM (50) 87th conclusions, CAB 128/18/47, TNA.

105 Cabinet minutes, 25 Jan. 1951, CM (51) 7th conclusions, CAB 128/19/7, TNA.

106 'Memorandum of Meeting Between British Ambassador and Secretary Acheson', 2 Apr. 1951, Memoranda of Conversations File, 1949–1953: April 1951, Acheson Papers (Truman Library).

107 G. R. Strauss, unpublished memoirs, p. 141, Strauss Papers, STRS 1/2.

108 Cabinet Secretary's notebook, CM 7 (51), 25 Jan. 1951.

109 Philip M. Williams, *Diary of Hugh Gaitskell*, p. 229 (entry for 2 Feb. 1951).

110 'Our London Correspondence', *Manchester Guardian*, 17 Feb. 1951.

111 Tom Williams, 'Parliament: Guns and Groundnuts', *New Statesman & Nation*, 24 Feb. 1951.

112 'Too Halting Steps to Safety', *Daily Telegraph*, 16 Feb. 1951.

113 Parliamentary Debates, House of Commons, Fifth Series, Vol. 484, 15 Feb. 1951, cols 734–5.

114 Campbell, *Nye Bevan*, pp. 227–8.

115 Philip M. Williams, *Hugh Gaitskell*, p. 248.

116 Parliamentary Debates, House of Commons, Fifth Series, Vol. 484, 15 Feb. 1951, col. 739.

117 Warner, *In the Midst of Events*, p. 54 (entry for 7 Jan. 1951).

118 '"Ernest Bevin": A Radio Portrait', Citrine Papers, 10/3.

119 Anne Sharpley, 'The Dirty Job of Axing Ministers – by Lord Attlee', *Evening Standard*, 25 July 1962.

120 Bevin to Acheson, 22 March 1951, Acheson Papers (Yale), 3/34.

121 Heffer (ed.), *Henry 'Chips' Channon*, p. 705 (entry for 19 March 1951).

122 Attlee, 'Bevan as Hero', in Field (ed.), *Attlee's Great Contemporaries*, p. 139.

123 Hugh Dalton, *High Tide and After*, p. 362.

124 Attlee, *The Granada Historical Records Interview*, p. 49; 'Inside Politics' (interview with Attlee), *News Chronicle*, 20 Apr. 1959.

125 Pearce, *Patrick Gordon Walker Diaries*, p. 192 (entry for 10 March 1951).

126 Donoughue and Jones, *Herbert Morrison*, p. 468; Interview with George Isaacs, 16 Feb. 1968, Morrison Papers (LSE), 6/2.

127 Office of Current Intelligence, Daily Digest of Significant Traffic, 10 March 1951, CREST database, CIA-RDP79T01146A000100090001-2.

128 Mariel Grant, '"Working for the Yankee Dollar": Tourism and the Festival of Britain as Stimuli for Recovery', *Journal of British Studies*, 45 (2006), pp. 581–601.

129 Attlee, *The Granada Historical Records Interview*, p. 49.

130 Harold Nicolson to Vita Sackville-West, 1 Aug. 1951, in Nigel Nicolson (ed.), *Harold Nicolson: Diaries and Letters 1945–1962*, Collins, London, 1968, p. 208.

131 Dalton, *High Tide and After*, p. 361. Dalton did not identify the individual who said this.

132 Interview with Lord Strang at the House of Lords, 22 Apr. 1969, Morrison Papers (LSE), 6/4.

133 Second interview between G. W. Jones and Lord Henderson, 22 Apr. 1970, Morrison Papers (LSE), 6/2.

134 Speech of 10 Jan. 1943, in Herbert Morrison, *Prospects and Policies*, Alfred A. Knopf, New York, 1944, pp. 80–1.

135 Attlee Chronology, 21 and 31 March 1951, Attlee Papers (Bodleian), MS.CRA.21; 'Our London Correspondence', *Manchester Guardian*, 17 March 1951.

136 Francis Williams, *A Prime Minister Remembers*, p. 246.

137 Strauss, unpublished memoirs, pp. 141–2, Strauss Papers, STRS 1/2.

138 Philip M. Williams, *Diary of Hugh Gaitskell*, pp. 238–47 (entry for 30 Apr. 1951); Cabinet minutes, 9 Apr. 1951, CM (51) 25th Conclusions, CAB 128/21/8, TNA; Pearce, *Patrick Gordon Walker Diaries*, pp. 193 (entry for 12 Apr. 1951) 'Bevan Has Happy Evening With Dockers', *News Chronicle*, 4 Apr. 1951; Nicklaus Thomas-Symonds, *Nye: The Political Life of Aneurin Bevan*, I.B. Tauris, London, 2018, pp. 188.

139 Cabinet minutes, 9 Apr. 1951, CM (51) 26th Conclusions, CAB 128/21/9, TNA.

140 Philip M. Williams, *Diary of Hugh Gaitskell*, pp. 238–47 (entry for 30 Apr. 1951). Emphasis in original.

141 Pimlott, *Political Diary of Hugh Dalton*, pp. 523–4 (entry for 10 Apr. 1951).

142 Benn, *Years of Hope*, pp. 146–8 (entry for 11 Apr. 1951).

143 '"Ernest Bevin": A Radio Portrait', Citrine Papers, 10/3.

144 Hugh Dalton to Attlee, 15 Apr. 1951, Attlee Papers (Bodleian), MS.CRA.5

145 Bevan to Attlee, 21 Apr. 1951, and Attlee's reply of the same day, in Francis Williams, *A Prime Minister Remembers*, pp. 247–8.

146 See Hugh Purcell, *A Very Private Celebrity: The Nine Lives of John Freeman*, The Robson Press, London, 2015.

147 Castle, *Fighting All the Way*, p. 190.

148 For his defence, see Hugh Gaitskell, 'Defence the Budget, and "Tribune"', *Tribune*, 28 Dec. 1951.

149 'Inside Politics', *News Chronicle*, 20 Apr. 1959.

150 Foot, *Aneurin Bevan; Vol. II*, pp. 295, 323; Campbell, *Nye Bevan*, p. 248; Brian Brivati, *Hugh Gaitskell*, Richard Cohen Books, London, 1996, p. 118.

151 Attlee, *The Granada Historical Records Interview*, p. 47.

152 Parliamentary Debates, House of Commons, Fifth Series, Vol. 487, 23 Apr. 1951, col. 42

153 Jay, *Change and Fortune*, p. 205.

154 James Bamberg, *The History of the British Petroleum Company; Vol. II: The Anglo-Iranian Years, 1928–1954*, Cambridge University Press, Cambridge, 1994, p. 513.

155 James Bamberg, *British Petroleum and Global Oil, 1950–1975: The Challenge of Nationalism*, Cambridge University Press, Cambridge, 2000, p. 40.

156 Joint Intelligence Committee, 21 March 1951, JIC (51) 31, CAB 158/12, TNA.

157 Warner, *In the Midst of Events*, p. 75 (entry for 24 June 1951).

158 Acheson, *Present At the Creation*, p. 507.

159 Foreign Office to Washington, 6 Oct. 1951, FO 800/653, TNA.

160 George W. Jones, interview with Philip Noel-Baker, 20 March 1969, Morrison Papers (LSE), 6/1.

161 Francis Williams, *A Prime Minister Remembers*, p. 255.

162 D. E. Butler, *The British General Election of 1951*, Macmillan, London, 1952, pp. 86, 116.

163 Sue Onslow, '"Battlelines for Suez": The Abadan Crisis of 1951 and the Formation of the Suez Group', *Contemporary British History*, 17 (2003), pp. 1–28.

164 LPACR 1951, p. 122.

165 In fact, the state of the King's health prevented him making the trip and he died the following year. Wheeler-Bennett, *King George VI*, pp. 792–3. There is some correspondence in Attlee Papers at the Bodleian Attlee Papers (MS.CRA.5) from George VI and Princess Elizabeth (the future Elizabeth II) that is not accessible to researchers. Conceivably, this could cast further light on these issues. For Attlee's thoughts on the timing of the election, see his letter to Morrison of 27 May 1951, Morrison Papers (LSE), 8/4.

166 Dalton, *High Tide and After*, p. 375.

167 Labour Party manifesto, 1951.

168 Attlee Chronology, 25 Oct. – 1 Nov. 1951, Attlee Papers (Bodleian), MS.CRA.21; Butler, *British General Election of 1951*, p. 236.

169 'Attlees Go to the Country – to Live', *Daily Mail*, 2 Nov. 1951.

170 Attlee, *The Granada Historical Records Interview*, p. 50.

CHAPTER 9

1 'Labour Strong and Unburdened', *Manchester Guardian*, 7 Nov. 1951.
2 Pimlott (ed.), *Political Diary of Hugh Dalton*, p. 567 (entry for end of October 1951).
3 'Let's Face the Future', *New Statesman & Nation*, 3 Nov. 1951.
4 Jay, *Change and Fortune*, p. 221.
5 Janet Morgan (ed.), *The Backbench Diaries of Richard Crossman*, Book Club Associates, London, 1981, p. 48 (entry for 6 Dec. 1951).
6 Woodrow Wyatt, 'The Secret of Clement Attlee', *New Statesman*, 13 Oct. 1967.
7 Cairncross, *Years of Recovery*, , p. 509.
8 Zweiniger-Bargielowska, *Austerity in Britain*, pp. 234–42.
9 Black, *The Political Culture of the Left in Britain, 1951–64*.
10 The word 'privatization' was not yet in use.
11 Howard Glennerster, *British Social Policy since 1945* (2nd edn), Blackwell Publishers, Oxford, 2000, Chapter 4.
12 Hugh Gaitskell to Kingsley Martin, 7 Nov. 1952, in Philip M. Williams (ed.), *The Diary of Hugh Gaitskell*, p. 324.
13 Speech by Tony Blair to a Fabian Society conference, 17 June 2003, https://www.theguardian.com/society/2003/jun/17/publicservices.speeches1 (consulted 14 Jan. 2023). For further discussion, see below.
14 T. Balogh, 'John Strachey's Golden Age', *Tribune*, 7 March 1952.
15 Bevan, *In Place of Fear*, p. 8.
16 Morgan, *Backbench Diaries*, p. 419 (entry for 3 May 1955).
17 Labour Party manifesto, 1955.
18 Memo on the 1955 election accompanying Brendon Sewell to Michael Fraser, 8 June 1955, CRD 2/48/54, Conservative Party Archive.
19 Alan Moorehead, 'Going Sober With Labour', *Sunday Times*, 6 Oct. 1963.
20 Clement Attlee to Douglas Jay, 10 Sept. 1962, Jay Papers, MS.6745/2.
21 Ivan Yates, 'Attlee's Little Joke', *Observer*, 11 Oct. 1964.
22 Douglas Jay, 'Attlee: A Memorial', *The House Magazine*, 15 Apr. 1963, copy in Jay Papers, MS.6745/140.
23 Lord Attlee, 'In the Driver's Seat', *Observer*, 18 Oct. 1964.
24 David Reynolds, *In Command of History: Churchill Fighting and Writing the Second World War*, Allen Lane, London, 2004.
25 See the correspondence in the Stow Hill Papers, STH/FS/1/ATT.
26 Lord Winster, 'Letter From London', *Baltimore Sun*, 2 May 1954.
27 'Weekend Competitions', *New Statesman & Nation*, 26 June 1954.
28 Broadcast on 3 Jan. 1959 on BBC TV. For the transcript, see 'A Prime Minister Remembers', *The Listener*, 22 Jan. 1959; 'TV: A Week-End of Accomplishments', *New York Times*, 1 Dec. 1958. The original of the Attlee–Truman film, originally broadcast by CBS, is held at the Truman Library (MP59-9). A digitized version can be found at https://www.trumanlibrary.gov/movingimage-records/mp59-9 (consulted 19 March 2023).
29 Attlee to Francis Williams, 1 Apr. 1959, Williams Papers, FRWS 8/1.
30 Published in the United States with the title *Twilight of Empire*.

31 Attlee, *The Granada Historical Records Interview*; 'Lord Attlee Remembers', BBC Home Service, 21 Apr. 1963.

32 Attlee to Paul Addison, 5 July 1965, Addison Papers. See also Addison's interview with him of 31 Jan. 1967.

33 For his involvement in the biographies written, respectively, by Patricia Strauss and Eric Estorick, see the various discussions in Clarke, *Cripps Version*.

34 Frank S. Stuart to Ernest Bevin, 9 Sept. 1937, and Bevin's reply of 16 Sept., Bevin Papers (Warwick), 126/EB/X/17/29-30. For Bevin's efforts to prevent the publication of Trevor Evans's 1946 biography of him, see the correspondence in the George Allen & Unwin Papers, AUC 247/5, that in the Bevin Papers (CAC), BEVN II 6/2, and the record of Paul Addison's discussion with Evans on 27 Sept. 1966, Addison Papers.

35 G. W. Jones, interview with F. G. Kay, 26 May 1967, Morrison Papers (LSE), 6/2; Donoughue and Jones, *Herbert Morrison*, p. 556.

36 Attlee to Arthur Moyle, 14 Aug. 1965, quoted in Harris, *Attlee*, p. 560.

37 Jones, interview with Kay.

38 Pimlott, *Hugh Dalton*, pp. 638–40.

39 Robert McKenzie, 'Witness At the Sick Bed of Socialism', *Observer*, 4 Feb. 1962.

40 Jennie Lee, 'Dalton's Hymn of Hate Against the Left', *Tribune*, 2 March 1962.

41 David Marquand, 'A Lusty Appetite for Power', *Guardian*, 5 Feb. 1962. Marquand's father Hilary had been Bevan's successor at the Ministry of Health (as noted in Chapter 8, above).

42 Alison Fenton to Frank and Susan Soskice, 26 Oct. [1967], Stow Hill Papers, STH/FS/1/ATT.

43 See those published in *The Times* and *Guardian* respectively on 9 Oct. 1967.

44 As an example of a thoughtful Conservative response, see T. E. Utley, 'Attlee: No Ordinary Man', *Daily Telegraph*, 9 Oct. 1967.

45 'As It Happened', *The Economist*, 14 Oct. 1967.

46 Philip Williamson, 'Baldwin's Reputation: Politics and History, 1937–1967', *Historical Journal*, 47 (2004), pp. 127–68; Ronald Butt, 'A Constitutional Revolutionary', *Financial Times*, 9 Oct. 1967.

47 'Clement Attlee', *The Times*, 9 Oct. 1967.

48 Kevin Theakston and Mark Gill, 'Theresa May Joint Worst Post-war Prime Minister, Say Historians and Politics Professors in New Survey', *The Conversation*, 6 July 2021, https://theconversation.com/theresa-may-joint-worst-post-war-prime-minister-say-historians-and-politics-professors-in-new-survey-163912 (consulted 19 Jan. 2023).

49 D. W. Hayton, *Conservative Revolutionary: The Lives of Lewis Namier*, Manchester University Press, Manchester, 2019, pp. 290–2; John L. Harvey, 'History and the social sciences', in Stefan Berger, Heiko Feldner and Kevin Passmore (eds), *Writing History: Theory and Practice* (3rd edn), Bloomsbury Academic, London, 2020, pp. 86–112.

50 Donoughue and Jones, *Herbert Morrison*, p. xi.

51 Simon Burgess, '1945 Observed: A History of the Histories', *Contemporary Record*, 5 (1991), pp. 155–70.

52 Paul Addison to David Machin, 10 June 1975, Jonathan Cape Papers, JC217.

53 Paul Addison, 'The Politics and Historiography of the Second World War', unpublished and undated paper, Addison Papers. Internal evidence dates this to soon after the 1976 Labour leadership contest.

54 Angus Calder, 'The Left in the War, 1939–1945: State of My Research', n.d., Calder Papers, Acc. 9851/1.

55 Angus Calder, *The People's War: Britain 1939–45*, Jonathan Cape, London, 1969, p. 575.

56 Paul Addison and Harriet Jones, *Companion to Contemporary Britain: 1939–2000*, Blackwell Publishing, Oxford, 2005, pp. 1–2.

57 Paul Addison, The *Road to 1945: British Politics and the Second World War* 2nd (edn), Pimlico, London, 1994, pp. 284–5.

58 Addison to Arthur Marwick, 6 Sept. [1974], Addison Papers.

59 Addison, *The Road to 1945*, p. 280.

60 Paul Addison, *No Turning Back: The Peacetime Revolutions of Post-War Britain*, Oxford University Press, Oxford, 2010, pp. 276–7.

61 Keith Joseph, 'Notes Towards the Definition of Policy', 4 April 1975, Thatcher Papers (2/6/1/156), http://www.margaretthatcher.org/document/110098; Lord Hailsham notes on a meeting of the Shadow Cabinet, 11 April 1975, http://www.margaretthatcher.org/document/111134; and the official minutes of the meeting, available at http://www.margaretthatcher.org/document/109958 (all consulted 27 Apr. 2020).

62 Parliamentary Debates, House of Commons, Fifth Series, Vol. 892, 22 May 1975, col. 1668.

63 Keith Harper, 'The Heights of Ingenuity by Benn (and Attlee)', *Guardian*, 2 Oct. 1975. Benn quoted from Attlee, *The Labour Party In Perspective*, pp. 15, 32.

64 LPACR 1975, p. 229.

65 'Return to Principles of 1945 Manifesto, Urges Benn', *Guardian*, 7 Sept. 1945.

66 'The Shrouded Spirit of '45', *Guardian*, 14 Dec. 1977.

67 'How Benn Would Liberate Britain, the Last Colony', *Guardian*, 29 Sept. 1980.

68 'Benn the Clear Target as Healey Puts the Boot in', *Guardian*, 22 May 1981.

69 Mike Finn, 'The promise of "Liberal Democracy", c. 1981–2010', in Thackeray and Toye (eds), *Electoral Pledges in Britain*, pp. 249–70, at pp. 253–4.

70 Richard Gott, 'By the Left', *Guardian*, 14 Dec. 1981. For the quotation, see Attlee, *The Labour Party In Perspective*, p. 60.

71 LPACR 1980, p. 67.

72 Paul Corthorn, 'Michael Foot as Labour leader: The uses of the past', in Richard Toye and Julie Gottlieb (eds), *Making Reputations: Power, Persuasion and the Individual in Modern British Politics*, I.B. Tauris, London, 2005, pp. 151–65.

73 Thatcher, *The Path to Power*, pp. 45, 120.

74 E. H. H. Green, *Thatcher*, Hodder Arnold, London, 2006, pp. 17–21, 38–9.

75 Peter Hennessy, *A Duty of Care: Britain Before and After Covid*, Penguin Books, London, 2023, p. 21.

76 Press conference, 10 June 1987, https://www.margaretthatcher.org/document/106882 (consulted 21 Jan. 2023).

77 Thatcher, *Path to Power*, p. 150.

78 For a cogent expression of this view, see Nigel Lawson, 'The New Conservatism' (Lecture to the Bow group), 4 Aug. 1980, https://www.margaretthatcher.org/document/109505 (consulted 21 Jan. 2023).

79 Correlli Barnett, *The Audit of War: The Illusion and Reality of Britain as a Great Nation*, Macmillan, London, 1986, p. 19.

80 Paul Addison, 'Warfare and Welfare', *London Review of Books*, 24 July 1986.

81 David Edgerton, 'The Prophet Militant and Industrial: The Peculiarities of Correlli Barnett', *Twentieth Century British History*, 2 (1991), pp. 360–79, at 363.

82 Correlli Barnett, *The Lost Victory: British Dreams, British Realities, 1945–1950*, Macmillan, London, 1995; Michael Heseltine, *Life in the Jungle: My Autobiography*, Hodder & Stoughton, London, 2000, p. 493.

83 Kenneth O. Morgan, *My Histories*, University of Wales Press, Cardiff, 2015, pp. 99–100.

84 Peter Clarke, 'High Tide for the Left', *Times Literary Supplement*, 16 March 1984.

85 Denis MacShane, 'Labour and the Lessons of Power', *Tribune*, 29 June 1984.

86 E. P. Thompson, 'Mr Attlee and the Gadarene Swine', *Guardian*, 3 March 1984.

87 Jackson, *The Case for Scottish Independence*, p. 115; Morgan, *Labour In Power*, pp. 306–12. The government did concede a Council of Wales, which, though toothless, paved the way for later developments, such as the creation of the position of Secretary of State for Wales in 1964.

88 Andrew Seaton, 'Against the "Sacred Cow": NHS Opposition and the Fellowship for Freedom in Medicine, 1948–72', *Twentieth Century British History*, 26 (2015), pp. 424–49.

89 Timmins, *The Five Giants*, pp. 392–3.

90 Parliamentary Debates, House of Commons, Sixth Series, Vol. 136, 5 July 1988, col. 908.

91 Audrey Leathard, *Health Care Provision: Past, Present and into the 21st Century* (2nd edn), Stanley Thomas (Publishers) Ltd, p. 108.

92 Speech of 2 Oct. 1983, in Neil Kinnock, *Thorns & Roses: Speeches, 1983–1991*, Hutchinson, London, 1992, p. 38.

93 Martin Westlake, *Kinnock: The Biography*, Little, Brown and Company, London, 2001, pp. 26–7, 710–11.

94 Neil Kinnock, *Making Our Way*, Basil Blackwell Ltd, Oxford, 1986, p. 7.

95 Kate Muir, 'Red Rose of Taxes', *The Times*, 14 March 1992; Mark Stuart, *John Smith: A Life*, Politico's, London, 2005, p. 243; Andy McSmith, *John Smith: A Life 1938–1994*, Mandarin, London, 1994, p. 327.

96 Martin Francis, *Ideas and Policies Under Labour, 1945–51: Building a New Britain*, Manchester University Press, Manchester, 1997

97 Fielding, Thompson and Tiratsoo, *'England Arise!'*, 1995.

98 David Marquand, *The Progressive Dilemma: From Lloyd George to Kinnock*, Heinemann, London, 1991, p. 2.

99 Speech of 5 July 1995 in Tony Blair, *New Britain: My Vision of a Young Country*, London, Fourth Estate, 1996, p. 11.

100 Peter Mandelson and Roger Liddle, *The Blair Revolution: Can New Labour Deliver?*, Faber and Faber, London, 1996, p. 23.

101 Donald Macintyre, *Mandelson and the Making of New Labour*, HarperCollins, London, 2000, p. 12; Philip Johnston, 'Mandelson Lets Mask Slip to Show that Spin Doctors Can Feel Emotions', *Daily Telegraph*, 16 May 1997.

102 Mandelson's foreword to Donoughue and Jones's reissued biography of Morrison, Phoenix Press, London, 2001, p. xi.

103 Tony Blair, 'My Radical Task', *Observer*, 15 Sept. 1996.

104 'Lord Attlee Goes for a Short Walk', *Guardian*, 7 March 1997.

105 Stephen Churchett, *Tom and Clem*, Faber and Faber, London, 1997; Paul Foot, 'Ghosts of Tom and Clem at No 10 and No 11', *Guardian*, 5 May 1997.

106 Tony Benn, 'Attlee and British Socialism' (Attlee memorial lecture), 9 Feb 1998, https://attleefoundation.org/a-homepage-section/ (consulted 28 Jan. 2023).

107 Tony Blair, speech of 28 Sept. 1999, http://www.guardian.co.uk/lab99/Story/0 ,2763,202187,00.html (consulted 28 Jan. 2023).

108 Blair speech of 17 June 2003; 'The Egoist', *New Statesman*, 24 Apr. 1954.

109 *One Night in 2012 – An Imagine Special*, BBC1, 17 July 2016.

110 John Cruddas, 'Attlee, the ILP and the Romantic Tradition', 4 Nov. 2011 (edited version of an Attlee Memorial Lecture delivered at University College, Oxford on 28 Oct. 2011), https://www.independentlabour.org.uk/2011/11/04/attlee-the-ilp -and-the-romantic-tradition/ (consulted 7 Feb. 2023).

111 Speech of 2 Oct. 2012, https://labourlist.org/2012/10/ed-milibands-conference -speech-the-transcript/ (consulted 7 Feb. 2023); Judi Atkins, 'Narrating One Nation: The Ideology and Rhetoric of the Miliband Labour Party', *Politics*, 35 (2015), pp. 19–31; Batrouni, *The Battle of Ideas in the Labour Party*, Chapter 3.

112 Patrick Wintour and Andrew Sparrow, 'Attlee Reformed in Austerity and So Can We – Miliband', *Guardian*, 22 June 2013.

113 Dave Calhoun, 'Film of the Week', *Time Out*, 12 March 2013.

114 Steven Fielding, 'Ken Loach's Spirit of '45 is a Fantasy', 8 March 2013, https:// www.theguardian.com/commentisfree/2013/mar/08/ken-loach-the-spirit-of-45 -fantasy (consulted 9 Feb. 2023).

115 Philip French, review of *The Spirit of '45*, *Observer*, 17 March 2013.

116 The speaker was Julian Tudor Hart (1927–2018), a pioneering GP and a Communist parliamentary candidate in the 1960s and 1970s, though he subsequently joined the Labour Party.

117 'Ken Loach on *The Spirit of '45*' – video, 13 March 2013, https://www.theguardian .com/film/video/2013/mar/13/ken-loach-spirit-45-video (consulted 9 Feb. 2023).

118 Steven Fielding, 'The shifting significance of "The Spirit of '45"', in Nathan Yeowell (ed.), *Rethinking Labour's Past*, I.B. Tauris, London, 2022, pp. 57–74, at 69.

119 Bew, *Citizen Clem*, p. xix.

120 Speech of 18 Feb. 2021, https://labour.org.uk/press/full-text-of-keir-starmer-speech -on-a-new-chapter-for-britain/ (consulted 9 Feb. 2023).

121 Phil Tinline, *The Death of Consensus: 100 Years of British Political Nightmares*, Hurst & Company, London, 2022, p. 320.

122 Martin Beckford, 'I'd Lead Like Attlee After WW2, Claims Under Fire Starmer', *Daily Mail*, 18 Feb. 2021; Andrew Fisher, 'Not McDonnell-esque But Bolder Than

Anything Done By Miliband', *i-paper*, 19 Feb. 2021; Miranda Green, 'Labour Battles Over Its Own History Hoping for "1945 and all that"', *Financial Times*, 25 Nov. 2021.

123 Janan Ganesh, 'Why Biden and Starmer Keep Beating the Critics', *Financial Times*, 31 Aug. 2022.

124 Colin Brown, 'Labour Prepares to Take Its New Show on the Road', *Guardian*, 10 March 1984.

CONCLUSION

1 Ben Pimlott, preface to the 1995 edition of *Hugh Dalton*, quoted in Peter Hennessy, 'Benjamin John Pimlott, 1945–2004', *Proceedings of the British Academy*, 150 (2007), pp. 161–79, at 169.

2 Geoffrey de Freitas and Helen de Freitas, *The Slighter Side of a Long Public Life*, privately published, 1985, p. 57.

3 Kit Kowol, 'The Lost World of British Conservatism: The Radical Tory Tradition, 1939–1951'. DPhil Dissertation, University of Oxford, 2014, pp. 237–46.

4 Woodrow Wyatt, 'The Secret of Clement Attlee', *New Statesman*, 13 Oct. 1967.

5 James K. Galbraith, *The End of Normal: The Great Crisis and the Future of Growth*, Simon & Schuster Paperbacks, New York, 2015, p. 34.

Bibliography

ARCHIVAL COLLECTIONS

UK

London

The National Archives, Kew
Institute of Education Archives
Union of Women Teachers Archive
Imperial War Museum
Albert Hird diary
Liddell Hart Centre, King's College London

Christopher Mayhew Papers

LSE Archives

Walter Citrine Papers
William Beveridge Papers
Hugh Dalton Papers
Evan Durbin Papers
John Parker Papers
Herbert Morrison Papers

Parliamentary Archives

Beaverbrook Papers
Levy Papers
David Lloyd George Papers
Stansgate Papers
Stow Hill Papers
University College London Special Collections
Hugh Gaitskell Papers

Aberystwyth

National Library of Wales
James Griffiths Papers
Bristol
University of Bristol, Special Collections
National Liberal Club collection
Caversham

BBC Written Archives

Cambridge
Cambridge University Library

Stanley Baldwin Papers

Churchill Archives Centre

Mark Abrams Papers
Paul Addison Papers
A. V. Alexander Papers
Leo Amery Papers
Clement Attlee Papers
Ernest Bevin Papers
Alexander Cadogan Papers
R. W. B. Clarke Papers
Henry Page Croft Papers
John Hynd Papers
Stephen King-Hall Papers
Valentine Lawford Papers
E. A. G. Robinson Papers
Enid Russell-Smith Papers
George Strauss Papers
Francis Williams Papers
Henry Willink Papers
Michael Young Papers

Edinburgh
National Library of Scotland
Angus Calder Papers
Emrys Hughes Papers

Manchester
People's History Museum
Ian Mikardo Papers

Labour Party Archive
Ellen Wilkinson Papers

Oxford
Bodleian Library
Clement Attlee Papers

Barbara Castle Papers
Conservative Party Archive
Stafford Cripps Papers
Douglas Jay Papers
Roy Jenkins Papers
Harold Macmillan Papers
Harold Wilson Papers
Earl Winterton Papers

Nuffield College
Herbert Morrison Papers

Reading
University of Reading Special Collections
George Allen & Unwin Papers
Jonathan Cape Papers
Warwick
Modern Records Centre, University of Warwick
Ernest Bevin Papers
Richard Crossman Papers
Trades Union Congress General Council minutes
Woking
Surrey History Centre
James Chuter Ede Papers

USA
College Park, Maryland
National Archives

New York
New York Historical Society
Time Inc. Records
New York Public Library
Arthur Hays Sulzberger Papers
Independence, Missouri
Harry S. Truman Presidential Library
Dean Acheson Papers
Oral history interviews with Winthrop G. Brown, Emilio Collado, and Joseph D.
    Coppock.
Fred M. Vinson Papers (consulted on microfilm)

DATABASES AND ONLINE SOURCES

Dean Acheson Papers (Yale)
CREST (CIA) database
Foreign Broadcast Information Service
Lord Halifax diaries

Neville Chamberlain Papers
Winston Churchill Papers
Mass Observation Archive
W. L. Mackenzie King diary
Oxford Dictionary of National Biography
Margaret Thatcher Papers

UK GOVERNMENT PUBLICATIONS

Beveridge, William, *Social Insurance and Allied Services*, HMSO, London, 1942.
Economic Survey for 1947, Cmd. 7046, Feb. 1947.
Financial Agreement Between the Governments of the United States and the United Kingdom, Cmd. 6708, 6 Dec. 1945.
Proposals for Consideration by an International Conference on Trade and Employment, Cmd. 6709, 6 Dec. 1945.
Report from the Select Committee on the Budget Disclosure, HMSO, London, 1947.
Statement on Personal Incomes, Costs and Prices, Cmd. 7231, Feb. 1948.
Minutes of Evidence Taken Before the Royal Commission on the Press, 29th April 1948, Cmd. 7480, July 1948.
Report of the Tribunal appointed to inquire into Allegations reflecting on the Official Conduct of Ministers of the Crown and other Public Servants, Cmd. 7616, Jan. 1949.
Anglo-French Discussions regarding French proposals for the Western European Coal, Iron and Steel Industries, May–June, 1950, Cmd. 7970, 1950.

LABOUR PARTY PUBLICATIONS

Annual conference reports
Labour and the Nation, 1928.
Hastings, Somerville, *The People's Health*, 1932.
For Socialism and Peace, 1934.
National Service For Health, 1943.
Labour Party, *Full Employment and Financial Policy*, 1944.
Speaker's Handbook 1945, 1945.
Ernest Bevin's Work in Wartime, 1940–1945, 1945.
Cards on The Table: An Interpretation of Labour's Foreign Policy, 1947.
Labour Believes in Britain, 1949.
Speakers' Handbook 1949–50, 1949.
Labour Party, *European Unity: A Statement by the National Executive Committee of the British Labour Party*, 1950.

CONSERVATIVE PARTY PUBLICATIONS

General Election 1945: Notes for Speakers and Workers, 1945.
The Right Road for Britain: The Conservative Party's Statement of Policy, 1949.

BIBLIOGRAPHY

TRADES UNION CONGRESS PUBLICATIONS

Annual Congress reports

PUBLISHED DOCUMENT SERIES

Documents on British Policy Overseas
Foreign Relations of the United States
Public Papers of the Presidents of the United States: Harry S. Truman

NEWSPAPERS AND PERIODICALS

Aberdeen Journal
Baltimore Sun
Belfast Telegraph
British Medical Journal
Chelmsford Chronicle
Chicago Tribune
Clarion
Cornhill Magazine
Daily Express
Daily Herald
Daily Mail
Daily Mirror
Daily Telegraph
Daily Worker
Derby Daily Telegraph
Dover Express
Dundee Courier
Dundee Evening Telegraph
Economic Weekly
Economist
Evening Standard
Exeter and Plymouth Gazette
Fabian Quarterly
Financial Times
Forward
Halifax Daily Courier
Independent
i-paper
Le Monde
Leicester Evening Mail
Listener
Lloyd George Liberal Magazine
London Review of Books

Maclean's Magazine
Man in the Street
Manchester Guardian/Guardian
Middletown Press (Connecticut)
Morning Post
New Leader
New Statesman & Nation/New Statesman
New York Herald Tribune
New York Times
News Chronicle
Newsweek
Northern Whig
Nottingham Evening Post
Observer
Picture Post
Popular View
Scotsman
Shipley Times & Express
Spectator
Spiritualist News
Sunday Post
Sunday Times
Time
Time Out
The Times
Times Literary Supplement
Town Crier (Birmingham)
Tribune
Western Daily Press
Western Mail
Yorkshire Post

BOOKS, ARTICLES AND THESES

Abel-Smith, Brian, 'Hospital Planning and the Structure of the Hospital Service', *Medical Care*, 2 (1964), pp. 47–51.

_____, *The Hospitals 1800–1948: A Study in Social Administration in England and Wales*, Heinemann Educational Books Ltd, London, 1964.

Acheson, Dean, *Present at the Creation: My Years in the State Department*, W.W. Norton & Co., New York, 1969.

ACCO, *Child Care 1949–1970: ACCO – A Souvenir Portrait 1949–1970*, Association of Child Care Officers, London, 1970.

Ackers, Peter and Jonathan Payne, 'Before the Storm: The Experience of Nationalization and the Prospects for Industrial Relations Partnership in the British Coal Industry, 1947–1972 – Rethinking the Militant Narrative', *Social History*, 27 (2002), pp. 184–209.

Acland, Richard, et al., *Keeping Left: Labour's First Five Years and the Problems Ahead*, New Statesman, London, 1950.

Adams, Jad, *Tony Benn*, Macmillan, London, 1992.

Adamthwaite, Anthony, 'Britain and the World, 1945–9: The View from the Foreign Office', *International Affairs*, 61 (1985), pp. 223–35.

Addison, Christopher, et al., *Problems of a Socialist Government*, Victor Gollancz Ltd, London, 1933.

Addison, Paul, *Churchill on the Home Front, 1900–1955*, Jonathan Cape, London, 1992.

_____, *The Road to 1945*, Jonathan Cape, London, 1975 (2nd edn, Pimlico, London, 1994).

_____, *No Turning Back: The Peacetime Revolutions of Post-War Britain*, Oxford University Press, Oxford, 2010.

Addison, Paul and Harriet Jones, *Companion to Contemporary Britain: 1939–2000*, Blackwell Publishing, Oxford, 2005.

Aldrich, Richard J. (ed.), *British Intelligence, Strategy and the Cold War, 1945–51*, Routledge, London, 1992.

Andrade, Jackie, 'What Does Doodling Do?', *Applied Cognitive Psychology*, 24 (2010), pp. 100–106.

Anon, *The Scottish Socialists: A Gallery of Contemporary Portraits*, Faber and Faber, London, 1931.

Anyonge, Nathan Jumba, 'British Groundnut Scheme in East Africa: Labour Government's Dilemma', MA thesis, Kansas State University, 1966.

Armstrong, William (ed.), *With Malice Toward None: A War Diary by Cecil H. King*, Sidgwick & Jackson, London, 1970.

Ashworth, Lucian M., 'Rethinking a Socialist Foreign Policy: The British Labour Party and International Relations Experts, 1918 to 1931', *International Labor and Working-Class History*, 75 (2009), pp. 30–48.

Atkins, Judi, 'Narrating One Nation: The Ideology and Rhetoric of the Miliband Labour Party', *Politics*, 35 (2015), pp. 19–31.

Attlee, C. R., *The Labour Party in Perspective*, Victor Gollancz Ltd, London, 1937.

_____, *Labour's Peace Aims*, Labour Party, London, 1939.

_____, *As It Happened*, William Heinemann Ltd, London, 1954.

_____, *Clem Attlee: The Granada Historical Records Interview*, Panther Books, London, 1967.

Auer, Peter (ed.), *Style and Social Identities Alternative Approaches to Linguistic Heterogeneity*, Mouton de Gruyter, Berlin, 2007.

Bailey, Victor, 'The Shadow of the Gallows: The Death Penalty and the British Labour Government, 1945–51', *Law and History Review*, 18 (2000), pp. 305–49.

Ball, Stuart (ed.), *Parliament and Politics in the Age of Churchill and Attlee: The Headlam Diaries 1935–1951*, Cambridge University Press for the Royal Historical Society, London, 1999.

Ball, Stuart and Ian Holliday (eds), *Mass Conservatism: The Conservatives and the Public since the 1880s*, Routledge, London, 2002.

Bamberg, James, *The History of the British Petroleum Company: Vol. II: The Anglo-Iranian Years, 1928–1954*, Cambridge University Press, Cambridge, 1994.

_____, *British Petroleum and Global Oil, 1950–1975: The Challenge of Nationalism*, Cambridge University Press, Cambridge, 2000.

Barclay, Roderick, *Ernest Bevin and the Foreign Office 1939–1969*, published by the author, London, 1975.

Barnett, Correlli, *The Audit of War: The Illusion and Reality of Britain as a Great Nation*, Macmillan, London, 1986.

_____, *The Lost Victory: British Dreams, British Realities, 1945–1950*, Macmillan, London, 1995.

Batrouni, Dimitri, *The Battle of Ideas in the Labour Party: From Attlee to Corbyn and Brexit*, Policy Press, Bristol, 2021.

Baylis, John, *The Diplomacy of Pragmatism: Britain and the Formation of NATO, 1942–1949*, Kent State University Press, Kent, Ohio, 1993.

Becker, Josef and Franz Knipping (eds), *Power in Europe? Great Britain, France, Italy and Germany in a Post-war World, 1945–50*, De Gruyter, New York, 1986.

Beckett, Francis, *Clem Attlee*, Richard Cohen Books, London, 1997.

Beers, Laura, 'Labour's Britain, Fight for It Now!', *Historical Journal*, 52 (2009), pp. 667–95.

_____, *Your Britain: Media and the Making of the Labour Party*, Harvard University Press, Cambridge, MA, 2010.

_____, 'A Model MP? Ellen Wilkinson, Gender, Politics and Celebrity Culture in Interwar Britain', *Cultural and Social History*, 10 (2013), pp. 231–50.

_____, *Red Ellen: The Life of Ellen Wilkinson, Socialist, Feminist, Internationalist*, Harvard University Press, Cambridge, MA, 2016.

Benn, Tony, *Years of Hope: Diaries, Letters, and Papers, 1940–1962*, Hutchinson, London, 1994.

_____, *Dare to be a Daniel: Then and Now*, Hutchinson, London, 2004.

Bennett, Gill, *The Zinoviev Letter: The Conspiracy That Never Dies*, Oxford University Press, Oxford, 2018.

Bennett, Huw, '"A very salutary effect": The Counter-Terror Strategy in the Early Malayan Emergency, June 1948 to December 1949', *Journal of Strategic Studies*, 32 (2009), pp. 415–44.

Berger, Stefan, Heiko Feldner and Kevin Passmore (eds), *Writing History: Theory and Practice* (3rd edn), Bloomsbury Academic, London, 2020.

Berthezène, Clarisse, *Training Minds for the War of Ideas: Ashridge College, the Conservative Party and the Cultural Politics of Britain, 1929–54*, Manchester University Press, Manchester, 2015.

Bevan, Aneurin ('Celticus'), *Why Not Trust the Tories?*, Victor Gollancz, London, 1944.

Bevan, Aneurin, *Democratic Values*, Fabian Publications Ltd and Victor Gollancz Ltd, London, 1950.

_____, *In Place of Fear*, William Heinemann Ltd, London, 1952.

Bevan, Aneurin, E. J. Strachey and George Strauss, *What We Saw in Russia*, Hogarth Press, London, 1931.

Bevan, Aneurin, W. J. Brown, John Strachey and Allan Young, *A National Policy: An Account of the Emergency Programme advanced by Sir Oswald Mosley*, Macmillan, London, 1931.

Bevin, Ernest, *Labor's Achievement and the Goal* (speech of 18 Aug. 1941), British Library of Information, New York, 1941.

Bevir, Mark, 'The Labour Church Movement, 1891–1902', *Journal of British Studies*, 38 (1999), pp. 217–45.

Bew, John, *Citizen Clem: A Biography of Attlee*, Riverrun, London, 2016.

Bhambra, Gurminder K., 'Relations of extraction, relations of redistribution: Empire, nation, and the construction of the British welfare state', *British Journal of Sociology*, 73 (2022), pp. 4–15.

Bingham, Adrian, '"Stop the Flapper Vote Folly": Lord Rothermere, the *Daily Mail*, and the Equalization of the Franchise 1927–28', *Twentieth Century British History*, 13 (2002), pp. 17–37.

Birkenhead, The Earl of, *Halifax: The Life of Lord Halifax*, Hamish Hamilton, London, 1965.

Bivins, Roberta, 'Picturing Race in the British National Health Service, 1948–1988', *Twentieth Century British History*, 28 (2017), pp. 83–109.

Black, Lawrence *The Political Culture of the Left in Britain, 1951–64: Old Labour, New Britain?*, Palgrave Macmillan, Basingstoke, 2002.

Blackburn, Dean, 'Reassessing Britain's "Post-war consensus": The Politics of Reason 1945–1979', *British Politics*, 13 (2018), pp. 195–214.

_____, *Penguin Books and Political Change: Britain's Meritocratic Moment, 1937–1988*, Manchester University Press, Manchester, 2020.

Blair, Tony, *New Britain: My Vision of a Young Country*, London, Fourth Estate, 1996.

Bland, Larry I. and Joellen K. Bland (eds), *George C. Marshall: Interviews and Reminiscences for Forrest C. Pogue*, George C. Marshall Research Foundation, Lexington, VA, 1991.

Bloom, Cecil, 'The British Labour Party and Palestine, 1917–1948', *Jewish Historical Studies*, 36 (1999), pp. 141–71.

Bohlen, Charles E., *Witness to History 1929–1969*, W.W. Norton & Company Inc., New York, 1973.

Booth, Alan, 'How Long are Light Years in British Politics? The Labour Party's Economic Ideas in the 1930s', *Twentieth Century British History*, 7 (1996), pp. 1–27.

Bostdorff, Denise M., *Proclaiming the Truman Doctrine: The Cold War Call to Arms*, Texas A & M University Press, College Station, 2008.

Boyd, Andrew, *Jim Connell: Author of the Red Flag*, Donaldson Archives/Socialist History Society Occasional Papers No. 13.

Brett, Teddy, Steve Gilliatt and Andrew Pople, 'Planned Trade, Labour Party Policy and US Intervention: The Successes and Failures of Post-War Reconstruction', *History Workshop*, 13 (spring, 1982), pp. 130–42.

Brivati, Brian, *Hugh Gaitskell*, Richard Cohen Books, London, 1996.

Brockway, Fenner, *Inside the Left: Thirty Years of Platform, Press, Prison and Parliament*, George Allen & Unwin Ltd, London, 1942.

Brogan, Colm, *Our New Masters*, Hollis and Carter, London, 1948.

Brome, Vincent, *Aneurin Bevan: A Biography*, Longmans, Green and Co., London, 1953.

Brooke, Stephen, *Labour's War: The Labour Party and the Second World War*, Oxford University Press, Oxford, 1992.

_____, 'The Labour Party and the 1945 General Election', *Contemporary Record*, 9 (1995), pp. 1–21.

Brookshire, Jerry H., *Clement Attlee*, Manchester University Press, Manchester, 1995.

Brown, George, *In My Way: The Political Memoirs of Lord George-Brown*, Victor Gollancz, London, 1971.

Brown, Judith and Wm. Roger Louis (eds), *The Oxford History of the British Empire; Vol. IV: The Twentieth Century*, Oxford University Press, Oxford, 1999.

Bullock, Alan, *The Life and Times of Ernest Bevin; Volume 1: Trade Union Leader 1881–1940*, Heinemann, London, 1960.

_____, *The Life and Times of Ernest Bevin; Vol. II: Minister of Labour 1940–1945*, Heinemann, London, 1967.

_____, *Ernest Bevin: Foreign Secretary*, Heinemann, London, 1983.

Burgess, Simon, '1945 Observed: A History of the Histories', *Contemporary Record*, 5 (1991), pp. 155–70.

_____, *Stafford Cripps: A Political Life*, Victor Gollancz, London, 1999.

Burridge, Trevor, *Clement Attlee: A Political Biography*, Jonathan Cape, London, 1985.

Butler, D. E., *The British General Election of 1951*, Macmillan, London, 1952.

Butler, Lord, et al., *The Jawaharlal Nehru Memorial Lectures: Being the four lectures given in the years between 1966 and 1971*, The Jawaharlal Nehru Memorial Trust, London, 1973.

Butler, R. A., *The Art of the Possible: The Memoirs of Lord Butler K.G., C.H.*, Hamish Hamilton, London, 1971.

Buttle, Geoffrey William, 'A Signal Failure? The Organisation and Management of British Railways 1948–1964', PhD thesis, Durham University, 2008.

Byrnes, James F., *Speaking Frankly*, William Heinemann Ltd, London, 1947.

Cairncross, Alec, *Years of Recovery: British Economic Policy 1945–51*, Methuen & Co. Ltd, London, 1985.

_____ (ed.), *The Robert Hall Diaries 1947–1953*, Unwin Hyman, London, 1989.

Calder, Angus, *The People's War*, Jonathan Cape, London, 1969.

Callaghan, James, *Time and Chance*, William Collins Sons & Co. Ltd, Glasgow, 1987.

Callaghan, John, 'British Labour's Turn to Socialism in 1931', *Journal of Political Ideologies*, 14 (2009), pp. 115–32.

Campbell, John, *Lloyd George: The Goat in the Wilderness, 1922–1931*, Jonathan Cape, London, 1977.

_____, *Nye Bevan: A Biography*, Hodder & Stoughton, London, 1994.

Carew, Anthony, 'The Anglo-American Council on Productivity (1948–52): The Ideological Roots of the Post-War Debate on Productivity in Britain', *Journal of Contemporary History*, 26 (1991), pp. 49–69.

Casey, Steven, *Selling the Korean War: Propaganda, Politics, and Public Opinion in the United States, 1950–1953*, Oxford University Press, New York, 2008.

Castle, Barbara, *Fighting All the Way*, Macmillan, London, 1993.

Chenier, John A., 'The Development and Implementation of Post-war Housing Policy Under the Labour Government', DPhil thesis, University of Oxford, 1984.

Church, Roy and Quentin Outram, *Strikes and Solidarity: Coalfield Conflict in Britain, 1889–1966*, Cambridge University Press, Cambridge, 1998.

Churchett, Stephen, *Tom and Clem*, Faber and Faber, London, 1997.

Clarke, Peter, *The Keynesian Revolution in the Making, 1924–1936*, Clarendon Press, Oxford, 1988.

_____, *The Cripps Version: The Life of Sir Stafford Cripps, 1889–1952*, Allen Lane, London, 2002.

_____, *The Last Thousand Days of the British Empire*, Allen Lane, London, 2007.

_____, 'In Memoriam: Duncan Tanner', *Twentieth Century British History*, 21 (2010), pp. 137–40.

Coates, W. P. and Zelda K. Coates, *A History of Anglo-Soviet Relations*, Lawrence & Wishart and the Pilot Press, London, 1945.

Cockett, Richard (ed.), *My Dear Max: The Letters of Brendan Bracken to Lord Beaverbrook, 1925–1958*, The Historians' Press, London, 1990.

Cole, G. D. H., *Guild Socialism*, Fabian Society, London, 1920.

_____, *History of the Labour Party from 1914*, Routledge & Kegan Paul, London, 1948.

_____, *Labour's Second Term: A Comment on the Draft: "Labour Believes in Britain"*, Fabian Publications Ltd and Victor Gollancz Ltd, London, 1949.

Cole, Margaret (ed.), *The Webbs and Their Work*, Frederick Muller Ltd, London, 1949, pp. 285–301.

Cooper, Duff, *Old Men Forget*, E. P. Dutton & Co., New York, 1954.

Corthorn, Paul, 'Labour, the Left, and the Stalinist Purges of the Late 1930s', *Historical Journal*, 48 (2005), pp. 179–207.

Costigliola, Frank (ed.), *The Kennan Diaries*, W.W. Norton & Company, New York, 2014.

Cowling, Maurice, *The Impact of Hitler: British Politics and British Policy 1933–1940*, Cambridge University Press, Cambridge, 1975.

Craig, F. W. S. (ed.), *British General Election Manifestos, 1959–1987*, Dartmouth, Aldershot, 1990.

Crang, J. A., 'Politics on Parade: Army Education and the 1945 General Election', *History*, 81 (1996), pp. 215–27.

Cripps, Richard Stafford, *Towards Christian Democracy*, The Philosophical Library, New York, 1946.

Crofts, William, *Coercion or Persuasion? Propaganda in Britain after 1945*, Routledge, London, 1989.

Crompton, Gerald, '"Good Business for the Nation": The Railway Nationalisation Issue, 1921–47', *Journal of Transport History*, 20 (1999), pp. 141–59.

Crosland, C. A. R., *The Future of Socialism*, The Macmillan Company, New York, 1957.

Crossman, R. H. S., et al., *Keep Left*, New Statesman, London, 1947.

_____, *A Nation Reborn: The Israel of Weizmann, Bevin, and Ben-Gurion*, Hamish Hamilton, London, 1960.

Crowcroft, Robert, *Attlee's War: World War II and the Making of a Labour Leader*, I.B. Tauris, London, 2011.

Dalton, Hugh, *With British Guns in Italy: A Tribute to Italian Achievement*, Methuen & Co. Ltd, London, 1919.

_____, *Practical Socialism for Britain*, George Routledge & Sons, London, 1935.

_____, *Call Back Yesterday: Memoirs 1887–1931*, Frederick Muller Ltd, London, 1953.

_____, *The Fateful Years: Memoirs 1931–1945*, Frederick Muller Ltd, London, 1957.

_____, *High Tide and After: Memoirs 1945–1960*, Frederick Muller Ltd, London, 1962.

Dalyell, Tam, *Dick Crossman: A Portrait*, Weidenfeld & Nicolson, London, 1989.

Daunton, Martin, *Just Taxes: The Politics of Taxation in Britain, 1914–1979*, Cambridge University Press, Cambridge, 2002.

Davenport, Nicholas, *Memoirs of a City Radical*, Weidenfeld & Nicolson, London, 1974.

Davies, Norman, 'Lloyd George and Poland, 1919–20', *Journal of Contemporary History*, 6 (1971), pp. 132–54.

Dawson, Michael, 'Liberalism in Devon and Cornwall, 1910–1931: "The Old-Time Religion"', *Historical Journal*, 38 (1995), pp. 425–37.

de Freitas, Geoffrey and Helen de Freitas, *The Slighter Side of a Long Public Life*, privately published, 1985.

Defty, Andrew, *Britain, America and Anti-Communist Propaganda 1945–53: The Information Research Department*, Routledge, London, 2013.

Dellar, Geoffrey (ed.), *Attlee As I Knew Him*, Tower Hamlets Library Service, London, 1983.

Dettman, Sean and Richard Toye, 'The Discourse of "The people's war" in Britain and the USA during World War II: A Reply to David Edgerton', *English Historical Review*, forthcoming.

Digby, Anne and Nick Bosanquet, 'Doctors and Patients in an Era of National Health Insurance and Private Practice, 1913–1938', *Economic History Review*, 41 (1988), pp. 74–94.

Dilks, David (ed.), *The Diaries of Sir Alexander Cadogan, 1938–1945*, Cassell, London, 1971.

Dixon, Piers, *Double Diploma: The Life of Sir Pierson Dixon, Don and Diplomat*, Hutchinson, London, 1968.

Dockrill, Michael and J. W. Young (eds), *British Foreign Policy, 1945–56*, Macmillan, London, 1989.

Donoughue, Bernard and G. W. Jones, *Herbert Morrison: Portrait of a Politician*, Weidenfeld & Nicolson, London, 1973 (2nd edn, Phoenix Press, 2001).

Dow, J. C. R., *The Management of the British Economy 1945–60*, Cambridge University Press, Cambridge, 1970.

Drucker, H. M., *Doctrine and Ethos in the Labour Party*, George Allen & Unwin Ltd, London, 1979.

Drury, Allen, *A Senate Journal 1943–1945*, McGraw Hill Book Company, New York, 1963.

Dupree, Marguerite (ed.), *Lancashire and Whitehall: The Diary of Sir Raymond Streat; Vol. II: 1939–57*, Manchester University Press, Manchester, 1987.

Duranti, Marco, *The Conservative Human Rights Revolution: European Identity, Transnational Politics, and the Origins of the European Convention*, Oxford University Press, Oxford, 2017.

Durbin, Elizabeth, *New Jerusalems: The Labour Party and the Economics of Democratic Socialism*, Routledge, London, 1985.

Dymond, Glenn, 'The Salisbury Doctrine', House of Lords Library Note (LLN 2006/006), 2006.

Eden, Anthony, *Full Circle*, Cassell, London, 1960.

_____, *The Reckoning*, Houghton Mifflin Company, Boston, 1965.

Edgerton, David, 'The Prophet Militant and Industrial: The Peculiarities of Correlli Barnett', *Twentieth Century British History*, 2 (1991), pp. 360–79.

_____, *Warfare State: Britain, 1920–1970*, Cambridge University Press, Cambridge, 2006.

_____, *The Rise and Fall of the British Nation: A Twentieth-Century History*, Allen Lane, London, 2018.

_____, 'The Nationalisation of British History: Historians, Nationalism and the Myths of 1940', *English Historical Review*, 136 (2021), pp. 950–85.

Einzig, Paul, *In the Centre of Things: The Autobiography of Paul Einzig*, Hutchinson, London, 1960.

Elder, A. T. 'Health Services of Northern Ireland', *British Journal of Preventive and Social Medicine*, 7 (1953), pp. 105–11.

Enderby, John Stephen, 'The English Radical Tradition and the British Left 1885–1945', PhD thesis, Sheffield Hallam University, 2019.

Englander, David, 'The National Union of Ex-Servicemen and the Labour Movement, 1918–1920', *History*, 76 (1991), pp. 24–42.

Estorick, Eric, *Stafford Cripps*, William Heinemann Ltd, London, 1949.

Evans, Neil and Dot Jones, '"A Blessing for the Miner's Wife": The Campaign for Pithead Baths in the South Wales Coalfield, 1908–1950', *Llafur*, 6 (1994), pp. 5–28.

Ewing, K. D., Joan Mahoney and Andrew Moretta, *MI5, the Cold War, and the Rule of Law*, Oxford University Press, Oxford, 2020.

Fabian Society, *Labour's Next Step: A Wartime Strategy*, Fabian Society, London, 1940.

Farmer, Richard, 'All Work and No Play: British Leisure Culture and the 1947 Fuel Crisis', *Contemporary British History*, 27 (2013), pp. 22–43.

_____, 'Suspension Or Suppression? The British Periodical Press and the 1947 Fuel Crisis', *Media History*, 19 (2013), pp. 153–68.

Fawcett, Louise, 'Revisiting the Iranian Crisis of 1946: How Much More Do We Know?', *Iranian Studies*, 47 (2014), pp. 379–99.

Ferrell, Robert H. (ed.), *Truman in the White House: The Diary of Eben A. Ayers*, University of Missouri Press, Columbia, MO, 1991.

Fforde, John, *The Bank of England and Public Policy 1941–1958*, Cambridge University Press, Cambridge, 1992.

Field, Frank (ed.), *Attlee's Great Contemporaries: The Politics of Character*, Continuum, London, 2009.

Fielding, Steven, 'What Did "the People" Want? The Meaning of the 1945 General Election', *Historical Journal*, 35 (1992), pp. 623–39.

_____, 'The Second World War and Popular Radicalism: The Significance of the "Movement Away from Party"', *History*, 80 (1995), pp. 38–58.

Fielding, Steven, Peter Thompson and Nick Tiratsoo, *'England Arise!' The Labour Party and Popular Politics in 1940s Britain*, Manchester University Press, Manchester, 1995.

Folly, Martin H., '"The impression is growing … that the United States is hard when dealing with us": Ernest Bevin and Anglo-American Relations at the Dawn of the Cold War', *Journal of Transatlantic Studies*, 10 (2012), pp. 150–66.

Foot, Michael, *Aneurin Bevan: A Biography; Vol. II: 1945–1960*, Davis-Poynter, London, 1973.

Foot, Rosemary J., 'Anglo-American Relations in the Korean Crisis: The British Effort to Avert an Expanded War, December 1950–January 1951', *Diplomatic History*, 10 (1986), pp. 43–57.

Frame, William, '"Sir Stafford Cripps and His Friends": The Socialist League, the National Government and the Reform of the House of Lords 1931–1935', *Parliamentary History*, 24 (2005), 316–31.

Francis, Martin, *Ideas and Policies Under Labour, 1945–51: Building a New Britain*, Manchester University Press, Manchester, 1997.

_____, 'Tears, Tantrums, and Bared Teeth: The Emotional Economy of Three Conservative Prime Ministers, 1951–1963', *Journal of British Studies*, 41 (2002), pp. 354–87.

French, Philip and Michael Sissons (eds), *Age of Austerity*, Hodder & Stoughton, London, 1963.

Gaddis, John Lewis, *The Cold War: A New History*, The Penguin Press, New York, 2005.

Galbraith, James K., *The End of Normal: The Great Crisis and the Future of Growth*, Simon & Schuster Paperbacks, New York, 2015.

Galbraith, John Kenneth, *A Life In Our Times: Memoirs*, Andre Deutsch, London, 1981.

Gallup, George H., *The Gallup International Opinion Polls: Great Britain 1937–1975; Vol. I 1937–1964*, Random House, New York, 1976.

Gannon, Philip, 'The Special Relationship and the 1945 Anglo-American Loan', *Journal of Transatlantic Studies*, 11 (2014), pp. 1–17.

Gardner, Richard N., *Sterling-Dollar Diplomacy: The Origins and the Prospects of our International Economic Order*, McGraw Hill, New York, 1980.

Garland, David, 'The Emergence of the Idea of "The Welfare State" in British Political Discourse', *History of the Human Sciences*, 35 (2022), pp. 132–57.

Geiger, Till and Richard Toye, 'Britain, America and the Origins of the European Payments Union: A Reassessment', Working Paper, 2008, https://ore.exeter.ac.uk/repository/handle/10036/31032.

Gildart, Keith, 'Séance Sitters, Ghost Hunters, Spiritualists, and Theosophists: Esoteric Belief and Practice in the British Parliamentary Labour Party, c. 1929–51', *Twentieth Century British History*, 29 (2018), pp. 357–87.

Gildart, Keith and David Howell (eds), *Dictionary of Labour Biography Vol. XV*, Palgrave Macmillan, London, 2019.

Gilroy, Paul, *Postcolonial Melancholia*, Columbia University Press, New York, 2005.

Glennerster, Howard, *British Social Policy since 1945* (2nd edn), Blackwell Publishers, Oxford, 2000.

Goldie, Grace Wyndham, *Facing the Nation: Television and Politics 1936–1976*, The Bodley Head, London, 1977.

Goodman, Geoffrey (ed.), *The State of the Nation: The Political Legacy of Aneurin Bevan*, Victor Gollancz, London, 1997.

Gorman, John, 'The Labour Party's Election Posters in 1945', *Labour History Review*, 61 (1996), pp. 299–308.

Gormly, James L., 'The Washington Declaration and the "Poor Relation": Anglo-American Atomic Diplomacy, 1945–6', *Diplomatic History*, 8 (1984), pp. 125–44, at 131.

Gorsky, Martin and John Mohan, 'London's Voluntary Hospitals in the Interwar Period: Growth, Transformation, or Crisis?', *Non-profit and Voluntary Sector Quarterly*, 30 (2001), pp. 247–75.

Gorst, Anthony, Lewis Johnman and W. Scott Lucas (eds), *Contemporary British History, 1931–1961: Politics and the Limits of Policy*, Pinter, London, 1991, pp. 1–16.

Gottlieb, Julie, 'An Epidemic of Nervous Breakdowns and the Crisis Suicides: Britain's War of Nerves, 1938–1940', forthcoming.

Gowing, Margaret, *Independence and Deterrence: Britain and Atomic Energy, 1945–1952; Volume 1: Policy Making*, Macmillan, Basingstoke, 1974.

'Gracchus', *Your MP*, Victor Gollancz, London, 1944.

Grant, Mariel, '"Working for the Yankee Dollar": Tourism and the Festival of Britain as Stimuli for Recovery', *Journal of British Studies*, 45 (2006), pp. 581–601.

Green, E. H. H., *Thatcher*, Hodder Arnold, London, 2006.

Green, E. H. H. and D. M. Tanner (eds), *The Strange Survival of Liberal England: Political Leaders, Moral Values and the Reception of Economic Debate*, Cambridge University Press, Cambridge, 2007.

Greener, Ian and Martin Powell, 'Beveridge, Bevan and Institutional Change in the UK Welfare State', *Social Policy & Administration*, 56 (2022), pp. 271–83.

Griffiths, Clare V. J., *Labour and the Countryside: The Politics of Rural Britain 1918–1939*, Oxford University Press, Oxford, 2007.

Griffiths, James, *Pages From Memory*, J. M. Dent & Sons Ltd, London, 1969.

Guldi, Jo, 'World Neoliberalism as Rebellion From Below? British Squatters and the Global Interpretation of Poverty, 1946–1974', *Humanity*, 10 (2019), pp. 29–57.

Gupta, Partha Sarathi, *Imperialism and the British Labour Movement, 1914–1964*, Holmes & Meier Publishers, New York, 1975.

Haapala, Taru and Teemu Häkkinen, 'Debating Federal Europe in the British Parliament, c. 1940–49', *European Review of History: Revue européenne d'histoire*, 24 (2017), pp. 801–16.

Harris, Jose, *William Beveridge: A Biography*, Clarendon Press, Oxford, 1997.

Harris, Kenneth, *Attlee*, Weidenfeld & Nicolson, London, 1982 (revised edn 1995).

Harrod, R. F., *The Life of John Maynard Keynes*, Macmillan, London, 1954.

Hart, Stephen, *James Chuter Ede: Humane Reformer and Politician*, Pen & Sword, Barnsley, 2021.

Hart-Davis, Duff (ed.), *King's Counsellor: Abdication and War: The Diaries of Sir Alan Lascelles*, Weidenfeld & Nicolson, London, 2006.

Hartill, Jeremy, 'British Railway Shipping 1948–1984: A Nationalised Success Story', MA research thesis, University of York, 2014.

Hatton, Timothy J., 'Infant Mortality and the Health of Survivors: Britain, 1910–50', *Economic History Review*, 64 (2011), pp. 951–72.

Hayes, Nick, 'Did We Really Want a National Health Service? Hospitals, Patients and Public Opinions before 1948', *English Historical Review*, CXXVII (2012), pp. 625–61.

Hayton, D. W., *Conservative Revolutionary: The Lives of Lewis Namier*, Manchester University Press, Manchester, 2019.

Healey, Denis, *The Time of My Life*, Michael Joseph, London, 1989.

Heffer, Simon (ed.), *Henry 'Chips' Channon: The Diaries 1943–57*, Hutchinson, London, 2022.

Hennessy, Peter, *Whitehall*, Fontana Press, London, 1989.

_____, *Never Again: Britain, 1945–51*, Jonathan Cape, London, 1992.

_____, *The Prime Minister: The Office and Its Holders Since 1945*, Allen Lane, London, 2000.

_____, 'Michael Young and the Labour Party', *Contemporary British History*, 19 (2005), pp. 281–4.

_____, 'Benjamin John Pimlott, 1945–2004', *Proceedings of the British Academy*, 150 (2007), pp. 161–79.

_____, *A Duty of Care: Britain Before and After Covid*, Penguin Books, London, 2023.

Heseltine, Michael, *Life in the Jungle: My Autobiography*, Hodder & Stoughton, London, 2000.

Hinton, James, 'Self-help and Socialism: The Squatters' Movement of 1946', *History Workshop Journal*, 25 (1988), pp. 100–126.

_____, 'Militant Housewives: The British Housewives' League and the Attlee Government', *History Workshop Journal*, 38 (1994), pp. 129–56.

Honeyman, Victoria, *Richard Crossman: A Reforming Radical of the Labour Party*, I.B. Tauris, London, 2007.

Hopkins, Michael F. (ed.), *British Financial Diplomacy With North America 1944–1946: The Diary of Fredric Harmer and the Washington Reports of Robert Brand*, Cambridge University Press for the Royal Historical Society, Cambridge, 2021.

Howell, David, *MacDonald's Party: Labour Identities and Crisis 1922–1931*, Oxford University Press, Oxford, 2002.

_____, *Attlee*, Haus, London, 2006.

Howson, Susan and D. E. Moggridge (eds), *The Collected Papers of James Meade; Vol. IV: The Cabinet Office Diary, 1944–1946*, Unwin Hyman, London, 1990.

_____ (eds), *The Wartime Diaries of Lionel Robbins and James Meade, 1943–45*, Palgrave Macmillan, Basingstoke, 1990.

Huxford, Grace, *The Korean War in Britain: Citizenship, Selfhood and Forgetting*, Manchester University Press, Manchester, 2018.

Hyam, Ronald, 'Africa and the Labour Government, 1945–1951', *Journal of Imperial and Commonwealth History*, 16 (1988), pp. 148–72.

Irving, Henry, 'The Birth of a Politician: Harold Wilson and the Bonfires of Controls, 1948–9', *Twentieth Century British History*, 25 (2014), pp. 87–107.

Jackson, Ben, *The Case for Scottish Independence: A History of Nationalist Political Thought in Modern Scotland*, Cambridge University Press, Cambridge, 2020.

Jarvis, David, 'British Conservatism and Class Politics in the 1920s', *English Historical Review*, CXI (1996), pp. 59–84.

Jay, Douglas, *Change and Fortune: A Political Record*, Hutchinson & Co., London, 1980.

_____, *Sterling: Its Use and Misuse – A Plea for Moderation*, Sidgwick & Jackson, London, 1985.

Jebb, Gladwyn, *The Memoirs of Lord Gladwyn*, Weybright and Talley, New York, 1972.

Jefferys, Kevin, 'R.A. Butler, The Board of Education, and the 1944 Education Act', *History*, 69 (1984), pp. 415–31.

_____ (ed.), *Labour and the Wartime Coalition: From the Diary of James Chuter Ede, 1941–1945*, Historian's Press, London, 1987.

_____, *The Churchill Coalition and Wartime Politics*, Manchester University Press, Manchester, 1991.

Jenkins, Andrew, 'Government Intervention in the British Gas Industry, 1948 to 1970', *Business History*, 46 (2004), pp. 57–78.

Jenkins, Roy, *Mr. Attlee: An Interim Biography*, William Heinemann Ltd, London, 1948.

_____, *A Life at the Centre*, Macmillan, London, 1991.

Jennings, W. Ivor, 'The Emergency Powers (Defence) (No. 2) Act, 1940,' *Modern Law Review*, 4 (1940), pp. 132–6.

_____, *The British Constitution*, Cambridge University Press, Cambridge, 1958.

Jobson, Richard, *Nostalgia and the Post-War Labour Party: Prisoners of the Past*, Manchester University Press, Manchester, 2018.

Jones, C. A., S. J. Davies and N. Macdonald, 'Examining the Social Consequences of Extreme Weather: The Outcomes of the 1946/1947 Winter in Upland Wales, UK', *Climatic Change*, 113 (2012), pp. 35–53.

Esyllt Jones, 'Nothing Too Good for the People: Local Labour and London's Interwar Health Centre Movement', *Social History of Medicine*, 25 (2012), pp. 84–102.

Jones, Harriet, 'The Conservative Party and the Welfare State 1942–1955', PhD thesis, University of London, 1992.

_____, '"This is magnificent!": 300,000 Houses a Year and the Tory Revival after 1945', *Contemporary British History*, 14 (2000), pp. 99–121.

Jones, Harriet and Michael Kandiah (eds), *The Myth of Consensus: New Views on British History, 1945–64*, Macmillan Press, Basingstoke, 1996.

Jones, Matthew, 'Great Britain, the United States, and Consultation Over Use of the Atomic Bomb, 1950–1954', *Historical Journal*, 54 (2011), pp. 797–828.

Jones, Russell, *Wages and Employment Policy 1936–1985*, Allen & Unwin, London, 1987.

Kelly, Saul, *Cold War in the Desert: Britain, the United States and the Italian Colonies, 1945–52*, Palgrave Macmillan, London, 2000.

Kelly, Scott, '"The Ghost of Neville Chamberlain": Guilty Men and the 1945 Election', *Conservative History Journal*, 5 (autumn 2005), pp. 18–24.

Kent, John, 'The Egyptian Base and the Defence of the Middle East, 1945–54', *Journal of Imperial and Commonwealth History*, 21 (1993), pp. 45–65.

Khan, Yasmin, *The Great Partition: The Making of India and Pakistan*, Yale University Press, New Haven, CT, 2017.

King, Anthony (ed.), *British Political Opinion 1937–2000: The Gallup Polls*, Politico's, London, 2001.

Kinnock, Neil, *Making Our Way*, Basil Blackwell Ltd, Oxford, 1986.

_____, *Thorns & Roses: Speeches, 1983–1991*, Hutchinson, London, 1992.

Klein, Rudolf, 'The National Health Service (NHS) at 70: Bevan's Double-edged Legacy', *Health Economics, Policy and Law*, 14 (2019), pp. 1–10.

Klos, Felix, *Churchill's Last Stand: The Struggle to Unite Europe*, I.B. Tauris, London, 2017.

Knox, W. W., 'Religion and the Scottish Labour Movement c. 1900–39', *Journal of Contemporary History*, 23 (1988), pp. 609–30.

Kowol, Kit, 'The Lost World of British Conservatism: The Radical Tory Tradition, 1939–1951', DPhil Dissertation, University of Oxford, 2014.

_____, '"I weep with shame and grief": The Feeling of the 1945 General Election in Letters to Winston Churchill', unpublished manuscript, 2023.

Kramnick, Isaac and Barry Sheerman, *Harold Laski: A Life on the Left*, Hamish Hamilton Ltd, London, 1993.

Krishnan, Y., 'Mountbatten and the Partition of India', *History*, 68 (1983), pp. 22–38.

Kumarasingham, H. (ed.), *The Rise of Labour and the Fall of Empire: The Memoirs of William Hare, Fifth Earl of Listowel*, Cambridge University Press, Cambridge, 2019.

Kunz, Diane B., 'The Marshall Plan Reconsidered: A Complex of Motives', *Foreign Affairs*, 76 (1997), pp. 162–70.

Kynaston, David, *Austerity Britain, 1945–51*, Bloomsbury, London, 2007.

Langham, Raphael, 'The Bevin Enigma: What Motivated Ernest Bevin's Opposition to the Establishment of a Jewish State in Palestine', *Jewish Historical Studies*, 44 (2012), pp. 165–78.

Langhamer, Claire, '"The Live Dynamic Whole of Feeling and Behavior": Capital Punishment and the Politics of Emotion, 1945–1957', *Journal of British Studies*, 51 (2012), pp. 416–41.

Lawrence, Jon, *Electing Our Masters: The Hustings in British Politics from Hogarth to Blair*, Oxford University Press, Oxford, 2009.

Lawson, Jack, *A Man's Life*, Hodder & Stoughton Ltd, London, 1944.

Leathard, Audrey, *Health Care Provision: Past, Present and into the 21st century* (2nd edn), Stanley Thomas (Publishers) Ltd, Cheltenham, 2000.

Lee, Jennie, *My Life with Nye*, Jonathan Cape, London, 1980.

Lee, Steven Hugh, 'The Korean War in History and Historiography', *Journal of American–East Asian Relations*, 21 (2014), pp. 185–206.

Leffingwell, R. C., 'Devaluation and European Recovery', *Foreign Affairs*, Jan. 1950, pp. 203–30.

Leslie, Peter, *Chapman-Andrews and the Emperor*, Pen & Sword, Barnsley, 2005.

Levene, Alysa, 'Between Less Eligibility and the NHS: The Changing Place of Poor Law Hospitals in England and Wales, 1929–39', *Twentieth Century British History*, 20 (2009), pp. 322–45.

Lockhart, R. H. Bruce, *Comes the Reckoning*, Putnam, London, 1947.

Lomas, Daniel W. B., *Intelligence, Security and the Attlee Governments, 1945–51*, Manchester University Press, Manchester, 2017.

Love, Gary, 'The Periodical Press and the Intellectual Culture of Conservatism in Interwar Britain', *Historical Journal*, 57 (2014), pp. 1027–56.

Ludlow, Piers, 'The Schuman Plan and the Start of Supranational European Integration', *Oxford Research Encyclopedia of Politics* [e-resource], Oxford University Press, Oxford, 2019.

Luff, Jennifer, 'Covert and Overt Operations: Interwar Political Policing in the United States and the United Kingdom', *American Historical Review*, 122 (2017), pp. 727–57.

Macintyre, Donald, *Mandelson and the Making of New Labour*, HarperCollins, London, 2000.

MacKenzie, Norman (ed.), *Letters of Sidney and Beatrice Webb; Vol. II: Partnership 1892–1912*, Cambridge University Press, Cambridge, 1978.

MacKenzie, Norman and Jeanne MacKenzie (eds), *The Diary of Beatrice Webb; Vol. IV 1924–1943, 'The Wheel of Life'*, Belknap Press, Cambridge, MA, 1985.

Malpass, Peter, 'The Wobbly Pillar? Housing and the British Post-war Welfare State', *Journal of Social Policy*, 32 (2003), pp. 589–606.

Mandelson, Peter and Roger Liddle, *The Blair Revolution: Can New Labour Deliver?*, Faber and Faber, London, 1996.

Mann, Jean, *Woman in Parliament*, Odham's Press Ltd, London, 1962.

Manning, Sam, *Cinemas and Cinema-Going in the United Kingdom: Decades of Decline, 1945–65*, University of London Press, London, 2020.

Mansergh, Nicholas and Penderel Moon (eds), *The Transfer of Power 1942–47; Vol. IX: The Fixing of a Time Limit 4 November 1946–22 March 1947*, HMSO, London, 1980.

Manton, Kevin, 'Labour and the 1949 Parliament Act', *Contemporary British History*, 26 (2012), pp. 149–72.

Margach, James, *The Abuse of Power: The War between Downing Street and the Media from Lloyd George to James Callaghan*, W. H. Allen, London, 1978.

Marquand, David, *Ramsay MacDonald*, Jonathan Cape, London, 1977.

_____, *The Progressive Dilemma: From Lloyd George to Kinnock*, Heinemann, London, 1991.

Martin, Kingsley, *Harold Laski, 1893–1950: A Biographical Memoir*, Victor Gollancz, London, 1953.

_____, *Editor: A Second Volume of Autobiography, 1931–45*, Hutchinson, London, 1968.

Matei, Alin-Victor, 'Secretary of State Byrnes, the US East European Policy and the Moscow Conference of December 1945', *Romanian Journal of History and International Studies*, 2 (2015), pp. 7–22.

Mayhew, Christopher, *Time To Explain: An Autobiography*, Hutchinson, London, 1987.

McCallum, R. B. and Alison Readman, *The British General Election of 1945*, Oxford University Press, London, 1947.

McCulloch, Gary, 'Labour, the Left, and the British General Election of 1945', *Journal of British Studies*, 24 (1985), pp. 465–89.

McKenzie, Francine, 'Renegotiating a Special Relationship: The Commonwealth and Anglo-American Economic Discussions, September–December 1945', *Journal of Imperial and Commonwealth History*, 26 (1998), pp. 71–93.

_____, *GATT and Global Order in the Post-war Era*, Cambridge University Press, Cambridge, 2020.

McKibbin, Ross, 'The Economic Policy of the Second Labour Government 1929–1931', *Past & Present*, 68 (1975), pp. 95–123.

McKinstry, Leo, *Attlee and Churchill: Allies in War, Adversaries in Peace*, Atlantic Books, London, 2019.

McSmith, Andy, *John Smith: A Life 1938–1994*, Mandarin, London, 1994.

Mercer, Helen, Neil Rollings and Jim Tomlinson (eds), *Labour Governments and Private Industry: The Experience of 1945–1951*, Edinburgh University Press, Edinburgh, 1992.

Merrick, Leigh Ann, '"In need of care and attention": Local Authorities and the Implementation of the Scottish NHS Act, 1948–1960', *Family & Community History*, 12 (2009), pp. 130–45.

Mikardo, Ian, *Back-Bencher*, Weidenfeld & Nicolson, London, 1988.

Miliband, Ralph, *Parliamentary Socialism: A Study in the Politics of Labour*, Allen & Unwin, London, 1961 (2nd edn, Merlin Press, 1972).

Millis, Walter (ed.), *The Forrestal Diaries: The Inner History of the Cold War*, Cassell & Company Ltd, London, 1952.

Millward, Robert and John Singleton (eds), *The Political Economy of Nationalisation in Britain 1920–1950*, Cambridge University Press, Cambridge, 1995.

Milward, Alan S., *The Rise and Fall of a National Strategy: The UK and The European Community; Vol. 1*, Routledge, London, 2002.

Minkin, Lewis, *The Labour Party Conference*, Manchester University Press, Manchester, 1980.

Mitchell, Austin, *Election '45: Reflections on the Revolution in Britain*, Bellew Publishing, London, 1995.

Montgomery, Lord, *The Memoirs of Field-Marshal Montgomery*, Collins, London, 1958.

Moon, Penderel (ed.), *Wavell: The Viceroy's Journal*, Oxford University Press, London, 1973.

Moran, Lord, *Winston Churchill: The Struggle for Survival, 1940–1965*, Houghton Mifflin, Boston, 1966.

Morgan, Janet (ed.), *The Backbench Diaries of Richard Crossman*, Book Club Associates, London, 1981.

Morgan, Kenneth O., *Labour in Power 1945–1951*, Clarendon Press, Oxford, 1984.

_____, *Michael Foot: A Life*, HarperCollins, London, 2007.

_____, *My Histories*, University of Wales Press, Cardiff, 2015.

Morgan, Kevin, 'The Problem of the Epoch? Labour and Housing, 1918–51', *Twentieth Century British History*, 16 (2005), pp. 227–55.

Morrison, Herbert, *Prospects and Policies*, Alfred A. Knopf, New York, 1944.

_____, *The Peaceful Revolution*, George Allen & Unwin Ltd, London, 1949.

_____, *Government and Parliament: A Survey From the Inside*, Oxford University Press, London, 1954.

_____, *Herbert Morrison: An Autobiography*, Odhams Press Ltd, London, 1960.

Morrison, Herbert, et al., *Forward From Victory! Labour's Plan*, Victor Gollancz Ltd, London, 1946.

Myers, Margaret G., 'The Nationalization of Banks in France', *Political Science Quarterly*, 64 (1949), pp. 189–210.

Nicholas, H. G., *The British General Election of 1950*, Macmillan & Co. Ltd, London, 1951.

_____ (ed.), *Washington Despatches 1941–1945: Weekly Political Reports from the British Embassy*, University of Chicago Press, Chicago, 1981.

Nicolson, Nigel (ed.), *Harold Nicolson: Diaries and Letters 1939–1945*, Collins, London, 1967.

_____ (ed.), *Harold Nicolson: Diaries and Letters 1945–1962*, Collins, London, 1968.

Noon, Ron, 'Goodbye, Mr Cube', *History Today*, Oct. 2001.

Norwich, John Julius (ed.), *The Duff Cooper Diaries, 1915–1951*, Weidenfeld & Nicolson, London, 2005.

_____ (ed.), *Darling Monster: The Letters of Lady Diana Cooper to Her Son John Julius Norwich, 1939–1952*, Overlook Press, New York, 2014.

Onslow, Sue, '"Battlelines for Suez": The Abadan Crisis of 1951 and the Formation of the Suez Group', *Contemporary British History*, 17 (2003), pp. 1–28.

Ortolano, Guy, *Thatcher's Progress: From Social Democracy to Market Liberalism through an English New Town*, Cambridge University Press, Cambridge, 2019.

Ovendale, Ritchie (ed.), *The Foreign Policy of the British Labour Governments 1945–51*, Leicester University Press, Leicester, 1984.

Owen, Nicholas, 'The Conservative Party and Indian Independence, 1945–1947', *Historical Journal*, 46 (2003), pp. 403–36.

Oxford and Asquith, Countess of (ed.), *Myself When Young, by Famous Women of Today*, Frederick Muller Ltd, London, 1938.

Paraskevov, Vasil, 'Conflict and Necessity: British–Bulgarian Relations, 1944–56', *Cold War History*, 11 (2011), pp. 241–68.

Parris, Matthew and Kevin Maguire, *Great Parliamentary Scandals: Five Centuries of Calumny, Smear and Innuendo*, Robson Books, London, 2004, pp. 122–4.

Parsons, Neil, 'The Impact of Seretse Khama on British Public Opinion 1948–56 and 1978', *Immigrants & Minorities*, 12 (1993), pp. 195–219.

Pasko, Brandon E., *The Role of the Operational Artist: General MacArthur in the Korean War from June 1950 to April 1951*, US Army Command and General Staff College Fort Leavenworth, KS, 2019.

Pater, John E., *The Making of the National Health Service*, King's Fund, London, 1981.

Paul, Kathleen, '"British Subjects" and "British Stock": Labour's Post-war Imperialism', *Journal of British Studies*, 34 (1995), pp. 233–76.

Pearce, Robert (ed.), *Patrick Gordon Walker: Political Diaries 1932–1971*, The Historians' Press, London, 1991.

Pelling, Henry, *A History of British Trade Unionism*, Macmillan, London, 1963.

_____, 'The 1945 General Election Reconsidered', *Historical Journal*, 23 (1980), pp. 399–414.

_____, *Britain and the Marshall Plan*, Palgrave Macmillan, Macmillan Press, Houndmills, Basingstoke, 1988.

Peplow, Emma, 'The Role of Britain in the Berlin Airlift', *History*, 95 (2010), pp. 207–24.

Perkins, Anne, *Red Queen: The Authorized Biography of Barbara Castle*, Macmillan, London, 2003.

Perry, Matt, *'Red Ellen' Wilkinson: Her Ideas, Movements and World*, Manchester University Press, Manchester, 2014.

Petrie, Malcolm, '"Contests of vital importance": By-elections, the Labour Party, and the Reshaping of British Radicalism, 1924–1929', *Historical Journal*, 60 (2017), pp. 121–48.

Phillips, Jim, 'Deindustrialization and the Moral Economy of the Scottish Coalfields, 1947 to 1991', *International Labor and Working-Class History*, 84 (2013), pp. 99–115.

Piketty, Thomas, *Capital in the Twenty-First Century*, The Belknap Press, Cambridge, MA, 2014.

Pimlott, Ben, *Labour and the Left in the 1930s*, Cambridge University Press, Cambridge, 1977.

_____, *Hugh Dalton*, Jonathan Cape Ltd, London, 1985.

_____, *Harold Wilson*, HarperCollins, London, 1992.

Pimlott, Ben (ed.), *The Political Diary of Hugh Dalton: 1918–40, 1945–60*, Jonathan Cape, London, 1986.

_____ , *The Second World War Diary of Hugh Dalton, 1940–45*, Jonathan Cape, London, 1986.

Plowden, Edwin, *An Industrialist in the Treasury: The Post-War Years*, Andre Deutsch, London, 1989.

Pottle, Mark (ed.), *Daring to Hope: The Diaries and Letters of Violet Bonham Carter, 1946–1969*, Weidenfeld & Nicolson, London, 2000.

Pressnell, L. S., *External Economic Policy Since the War; Vol I: The Post-war Financial Settlement*, HMSO, London, 1986.

Pugh, Martin, 'The Daily Mirror and the Revival of Labour 1935–1945', *Twentieth Century British History*, 9 (1998), pp. 420–38.

Purcell, Hugh, *A Very Private Celebrity: The Nine Lives of John Freeman*, The Robson Press, London, 2015.

Radice, Giles (ed.), *What Needs to Change: New Visions For Britain*, HarperCollins, London, 1996.

Ramsden, John, *The Age of Churchill and Eden, 1940–1957*, Longman, London, 1995.

Ravndal, Ellen Jenny, 'Exit Britain: British Withdrawal From the Palestine Mandate in the Early Cold War, 1947–1948', *Diplomacy & Statecraft*, 21 (2010), pp. 416–33.

Rees, D. Ben, *Jim: The Life and Work of the Rt. Hon. James Griffiths*, Modern Welsh Publications, Allerton, Liverpool, 2021.

Rees, Russell, *Labour and the Northern Ireland Problem 1945–1951: The Missed Opportunity*, Irish Academic Press, Dublin, 2009.

Reilly, Joanne, *Belsen: The Liberation of a Concentration Camp*, Routledge, London, 1998.

Reynolds, David, *In Command of History: Churchill Fighting and Writing the Second World War*, Allen Lane, London, 2004.

Rhodes James, Robert (ed.), *Winston S. Churchill: His Complete Speeches, 1897–1963*, 8 vols, Chelsea House Publishers, New York, 1974.

Richardson, Adam, 'Orme Sargent, Ernest Bevin and British Policy Towards Europe, 1946–1949', *International History Review*, 41 (2019), pp. 891–908.

Riddell, Neil, *Labour in Crisis: The Second Labour Government, 1929–1931*, Manchester University Press, Manchester, 1999.

Ritchie, Chris, '"Only Mugs Work": The Spiv in British Comedy', *Comedy Studies*, 2 (2011), pp. 13–20.

Robertson, David, *Sly and Able: A Political Biography of James F. Byrnes*, W. W. Norton & Company, New York, 1994.

Robinson, E. A. G., *Economic Planning in the United Kingdom: Some Lessons*, Cambridge University Press, Cambridge, 1967.

Robock, Alan, 'Nuclear Winter', *WIREs Climate Change*, 1 (2010), pp. 418–27.

Rodgers, W. T. (ed.), *Hugh Gaitskell 1906–1963*, Thames and Hudson, London, 1964.

Roll, Eric, *Crowded Hours: An Autobiography*, Faber and Faber, London, 1985.

Rollings, Neil, 'Whitehall and the Control of Prices and Profits in a Major War, 1919–1939', *Historical Journal*, 44 (2001), pp. 517–40.

Roodhouse, Mark, 'The 1948 Belcher Affair and Lynskey Tribunal', *Twentieth Century British History*, 13 (2002), pp. 384–411.

_____, *Black Market Britain: 1939–1955*, Oxford University Press, Oxford, 2013.

Rose, Sonya O., *Which People's War? National Identity and Citizenship in Britain 1939–1945*, Oxford University Press, Oxford, 2003.

Roy, Anwesha, *Making Peace, Making Riots: Communalism and Communal Violence, Bengal 1940–1947*, Cambridge, Cambridge University Press, 2018.

Ruggie, John Gerard, 'International Regimes, Transactions, and Change: Embedded Liberalism in the Post-war Economic Order', *International Organization*, 36 (1982), pp. 379–415.

Ryan, Michael, 'Health Centre Policy in England and Wales', *British Journal of Sociology*, 19 (1968), pp. 34–46.

Schneer, Jonathan, 'Hopes Deferred or Shattered: The British Labour Left and the Third Force Movement, 1945–49', *Journal of Modern History*, 56 (1984), pp. 197–226.

Scott, L. V., *Conscription and the Attlee Governments: The Politics and Policy of National Service 1945–1951*, Oxford University Press, Oxford, 1993.

Seaton, Andrew, 'Against the "Sacred Cow": NHS Opposition and the Fellowship for Freedom in Medicine, 1948–72', *Twentieth Century British History*, 26 (2015), pp. 424–49.

Self, Robert (ed.), *The Neville Chamberlain Diary Letters; Vol. IV: The Downing Street Years, 1934–1940*, Ashgate, Aldershot, 2005.

Sellers, Owen, 'Labour in the South East: A Regional Study of Political Culture & Practices circa 1931–1945', DPhil thesis, University of Oxford, 2021.

Shawcross, Hartley, *Life Sentence: The Memoirs of Lord Shawcross*, Constable, London, 1995.

Shephard, Ben, *The Long Road Home: The Aftermath of the Second World War*, Alfred A. Knopf, New York, 2011.

Shepherd, John and Keith Laybourn, *Britain's First Labour Government*, Palgrave Macmillan, Houndmills, Basingstoke, 2006.

Shinwell, Emanuel, *Conflict Without Malice*, Odhams Press Ltd, London, 1955.

Sitariu, Mihaela, 'The British–Romanian Relations during the Cold War', *Studia Politica: Romanian Political Science Review*, 6 (2006), pp. 959–72.

Skidelsky, Robert, *Politicians and the Slump: The Labour Government of 1929–1931* (2nd edn), PaperMac, London, 1994.

_____, *John Maynard Keynes; Vol. 3: Fighting For Britain 1937–1946*, Macmillan, London, 2000.

Skinner, Geoffrey, 'The Development of Military Nuclear Strategy and Anglo-American Relations, 1939–1958', PhD thesis, University of Exeter, 2018.

Smart, Nick, 'Four Days in May: The Norway Debates and the Downfall of Neville Chamberlain', *Parliamentary History*, 17 (1998), pp. 215–43.

Smith, Lyn, 'Covert British Propaganda: The Information Research Department: 1947–77', *Millennium*, 9 (1980), pp. 67–83.

Snell, Henry, *Daily Life in Parliament*, G. Routledge & Sons, London, 1930.

Stanford, Peter, *The Outcast's Outcast: A Biography of Lord Longford*, Sutton Publishing, Stroud, 2003.

Stewart, John, 'Socialist Proposals for Health Reform in Inter-War Britain: The Case of Somerville Hastings', *Medical History*, 39 (1995), pp. 338–57.

_____, '"The finest municipal hospital service in the world"? Contemporary Perceptions of the London County Council's Hospital Provision, 1929–39', *Urban History*, 32 (2005), pp. 327–44.

Strang, Lord, *Home and Abroad*, Andre Deutsch, London, 1956.

Sulzberger, C. L., *A Long Row of Candles: Memoirs and Diaries, 1934–1954*, The Macmillan Company, Toronto, 1969.

Supple, Barry, *The History of the British Coal Industry; Vol. 4, 1914–1946: The Political Economy of Decline*, Clarendon Press, Oxford, 1987.

Tanner, Duncan, 'The Parliamentary Electoral System, the "Fourth" Reform Act and the Rise of Labour in England and Wales', *Historical Research*, 56 (1983); pp. 205–19.

Tanner, Duncan, Pat Thane and Nick Tiratsoo (eds), *Labour's First Century*, Cambridge University Press, Cambridge, 2000.

Tarling, Nicholas, '"Some Rather Nebulous Capacity": Lord Killearn's Appointment in Southeast Asia', *Modern Asian Studies*, 20 (1986), pp. 559–600.

Tawney, R. H., *The Attack and Other Papers*, George Allen & Unwin, London, 1953.

Taylor, Andrew J., 'The Miners and Nationalisation, 1931–36', *International Review of Social History*, 28 (1983), pp. 176–99.

Taylor, Richard, *English Radicalism in the Twentieth Century: A Distinctive Politics?*, Manchester University Press, Manchester, 2020.

Temple, John Robert, 'A Radical and Progressive Legacy: Labour's Housing Record, 1945 to 1951', *Labour History Review*, 87 (2022), pp. 65–89.

Thackeray, David and Richard Toye (eds), *Electoral Pledges in Britain since 1918: The Politics of Promises*, Palgrave Macmillan, Cham, Switzerland, 2020.

_____ (eds), *Age of Promises: Electoral Pledges in Twentieth Century Britain*, Oxford University Press, Oxford, 2021.

Thatcher, Margaret, *The Path to Power*, HarperCollins, New York, 1995.

Thomas, Geraint, *Popular Conservatism and the Culture of National Government in Inter-War Britain*, Cambridge University Press, Cambridge, 2020.

Thomas-Symonds, Nicklaus, *Attlee: A Life in Politics*, I.B. Tauris, London, 2010.

_____, *Nye: The Political Life of Aneurin Bevan*, I.B. Tauris, London, 2018.

Thompson, Alan, *The Day Before Yesterday: An Illustrated History of Britain from Attlee to Macmillan*, Granada Publishing Limited, London, 1971.

Thompson, Noel, 'To See Ourselves: The Rhetorical Construction of an Ideal Citizenry in the Perorations of Twentieth-century Budget Speeches', *British Politics*, 12 (2017), pp. 90–114.

Thompson, Steven David, 'A Social History of Health in Interwar South Wales', PhD thesis, Aberystwyth University, 2001.

Thorpe, Andrew, *The British General Election of 1931*, Clarendon Press, Oxford, 1991.

_____, *Parties at War: Political Organization in Second World War Britain*, Oxford University Press, Oxford, 2009.

_____, 'Reconstructing Conservative Party Membership in World War II Britain', *Parliamentary Affairs*, 62 (2009), pp. 227–41.

_____, 'Locking out the Communists: The Labour Party and the Communist Party, 1939–46', *Twentieth Century British History*, 25 (2014), pp. 221–50.

_____, *A History of the British Labour Party* (4th edn), Palgrave, London, 2015.

Timmins, Nicholas, *The Five Giants: A Biography of the Welfare State*, HarperCollins, London, 1995.

Tinline, Phil, *The Death of Consensus: 100 Years of British Political Nightmares*, Hurst & Company, London, 2022.

Tomlinson, Jim, 'Welfare and the Economy: The Economic Impact of the Welfare State, 1945–1951', *Twentieth Century British History*, 6 (1995), pp. 194–219.

_____, *Democratic Socialism and Economic Policy: The Attlee Years, 1945–1951*, Cambridge University Press, Cambridge, 1996.

_____, 'Correlli Barnett's History: The Case of Marshall Aid', *Twentieth Century British History*, 8 (1997), pp. 222–38.

_____, 'Marshall Aid and the "Shortage Economy" in Britain in the 1940s', *Contemporary European History*, 9 (2000), pp. 137–55.

Tookey, Mark, 'The Labour Party and Nationalisation from Attlee to Wilson, 1945–1968: Beyond the Commanding Heights', PhD thesis, University of Durham, 2000.

Toye, Richard, *The Labour Party and the Planned Economy, 1931–1951*, Boydell and Brewer for the Royal Historical Society, Woodbridge, 2003.

Toye, Richard and Julie Gottlieb (eds), *Making Reputations: Power, Persuasion and the Individual in Modern British Politics*, I.B. Tauris, London, 2005.

Trentmann, Frank, *Free Trade Nation: Commerce, Consumption, and Civil Society in Modern Britain*, Oxford University Press, Oxford, 2008.

Truman, Harry S., *Year of Decisions*, Doubleday, New York, 1955.

_____, *Memoirs; Vol. II: Years of Trial and Hope*, Doubleday and Company Inc., New York, 1956.

Vandenberg Jr, Arthur H. (ed.), *The Private Papers of Senator Vandenberg*, Houghton Mifflin Company, Boston, 1952.

Vernon, Betty D., *Ellen Wilkinson*, Croom Helm, London, 1982.

Vickers, Rhiannon, *Manipulating Hegemony: State Power, Labour and the Marshall Plan in Britain*, Macmillan Press Ltd, Houndmills, Basingstoke, 2000.

Ward, Paul, *Red Flag and Union Jack: Englishness, Patriotism, and the British Left, 1881–1924*, Boydell Press for the Royal Historical Society, Woodbridge, 1998.

_____, 'Preparing for the People's War: Labour and Patriotism in the 1930s', *Labour History Review*, 7 (2002), pp. 171–85.

Ward, Stuart, 'The European Provenance of Decolonization', *Past & Present*, 230 (2016), pp. 227–60.

_____, *Untied Kingdom: A Global History of the End of Britain*, Cambridge University Press, Cambridge, 2023.

Warner, Geoffrey, 'The Study of Cold War Origins', *Diplomacy and Statecraft*, 1 (1990), pp. 13–26.

Warner, Geoffrey (ed.), *In the Midst of Events: The Foreign Office Diaries and Papers of Kenneth Younger*, February 1950–October 1951, Routledge, London, 2005.

Webb, Sidney and Beatrice Webb, *A Constitution for the Socialist Commonwealth of Great Britain*, London, 1920.

Webster, Charles, *Problems of Health Care: The National Health Service Before 1957*, HMSO, London, 1988.

_____, 'Conflict and Consensus: Explaining the British Health Service', *Twentieth Century British History*, 1 (1990), pp. 115–51.

_____, *The National Health Service: A Political History* (2nd edn), Oxford University Press, Oxford, 2002.

Weinbren, Daniel (ed.), *Generating Socialism: Recollections of Life in the Labour Party*, Sutton Publishing, Stroud, 1997.

Weir, L. MacNeill, *The Tragedy of Ramsay MacDonald: A Political Biography*, Secker & Warburg, London, 1938.

Westad, Odd Arne, *The Cold War: A World History*, Penguin Books, London, 2017.

Westcott, Nicholas, *Imperialism and Development: The East African Groundnut Scheme and Its Legacy*, James Currey, Woodbridge, Suffolk, 2020.

Westlake, Martin, *Kinnock: The Biography*, Little, Brown and Company, London, 2001.

Wevill, Richard, *Britain and America After World War II: Bilateral Relations and the Beginnings of the Cold War*, I.B. Tauris, London, 2012.

Wheeler-Bennett, John W., *King George VI: His Life and Reign*, St Martin's Press, New York, 1958.

Whiting, Richard, *The Labour Party and Taxation: Party Identity and Political Purpose in Twentieth-Century Britain*, Cambridge University Press, Cambridge, 2001.

Whittaker, Jason, *Jerusalem: Blake, Parry, and the Fight for Englishness*, Oxford University Press, Oxford, 2022.

Williams, Francis, *Ernest Bevin: Portrait of a Great Englishman*, Hutchinson, London, 1952.

_____, *A Prime Minister Remembers: The War and Post-War Memoirs of the Rt. Hon. Earl Attlee*, William Heinemann Ltd, London, 1961.

_____, *Nothing So Strange: An Autobiography*, Cassell, London, 1970.

Williams, Philip M., *Hugh Gaitskell*, Jonathan Cape, London, 1979.

Williams, Philip M. (ed.), *The Diary of Hugh Gaitskell, 1945–1956*, Jonathan Cape, London, 1983.

Williams, Shirley, *Climbing the Bookshelves*, Virago Press, London, 2009.

Williamson, Philip, '"Safety First": Baldwin, the Conservative Party, and the 1929 General Election', *Historical Journal*, 25 (1982), pp. 385–409.

_____, 'A "Bankers' Ramp"? Financiers and the British Political Crisis of August 1931', *English Historical Review*, XCIX (1984), pp. 770–806.

_____, 'Baldwin's Reputation: Politics and History, 1937–1967', *Historical Journal*, 47 (2004), pp. 127–68.

Williams-Thompson, Richard, *Was I Really Necessary?*, World's Press News Publishing Co., London, 1951.

Wilson, Harold, *A Prime Minister on Prime Ministers*, Book Club Associates, London, 1977.

_____, *Memoirs: The Making of a Prime Minister, 1916–64*, Weidenfeld & Nicolson and Michael Joseph, London, 1986.

Winter, J. M., 'The Impact of the First World War on Civilian Health in Britain', *Economic History Review*, 30 (1977), pp. 487–507.

_____, 'Infant Mortality, Maternal Mortality and Public Health in Britain in the 1930s', *Journal of European Economic History*, 8 (1979), pp. 439–62.

Wood, Ian, *John Wheatley*, Manchester University Press, Manchester, 1990.

Worley, Matthew, *Oswald Mosley and the New Party*, Palgrave Macmillan, London, 2010.

Wyatt, Woodrow, *Confessions of an Optimist*, Collins, London, 1985.

Wyburn-Powell, Alun, *Defectors and the Liberal Party 1910–2010: A Study of Inter-Party Relationships*, Manchester University Press, Manchester, 2012.

Yeandle, Peter, Katherine Newey and Jeffrey Richards (eds), *Politics, Performance and Popular Culture: Theatre and Society in Nineteenth-Century Britain*, Manchester University Press, Manchester, 2016.

Yeowell, Nathan (ed.), *Rethinking Labour's Past*, I.B. Tauris, London, 2022.

Young, J. W., 'Churchill's "No" to Europe: The "Rejection" of European Union by Churchill's Post-War Government, 1951–1952', *Historical Journal*, 28 (1985), pp. 923–37.

Younger, Kenneth, review of *The Memoirs of Lord Gladwyn*, *International Affairs*, 48 (1972), pp. 637–8.

Ziegler, Philip, *Mountbatten*, Alfred A. Knopf, New York, 1985.

Zweiniger-Bargielowska, Ina, 'Rationing, Austerity and the Conservative Party Recovery after 1945', *Historical Journal*, 37 (1994), pp. 173–97.

_____, *Austerity in Britain: Rationing, Controls, and Consumption, 1939–1955*, Oxford University Press, Oxford, 2000.

Index